Critical Literacy
Politics, praxis, and the postmodern

Edited by
Colin Lankshear and Peter L. McLaren

With a foreword by
Maxine Greene

State University of New York Press

Published by
State University of New York Press, Albany

© 1993 State University of New York

Printed in the United States of America

For information, address the State University of New York Press,
State University Plaza, Albany, NY 12246

Production by Bernadine Dawes
Marketing by Fran Keneston

Library of Congress Cataloging-in-Publication Data
Critical literacy : politics, praxis, and the postmodern / edited by
   Colin Lankshear and Peter L. McLaren ; with a foreword by Maxine
   Greene.
         p.   cm.—(SUNY series, Teacher enpowerment and school
   reform)
      Includes bibliographical references and index.
      ISBN 0-7914-1229-6 (alk. paper) : $57.50. -- ISBN 0-7914-1230-X
   (pbk. : alk. paper) : $18.95
      1. Critical pedagogy.   2. Literacy--Social aspects.
   I. Lankshear, Colin.   II. McLaren, Peter, 1948-   .   III. Series:
   Teacher empowerment and school reform.
   LC196.C75   1993
   302.2'244—dc20   91-39669
                                                                                    CIP

10   9   8   7   6   5   4   3   2   1

To my son, Tomás;
to Nancy Bell;
to Elsa Richmond;
and to Paulo Freire

—Colin Lankshear

———

To Jenny and my two children,
Laura and Jonathan; to my son-in-law, Marcelo;
to my editor,
Priscilla Ross;
and to
Paulo and Nita Freire

—Peter L. McLaren

Contents

Foreword

Across the world there has been a slippage of familiar foundations. Old authorities have become questionable, along with the long-sanctioned narratives explaining what has been and what will be. There is a restiveness with regard to categorizations once taken for granted. Persons of all ages are rejecting mere acquiescence to tradition; they are struggling to name the relations of power, to open spaces where they can be free. It is no longer a matter of either/or, of one ideology in tension with another; and the novel complexities of the present demand multi-perspectival responses, the sounds of many voices, the shadings of different points of view.

The uniqueness of this book lies in the diversity of the contributors' vantage points. Not only do they come from a range of disciplines: sociology, ethnography, philosophy, literary criticism, semiotics. They speak about a great spectrum of significant themes: pedagogy, feminism, colonialism, media, popular culture, sexuality. Also, they are located in various places: England, Grenada, Palestine, Australia, the United States. They offer, in consequence, rows of windows through which their readers can see; and what we see has focally to do with education, with the *praxis* of pedagogy in these postmodern times, and with the always unsettled problems of literacy.

Critical literacy, of course, lies at the heart of the text; and, if we are to associate it with any one individual thinker, it is clearly with the Brazilian educator Paulo Freire. Like other committed philosophers of *praxis*, however, Freire has moved others to identify their own commitments, to take reflective action on the grounds of their own lived situations in the human worlds they share. It is not surprising, therefore, to find ourselves moving from public schools in this country to literacy campaigns in Cuba or Nicaragua or Grenada. Nor is it surprising to find ourselves considering the plight of immigrant women in Australia seeking emancipation through solidarity and truly critical literacy and, soon afterwards, the tensions around what is called "Woman-women" and the relation of women to public and private spaces. The crucial issue in all the chapters has to do with human liberation and its connection with social justice.

We are reminded to hold these in mind when we read the poetry of children caught in the *intifada* in Jerusalem, the stories of Black city children, the accounts of young people's responses to the Gulf War. We are made to see the relation between these articulations and the regulations imposed by textbooks. We are made to confront, again with human emancipation and dignity in mind, the so-called "crisis" in English Studies and rhetoric and the relation between student narratives and works of literary art. Not only is it considered important to identify the intersections of aesthetic codes with economic and political ones; it is important as well to discover a pedagogy that will in time become transformative. Here and in other discussions, emphasis is placed on narrative and voice, on contesting meanings, on multiple meanings. These are set in opposition to the one-dimensional, and monological emphases in talk of "cultural literacy," analytic philosophy, and in the ongoing current preoccupations with school restructuring and "reform."

The attention paid to discourse, textuality, difference, and the structures of power brings this anthology into the culture-wide dialogue regarding postmodernism. Linking some of the dominant themes of this dialogue to the problems of oppression, equality, and justice, the authors move the conversation to domains of action and to realizable possibility. The editors themselves ask the readers of this book to engage with the text in a way that launches them into questioning, into judgment, and into a kind of collective interpretation. The encounter that lies ahead is not intended to be precious, purely private, or hermetically "intellectual." It can be—it ought to be—the

kind of encounter that makes readers curious, uneasy—and, in some manner, hopeful. There are no promises in a book like this; nor are there any
final answers. Rather, there are openings as well as windows, metaphorical
doorways through which we can move in a new-found solidarity in search of a
somewhat better world.

Maxine Greene
Teachers College
Columbia University

Preface

════════

Critical and *literacy* are both buzzwords at present. We do well to treat them cautiously. If anything, buzzwords are more likely to be avenues to nowhere much worth going to than to provide helpful guidance to reflection and practice. Take the case of *literacy*. It is now commonplace for people who until recently presented their activities—whether of research, teaching, or both—in terms of a concern for *reading* and *writing* to now portray themselves as working in the field of literacy. The case is similar to the situation of social or political theorists who previously talked about *government*, but who have latterly taken to talking about the *state*. In many cases their practice is little different from how it was previously. (In other cases, of course, it *is* different to a greater or lesser extent.) It is worth asking, then, why it is that literacy has come to usurp linguistic space previously occupied by reading and writing, especially where theorists feel they can make the shift without significantly altering their perspective or practice. This will help to reveal some of the characteristics of literacy as a buzzword, as well as to clarify how we perceive the difference between a concern for literacy and a concern for reading and writing. This in turn will help define our intended audience and our particular project. It will also help determine what point is served by adopting a new terminology, for it is by no means certain that any productive point *will* be served. On the contrary, crucial issues may be blurred, trivialized, or mystified by such a shift. Our commitment here is to serving an educationally productive purpose, and our effort should be judged accordingly.

It is quite easy to locate several motives for educationists making the shift from casting their enterprise in the language of reading and writing to that of literacy without making any significant shift in their conceptual, theoretical, or practical orientation. Three of these should be sufficient to make our point. We call these "getting with it," "getting trendy," and "getting relevant." Let us take these in turn, looking at events lying behind them.

Chris Searle[1] suggests that an impediment to the language of literacy hitherto entering school and school-based research talk has been precisely the value that *literacy*, in its primary habitat of adult learning among the disadvantaged of First and Third World nations alike, "puts upon transforming *consciousness*, and in particular social and political consciousness." School educators have long seen "'teaching children to read and write' . . . as a routine, unpolitical, non-consciousness-raising process." Insofar as teaching reading and writing is perceived as teaching decontextualized mechanical skills "to achieve just and only that with a child," a commitment to literacy and its "ingredient of raising consciousness through the selection of 'provocative' or 'propagandist' contents or contexts" goes against the grain of the formal educator's perceived vocation. At the same time that this provides a rationale for what Searle sees as the continuing reluctance to invoke literacy talk in British schools, it also provides a clue to the increasing trend *toward* such talk within other school systems and in the school-directed research of the academy.

The assumption that schooling is a politically neutral activity which should not overtly address "consciousness," at least in its political and social dimensions, took a severe pounding during the 1970s and 1980s. In part this derived from work undertaken in peripheral nations by people like Paulo Freire. It also emanated from academies at the center, where theorists returned to Marxist and other radical traditions across a range of disciplines. Many were influenced by readings of lived realities in peripheral societies and attempts to address those realities, engaging them in a dialectic with what they perceived at home.

Gradually, the assumption of neutrality was worn down—not entirely, of course, but at least to the point where it was no longer novel or mysterious to proclaim it a myth. Even where educators and educational theorists were not directly acquainted with the literature that spoke of these matters, the general impact of that literature occasioned among many a felt need to "get with it," to at least display some recognition that new ways of thinking about the politics of education had emerged. We are suggesting that one index of this is the tendency among certain educationists now to represent their work in reading and writing as an engagement with *literacy,* even though little or nothing about their reading, theorizing, or practical activity may have changed.

The period from the 1960s through the early 1980s also witnessed some highly effective and imagination-arresting literacy initiatives within the Third World and the urban First World alike. Although these were neither as widely nor as well publicized as they might have been, they nevertheless made their presence felt within educational circles in our society. The singular success of the Cuban literacy campaign of 1961 prompted UNESCO to rethink its adult education programs. Freire's work in Brazil and Chile took him to Harvard, among other places, and introduced him to an enormous First World readership via American and British publishers. Nicaragua's 1980 National Literacy Crusade won the UNESCO price for literacy endeavor, and the numerous subsequent accounts of that campaign fired imaginations with a sense of the romance (as well as the frustrations) that literacy work can hold.

Once again, there was seemingly something to be had from representing work in reading and writing as addressing literacy. "Getting trendy," it seemed, could be as easy as shifting linguistic usage. This, of course, is just one more variation on a very old theme. And when work is as difficult and unrewarding as the teaching of reading and writing often is, it seems churlish to resent the will to derive whatever satisfaction may come from "getting trendy," as well as "getting with it," except that there is much of value and importance to be derived from those theories and practices of literacy that conjure up exotic and romantic images among theorists and practitioners in our own schools and universities. Consequently, if nothing changes other than the terminology used to name the focus of activity, any increased satisfaction flowing from that minimal change will probably be outweighed by the

missed opportunities and dangers of mystification and language abuse involved in taking the name without the substance.

The third aspect to be considered is, perhaps, the most obvious and
compelling. This is what has variously been described as the discovery or
invention[2] of a literacy crisis in the 1970s. Considerable adult illiteracy—
and *illiteracy* was the term used—was "discovered" in the United States and
Britain during the early 1970s: a "discovery" which was quickly replicated in
Australia, Canada, New Zealand, and elsewhere. A *Newsweek* story made
this alleged crisis into a major public issue in the United States in 1975, and
from that point the literacy business took off. Policies and funding to address
literacy needs and to create programs to eradicate what was widely represented as a "disease" which had reached "epidemic proportions" soon
emerged, though rarely on the scale seen as necessary and desirable by
researchers and practitioners in the field. Funding was available for *literacy*.
Illiteracy was a major "problem." Attention, not surprisingly, turned to addressing literacy. The first task of schools became redescribed as that of
ensuring that pupils became literate. Researchers dressed up their funding
applications in the language of literacy, whether they were working with
adults or children, in school or out of it. Publishing lists addressing literacy
burgeoned. Teacher education and other university courses emerged in the
language of literacy. Research and practical programs seemingly derived new
power from their identification as literacy initiatives. Dealing with *literacy*
had become a way of "getting relevant." Yet often little or nothing changed
other than the descriptor terminology.

Of course there is some linguistic warrant for identifying the two languages as synonymous. The *Oxford Paperback Dictionary*, for example, defines *literacy* as a noun denoting "the ability to read and write," and *literate*
as an adjective which describes a person as "able to read and write."[3] So far
as dictionary definition is concerned, therefore, it is perfectly acceptable for
those hitherto involved with reading and writing to re-present their concerns
in the language of literacy *without* making any significant theoretical or
practical changes.

There are at least three ways to address this situation, and it should be
addressed because human interests are vitally at stake in educational activity. One is to accept that ordinary usage, as recorded by dictionaries, speaks

with some authority and that an onus rests with those who would require the linguistic shift to be matched with theoretical and/or practical shifts to make their case. A second is to deny that ordinary language has this authority, and to assert that if *literacy* has the sorts of connotations ascribed to it by Searle, it is reasonable for the differences between *literacy* and *reading and writing* to be recognized and reflected one way or another in the theory and practice of those who move from addressing the latter to addressing the former. The linguistic shift, in other words, should count for something. The third is to say that whatever the "facts" are about ordinary language and its authority, the truth is that some important insights have emerged within the field of literacy studies and the practice of literacy in the adult education arena, and the opportunity should be taken to make these known and to encourage their engagement and further elaboration by those who would identify themselves as concerned with literacy. This puts the discussion into the realm of substantive debate, where, we believe, it properly belongs.

In taking this third option we are placing faith in the power of this book and other similarly intentioned books to demonstrate the advantages of adopting a more rigorous conception of literacy and of receiving the theoretical, ethical, political, and practical benefits and challenges it affords. Consequently, much of our concern here will be to further reveal the insights of literacy studies as a specialized field and to develop them beyond the point they have already reached. To that extent, then, our intended audience comprises those who wish to participate in this endeavor. In other words, we aim to speak to people who require of literacy that it be more than a buzzword and that it reveal its capacity to contribute to real educational advance.

Critical is also a buzzword which is currently enjoying a moment of vogue. Roger Dale sounds a warning note we do well to heed here. He notes that there has been a noticeable increase in reference to *the state* to explain recent educational changes. Although an important purpose can be served by understanding such change in relation to the state (and vice versa), the mere invocation of the term has its dangers. For

'the state' may be in danger of becoming an example of a vital concept drained of its original value through promiscuous use in exercises of theoretical painting by numbers, and consequently at risk of joining 'resistance' and 'critical' . . . on the shelves of theoretical banality. The danger is that, like them, 'the state' has come to be used to *name* the space where theoretical work is needed rather than to fill that space, and worse, by such naming, to apparently preclude the need for more theoretical work.[4]

We see an important parallel here with the use of *critical* as a qualifier and are concerned to redress uses which commit the kind of offense Dale has identified in relation to *the state*. The specific point we wish to make about the qualifier *critical* in relation to literacy turns on discoveries made in recent years within literacy studies. One of the most salient is well captured in Brian Street's words, when he says that literacy is best understood as "a shorthand for the social practices and conceptions of reading and writing."[5]

The idea here is that reading and writing are not all of a piece. Literacy must not be seen as referring to something singular, like an essential technology, a specific skill, or a universal phenomenon such as print or script. Rather, reading and writing consist in myriad social and socially constructed *forms*. There is no such thing as a "literacy essence" lying behind the actual social practices and conceptions of reading and writing. Reading and writing are made, socially, into many and diverse forms. The approach to understanding literacy favored by people like Street, and which we endorse here, "concentrates on the specific social practices of reading and writing,"[6] on the forms that literate practice actually takes and the ways print skills are used, rather than on some abstracted technology or other essence. What literacy *is* is entirely a matter of how reading and writing are conceived and practiced within particular social contexts: and this varies markedly. Indeed, for many social settings we do better to think in terms of litera*cies* rather than literacy.

Given that literacy is many rather than singular, we need ways of classifying and distinguishing the different forms that exist. These, of course, like all bases for differentiating and classifying, will reflect purpose. This fact speaks to *critical* as a qualifier and, indeed, as a basis for classification. To see this we must turn to a second salient insight from literacy studies, which concerns the *politics* of literacy.

Literacies are socially constructed within political contexts: that is, within contexts where access to economic, cultural, political, and institutional power is structured unequally. Moreover, these same literacies evolve and are employed in daily life settings which are riven with conflicting and otherwise competing interests. In short, literacies are ideological. They reflect the differential structured power available to human agents through which to secure the promotion and serving of their interests, including the power to shape literacy in ways consonant with those interests. Consequently, the conceptions people have of what literacy involves, of what *counts* as being literate, what they see as "real" or "appropriate" uses of reading and writing skills, and the way people actually read and write in the course of their daily lives—these all reflect and promote values, beliefs, assumptions, and practices which shape the way life is lived within a given social milieu and, in turn, influence which interests are promoted or undermined as a result of how life is lived there. Thus literacies are indices of the dynamics of power.

As we are using the term here, *critical* is tied to this point. We are faced with the reality of multiple literacies which can be distinguished from one another and classified according to a range of purposes. One such purpose is to distinguish and classify literacies in terms of their politics. In addressing *critical* literacy we are concerned with the extent to which, and the ways in which, actual and possible social practices and conceptions of reading and writing enable human subjects to understand and engage the politics of daily life in the quest for a more truly democratic social order. Among other things, critical literacy makes possible a more adequate and accurate "reading" of the world, on the basis of which, as Freire and others put it, people can enter into "rewriting" the world into a formation in which their interests, identities, and legitimate aspirations are more fully present and are present more equally.

In the essays which follow, then, *critical* assumes much more than buzzword status. It will be theorized and exemplified in accordance with a conscious radical intent. We believe that there is point in referring to critical literacy *only* where concerted efforts are being made to understand and practice reading and writing in ways that enhance the quest for democratic emancipation, for empowerment of the subordinated, the marginalized Other.

Accordingly, this book will theorize literacy in nontechnocratic and nonessentializing ways. It will explore the special understandings of literacy that come only when we go beyond commonsense conceptions of reading and writing as so many mechanical and decontextualized skills which, as they stand, are more or less neutral. Beyond this, it will theorize *the critical*, revealing differences in emphasis and focus between those, for example, who operate largely from within modernist discourses and others who have more fully embraced postmodern discourses of one form or another. Despite such differences as arise here, the contributors are all committed to the broad democratic concern espoused above.

Some of the essays will be less concerned with theorizing *literacy* and *the critical* than with providing real-life examples of literacy programs and other initiatives informed by a critical literacy concern. In each case, however, the assumptions that lie behind the practices described will be amply clear. Other essays will address specific antidemocratic and antiemancipatory practices, revealing them for what they are and endeavoring to point a way ahead. Others will address research issues and lay down elements of a critical literacy research agenda.

Above all of this, however, the book is intended to provide concrete illustrations of differences and similarities that exist between theorists of critical literacy who represent predominantly modernist and postmodernist stances, and to suggest ways in which the insights and strengths of both can best be brought together in the progressive search for enhanced practices and conceptions of critical literacy.

Colin Lankshear   Peter L. McLaren
Auckland, 1991   Oxford, OH, 1991

NOTES

1. Searle, C., "Words to a Life-Land: Literacy, the Imagination, and Palestine," in this volume, p. 169–170. Note that in the introduction we will draw on the work of John Searle. The two Searles come from radically different ideological positions, and it is important not to confuse them.

2. Shor, I. *Culture Wars: School and Society in the Conservative Restoration, 1969–1984* (New York: Routledge/Methuen, 1986), p. 64.

3. Hawkins, J. M. (compiler), *The Oxford Paperback Dictionary* (Oxford: Oxford University Press, 1986), p. 381.

4. Dale, R., "Review of Andy Green, *Education and State Formation: The Rise of Educational Systems in England, France, and the USA,*" *Journal of Education Policy.* 6, 4, 1991, p. 417.

5. Street, B., *Literacy in Theory and Practice* (Cambridge: Cambridge University Press, 1984), p. 1.

6. *Ibid.*, p. 2.

Acknowledgments

We acknowledge the generous contributions made by family, friends, and colleagues to the creation of this book.

We thank Priscilla Ross of SUNY Press for her supportive collaboration throughout the entire project. In addition to completing the usual editing tasks promptly and with care, Priscilla has offered valued assistance on matters of content and format, accommodated our editorial wishes with grace and flair, and provided morale boosts when needed.

Nancy Bell and Jenny McLaren have been constant and supportive companions along the way, for which we thank them in full measure.

Henry Giroux, Honor Fagan, Martin O'Neil, Steve Haymes, Adriana Hernández, Richard Quantz, Marcia Moraes, Khaula Murtandas, Dennis Carlson, Jeanne Brady Giroux, Donaldo Macedo, and Roger Dale have contributed in the best manner of collegial friendship. This book owes much to them, and we hope they take some pleasure from it.

We especially thank our authors for giving generously of their labors and insights, and for believing in the idea we wished to explore. They are an exemplary team. It has been a privilege to work with them.

Brenda Liddiard Laurent and Marianne Hill went out of their way to ensure that the typescript was ready on time. They frequently put their own time and convenience second to our deadline—invariably with humor and goodwill. Their professional expertise and collegial solidarity are greatly appreciated.

Laura McLaren brought all her skills to the quest for a suitable photograph of the editors. We thank her for her time and her sense of humor, as well as for the many photos we did not use but which will stand as mementos of the ever-growing friendship between the editors.

Finally, we thank Maxine Greene for writing the Foreword and, more importantly, for the outstanding example she has set over the years in theorizing and practicing critical literacy. The spirit and cause of critical literacy are writ large in *Teacher as Stranger, Landscapes of Learning, The Dialectic of Freedom,* "How do we think about our craft?", and a host of other writings. Her efforts to keep an Other voice and other perspectives alive and visible against a swamping positivist tide in educational philosophy, and from a singularly marginal position, proved inspirational to a generation of educationists who are now making their critical presence felt. Her life and work make Maxine a "natural" choice for writing the Foreword. We are honored that she accepted. Had she not, she would have joined those to whom this book is respectfully dedicated.

Introduction

Colin Lankshear and Peter L. McLaren

Literacy in the age of "new times"

We are living in a "post" age, wherein intellectuals and other social commentators are consciously identifying the present historical moment in comparison with that which preceded it. This, of course, is not a wholly new phenomenon. Humans have often consciously portrayed their immediate times as being "post":postwar, postdepression, post-Hiroshima, post-Stalin, post-Kennedy, and so on. A notable feature of the post-age we have in mind here, however, is that the present is being set not against a more or less *specific* event, figure, dynasty or crisis, but rather against an enduring and *complex epoch*, and that this is being done scarcely from hindsight but in the very moment of transition itself. It is almost as if we are seeing the flowering of a conscious recognition of history as a social construction wherein structured relations and practices, ideologies and institutions, modes of production, distribution and exchange, and the like are seen as constituting the "stuff" of ages, and that more or less coherent and identifiable—but complex— amalgams of these are presently being superseded. Currents, themes, and modes from the age that was are set against the new history that is being made, lived, and lived through. We are beginning to recognize that history itself is quintessentially a semiotic process created, as Brooke Williams

1

notes, in the relationship between mind-independent and mind-dependent orders of being. It is *enacted* through the mediacy of the sign through which the mind structures its experiences of the real. The postmodern challenge of historical knowledge is to participate in both past and present sign systems at once.[1]

And so, in different ways and on various dimensions, the age of modernity is set against the unfolding postmodern age,[2] the industrial social order is set against the postindustrial, the colonial and neocolonial ages against postcolonialism, and so on. Within academic discourse, modernist and structuralist currents are set against an emergent postmodernist and poststructuralist temperament.

Stuart Hall describes some of the hallmarks of these transitional "new times" as shifts in the technical organization of industrial-capitalist production toward information technologies and more flexible and decentralized forms of labor process, work organization, and increased product differentiation—what some critics are referring to as "post-Fordism."[3] Hall notes that post-Fordism is also concerned with broader social and cultural changes connected to the construction of new human identities associated with the politics of personal consumption, consumer ethics, and shifting economies of pleasure and desire. This had led, in Hall's terms, to a "return of the subjective," that is, to a return to a concern with subjectivity and identity as they have been culturally, ideologically, and historically produced.

The charred and consumptive iron smokestacks of the capitalist manufacturing plant set within the predatory, post-Holocaust landscapes of entropic American inner cities have been replaced by the high-tech boardrooms of the transnational corporate elite who oversee vast technocenters that extend the global neocortex through fiber optics and microchips. Visions for contemporary citizenship no longer depend as much on the grass-roots struggles of oppressed and peripheralized peoples but are conjured up in the chrome and steel offices of Silicon Valley. It is not so much the "time of the sign" as the "time of the cyn," as in *cyborg, cybernetics, cyberpunk*. A new cybercitizenry of specular beings is being produced through the interlocking forces of history, economics, politics, media, and gender in ways that allow the personal to be both informed by and calibrated against new modes of domination and surveillance.

The break is neither abrupt nor absolute, however. Themes and insights are carried over. Enduring concerns and projects take on new shapes. New ways of theorizing them, new vocabularies for conceptualizing them, and new strategies for addressing them are forged. No doubt epochal themes *are*, at some level, exhausted when the tasks called out by those themes finally prove adequate to their calling.[4] At such junctures, as Freire notes, we may indeed talk of one epoch being superseded by another. Yet certain historical threads have remained unbroken over successive epochs for as long as recorded history extends. These include, crucially, the distinctively human quests for liberation, emancipation, and justice.

The fact is that every age has its politics. History is always, necessarily, lived within relations, structures, and configurations of power. Hitherto, these have been characterized by inequalities. The dimensions and specifics of domination and subordination, elites and subalterns, change regularly: sometimes on grand scales, almost constantly in detail.

Conceptions of politics and the political dimension of human existence likewise change, and they are forever contested. Notions of what constitutes the political are irredeemably ideological. Conceptions of what are the political issues of the day and which groups are lined up in political contest are likewise disputed. What remains constant, however, is the *reality* of politics: the reality that human beings live, and endure the shaping effects on their *being* of so living, within social relations and practices in which opportunities to claim power for the end of achieving personal and collective fulfillment are structured unequally. And whether we limit our view of politics and the political to human interactions mediated by the state, or operate with a broader view which identifies the political with any human interaction conditioned by structured power, or take up some intermediate position, the conceptual kernel of politics is, precisely, *power*.

Our interest resides in the specificity of the means by which the "new times" have produced new economies of subjectivity and new regimes of desire through a proliferation of new literacies. If literacies largely inform how we read the world and the word, but also how such a reading produces who we are and how we dream our social present, then we need to explore the changing relationship between literacy and culture in the era of "new times."

During the past two decades scholars have paid increasing attention to the connections between literacy and power. We are now much more aware than previously of the nature and role of extant literacies within established configurations of power and advantage, of centers and margins, and how literacies impact on the satisfaction of human needs and interests. We understand more fully, but still imperfectly, how literacies are implicated in the shaping of human subjects, the ideologies they bear, and their placement within social hierarchies.

Literacy: Perspectives, promises, and politics

Burgeoning historical and sociological studies reveal how the forms taken by literacy in everyday life are shaped and defined *within* processes of competing social groups struggling to meet their respective interests and to have their voices heard and acknowledged.[5] We see how agents acting within established power structures and dominant ideologies effectively determine what literacy will be for others. Although, as in the case of most teachers, this is more or less unwitting, the political and ethical effects are real. More specifically, such studies trace how the varying ways that people are taught (and not taught) to use (and not to use) reading, writing, and publishing skills, the conditions or restrictions imposed upon their use, and prevailing conceptions of the legitimate or "correct" uses of reading and writing are important factors in shaping whose and which interests and aspirations are best satisfied and whose voices are heard within established daily routines.

A brief selection of typical examples will sharpen the point. Working from a historical perspective, Harvey Graff details the social construction of a particular form of school literacy in a selection of Ontario schools serving working-class children during the midnineteenth century. He examines the wider social, economic, and moral order and situates his analysis of working-class school literacy within this frame of values, practices, and expectations.

According to Graff, the distinctive form of literacy constructed on the school site was conditioned and shaped by identifiable sector interests and a value position and specific pedagogy consistent with those interests. The strong commitment of those who promoted schooling as a means to ensuring universal literacy was grounded in a clearly defined aim. This was to bring about moral development and social control through school learning, discipline, and order mediated by a "properly" conceived literacy.

Promoting literacy for its own sake, or in the interests of whatever ends individuals might choose to employ it, was never on the agenda of Ontario's promoters of working-class schooling. Indeed, "literacy alone . . . —that is, isolated from its moral base—was feared as potentially subversive."[6] The Christian ethos espoused by Education Superintendent Ryerson and the influential newspaper *The Christian Guardian* (formerly edited by Ryerson) stressed the need to control literacy in home and school alike. The "selection of proper books" was crucial. "Exciting works of fiction," along with politically subversive works of people like Voltaire and Paine, were especially feared. The Bible was seen as the best possible literature for guiding daily life.[7] Literacy was valued as a means for adjusting working-class children to a *morally restrained* social order and for establishing a hegemony attuned to industrial capitalism.

The actual physical characteristics and dynamics of the classroom, together with the pedagogy employed and the values associated with reading, contrived to produce a learning context admirably suited to promoting the required "moral" development and social control among working-class children. Teacher-pupil ratios of 1:70 by typical attendance made maintaining order a major priority. Heavy emphasis placed on sheer classroom management had obvious implications for the sorts of attitudes and habits each child had to develop for learning to proceed. Children were required to be docile and quiet, except when called on to recite their ABCs. The prevailing pedagogy was highly conducive to promoting obedience, quietness, and discipline. The method of rote repetition of letters militated against reading or writing with genuine comprehension. Consequently, it was "safe" in the sense that it was virtually impotent to foster a critical literacy that might encourage questioning social practices and arrangements or the values sought by ruling interests. The method did, however, assert teacher and adult authority, establish values and habits of drill, and promote passive attitudes and responses on the part of pupils.

We see here the social construction of a particular form—a social practice and conception—of literacy. At the same time, in other sites, among other groups, quite different literacies were conceived and transmitted: for example, among students (of other classes) bound for professions, higher learning, careers as writers, and so forth. Such students learned within very different instructional settings from those described by Graff, via significantly different pedagogies—often more "open" or liberal. Of course, these other literacies all had their specific articulations with prevailing structures of power and hierarchies of interests. Some were well suited to the development of personal agency (although not necessarily *critical* agency), fluency, and individual advancement. This marks a major difference from the literacy described by Graff. The link between literacy and power in Graff's example is abundantly clear. So are its implications for whose interests were served (and whose were not), which interests were served, and how they were served.

The same broad theme can be approached from other angles. Freire's concept of banking education[8] has been useful in examining the political significance of literacy within school and nonschool settings alike. Freire claims that within pedagogies based on the model of a narrating subject (the teacher) and patient, listening objects (the students), the content, "whether values or empirical dimensions of reality, tend in the process of being narrated to become lifeless and petrified."[9] The "acts" of reading and writing are effectively robbed of their transformative potential. Teachers talk about reality "as if it were motionless, static, compartmentalized, and predictable."[10]

The political implications of making reading and writing into acts of receiving and re-presenting narrated (whether by voice or print) material are important. Social and cultural reality is reified into an extension or analogue of the natural world, which, as Freire reminds us (*and unlike the world of culture*), "humans did not make."[11] Reality is portrayed as something to be received, not as something which is to a crucial extent made and transformed by human action. "Facts" are approached as more or less fixed and given. Social phenomena like hierarchies of class and privilege, moral and social norms and values, stereotypes of race and gender, structured and patterned practices and routines of daily life, and so forth are received as natural and immutable realia. Banking pedagogy and the literacy it fosters encourages passive acceptance of the way things are: at the very least to the extent that it undermines conceptions and capacities conducive to a more active orientation. This has obvious import for preserving established structures and routines and the hierarchies of interests and satisfactions they ordain.

It must not be thought that this is a simplistic analysis applicable only to more elementary and less academic levels and tracks of education. It applies to the highest reaches of the academy. For trained and certificated college graduates, the habits of passive acceptance and responsiveness to given tasks and information frequently underwrite involvement in some of the most prestigious, well-paid, and politically potent pursuits of our times. The work of industrial scientists, who can blithely apply theory to great effect in the manufacture of consumerables and other products without foreseeing or having to consider the social and environmental corollaries of this work, is an obvious case in point. The burgeoning field of policy analysis provides a further instance. Dale says that the roots of policy analysis "lie not in trying to change the content of social policy in a particular direction, but in the search for ways of ensuring the efficient and effective delivery and implementation of social policies, irrespective of their content. It arises from studies that revealed how ineffective social policy is in bringing about its stated ends."[12]

Of course, the interest-serving directions of contemporary education policy are all too evident. Some of these are considered in detail in later chapters by Carlson, Harris, and Apple.

Other approaches also contribute to our understanding of how agents working within established structures of power participate in the social construction of literacies, revealing their political implications. One important body of work here deals with functional literacy initiatives.[13] Numerous studies now exist which analyze specific approaches to functional literacy, documenting their aims and content and seeking to understand them in relation to wider sociocultural practices and values. Such studies document conscious attempts to create discrete forms of reading and writing instruction which will, allegedly, make currently "dysfunctional" people functional. Most of these studies go on to identify interests at stake in functionalist programs and, in some cases, argue the propensity of such programs to promote the interests of certain groups or sectors at the expense of others.[14]

A further corpus of studies focuses on the content of classroom literature and texts. In relatively early treatments of content, Anyon[15] and MacDonald[16] identify legitimated views of what students should read in school (the required texts and other literature defining the syllabus) and suggest their political implications for working people, ethnic minorities, and women. Writing in 1979, Anyon claims that even updated social studies texts used in U.S. schools portray native Americans, blacks, women, and the working class in terms that favor the interests of those who dominate over them. She argues that texts are replete with interest-serving omissions, stereotypes, and distortions. History schoolbooks "provide no label with which to identify as one group with a set of distinct concerns all those wage and salaried persons who are industrial laborers, craftspersons, clerical workers, or service, sales, and technical workers." School texts thus present an impediment to such people calling themselves to mind as a group, predisposing "workers and others against actions on behalf of the interests working people have in common."[17] At a similar level of analysis, MacDonald surveyed studies which examine the ways in which women in particular are represented in school and university texts. She concludes that the general impression conveyed in official texts "is one of woman's inferiority, her domesticity, her lack of adventure, ability, sense of adventure or creativity." The implication is that school literacy is submerged in ruling bourgeois, patriarchal, and ethnic majority views and values, with accordant implications for inequality, discrimination, and disadvantage.[18]

The limitations of such work for the analysis of school texts have been exposed from a range of positions, several of them nicely summarized by Geoff Whitty.[19] One line of criticism stresses the need to address the *form* as well as the content of specific texts.[20] Another notes the failings involved in assuming that literacies defined by specific content actually determine (or strongly shape) attitudes and values in their readers. In fact, "studies of texts . . . need to be related to the broader discursive contexts in which they circulate."[21]

A complementary line of argument insists on the importance of recognizing the mediating role of pedagogy in textbook use. Although "in some cases, there may be a . . . correspondence between the ideology of textbooks and the ideology of teaching style, in other cases the relationship may be a contradictory one."[22] Teachers using the most "reactionary" texts *might* use them to help students understand the nature and implications of the ideology on parade: and in so doing might engage students in reflection upon their *own* ideological investments.

The most recent developments in the line of progression from work like that of Anyon and MacDonald seek to understand the process by which human subjectivity is constituted and transformed through discourse, experience, and material practices: in education generally, and through literacy specifically.[23] In arguing that more limited, reproductivist, one-dimensional analyses of textual content cannot account for the "tenuousness, disjunction, interruption and possibility" inherent in educational practices at large, Wexler advocates a critical semiotics of texts.[24] More recently, Giroux has rejected the "reductionist . . . practice of limiting critique to the analyses of cultural products such as texts, books, films, and other commodities." The more narrowly defined views and theories of literacy tied to such critique "obscure the *relational* nature of how meaning is produced, i.e., the intersection of subjectivities, objects, and social practices with specific relations of power."[25]

In its positive contribution as well as through the critique it has invited, analysis of textbook content focuses attention on the extent to which differences in content may comprise different literacies. And given the links between content and wider human purposes, value systems, and modes of life and being, these differences can have great political significance. It is failure to recognize literacy as many and varied, which precludes the possibility of focusing closely on the significance of differences between various forms taken by reading and writing, that marks the main weakness of many technocratic views of literacy as "reading and writing." Analysis of textbook content both recognizes the multiplicity of literacy and documents important dimensions of difference. In so doing it helps remind us of points at which it is important to resist unreflective shifts from the language of reading and writing to that of literacy.

Let us turn now to recent developments in understanding and theorizing literacy, in its relation to structures and economies of power associated with various postmodernist and poststructuralist currents in social theory. In Chapter 13 Giroux claims that literacy "in its *varied versions* is about the practice of representation as a means of organizing, inscribing, and containing meaning."[26] Literacy must be approached as discursive practice, as discourse or, more accurately, as so many discourses which in inscribing meaning are crucially involved in the formation of human subjects. Literacy researchers must uncover the *relational* manner in which meaning is produced, unveiling the interplay between subjectivities, objects, and social practices within specific relations of power. Literacies, and knowledge more generally, are identified as forms of discursive production which organize ways of thinking into ways of doing and being. As discourse, literacies shape social practices of which they are mutually constitutive. This makes literacy inherently political. What does this mean?

The notion of *meaning* itself provides an important clue here. Meaning is central to *human* life and human *being*. This is not simply linguistic meaning, but the idea also that human life is meaningfully ordered: around concepts, purposes, values, ideas and ideals, rules, notions of reality, and so on.

Of course, linguistic meaning and meaning in the wider sense are mutually entangled. Language and communication are essential to human being. It is through the medium of language that biological human life becomes *social* (cultural, economic, and so on) life: that is, life organized into some form or shape (more or less consciously recognized and understood by participants) and within which human identities emerge. Meaning, and hence being and human subjectivity, are constituted within and through discourse.

Discourses have been defined as "modalities which to a significant extent govern what can be said, by what kind of speakers, and for what types of imagined audiences."[27] To draw out the concept of discourse we need to read phrases like *what can be said, by what kind of speakers,* and *to what kind of audiences* in a double way—parallel to the double reading of *meaning* mentioned above.

Discourse is like (and includes) language in the sense that only once norms and rules for use are established and observed can linguistic meaning be "stamped" and communicated, and people participate in speaking the language. Only with rules, norms, and meanings in place can language operate as a medium for giving shape to human life. Beyond the dimension of language—albeit the central dimension—*discourse* refers to the larger project of creating, shaping, and bounding social life, and this includes the metaphors that both live through us and give meaning to the flesh of our desire. From a strictly biological standpoint, human life has the potential to take on any of a vast array of shapes or none at all. A baby which dies shortly after birth has existed briefly as a biological entity but scarcely, in its own right, as a social being. It has been social only by virtue of having been, momentarily, a member of a family, a much-looked-forward-to arrival, and so on. Its death is a tragedy to the family and the wider network of kin and friends it would have entered. But this social status reflects the discursive ordering of human life into "units" like families, within and around which various ideas, hopes, dreamed-of futures, expectations, identities, relationships, and modes of living are centered.

Discourses are norm-governed practices and involvements around and within which forms of human living are constructed and identities and subjectivities shaped. Discourses of classroom learning, for instance, are by no means confined to the language of conducting lessons, in the narrower everyday sense of *language*. Rather, the "language" or discourse of the classroom is closer to what Wittgenstein meant by language and its place within "forms of life."[28] Classroom discourse, then, includes the norms and processes by which authority is established and exercised, discipline maintained, and decisions made about what will be learned, via what media, and how, plus the myriad other ingredients which collectively explain why what is going on at a particular moment in a given physical and social or cultural space— namely, *this* classroom and others more or less like it—*is* going on. Discourse, therefore, is often hidden and implicit. The discourses that police the body, shape desire, and mobilize consent will necessarily have a direct and discernible bearing on the process through which ideologies develop into specific teaching and learning practices.

'Discourse', then, is a large concept. At the level of research and study, discourses define what counts as doing research in an area or studying an issue or field "properly," and how such matters are determined. They also sanction "appropriate" activity. (In his chapter in this volume, Harris provides an elaborate case study of analytic philosophy of education as discursive practice.) At the level of child rearing, there are discourses of appropriate behavior, of procedures for nurturing children, of socializing them, and so on. Educational discourses consist in so many structured, ideologically informed, and sanctioned views about what should be done, how, and why it should be done. These make human activity in the name of education into so many forms, lending meaning to such activity and, in the process, shaping how educatees "turn out" and how they don't turn out.

A crucial point here is that meanings and the discourses through which they are inscribed—whether in research, child rearing, education, or whatever site of human practice—are never *givens*. Although they may be inherited by culture and sedimented by the dead weight of tradition into social facts that we mistakenly take for granted, they are neither ontologically nor epistemologically *prior* to human living in the sense of being natural or transcendent; nor are they fixed. Indeed, they are always in principle, and typically in practice, contested, since competing discourses are always potentially or actually in operation. Discourses are generated and lived out within political contexts, within structures and relations of power inherited by humans inhabiting a given cultural and social time and space, these themselves reflecting previous discursive production. But these contingent historical facts of discursive production and inheritance are precisely that: contingent and historical. And *contested*. To that extent, so also are the forms that human subjectivity takes on within the discursive economies of their formation. Human subjectivity, then, is never closed. It is never fixed. The particular forms it takes are never essentially or transcendentally dictated. What individual and collective human subjectivities reflect are the dynamics and processes of discursive production in their current historical and cultural *contingency*. At the same time, given the contingent facts of discursive production within a particular space and time, there is *that degree of historical "determination"* of human subjectivity. But that determination is, ultimately, a contingent matter. Three quotations from this book help concretize these matters.

> Discourses are not single-minded positivities but are invariably mutable, contingent, and partial. Their authority is always provisional as distinct from transcendental . . . Discourses may in fact *possess* the power of truth, but in reality they are historically contingent rather than inscribed by natural law; they emerge out of social conventions. In this view, any dis-

course of conducting is bounded by the historical, cultural, and political conditions and the epistemological resources available to articulate its meaning . . . [P]eople do not possess power but produce it and are produced by it in their relational constitution through discourse.[29]

[Poststructualism places much emphasis] on meaning as *a contested event,* a terrain of struggle in which individuals take up often conflicting subject positions in relation to signifying practices [in both the narrower and the wider sense of "language" and "signs"]. Poststructuralists acknowledge explicitly that meaning consists of more than signs operating and being operated in a context. Rather, there is struggle over signifying practices. This struggle is eminently *political* and must include the relationship among discourse, power, and difference. Poststructuralists place much . . . emphasis on discourse and the contradictions involved in subjective formation.[30]

"The subject is a consequence of certain rule-governed discourses that govern the intelligible invocation of identity. The subject is not *determined* by the rules through which it is generated because signification is *not a founding act, but rather a regulated process of repetition* that both conceals itself and enforces its rules precisely through the production of substantializing effects . . . There is no self that is prior to the convergence or who maintains 'integrity' prior to its entrance into this conflicted cultural field. There is only a taking up of the tools where they lie, where the very 'taking up' is enabled by the tool lying there." . . . We construct our future selves, our identities, through the availability and character of signs of possible futures. The parameters of the human subject vary according to the discursive practices, economies of signs, and subjectivities (experiences) engaged by individuals and groups at any historical moment. We must abandon the . . . idea that we possess as social agents a timeless essence or a consciousness that places us beyond historical and political practices. Rather, we should understand our "working identities" as an effect of such practices . . . Our identities as subjects are . . . constitutive of the literacies we have at our disposal through which we make sense of our day-to-day politics of living.[31]

To approach literacy as discursive production, then, is to seek understanding of *how* literacies are created, what they are created *as* (undertaking, perhaps, some kind of "archeology" of extant literacy discourses), and what they entail for the shape and texture of human life and subjectivity. This throws us back on Giroux's idea of literacy as "a means of organizing, inscribing, and containing meaning." In doing this kind of work we have to bear in mind the sorts of challenges issued by Wexler, Whitty, and others noted earlier, and much more besides. For Giroux's conception of literacy is a complex idea to handle. An important part of handling it involves looking at earlier positions, such as those of Wittgenstein, Marx and neo-Marxists, advocates of hermeneutical and phenomenological approaches, and so forth, which have important historical and intellectual links to contemporary views. The real challenge of the postmodern turn in social theory, particularly as applied to literacy, involves coming to understand the similarities and differences that obtain between it and its theoretical forebears.

The colonization of culture

With that said, however, let us turn briefly to a theme which has been rehearsed by a number of literacy researchers operating from the broad perspective in question: namely, recent attempts within the United States to establish a discourse of *cultural* literacy. Attempts to define cultural literacy and to suggest broad approaches and programs schools should undertake to advance cultural literacy represent answers to the question of what kind of knowledge our young must acquire in order to be able to participate in society as active, informed citizens. As such, cultural literacy overlaps to some extent with functional literacy but goes beyond it to name a broad range of meanings, values, and views that students should come to bear. Being culturally literate has become synonymous with "acquiring a knowledge of selected works of literature and historical information necessary for informed participation in the political and cultural life of the nation."[32]

The foremost proponents of cultural literacy identified by writers intent on understanding and critiquing it as a discursive practice include Allan Bloom, E.D. Hirsch, Jr., Diane Ravitch, William Bennett, Chester Finn, and Nathan Glazer. Interpreters and critics of cultural literacy as discourse include Stanley Aronowitz, Henry Louis Gates, Jr., Henry Giroux, and Peter

McLaren. Since these writers typically identify their work as proceeding from a critical literacy perspective, this section will provide a bridge to subsequent discussion of what is involved in being critical and what should be understood by critical literacy.

The points we seek can best be made by referring to the enormously influential work of E.D. Hirsch, Jr. In *Cultural Literacy: What Every American Needs to Know,* Hirsch maintains that students are unable to read and write adequately if they lack "the relevant background information, a particular body of shared information that expresses a privileged cultural currency with high exchange value in the public sphere." Moreover, students who do not have this "canon" will be unable "to function adequately in society." Hirsch sees the new illiteracy as "embodied in those expanding ranks of students who are unable either to contextualize information or to communicate with each other within the parameters of a wider national culture."[33]

Hirsch, then, argues for the transmission of a uniform cultural "canon"—a traditional literate culture—through the medium of standard English. He sees literacy as having declined because schools have emphasized process to the detriment of adequate content. Schools need to redress the balance by moving background knowledge to the center. The appropriate body of prescribed content will allegedly give students access to mainstream economic and political life, thereby becoming a route to greater social and economic justice for marginal groups. In Hirsch's view the requisite content is derived from "common culture." It is not so much information from *elite* culture (in the manner of Bloom) as information possessed by people Hirsch regards as "literate Americans." To this extent he defines the content of cultural literacy ostensively: by reference to what civically capable, culturally endowed Americans know.

Aronowitz and Giroux seize on a potentially disarming feature of Hirsch's position to reveal its real political character. This provides a springboard for a sustained unpacking and critique of Hirsch's version of cultural literacy. They say the prescribed content of cultural literacy

> is drawn from what Hirsch calls the common culture, which in his terms is marked by a history and contemporary usefulness that raises it above issues of power, class, and discrimination. In Hirsch's terms, this is "everybody's

culture," and the only real issue, as he sees it, is that we outline its contents and begin to teach it in schools. For Hirsch, the national language, which is at the center of his notion of literacy, is rooted in a civic religion that forms the core of stability in the culture itself. "Culture" in these terms is used in the descriptive rather than anthropological and political sense; it is the medium of conservation and transmission. Its meaning is fixed in the past, and its essence is that it provides the public with a common referent for communication and exchange. It is the foundation upon which public life interacts with the past, sustains the present, and locates itself in the future . . . Culture for Hirsch is a network of information shrouded in innocence and goodwill. [This interpretation is evident] in his reading of the relationship between culture and what he describes as nation building; "nation builders use a patchwork of scholarly folk materials, old songs, obscure dances, and historical legends all apparently quaint and local, but in reality selected and reinterpreted by intellectuals to create a culture upon which the life of the nation can rest."[34]

The legacy bequeathed to a nation's young by its nation builders is, allegedly, the promise of a basis for informed, adequate, and satisfying participation in social and civic life.

Whereas Hirsch represents the common culture to himself and his readers in this ideological manner, a reading of cultural literacy as discursive practice tells a very different story. Perhaps the most sophisticated analysis and critique of Hirsch's approach to cultural literacy as discursive practice is that provided by Aronowitz and Giroux. They argue that for Hirsch mainstream or American culture is simply "there." There is a common pool of information that defines what it really means to be American, a kind of "essence" of being an American citizen. To live and participate effectively as an American citizen presupposes possessing this canon of information and being able, with its assistance, to read, write, and speak effectively. This possession is simultaneously the *sine qua non* and the *guarantee* of automatic membership as a full citizen.[35] Hirsch presents this common culture as "existing beyond the realm of politics and struggle." It is somehow transcendental—like the ideas which, for Hirsch, seem to drive history itself—"'presenting' itself for all to participate in its meanings and conventions."[36] Hirsch acknowledges that we can distinguish between mainstream and ethnic culture(s), but in the end mainstream culture is a kind of transcendent American common denominator which is politically innocent. He does not conceive of mainstream culture as what has prevailed in a process of struggle between competing groups occupying positions of unequal access to power within the social structure to establish dominant meanings, knowledges, values, interpretations, practices, relations, and so forth, any more than he would see ethnic cultures as the outcome of struggles over collective memory and how to "live out and make sense of the given circumstances and conditions of life" within the various ethnic groupings that exist within a society.[37]

What, then, are the implications and consequences of asserting the existence of a transcendent, essential, apolitical shared culture of being American, and seeking to ground educational practice in such a discourse of culture? In the first place, education is represented as a neutral activity with the potential for fair and equal outcomes at the point that really matters. After all, culture is itself represented as divorced from "the struggle for moral and social regulation"; hence this struggle is not inscribed in mainstream cultural meanings.[38] For Hirsch there is no struggle, just a common culture. From this viewpoint, Freire's claim that education cannot be neutral but must be an instrument either of domestication or of liberation is mistaken. Education faces no such choice. From Hirsch's perspective, the only choice it faces is the technical one of whether schooling will promote or fail to promote among all learners an adequate grasp of what is involved in being what they "really" are. The common culture belongs to all equally and in principle is available to all. The problem simply is that at present it *is* excluded to some in practice. All that is required is a curriculum and a pedagogy adequate to the task of making available to all equally the heritage they share equally. The fact that different people will end up with different qualities of employment, different levels of qualification, different incomes, and the differences—inequalities—that these entail is no more than is inevitable given the natural transcendent historical order of things. As such, this is not a political outcome, and it in no way speaks to the lack of *educational* neutrality. The important educational outcome, which all *can* share equally, is satisfying participation in American society as full-fledged citizens.

The reality, however, is completely different. Cultural literacy, thus conceived, becomes an ideological mechanism which performs the same role as conventional approaches to functional literacy. It serves as a medium for recouping or further immersing those who are objectively disadvantaged economically, socially, and politically in a view of the world that leads them to accept as inevitable, and to participate actively in, the very social practices and relations that disadvantage them.[39]

Second, this educational discourse of cultural literacy implies the denial of cultural difference as educationally valid and legitimate. Hirsch's conception of culture "maintains an ominous ideological silence . . . regarding the validity and importance of the experiences of women, Blacks, and other groups excluded from the narrative of mainstream history and culture."[40] This has implications for silencing the voices of these groups, sentencing their lived meanings and their representations of their lives, conditions, and struggles to exile at the margins, while all the time they are measured by their "performance" against criteria and demands of the dominant culture. This is oppressive.

The educational implications are what are of immediate interest. These are implications of pedagogical exclusion. Hirsch's model of cultural literacy effectively excludes a practice of school literacy and learning which can take the voices and experiences of the Other as material for educational work. The rich possibilities for taking the histories, memories, and struggles of marginal groups as a basis for working toward understanding daily life, its demands, and its shortfalls in democratic terms are simply denied, if not made invisible, through a politics of exclusion. So also are the categories of meaning that Others bring to school learning, which offer them a basis, given an appropriate pedagogy, for producing and interpreting knowledge.

Hirsch's position is a decidedly antimaterialist and antiquarian theory of interpretation and the role of the citizen. Human agents are formed in the waxworks of history in which human capacity remains frozen in the shape of traditions, traditions that serve as the faceless curators of Western culture. The answer is not simply to take the voices and meanings of Others as givens, to be celebrated naively and accepted as educational knowledge in their own right. They have to be worked on responsibly and critically. The literacies they enfold are not to be assumed to have equal weight with any other literacy form(s). "On the contrary . . their differences are to be weighed against the capacity they have for enabling people to locate themselves in their own histories *while simultaneously establishing the conditions for them to function as part of a wider democratic culture*."[41] This, from a *critical* perspective, should be the educational test for all literacies. Like nationalism more generally, cultural literacy bolsters a social order which is unequal and oppressive, one that demonizes the Other and translates difference into deviancy. Where marginal and disadvantaged groups are made to think of themselves as Americans or Germans they will fight and die for what they believe to be the shared national interest. In fact, however, the shared national interest is no such thing. It is really an ideological umbrella for ruling or dominant interests. "The nation" is effectively the prevailing order, comprising the hierarchies, injustices, repression, denial of opportunities for full development of human potential, mistreatments, and so forth that inhere in it. The fact that many people are drawn to forms of nationalism as a route to vicarious identity precisely because their own has been denied, denigrated, or thwarted makes the point even more poignant.

Cultural literacy simultaneously distorts the true nature of what has been called the current crisis in education and democratic life and further entrenches it. It refuses to recognize that withdrawal from education and public life has much to do with being silenced and forced to engage in activities and modes of being that are profoundly alien, while at the same time having generations of history to draw on which attest to the fact that wholehearted and successful participation in the educational mainstream does not deliver on its promise of an enhanced quality of life. There is good reason for schooling having come to be strongly disvalued by those who have long experienced it as a route to inevitable failure and disadvantage.

Hunter and Harman relate this tendency to Collins's notions of education as a market for cultural goods and the inflation of education credentials since the middle of the last century. They note how groups at the bottom of the social and economic heap in the United States were led to believe that literacy and other educational achievements would enhance their life prospects. But as the number of people within these groups gaining educational credentials increased, so too did the level of qualifications demanded for the same jobs.

> Each time competing ethnic minorities reached the educational levels they had been told would lead to economic success and prestige, the game rules were changed . . . [Given] the resulting inflation of educational credentials . . . disillusionment is likely among those who purchase such credentials through school attendance when the promised pay-off fails to materialize. The disappointed groups may drop out of the difficult process of schooling.[42]

The problem in evidence here is deeply structural. It goes to the heart of a social order which is structurally unequal, and where the patterns of advantage and disadvantage are structured by social class, culture, race-ethnicity, and gender. Cultural literacy is impotent to address this structural malaise. At most it might put marginal groups back into the position of their forebears who gained credentials, only to find them inflate. To be sure, there are advantages for elite interests in having a culturally educated population. But the deeper structural—antidemocratic—realities militate against the interests of subordinate groups being promoted.

Moreover, it is no answer to say that cultural literacy does provide "hooks" for Others to connect with and relate to because Hirsch's canon of cultural knowledge contains items that appear to reflect the knowledge and experience of marginal groups. Tokenism does not constitute *recognition*. Culture is not a surface phenomenon only as "thick" as print on a page or as "deep" as a curriculum item (in Hirsch's case, one of 4,700 to be covered) treated verbally by a teacher or by reference to a bookish source. Cultural meanings, values, and experiences are deeply layered and have a complex texture. They are lived practices and representations, as deep as life itself because they *are* life. They are the outcomes of struggle, mediation, resolution, and creation. They whirl across the stage of history like a semiotic storm. To treat them as less than this, as a form of semantic inevitability, as in the literacy and pedagogy championed by Hirsch, is to deny and distort them. It is to risk premature closure on meaning. Worse, it is to practice pedagogy as domestication, to "shore up the status quo."[43]

What, then, is to be done? The answer provided by proponents of *critical* literacy is to create and practice forms of literacy that have genuine democratic and emancipatory potential. This involves recognizing the other side of literacy, which so far we have not addressed. In our discussion of recent developments in the politics of literacy we have focused on studies which reveal the nature and role of literacy as a buttress of prevailing social structures and relations and the hierarchies of interests inherent in them. Literacy, however, can be and has been made into forms which play an important part in attempts by subordinate groups to politicize themselves and to engage in action aimed at challenging existing structures of inequality and oppression and pursuing democratic alternatives. This theme has important contemporary associations with Paulo Freire and numerous lesser-known radical educators, as well as with a wide range of popular and community-based initiatives. The chapters by Bee, Jules, Searle, Rockhill, and Anderson and Irvine in this volume provide empirical examples of work in this tradition, which also has important roots in the past, notably within self-education initiatives undertaken by working-class folk in England during the nineteenth century.[44]

This is the tradition embraced by the emergent critical literacy project. To situate this project intellectually and politically and to distinguish it from other projects that might lay claims to the same name, it is helpful to consider a range of meanings that have been given to the qualifying term *critical*. Although the meanings that follow are by no means exhaustive, they are sufficient to distinguish liberal and conservative appropriations from emancipatory democratic versions and to account for the various positions represented in this book.

Critical literacy as paradigm and pluralism

The first meaning of *critical* we will consider is one which has long been associated with the idea of liberal education as an engagement aimed at promoting intellectual freedom or freeing the mind from error, delusion, or prejudice. Wider and narrower variations on this theme exist, but in both cases the critical ideal is typically celebrated as detached and politically neutral. After coming under sustained attack during the 1970s and 1980s, this view is currently being reasserted by liberal/conservative academics, some of whom, like Bloom, are couching their offensive in terms of literacy.[45]

The underlying notion is that in their attempts over the millennia to make their world meaningful and to discover truths about it, humans have fashioned public traditions of thought and reasoning which enshrine impersonal procedures and content. These are critical traditions, or "systematic developments of reasoning"[46] exemplified in the academic disciplines like science, philosophy, history, and mathematics. They are rule-governed modes of inquiry: *discourses*. To engage them is to follow those rules and meanings—concepts, principles of correct procedure, evaluation, testing, and inference—that define what it is to *think*. In the words of Richard Peters,

> Developed forms of reasoning, which involve criticism and the production of counter examples, can best be understood as the internalization of public procedures and the different points of view of others [arrived at by way of employing these same public procedures]. The individual who reasons in this developed sense is one who has taken a critic into his own consciousness, whose mind is structured by the procedures of a [critical rational] public tradition.[47]

In this way, humans are able to rise above arbitrariness, irrelevance, prejudice, distortion, and falsehood. Learners must be initiated, through schooling, into awareness of these critical traditions and the ability to work within them. In part this is a matter of mastering concepts, techniques, and standards. It also, however, involves imbibing a range of attitudes such as concern for truth, consistency, relevance, impartiality, clarity, and honesty in appraisal and interpretation of evidence, and avoiding contradiction in thought and action.

These discourses are not entirely fixed and static, as even the most cursory reading of their histories reveals. But within a given time-space there tend to exist dominant paradigms of each: roughly, what Kuhn refers to as "normal science"[48] and Harris as "mainstream or orthodox discourses."[49] Competing discourses typically exist alongside the dominant ones. But insofar as official curricula and syllabuses exist at the school level, the disciplines will tend to be taught as if the dominant paradigm were the only one.

Critical literacy as disciplinary knowledge

Given this general model of a liberal education, what counts as *critical* inquiry, or operating in a critical mode? Narrower and wider positions can be discerned here. The narrow view proceeds from the assumption that there is a single identifiable paradigm that represents what really constitutes the discipline in question. Take, for example, the case discussed by Harris, wherein Peters claims that "the important thing in the philosophy of education is that something should be there *to indicate what it is and to provide a determinate structure on which students can train their critical faculties.*"[50] From this stance, critical inquiry is a matter of observing the rules of the discipline within debate and dialogue with other views generated inside the same paradigm.

As such, being critical is not a matter of imbibing content (even "true" content) for its own sake, although it presupposes close familiarity with content, both in the process of becoming competent in a discipline and in interacting with other views in the critical quest for truth. Rather, it is a matter of trying to improve on other positions—to get closer to truth—by interacting with them from within the discursive parameters of their own creation. Such criticism, then, is internal and nonreflexive. It is internal to the paradigm and nonreflexive in the sense that it does not subject the paradigm itself to critical scrutiny. What passes for critical endeavor here is often little more than producing minor variations on existing positions, or successive refinements of them. A classic example of this kind of critical inquiry was apparent within analytic philosophy of education during the 1960s–1980s, as Harris discusses in the next chapter.

The wider view is implied in a recent article by John Searle. Commenting on the position of Michael Oakeshott, who eloquently championed the narrower view over a long career, Searle notes that Oakeshott "does not have much to say about the critical purpose of education. His educated person does not look as if he would produce any intellectual revolutions, or even upset many intellectual apple carts."[51]

Critical literacy as pluralism

A more pluralistic view of what it means to be critical can be gleaned from Searle's concern to sketch some features of a general theory of education, where education is seen as including among its purposes a critical intent. He plainly sees a place for critical thinkers who can upset intellectual apple carts and/or engender intellectual revolutions of one order or another. Although he values critical endeavor that produces less dramatic outcomes, his reference to *intellectual* achievements and the manner in which he construes them is the real key to his view of "the critical."

For Searle, the defining characteristic of education is that it is properly an intellectual engagement. It must *not* be construed as having a political intent, although he recognizes that what is done and not done in education, as elsewhere, will inevitably have political consequences. The main thing is to ensure that education is not conceived and practiced as a political engagement. It is to be detached, its emphasis intellectual, and its aim to enable people to attain the best intellectual understanding of the world that they can.

Searle construes *intellectual* in a detached and heavily bookish sense, although liberally educated persons may choose to apply their understanding and knowledge to critiquing material aspects of daily life. He claims that earlier generations, including his own,

> found the critical tradition that runs from Socrates through the *Federalist Papers*, through the writings of Mill and Marx, down to the twentieth century, to be liberating from the stuffy conventions of traditional American politics and pieties. Precisely by inculcating a critical attitude, the "canon" served to demythologize the conventional pieties of the American bourgeoisie and provided the student with a perspective from which to critically analyze American culture and institutions.[52]

Furthermore, one of the most liberating effects of "liberal education" lies in the opportunities it provides through the study of great works for "coming to see one's own culture as one possible form of life and sensibility among others."[53]

Education, then, is about "seeing" and "knowing," academically and bookishly conceived. The works to be studied—and study *is* to be grounded in *works*—must be the best. The best works are those which display academic rational virtues of the type identified by Oakeshott, Peters, and Scheffler, at the highest level. Searle insists, for example, on knowing at least one foreign language well enough to be able to read in the original "the best literature that the language has produced," on having enough philosophy "so that the methods of logical analysis are available to you to be used as a tool, and to acquire "the skills of writing and speaking that make for candor, rigor, and clarity."[54]

The quality of knowledge he has in mind is revealed in his account of how students will get to know how their culture got to be the way it is, which simultaneously betrays his understanding of culture, placing him close to Hirsch. Students must be exposed to political and social history, and master some of the great philosophical and literary texts of that culture. This means "reading not only texts that are of great value, like those of Plato, but many less valuable that have been influential, such as the works of Marx." It worries him not at all that Aristotle and Tocqueville might be taught along with Frantz Fanon, so long as social and political histories are taught "intelligently," by which he means in a detached, intellectual, and neutral manner. In this way, the histories of "all the major components of European and American society, including those that have been treated unjustly," should be recognized.[55]

Searle's notion of what it means to be educated for critical capacities is simply a less monopolistic, more plural version of the narrower view already described. He is more catholic in the "literatures" (in Oakeshott's sense) that students should be exposed to, and will tolerate "languages" other than the *dominant* paradigm discourses. Students should be free and enabled to range over paradigms and content (so long as they are legitimate, rational, and not "crankish") in order to make the best intellectually disciplined sense of things, and to apply their trained minds to evaluating the relative intellectual merits of varying methodologies and positions. The world is to be approached through theory and canon. It is implied that critical activity might largely be addressed to intellectual products alone, with application to daily life being an optional extra that educated people might choose to engage.

The implications of these liberal/conservative positions for a social conception and practice of literacy are clear. Texts are to be approached as media through which teachers enable students to master the know-how of thinking and judging in an academic manner. Students are to read and write in a context of learning how to do the kind of thing that those who produced the texts have done. In this they learn to maintain vigilance over logic, clarity, consistency, impartiality, and so forth and to become committed to the possibility of approximating objective truth and to see its pursuit as an imperative. Their stance is to be intellectually detached, their emphasis on trying to uncover an accurate picture of how things are. In reading and writing students must learn how to abstract and to relate particulars to universals and principles. In ethical, political, and other normative spheres, their primary concern will be to understand, construct, and evaluate principles. In short, critically informed reading and writing, and the use of reading and writing for critical ends, is exemplified in the ideals and practices of liberal academics cast in the mold of those whose account of this position we have described.

Critical literacy as transformative praxis

If such a literacy is to be described as a *critical* literacy, it is one whose intent and basic character is explicitly rejected by advocates of the critical literacy tradition represented in this book. For such a literacy has some very obvious status quo-maintaining tendencies. Rather than attempting to confront and subvert the sublime aura of the established social order in order to desacralize its power to commodify desire and to generate the mandates of technocratic reason, the very acts of learning to become critical and practicing criticism will tend to preserve established modes of inquiry which, whether they are *dominant* paradigms or not, will have recognized legitimacy within the academy. This almost certainly means that they have their own "agreements" with the established order.[56] Indeed, this is a precondition for their becoming dominant or otherwise legitimate in the first place within educational institutions sanctioned by the state. In some cases, as with Marxist paradigms, the liberal approach described here effectively "domesticates" or contains them within acceptable limits by channeling criticism into *theoreti-*

cal endeavor which keeps their radical potential one step removed from direct action on the world.

This kind of critical literacy is consciously detached from the world of social relations and practices. Criticism is much more of books and articles than of lived practices. Of course, the critical products addressed have typically been produced by people who enjoy (or enjoyed) relative economic, political, and cultural privilege, who inhabit ideological spaces remarkably consistent with the imperatives of dominant interests. Here the interests of criticism are necessarily collusive with the role of the West as a colonizing power. The social effects of such a position have led to benighted attacks on affirmative action and attempts by cultural workers to develop curricula and cultural practices that contest racism, sexism, homophobia, and white supremacist views on knowledge and identity. Such a view endorses a politics of diversity rather than of difference. A politics of diversity wraps itself in a counterfeit democracy and pseudo equality—as if diversity were simply accretive, benevolently allowing other voices to add themselves to the already assimilated mainstream, like different flavorings atop a vanilla ice-cream sundae. The conception of critical literacy endorsed within this volume sees diversity as a quest for something more than a collection of ethnic "add-ons" but rather as a politics of *thinking from the margins,* of possessing integral perspectives on the world. This is a far cry from the conservative and liberal view of diversity that is steeped in social amnesia and imperialist nostalgia, a view in which interest groups are simply added on to a preexisting pluralism, and in which negotiation takes place among culturally diverse groups against a backdrop of presumed cultural homogeneity. This misses the point raised by Chandra Mohanty, who argues that a politics of difference recognizes that all cultural knowledges are forged at particular historical moments and within shifting relations of power.[57]

This is not to say that liberal tools and standards of criticism cannot have their place within transformative and emancipatory criticism. For they do, although, as we shall see, further concepts, "tools," and attitudes and an entirely different orientation toward the world are required. Nor is it to say that more "radically" critical minds cannot evolve out of such an educational experience, for sometimes they do. But is not the intention of those who advocate this form of critical literacy to actively encourage, far less *ensure,* this as an outcome. Moreover, where more radically critical minds *do* emerge, their bearers necessarily conceive and practice an entirely different critical literacy.

A second meaning of *critical* can be gleaned from elements of Freire's distinction between critical and naive consciousness. In *Education: The Practice of Freedom*, Freire claims that naive consciousness is characterized by (among other things) "an oversimplification of problems" and "a lack of interest in investigation." By contrast, critical consciousness "is characterized by depth in the interpretation of problems," the application "of causal principles," "refusal to transfer responsibility," and "the attempt to avoid distortion when perceiving problems and to avoid preconceived notions when analyzing them."[58] These ideas have interesting dimensions when applied to understanding social problems which currently beset us and seeking effective solutions to them. For we often find a proclivity for oversimplifying and distorting such problems. This results in failure to identify their true causes, such that we confuse causes with symptoms and arrive at "solutions" which either transfer responsibility to the wrong people or which are otherwise simply inadequate to solving the problem.

Many common and powerful ideologies can be understood as elements of naive consciousness in this restricted sense. Very importantly, these include diverse forms of blame-the-victim reasoning in which agents who should be assuming responsibility for their part in the problem and/or for addressing it effectively are enabled to escape, and those who suffer the consequences of the problem either see the situation as being of their own making or inadequacy, or else assume that their condition is inevitable and must simply be endured or adapted to.

An illuminating angle on this species of ideological confusion is evident in C. Wright Mills's account of "sociological imagination." Mills notes the widespread feeling among people that they are trapped; the troubles they experience cannot be overcome. They feel helpless, caught in circumstances and processes of change they understand but dimly and which they sense to be beyond their control. Ironically, the more information people have about the world the more powerless they feel, the less they seem to understand "the meaning of their epoch for their own lives."[59] A major reason for this, says Mills, is the pervasive failure of people to grasp the relationship between biography and history, between feelings of personal entrapment and "the seemingly impersonal changes in the very structure of continent-wide societies."[60] A precondition for overcoming this feeling of powerlessness and confronting realistically the possibilities for asserting some control over our circumstances is an orientation toward the world which Mills calls "sociological imagination." By imagining sociologically we can perceive more clearly the relationship between what is going on in the world and what is happening to and with ourselves.

There is an intimate connection between *history* and *biography,* between social *structures* (and changes in these) and our private experience of life. "The facts of contemporary history are also facts about the success and failure of individual men and women. When a society is industrialized, a peasant becomes a worker . . . When classes rise or fall a man is employed or unemployed . . . Neither the life of an individual nor the history of a society can be understood without understanding both."[61] This involves attending to the "depth grammar" of a society, going beyond its "surface grammar."[62]

By grasping history and biography and the relations between the two in society, we can distinguish between "the personal troubles of milieux" and "the public issues of social structure." We can keep the two distinct, avoiding misconstruing afflictive conditions experienced by individuals which have their origins in the social structure as conditions which arise from purely personal or private factors. *Troubles* are more or less private matters, arising from the personality and immediate social context of individuals. *Issues* are public matters arising from "the larger structure of social and historical life."[63] When we confuse the two we will misconstrue problems, identify false causes, and perceive what are really personal *symptoms* of public issues as causes originating within individuals. Many ideologies prevalent within everyday life originate precisely from absence of sociological imagination. In their grip we readily blame victims and construct "solutions" to their problems which require them to attend to their own shortcomings but which, on their own, cannot work.

A classic example here concerns the link between literacy and personal success or effectiveness. Being unemployed or at risk of unemployment, for instance, is often construed as a matter of individuals being *unemployable—*

because, say, they are illiterate. The solution is seen in terms of "fixing individuals up," making them functionally or culturally literate. In fact, the origins of mass unemployment lie deep in the logic of capitalism, and in economic restructuring and lesser adjustments made imperative by the quest for capital accumulation. Where jobs are scarce, one person may become "employable" upon attaining functional literacy, but she or he will displace another worker or take a job that some other newly functional literate person might have taken. Moreover, illiteracy itself seems to be much more a *symptom* of economic marginality and its associated experiences than a *cause* of it. Critiques of Hirsch's view of cultural literacy may be couched in terms of his lacking sociological imagination, thereby confusing symptoms with causes and prescribing a solution which is no such thing. The same is true for functional literacy. This kind of analysis has also been employed to critique popular ideological representations of the underclass and the "solutions" advanced for addressing the "underclass problem."[64]

Given those elements of Freire's distinction between critical and naive consciousness identified above, we would argue that a conception of what it is to be critical and to practice critical literacy can proceed from Mills's notion of sociological imagination. To address social problems of the type we have identified in a *critical* manner, including examples where causes would properly be sought in structured patriarchal and/or racist social relations and practices, presupposes a sociological imagination that postulates a necessary connection between literacy as an act of knowing and as a form of advocacy. Failure to employ it almost inevitably results in oversimplifying and distorting problems. It indicates a lack of interest in serious investigation or an ability to perform it, and an inability to avoid distortion when perceiving problems or to transcend preconceived notions when analyzing them. Sociological imagination brings *depth* to analysis because it gets beneath the surface of prejudices and mystifying ideologies and goes to the deeper level of structured relations and practices within which humans live their lives and their lives are shaped. It is to see, for example, that although functional literacy may be necessary for personal effectiveness it is by no means sufficient. We must attend also to the structured routines which marginalize and diminish human subjects and their possibilities.

To teach and practice critical literacy in this sense involves employing texts and the capacity to read, write, and discuss in a context where teachers are consciously striving to engender a sociological imagination. This marks a major difference from the form of literacy previously described. On the surface it may appear that John Searle's requirement that educated people come to understand their culture and how it got to be that way is really a call to sociological imagination. This is not so. To take up promoting a sociological imagination as an educational task is an explicitly *political* commitment. It requires adopting a theoretical perspective, distinctive concepts, and a pedagogical stance almost entirely at odds with Searle's position.

It requires, for example, getting beyond bland, surface talk of our cultural tradition and understanding how it got to be what it is by exploring seminal texts seen as constitutive of its nature and shape, and by reference to orthodox social and political histories. It means adopting the view that society is not merely structured, but that under capitalism, patriarchy, race and ethnic hierarchy, and so on it is structured in a way that creates conflict between the interests of different groups of human beings, and systematically privileges the interests of certain groups at the expense of others. It presumes that ideological representations of reality will typically mask and distort the "real" nature of social practices and relations in their informal and institutionalized forms alike. Concepts which assume history to be riven with conflict and struggle rather than comprising an orderly progression of ideas and associated practices that are innocent in respect of privilege, discrimination, and struggle must often be employed: for example, concepts of social class and class struggle, competing interests, ideology, patriarchal domination, capitalism, and structured relations of power. Finally, a pedagogy of sociological imagination cannot be merely or principally bookish. Relevant texts, including many that Searle and others like him identify, must be employed, but not as material to be read in pursuit of surface understanding. Their reading must be mediated by serious attention to "voice," the struggles that have historically shaped the voices, meanings, and experiences of Others, and the structured conditions that have confined them to the margins. Texts are a call to the act of interpreting the experiences of elite and marginal groups alike in *deep* ways, not a stand-in for those experiences themselves or their interpretation.

This conception and practice of critical literacy can be expanded into a more elaborate position. Once again, the work of Roger Dale in education policy studies is helpful here.[65] Dale draws on ideas from Robert Cox and Claus Offe to suggest an approach to education policy studies which makes it into a species of critical theoretic activity which involves the practice of a critical form of literacy. Cox argues all theories are *interested* in the sense that they are for someone or other, and for some purpose or other, and they have a perspective in that they derive from some position in social and political time and space that constitutes a standpoint from which the world is seen. There is no such thing as theory in itself. "When any theory so represents itself, it is the more important to examine its ideology, and to lay bare its concealed perspective."[66]

The perspective of a theory circumscribes and shapes the issues and problems that theorists perceive as presented by the world. Issues, questions, and topics framed within a theoretical stance and which the theorist seeks to explain constitute its *problematic*. So far as their problematics are concerned, theories can serve two distinct purposes. The first is to make a response to the problem(s) posed by providing a guide to solving them. This gives rise to "problem-solving theory" which presumes the world as it is. *Existing* relations of power and their institutional organization provide the framework for problem-solving action. The problem is to be solved by action in the immediate sphere, taking the status quo in the wider spheres for granted, assuming it to be static. Theorists define and limit the problem as closely as necessary for effective action, breaking its elements down into subunits and identifying the variables to be acted on. Much policy analysis represents a good example of problem-solving theory. The other purpose is more reflective and introspective. It is concerned with examining "the process of theorizing itself: to become clearly aware of the perspective which gives rise to the theorizing [in the particular case], and its relation to other perspectives; and to open up the possibility of choosing a different valid perspective from which the problematic *becomes one of creating an alternative world*."[67]

Whereas problem-solving theory looks inward toward the specific focus of the problem rather than outward to examine the wider picture of social and political structures within which the problem arises, critical theory is consciously directed "to the social and political complex as a whole rather than to the specific parts."[68] Moreover, it involves trying to understand how the wider order came about and how it works in terms of human interests and concerns. It is an attempt to understand the prevailing social order structurally and dynamically. Theorists who take on this complex task do so for two distinctively critical ends that go far beyond the purpose of finding technical solutions to a technically defined problem. One is to call into question rather than take as given the very institutions and social and power relations within which the initial problem is located. It is recognized that a real solution may call for changing these wider conditions rather than trying to work within them. The *real* problem may consist in the social and political structures themselves rather than in specific symptoms caused by them, in the manner noted earlier in relation to literacy and employment under capitalism. The second critical dimension involves scrutiny of the very theory problematic itself. In particular, critical theorists try to understand their problematic in relation to the prevailing order and to see whether their perspective is itself part of a/the real problem. For example, given who and what the theory is for in the first place, will it actually work against asking the right questions, undermine promoting interests in a just manner, confuse causes and symptoms, and so on? As we claim in a later chapter,

> what characterizes a research as "critical" is an attempt to recognize its own status as discourse and to understand its role as a servant of power. Critical researchers try to understand how the research design and process are themselves implicated in social and institutional structures of domination . . . Critical research must be undertaken in such a way as to narrate its own contingency, its own situatedness in power and knowledge relations.[69]

Dale works from these ideas to advocate a critical theoretical approach to education policy studies as a scientific pursuit. He notes three important features of such a project which make it especially valuable. In approaching education policy *critically*, students will attain a "perspective on perspectives." This provides a basis for better understanding on the part of all involved in analyzing, framing, or evaluating education policy, of what they are putting together, why, and with what implications.[70] There are clear advantages in extending such a perspective to those involved in policy analysis.

Second, a critical approach to education policy studies gives priority to "asking further questions over seeking solutions to a list of problems." "It is at least as important and difficult to ask the right questions about education policy (or anything else) as to come up with the answers."[71] Functional literacy and cultural literacy are answers to the wrong questions.

Third, Dale stresses the importance in areas of social practice of achieving "more accurate perceptions of problems" and "framing . . . more answerable questions." A first step here is "to identify problems that *can* be solved at a particular level, and to distinguish them from those that *cannot* be solved there."[72] He introduces Offe's distinction between "dilemmas" and "contradictions" as a valuable theoretical tool here. The use of print in attuning learners to contradictions and contradictoriness in the relevant sense becomes a key aspect of critical literacy.

Offe claims that dilemmas occur almost universally in social relationships. They are conflicting pressures or tensions which have to be and, in practice, can be absorbed within institutional settings. They can be managed by reform, structural adjustment, or institutional tinkering within the arena in which they arise. Contradictions, however, are inherently insoluble problems inside existing arrangements. Offe's notion of contradiction is linked to the historical phenomenon of societal modes of material production. Part of what characterizes a given society is the mode of material production through which it reproduces itself, such as capitalism. Among the institutionalized rules through which a society operates are those which determine the process of material production. In any society—that is, under any given mode of production—three things must be regulated: "effective control over labour power, over the material means and resources of production, and over the product itself."[73] Every mode of production must meet the specific economic, political, and cultural requirements necessary for its continuation as a societal mode.

Offe notes that there are two ways in which this requirement might fail to be met. One is where certain necessities—such as labor power or materials—are either (or become) absent or in insufficient supply. In practice it is often possible to overcome such situations, such as by finding new sources of power or labor. The other is where contradictions exist. These cannot in principle be overcome. A contradiction "is the tendency inherent within a specific mode of production to destroy those very preconditions on which its survival depends. Contradictions become manifest in situations where . . . a collision occurs between the constituent pre-conditions and the results of a specific mode of production, or where the necessary becomes impossible and the impossible becomes necessary."[74]

Dale links this notion of contradiction to the quest of critical theorists to address and understand the broad historical and social context. Only by attending to "the prevailing social and power relationships and the institutions into which they are organized" can theorists seek out contradictions.[75] In so doing, they can reveal problems—as in education—that are insoluble given the imperatives of capitalism. All the tinkering and reform in the world cannot solve them. It may, at best, buy some time, helping maintain the status quo, but at the price of "squeezing" certain groups, adapting them to immiserating conditions and otherwise further oppressing them, or muddling through until a change in some other sphere eases the particular burden and creates a new one elsewhere. (For example, local unemployment might be eased by lowering wages until they are competitive with Third World labor.)

Critical theorizing which employs this notion of contradiction can identify and explain the inherent tendency within capitalism to marginalize certain people as a precondition for its very continuation. Mere reform cannot change this. It can only alter details of who is marginalized (as where women are admitted to the labor force but displace black males). If marginalization is historically necessary and inevitable under capitalism, such remedies as functional or cultural literacy cannot change much. If enabling capital accumulation and/or legitimating different material outcomes for individuals presupposes assessment by which some students do better than others or are tracked into higher-prestige courses than others, academic failure is made inevitable. When failure becomes patterned—say, by race and ethnicity and/or social class—*as it does*, apathy, truancy, disruption, illiteracy, and a host of other patterned conditions in turn become inevitable. To address these conditions would necessarily entail a societal mode and accordant social structures that do not give rise to such presuppositions in the first place. This is precisely what educational theorists have in mind when they speak of a *crisis* existing in education and democracy under present conditions.[76] Dale identifies inevitable contradictions arising from the requirement that capitalist schooling simultaneously assists in the process of capital accumulation, in providing a social context conducive to capital accumulation, and in legitimating the accumulation process.[77]

At a less comprehensive level, theorists employ the notion of contradiction in practicing immanent critique. This, says Harris, is "the most effective immediate critique of any thesis, stance, theory, body of thought [or] ideology." It is a form of critique "that attempts to show what is being criticized cannot . . . attain the end that it proposes for itself, and/or a critique that points out anomalies and contradictions that are otherwise comfortably contained and accommodated in the theory under scrutiny."[78]

In Chapter 1, Harris employs an immanent critique to show how Helen Nugent's economic rationalism necessarily undercuts one of the educational desiderata she explicitly endorses. The point is not that Nugent simply makes a slip in her argument. Rather, the critique shows where, how, and why Nugent's theoretical position necessarily cannot accommodate what she sets out to accommodate. The problem exists in the very structure of the theory itself and the social reality it is intended to address. Immanent critique presupposes the very virtues characteristic of critical theory in the present sense: namely, a perspective on perspectives, a commitment to scrutinizing the wider social and political context, and willingness to withdraw from a discourse of technical problem solving in the interests of giving priority to asking further questions in the hope of asking the *right* ones.

It is possible to construct a social practice and conception of critical literacy based on this view of critical theorizing. Critical literacy uses texts and print skills in ways that enable students to examine the politics of daily life within contemporary society with a view to understanding what it means to locate contradictions within modes of life, theories, and substantive intellectual positions, *and to actively seek out such contradictions*. It means enlisting the literate and intellectual capacities of learners in the task of understanding how theories and practices based upon theories, including education itself, cannot be neutral. And it calls for engaging them seriously in the acts of theorizing and evaluating theory in politically informed ways.

Although our elaboration of critical theory has drawn on its specific development in relation to capitalism as a mode of material production, we do not imply that this exhausts its conception or application. Parallel applications can and must be evolved for understanding and critiquing the structural logics of racism, sexism and patriarchy, and other modes—political, social, and cultural—of producing marginalized Others. Here, as elsewhere, it is essential to avoid constraining and distortive forms of economic reductionism. Several of the papers which follow[79] are contributions to this end. It is especially important to note the extent to which recent developments in critical postmodernist and critical poststructuralist social theory add to our understanding of what this entails, and the distinctive discursive means by which they are often able to undermine the conceptual coordinates that have been employed to fix language in familiar contexts.

Thus construed, critical theorizing presupposes social praxis, but does not necessarily actually *engage* praxis. In other words, critical theorists can and do produce critical theoretical products which are not in and of themselves *praxis*, and may not even reflect or report praxis. A number of researchers, including Wilfred Carr and Stephen Kemmis, mark the distinction between critical theory which is not "praxical" and that which is by distinguishing critical *theory* from critical *social science*. We turn, now, to critical social science and to Freire's idea of a problem-posing education as praxis, for clues to a further meaning of *critical* as a basis for conceiving and practicing critical literacy.

In *Becoming Critical: Knowing Through Action Research*, Carr and Kemmis critique positivist and interpretivist models of educational theory and argue for a critical social science approach.[80] In particular, they recognize the ways and the extent to which scientistic approaches to theorizing and addressing problems harbor fatal weaknesses, and may proceed from ideological distortions of the world that actually impede the pursuit of rational goals. Any adequate social science, and social practice informed by that science, must meet certain criteria and ensure certain outcomes. Those of direct concern to us may be summarized as follows.

1. Critical theorizing "must provide ways of distinguishing interpretations [of the world, problems, social practice, and so on] that are distorted by

ideology from those that are not [and] provide some view of how any distorted self-understanding is to be overcome."

2. Critical theorizing "must be concerned to identify and expose those aspects of the existing social order which frustrate the pursuit of rational goals and . . . be able to offer theoretical accounts which make [human actors] aware of how they can be eliminated or overcome."

3. Critical theorizing must be *practical*, "in the sense that the question of its truth will be determined by the ways in which it relates to practice." It

> must always be orientated towards transforming the ways in which [human subjects] see themselves and their situation so that the factors frustrating the rational development of their practices can be recognized and eliminated. Equally, it must be oriented towards transforming the situations which place obstacles in the way of achieving [social, especially *educational*] goals, perpetuate ideological distortions, and impede rational . . . work in [practical human] situations.[81]

To this extent, *critical* reflection is consciously guided by the intention to change understanding of the world and, in the same process, to change that very world we inhabit and are trying to understand. Theory and practice are to be brought together (rather than kept separate) within explicit acts of transformation, where the object to be transformed is not merely theory itself, or understanding, but the lived relations and practices of social reality. Critical social science proceeds from the insight that all theory is "interested" and a conviction that it is necessary to escape from the theory-practice divide which is precisely "an ideological reflection of a way of life in which 'theory' has been enlisted to serve, legitimate, and perpetuate the status quo."[82] This is critical engagement as *praxis*, which may be understood along the lines of Habermas's idea of *emancipatory* knowledge or, alternatively, by reference to Freire's model of a problem-posing pedagogy of liberation.[83] It is not enough for praxis that it transform consciousness of the world without also transforming social relations and practice in the world in the knowledge process.

This presupposes a very different epistemology from that underlying liberal rationalist approaches, which presume a given world to be known and then, perhaps, responded to. The epistemology of praxis is *constructivist*. "It sees knowledge as developing by a process of active construction and reconstruction of theory and practice by those involved."[84] The world to be known includes these active constructions and reconstructions themselves. It cannot be hived off from the way humans want it to be, and explored through inert, objective, detached means. The world to be known is itself partly constituted by the interested theories, domain assumptions,[85] and projects[86] that human knowers necessarily bring with them to their acts of knowing. In this view, the act of knowing necessarily reflects and refracts the world; it is always a situated practice, that is, an embedded or located "event" in that it is created in a particular context that has both material and interpretive dimensions. Different knowledges compete for legitimation at multiple levels of interaction and according to the various interests of the participants in such acts of knowing. In the case of critical social scientists, the world-to-be-known includes an emancipatory agenda that reflects what they are seeking through praxis to make it into.

In developing their account of action research as a critical praxis of knowing, Carr and Kemmis highlight the work of Habermas. Habermas identifies knowledge as the result of activity motivated by the natural needs and interests of human beings. He conceives humans as beings with the capacity to think rationally, to be self-reflective and self-determining. Beyond their biology, humans as a species are self-forming through their social practice, which is based on refined development of the technical power of production and ongoing development in the practical dimension of law, morality, and worldviews mediated by language.[87]

Habermas refers to those interests which motivate acts of knowing as "knowledge-constitutive interests" "because they are interests which guide and shape the way knowledge is constituted in different activities of inquiring or knowing."[88] According to Habermas, humans have three knowledge-constitutive interests, which define the types and spheres of legitimate knowledge: technical, practical, and emancipatory. Each yields a legitimate and necessary type of knowledge given what humans are. A problem here is that under the domination of positivist discourses and "scientism" in particular, the technical has tended to usurp a virtual monopoly over the claim to paradigm status, subordinating and distorting practical and emancipatory concerns, with disastrous consequences for human advancement.[89] Habermas seeks to demonstrate the just claims to legitimacy of the practical and emancipatory sciences and, especially, to elucidate and champion "the emancipatory" as a necessary precondition for the proper practice of the others.

Humans have a technical interest in understanding the natural world in ways that yield knowledge by which we can achieve control over natural objects. This is the realm of natural science, which issues in "typically instrumental knowledge taking the form of causal explanations."[90] Humans likewise have an interest in understanding and clarifying "the conditions for meaningful communication and dialogue" among them. The kind of knowledge yielded by the interpretive or hermeneutic sciences can, under optimal conditions, promote forms of understanding which provide valuable information and guidance for practical judgment in the interests of enhanced self-formation as a species.

There is, however, a complication here which connects with the emancipatory interest humans have in "securing freedom from self-imposed constraints, hypostasized forces and conditions of distorted communication."[91] This concerns social meanings and their potential for distorting our consciousness of social reality. The very fact that concepts and the theories housing them are *interested*, in the sense of being framed and employed within social settings characterized by unequal relations of power which are structured, underwrites a tendency for existing forms of communication to be "systematically distorted by prevailing social, cultural, or political conditions."[92] To this extent, communication and interaction between human beings will alienate them from their capacity to act rationally, to be self-determining and self-reflective. As Roderick puts it,

> The process of self-formation of the human species is, at least potentially, a process in which history can be made with "will and consciousness." But it is apparent that history embodies unreason in the form of domination, repression and ideological constraints on thought and action. Thus, it is also apparent that human self-understanding is limited by systematically unacknowledged conditions. If the rational capacity of humans is to function truly, if their rational potential is to be fulfilled, [self-reflection] becomes necessary to overcome and abolish these constraining conditions . . . "Self-reflection brings to consciousness those determinates of a

self-formative process of cultivation and self-formation which ideologically determine a contemporary practice and conception of the world . . . [generating] insight due to the fact that what has previously been unconscious is made conscious in a manner rich in consequences" . . . Self-reflection can, by revealing the structure of distortions, aid human beings in overcoming them.[93]

Praxis aims at enabling social groups to find the origins of their collective misunderstandings in ideology. In the grip of ideological distortions, social groups misunderstand their true situation and accept representations of reality that impede their recognition and pursuit of the interests and goals they have in common. At the same time, ideological views of reality and the situation of social groups are not entirely false. The ideas and beliefs humans have of the world, and their place and circumstances within it, "contain some indication of the real aims and interests of individuals and thereby imply some alternative self-conception based on their true meaning." Praxis is to make explicit the genuine self-conceptions implicit in ideological views, and to indicate how contradictions and inadequacies contained in existing "knowledge" and self-understanding can be overcome.[94]

Praxis is a social or pedagogical process which enlists human efforts to understand the world more accurately in conjunction with a political will to transform social practices and relations in a way that resolves contradictions "in the rationality and justice of social action and social institutions." Enhanced understanding is brought to bear on the world in transformative social action which addresses the very structures that encourage and house ideological misrepresentations of reality in the first place.

The most comprehensive and influential account of praxis to have made an impact on educationists concerned with articulating an ideal of critical literacy is that provided by Freire. Although the details of his metaphysic, ontology, and epistemology differ in significant ways from that of Habermas, his emancipatory project has a remarkably similar intent. His towering influence on the current thinking and practice of educationists involved in the critical literacy project makes attention to his model of critical praxis imperative.

Freire argues that in order to reclaim their right to live *humanly* marginalized groups must confront, in praxis, those institutions, processes, and ideologies that prevent them from "naming their world."[95] They must address, simultaneously, the reality they inhabit *and* their consciousness of that reality. This is an *epistemological* necessity. Human subjects can only *know* through direct action on the object of knowledge. For example, they can only know whether their diagnosis of how they are being oppressed or marginalized in a specific context or instance is correct by *acting* on that context in accordance with their analysis of it: by performing a limit act suggested by their identification and analysis of a limit situation and observing the consequences.[96] Knowledge, then, presupposes *transformative* action—on the world.

Integral to his model of emancipatory knowledge as praxis is the shift from what Freire calls "naive consciousness" to "critical consciousness." This is best expressed by Freire himself.

> True dialogue cannot exist unless it involves critical thinking—thinking which discerns an indivisible solidarity between the world and [humans] admitting of no dichotomy between them—thinking which perceives reality as process and transformation, rather than as a static entity—thinking which does not separate itself from action, but constantly immerses itself in temporality without fear of the risks involved. Critical thinking contrasts with naive thinking, which sees "historical time as a weight, a stratification of the acquisitions and experiences of the past," from which the present should emerge as normalized and "well behaved." For the naive thinker, the important thing is accommodation to this normalized "today." For the critic the important thing is the continuing humanization of people.[97]

The distorted perceptions which hold marginalized groups in oppression and passivity, or which send them down false trails, must be exploded. This can only occur where people's critical transforming action upon the world reveals myths and distortions for what they are. One becomes a critical thinker in the *act* of practicing critical thought.

Freire's model of problem-posing education is precisely a pedagogy for moving from naive to increasingly critical consciousness. It involves two structurally parallel phases: a literacy phase and a postliteracy phase. The former is galvanized around generative *words*, the latter around generative *themes*. Both are necessary because the ultimate "text" to be read and written is the world itself. Learning to read and write words is an important and integral part of coming to "read" and "write"—to understand and name— the world itself. The full flowering of the literacy phase is achieved only in exploring generative *themes* and in confronting the limit situations revealed in this exploration with limit acts. Of course, the practice of critical literacy within school classrooms under prevailing normalized conditions is precisely a limit act in Freire's sense, grounded in an analysis of limit situations imposed by ruling conceptions and practices of curriculum and pedagogy, and "legitimated" by the ruling ideologies of educational discourse.

Six important learning principles are called out by Freire's view.

1. The world must be approached as an object to be understood and known by the efforts of learners themselves. Moreover, their acts of knowing are to be stimulated and grounded in their own being, experiences, needs, circumstances, and destinies.

2. The historical and cultural world must be approached as a created, transformable reality which, like humans themselves, is constantly in the process of being shaped and made by human deed in accordance with ideological representations of reality.

3. Learners must learn how to actively make connections between their own lived conditions and being and the making of reality that has occurred to date.

4. They must consider the possibility for "new makings" of reality, the new possibilities for *being* that emerge from new makings, and become committed to shaping a new enabling and regenerative history. New makings are a collective, shared, social enterprise in which the voices of all participants must be heard.

5. In the literacy phase learners come to see the importance of print for this shared project. By achieving print competence within the process of bringing their experience and meanings to bear on the world in active construction and reconstruction (of lived relations and practice), learners will actually *experience* their own potency in the very act of understanding what it means to be a human subject.[98] In the postliteracy phase, the basis for action

is print-assisted exploration of generative *themes*. Addressing the theme of "Western culture" as conceived by people like Hirsch and reified in prevailing curricula and pedagogies, and seeking to transcend this conception in the kinds of ways elaborated in later chapters, involves exactly the kind of praxis Freire intends.

6. Learners must come to understand how the myths of dominant discourses are, precisely, myths which oppress and marginalize them—but which can be transcended through transformative action.

How might this work in practice? In Latin America Freire and his teams would spend time among the illiterate groups they were to work with, observing their language and lives and discovering their felt concerns and aspirations. On the basis of this experience they would select approximately twenty words from the "vocabular universe" of the learners. These generative words provided the building blocks for learning to read and write.[99] For each of the generative words a codification—a drawing, photograph, or slide—was produced. Before moving to the act of learning to recognize and read the word and to create new words out of its syllables and syllable families, the group would address the situation depicted in the codification. This codification "stood in" for an aspect of the learners' reality. They would stand back from it, relate to it existentially, and, with assistance from the coordinator, move to understand it more critically and to scrutinize their own initial understandings of it, thereby engaging in a critique of their own ideologically mediated perceptions of the situation in question, sorting out the "truth" and "distortions" in their self-conceptions.

One of the words used in the state of Rio de Janeiro was *poco*, a well. Critical discussion of its codification included reference to aspects of daily life, like health and endemic diseases, water supply, and sanitary education. It is easy to see how a critical praxis might unfold here. Very likely the learners would not have easy access to a well. Perhaps the only well nearby belonged to the landowner and was for the exclusive use of his family. Peasants would have to use the river for washing, drinking, and ablution. Diarrhea and other diseases are natural consequences, leading to physical debilitation and high infant mortality rates.

In discussing this situation and its implications, learners would come to see how their lack of access to land and their individual lack of resources—resulting from low wages, high rates of seasonal unemployment, and unequal distribution of land—are linked to their health problems. They had become resigned to their circumstances, thinking nothing could be done to change them. In fact, the reality depicted in the codification calls for action on their part in the light of reflection and greater understanding of its structured social dimensions. This might range from organized struggle to secure land down to pooling resources and labor to build wells of their own as a source of better quality water. They might, thereafter, use the river for washing clothes but use well water for drinking, cooking, and food preparation. They might construct simple hand pumps to make drawing water (typically women's work) easier, allowing more water to be used to improve food preparation and general hygiene. They could build latrines away from the well to avoid polluting its water. Over time they could observe improvements in health that followed. From such informed bases they could move more radically to challenge the system of land ownership, organize labor to negotiate higher wages, etc. This, in fact, is precisely the kind of educational activity that underpinned organized struggle by peasants in the Cuban and Nicaraguan revolutions.[100]

A more familiar example for First World readers is provided by Shor.[101] Teaching "open admissions" students at the City University of New York, Shor employed a range of codifications to instigate problem-posing dialogues. In one case, a hamburger was used, and the "sociology" of the hamburger was addressed through discussion and written work. The class drew a distinction between junk food and healthy food, and posed why many people like themselves undermined their health and nutritional well-being by eating so much junk food. More generally, the nexus between motorcar and hamburger was explored for the clues it gives to the social and historical construction of American society, and the differences between the society that has been constructed in the United States and others elsewhere.

> The kind of imagination which gets stimulated can serve as a base for discussing alternatives to the present society. For now, the burger and the car may be two ruling forces within daily life, but they weren't always with us and may not remain forever. At a certain point in time, society changed

so as to produce hamburgers and cars, and in turn these phenomena worked to change society. Students who gain the power to understand the transformation of society also gain the critical consciousness needed to invent their own transformations. Through our investigation, their perceptions of transport and food change. Talk emerges about non-polluting mass transit, about cooperative food service replacing the cafeteria's junk meals. [102]

Out of this pedagogical work "a class organizing committee emerged to cooperatize the college cafeteria, and have it offer a nutritious, fixed-price lunch."[103]

Such examples give clues to how critical literacy might be conceived and practiced within classroom settings. Whether at the point of students learning to read and write (more efficiently) or at the stage of using it more or less fluently within curricular study, print becomes a medium for exploring anti-democratic ideologies and lived practices in reflection-action. Several of the chapters which follow provide further indications of what may be involved. Those by Anderson and Irvine, Bee, Jules, and Searle approach the task in terms that broadly reflect the concepts and categories employed in late modernist projects. The positions developed by Berlin, Brady and Hernández, Gee, Giroux, Rockhill, and Sholle and Denski are more explicitly informed by concepts and categories that have emerged from recent developments in postmodern social theory.

Several points should be noted here. The first is that learning should always be linked as closely and directly as possible to the lived experience and immediate reality of learners. Praxis, after all, implies transformative action on the learners' world.

Second, where tight curricular guidelines are mandated, teachers will have to seek creative ways of turning the curriculum into pedagogical opportunities for critical activity. This is challenging but by no means beyond the capacities of teachers committed to a more truly praxical approach to education. Promoting class, gender, and race and ethnic consciousness can be done by using whatever freedom and control teachers have over curriculum, although the spaces are becoming increasingly constrained under the conservative restoration. Fortunately, engagement in critical literacy can be under-taken "in a subtle manner in all subjects and at all levels. Don't dig into the 'hard core' material; it isn't necessary and it could get you into trouble. Kids don't have to be confronted with 'The Communist Manifesto': a *sensitive* reading of Dickens will do very well."[104]

Third, teachers must themselves be widely enough read to know where to locate content that can help learners investigate curriculum issues from a more critical standpoint than those represented in prescribed texts. Access to alternative literatures is important, especially at higher levels of school-ing. The works of Alice Walker, Maya Angelou, Paule Marshall, Ann Petry, and Toni Morrison, for example, provide excellent correctives to the kind of status quo—maintaining tokenism that would reduce participation of female authors in the canon to the time-honored novels of George Elliot, Jane Austin, Virginia Woolf, and the Brontes, important and valuable as these may be. In any event, alternative literatures must not stand in for experience to the exclusion of direct, serious, and sociologically informed engagement with the lived cultures and accumulated cultural experience of marginal groups of learners.

Finally, it is important to note here that in the very act of practicing critical literacy teachers and learners are necessarily involved in living new social relations of learning and addressing the hierarchies of power and privilege inherent in conventional schooling. This speaks powerfully to the call to create a more truly and emancipatory educational practice. Even so, a growing number of writers working within emergent postmodernist and post-structuralist currents are identifying issues and themes which directly or indirectly present challenges to the conception and practice of critical liter-acy as praxis along the lines broadly described here. Several of these are discussed in later chapters.

An initial concern is that positions adopted within critical theory bear-ing a Frankfurt School imprint, together with more overtly modernist stances taken within a Freirean perspective, are too closely wedded to the Enlighten-ment ideal of a unified human subject. Poststructuralist and feminist theor-ists alike have criticized educators for working within a discourse of critical rationalism which reifies the human subject—the rational autonomous agent—as a subject of history, change, and resistance. To the extent that these criticisms are valid, the conception of the human subject as an agent of praxis warrants further theorizing: together with wider categories and constructs that will coalesce around subjecthood and agency.

The question of agency is particularly urgent in these politically troubling times. Following some poststructuralist lines of thought, we can argue that we are all subject to ideological inscriptions and multiple organized discourses of desire, and to a certain extent we are structured as social agents through a type of discursive ventriloquism. Although it is true that the social and semiotic structures of meaning "speak" us into existence as social agents, we do not need to give up the idea of constructing our identities "from the inside" altogether. Rather than "willing" ourselves into a new politics of resistance and refusal, we can begin to transform the codes, cultural forms, and social practices (and their anchoring institutions) through which identities and subjectivities are produced. We do not need to give up the idea of truth, but rather the idea of a single truth. We do not need to give up the project of liberatory pedagogy but rather learn to defamiliarize pedagogy's taken-for-granted strategies. We need to lay claim to a new vocabulary of interpretation that has the power to contest the current legitimizing of cultural texts as normative or aberrant. We need to work toward a politics of refusal that can rupture and offset the conventions of teleological closure that operate as a centralizing force in the construction of meaning systems.

The concern among postmodernist social theorists to radically decenter the subject has itself been exposed to ideological critique on the grounds that it undercuts political struggles by marginalized groups at precisely the moment when they have begun to demand the right to name themselves and act as subjects rather than objects of history. There is obviously an important issue to clarify and resolve here. In the process, we might ask to what extent ideas employed within critical theory, such as the notion of contradictory self-conceptions, actually reflect and overlap with recent concerns about unified subjects, contradictory subject positions, and so on. These matters point to a wider issue. Right now it is not clear how far the project of critical postmodernism and poststructuralism is *distinct* from that of critical modernity, or how far it should be understood as an extension of it. Although the papers in this book cannot finally answer such questions by themselves, they represent the contending positions in their current state of development within educational discourse and sharpen the points on which our attention should be focused, such as the relationship between ideology and discourse, questions about the nature and basis of meaning, and so on.

Further issues relate to the underlying epistemology and ontology of critical theory and praxis as described above. The problems facing those working from a position like Habermas's are different from those facing educationists working from a Freirean position. But the postmodern turn presents challenges to both positions. Take, for example, the question of how we are to define the "nonideological." Many postmodernists would argue against Habermas that his answer relies on a master narrative which, like all master narratives, must be rejected because of its tendency to "totalize" thought. Against Freireans, as Allan Luke notes, the argument may be that they cannot provide a positive account of the nonideological. "Everything that is ideological is ascertained by reference to the 'Other' (the oppressor, dominant classes, etc.)."[105] This creates problems for building emancipatory pedagogies around a politics of difference. Alternatively, the justificatory weight borne by Freire's metaphysic of humans having an ontological vocation might be criticized for its transcendent essentializing trappings, which do not sit easily with the postmodern turn of mind.

Similarly, there is a residual tendency within modernist critical projects to fix meanings and claim authority for "emancipatory" meanings over those of other discourses. By contrast, several of the papers included here assume that literacy only becomes critical "to the degree that it makes problematic the very structure and practice of representation [and focuses] attention on the importance of acknowledging that meaning is not fixed and that to be literate is to undertake a dialogue with others who speak from different histories, locations, and experiences." The chapters by Berlin, Brady and Hernández, Gee, Giroux, Rockhill, Sholle and Denski, and McLaren and Lankshear are especially apposite here.

In some forms critical praxis leaves itself open to the charge that it is itself a colonizing and patronizing practice, distinctively male and Eurocentric in tone. It is easy to see why such charges arise when critical engagement is construed, for example, as practice which "names the people for whom it is directed; it analyses their suffering; it offers enlightenment to them about what their real needs and wants are; it demonstrates to them in what way their ideas about themselves are false and at the same time extracts from these false ideas implicit truths about them."[106] A concern for how to take up a critical literacy praxis without falling into a colonizing logic is especially evident in the chapters by Berlin, Brady and Hernández, Giroux, Rockhill, and McLaren and Lankshear.

It is also argued that discussions and practices of critical literacy are too often confined to being pedagogies of the *oppressed* and do not pay sufficient attention to how the consciousness of elites is to be addressed. Much of the work that follows bears on this concern, particularly that which emphasizes the importance of critical literacy being grounded pedagogically in a politics of difference that offers learners, regardless of their particular classed, raced, or gendered subjectivities, opportunities to be "border crossers."

> As border crossers, students not only refigure the boundaries of academic subjects in order to engage in new forms of critical inquiry, but they are also offered the opportunities to engage the multiple references that construct different cultural codes, experiences, and histories . . . a pedagogy of difference provides the basis for students to cross over into diverse cultural zones that offer a critical resource for rethinking how the relations between dominant and subordinate groups are organized, how they are implicated and often structured in dominance, and how such relations might be transformed in order to promote a democratic and just society.[107]

Consequently, beyond the conceptions and practices of critical literacy described at length above, it is necessary also to recognize and explore contributions offered by progressive developments within postmodern social theory. At the same time we must acknowledge that these new insights and directions are at an early stage of their development within educational inquiry. We have tried to emphasize that the question of literacy is inescapably intertwined with the project of intellectual inquiry at the level of everyday life. Today the leftist public intellectual lies in splinters, face down in the back alley of history. Prophesized by Nietzsche and prefigured by Benjamin's suicide at the Spanish border, the current crisis of authority and meaning is also reflected in the present gloating calm of the West after the demise of communism as the preparation continues for a majestic spiral of consumer desire on a global basis.

Since meanings and identities are being forged in such a polyvalent nexus of new postmodern discourses and in the absence of leftist public intellectuals who are able to both interpret the crisis and coordinate and develop strategies and tactics for social and cultural resistance, we believe that it is important to both consider and expand the ways that are presently available for transforming the self into thought and structures of meaning necessary for an emancipatory praxis. That is, we wish to bring teachers and students face to face with the violent contingencies of the social present by posing questions for which no current criteria of engagement are satisfactory. We propose to at least begin this task by interrogating the literacies available for understanding and disclosing the technologies of the self that make us who we are, that produce us within the natural, self-evident condition of everyday discourse.

Collectively, the essays in this book reflect the point reached to date in theoretical and practical work on critical literacy—revealing its strengths and limitations. They also recognize the need for considerable further work, indicate some of the directions in which this work may lie, and call us to engage it. It is to this calling that the book is ultimately dedicated. Its contents will lead us to the best reformulation of a theory and practice of critical literacy currently possible.

Notes

1. Williams, B., *History and Semiotic* (Toronto, Canada: Victoria University, Toronto Semiotic Circle Monograph, No. 4, 1985).

2. Harvey, D., *The Condition of Postmodernity* (Oxford: Basil Blackwell, 1989), provides a valuable introduction to the wider literature and issues. An earlier landmark work here, from which much subsequent theorizing derives, is Mandel, E., *Late Capitalism* (London: Verso, 1978). See also Sarup, M., *Post-structuralism and Postmodernism* (Athens: University of Georgia Press, 1989).

3. Hall, S., "Brave New World," *Socialist Review,* 21, 1, 1991, pp. 57–64. See also McLaren, P., "Postmodernism, Postcolonialism and Pedagogy," *Education and Society* 9, 2 (1991) pp. 136–158.

4. Freire, P., *Education: The Practice of Freedom* (London: Writers and Readers, 1976), p. 5; and *Pedagogy of the Oppressed* (Harmondsworth: Penguin, 1972), pp. 73–75.

5. Examples include Graff, H., *The Literacy Myth* (New York: Academic Press, 1979), and (ed.), *Literacy and Social Development in the West* (Cambridge: CUP, 1982); Freire, P. (1972) and (1976), *op. cit.*, as well as *Cultural Action for Freedom* (Harmondsworth: Penguin, 1973), *The Politics of Literacy* (London: MacMillan, 1985), and with Macedo, D., *Literacy: Reading the Word and the World* (South Hadley, Mass.: Bergin and Garvey, 1987); de Castell, S., Luke, A., and Egan, K. (eds.), *Literacy, Society and Schooling* (Cambridge: CUP, 1986); Mackie, R. (ed.), *Literacy and Revolution* (London: Pluto Press, 1980); Hoyles, M. (ed.), *The Politics of Literacy* (London: Writers and Readers, 1977); and Arnove, R., and Graff, H. (eds.), *National Literacy Campaigns* (New York: Plenum, 1987). The Ontario study referred to here is from Graff (1979).

6. Graff (1979), *ibid.*, p. 23.

7. *Ibid.*

8. Freire (1972), *op. cit.*, Chapter 2, especially pp. 45–50.

9. *Ibid.*, p. 45.

10. *Ibid.*

11. Freire (1976), *op. cit.*, p. 46.

12. Dale, R., "Perspectives on Policy Making," being Part 2 of *Introducing Education Policy: Principles and Perspectives* (Milton Keynes: Open University Press, 1986), p. 58.

13. Levine, K., "Functional Literacy: Fond Illusions and False Economies," *Harvard Educational Review*, 52, 3, 1982, and *The Social Context of Literacy* (London: Routledge, 1986). See also Lankshear, C., "Humanizing Functional Literacy," *Educational Theory*, 36, 4, 1986; and McLaren, P., "Culture or Canon?," *Harvard Educational Review*, 58, 2, 1988.

14. Compare Levine (1982), *ibid.*; Lankshear, C., Lawler, M., *Literacy, Schooling and Revolution* (London: Falmer Press, 1987), Chapter 2; and McLaren, *ibid.*

15. Anyon, J., "Ideology and United States History Textbooks," *Harvard Educational Review*, 49, 3, 1979, and "Social Class and School Knowledge," *Curriculum Inquiry*, 11, 1, 1980.

16. MacDonald, M., "Schooling and the Reproduction of Class and Gender Relations," in Dale, R., et al. (eds.), *Education and the State*, vol. 2 (Lewes: Falmer Press, 1982).

17. Anyon, *op cit.*, pp. 383–384.

18. MacDonald, *op cit.*, pp. 170–171.

19. Whitty, G., *Sociology and School Knowledge* (London: Methuen, 1985), Chapter 2.

20. *Ibid.*, p. 44. See also Taxel, J., "The American Revolution: An Analysis of Literary Content, Form and Ideology," in Apple, M., and Weis, L. (eds.), *Ideology and Practice in Schooling* (Philadelphia: Temple University Press, 1983).

21. Whitty, *op. cit.*, p. 43.

22. *Ibid.*

23. Examples include Giroux, H., *Schooling and the Struggle for Public Life* (Minneapolis: University of Minnesota Press, 1988), Chapter 5; Apple, M., and Christian-Smith, L., *The Politics of the Textbook* (London and New York: Routledge, 1991); Luke, A., *Literacy, Textbooks and Ideology* (London: Falmer Press, 1988); and Gee, J., "Postmodernism and Literacies," Chapter 9 below.

24. Wexler, P., "Structure, Text and Subject," in Apple, M. (ed.), *Cultural and Economic Reproduction in Education* (London: Routledge, 1982).

25. Giroux, *op. cit.*, p. 155.

26. Giroux, H., "Literacy and the Politics of Difference," Chapter 13 below.

27. This conception is adopted by Weedon, C., *Feminist Practice and Post-structuralist Theory* (Oxford: Basil Blackwell, 1987).

28. Wittgenstein, L., *Philosophical Investigations* (Oxford: Basil Blackwell, 1972).

29. McLaren, P., and Lankshear, C., "Critical Literacy and the Postmodern Turn," Chapter 14 below, p. 382.

30. *Ibid.*, p. 385.

31. *Ibid.*, p. 385–386.

32. McLaren (1988), *op. cit.*, p. 213.

33. Aronowitz, S., and Giroux, H., "Schooling, Culture, and Literacy in the Age of Broken Dreams," *Harvard Educational Review*, 58, 2, 1988, p. 185.

34. *Ibid.*, pp. 185–186. The quotation is from Hirsch, E.D., Jr., *Cultural Literacy: What Every American Needs to Know* (Boston: Houghton Mifflin, 1987), p. 83.

35. Hirsch, *ibid.*, p. 22. See his position in Chapter 1 generally.

36. Aronowitz and Giroux, *op. cit.*, p. 191.

37. *Ibid.*

38. *Ibid.*

39. Cf. Lankshear with Lawler, *op. cit.*, p. 67.

40. Aronowitz and Giroux, *op. cit.*, p. 191.

41. *Ibid.*, p. 193.

42. Hunter, C., and Harman, D., *Adult Illiteracy in the United States* (New York: McGraw Hill, 1979), pp. 19–20.

43. Cf. McLaren, and Aronowitz and Giroux, both *op. cit.*

44. See Searle, C., "From Foster to Baker: The New Struggle for Education," *Race and Class*, 30, April–June, 1989; Lankshear with Lawler, *op. cit.*, Chapter 3.

45. Bloom, A., *The Closing of the American Mind* (New York: Simon and Schuster, 1987).

46. Peters, R., "The Development of Reason" in his *Psychology and Ethical Development* (London: Allen and Unwin, 1974), p. 126.

47. *Ibid.*, p. 124.

48. Kuhn, T., *The Structure of Scientific Revolutions* (Chicago: University of Chicago Press, 1973).

49. Harris, K., *Education and Knowledge* (London: Routledge, 1979), Chapter 3.

50. Peters, R., *Ethics and Education* (London: Allen and Unwin, 1966), p. 8.

51. Searle, J., "The Storm Over the University," *New York Review of Books*, 6 December 1990, pp. 34–42. The quotation is from p. 41. Note again that it is the work of John Searle and not Chris Searle that is being referred to here. For typical expressions of Oakeshott's views, see Oakeshott, H., "Rational Conduct" and "The Study of 'Politics' in a University," in his *Rationalism in Politics* (London: Methuen, 1962).

52. *Ibid.*, p. 36.

53. *Ibid.*, p. 39.

54. *Ibid.*, p. 42.

55. *Ibid.*

56. Cf. Harris, *op. cit.*, for an excellent sustained discussion of this point.

57. Mohanty, C.T., "On Race and Voice: Challenges for Liberal Education in the 1990s," *Cultural Critique*, 1989/90, pp. 179–208.

58. Freire (1976), *op. cit.*, p. 18.

59. Mills, C. Wright, *The Sociological Imagination* (New York: OUP, 1959), p. 5.

60. *Ibid.*, p. 3.

61. *Ibid.*

62. The idea here trades on an analogy with Chomsky's renowned distinction between depth and surface grammar in language.

63. Mills, *op cit.*, p. 8.

64. Lankshear, C., "Reading and Righting Wrongs: Literacy and the Underclass," *Language and Education*, 3, 3, 1989.

65. Dale, *op. cit.*

66. Cox, R., "Social Forces, States and World Orders," *Millenium*, 10, 2, 1980, p. 128.

67. *Ibid.*, p. 129.

68. *Ibid.*, p. 130.

69. McLaren and Lankshear, *op. cit.*, p. 382.

70. Dale, *op. cit.*, p. 68.

71. *Ibid.*, p. 64.

72. *Ibid.*, p. 65, our italics.

73. Offe, C., *Contradictions of the Welfare State* (London: Hutchinson, 1984), p. 131.

74. *Ibid.*, p. 132.

75. Cox, *op. cit.*, p. 129.

76. See, for example, Aronowitz, *op. cit.*, p. 188.

77. Dale, *op. cit.*, p. 66.

78. Harris, *op. cit.*, p. 118.

79. The authors in the present volume who most explicitly reject economic reductionism are Anderson and Irvine, Apple, Bee, Berlin, Sholle and Denski, Gee, Giroux, Brady and Hernández, McLaren and Lankshear, and Rockhill.

80. Carr, W., and Kemmis, S., *Becoming Critical: Knowledge through Action Research* (Victoria: Deakin University Press, 1983).

81. *Ibid.*, pp. 127–128.

82. *Ibid.*

83. See especially the following works by Habermas, J.: *Knowledge and Human Interests* (London: Heinemann Educational, 1972), *Theory and Practice* (Boston: Beacon Press, 1973), *The Theory of Communicative Action* (Boston: Beacon Press, 1984), *On the Logic of the Social Sciences* (Cambridge, Mass.: MIT Press, 1988), *Moral Consciousness and Communicative Action* (Cambridge, Mass.: MIT Press, 1990). See also Freire (1972), *op. cit.*; and Shor, I., and Freire, P., *A Pedagogy for Liberation* (South Hadley, Mass.: Bergin and Garvey, 1987).

84. Carr and Kemmis, *op. cit.*, p. 146.

85. Gouldner, A., *The Coming Crisis of Western Sociology* (London: Heinemann, 1971).

86. Dale, *op. cit.*, pp. 56–57.

87. Habermas (1972), *op. cit.*, and (1973) *op. cit.*, pp. 142–169. See also McCarthy, T., *The Critical Theory of Jürgen Habermas* (Cambridge, Mass.: MIT Press, 1978), pp. 16–40.

88. Carr and Kemmis, *op. cit.*, p. 133.

89. Marcuse, H., *One Dimensional Man* (Boston: Beacon Press, 1964).

90. Carr and Kemmis, *op. cit.*, p. 133.

91. Roderick, R., *Habermas and the Foundations of Critical Theory* (London: MacMillan, 1986), p. 56.

92. Carr and Kemmis, *op. cit.*, p. 134.

93. Roderick, *op. cit.*, p. 56. The quotation is from Habermas (1973), *op. cit.*, pp. 22–23.

94. Carr and Kemmis, *op. cit.*, p. 137.

95. Freire (1972), *op. cit.*, Chapter 3.

96. *Ibid.*, especially pp. 73–85.

97. *Ibid.*, pp. 64–65.

98. Freire (1976), *op. cit.*, pp. 4–5, 12.

99. *Ibid.* See pp. 49–55 for an account of the nature and purpose of generative words. For a full description of the literacy process, see pp. 41–84.

100. See Cabezas, O., *Fire from the Mountain* for a fascinating account of educational episodes within the Sandinista guerrilla insurrection in Nicaragua.

101. Shor, I., *Critical Teaching and Everyday Life* (Boston: South End Press, 1980).

102. *Ibid.*, p. 166.

103. *Ibid.*, p. 163.

104. Harris, K., *Teachers and Classes* (London: Routledge, 1982), p. 151.

105. Allan Luke in personal communication.

106. Fay, B., *Social Theory and Political Practice* (London: Basil Blackwell, 1977), p. 109.

107. Giroux, below p. 375. For an excellent example of border crossing at the level of critical theory development with profound implications for educational practice, refer to the work of Maxine Greene. *The Dialectic of Freedom* (New York: Teachers College Press, 1988), *Landscapes of Learning* (New York: Teachers College Press, 1978), and *Teacher as Stranger* (Belmont, Calif.: Wadsworth, 1973), are good starting points. See also "How do we go about our craft?" *Teachers College Record*, 86, 1, 1984, pp. 55–67. See also Peter McLaren, "Multiculturalism and the Postmodern Critique: Towards a Pedagogy of Resistance and Transformation," *Cultural Studies*, in press.

Critical literacy as political intervention: Three variations on a theme

Kevin Harris

Variation 1 (lightly and frivolously; then moderately)

> Such labour'd nothings, in so strange a style
> Amaze the unlearn'd, and make the learned smile.
> —Alexander Pope

On 27 February 1977 I attended a performance of Beethoven's Third Piano Concerto at Royal Festival Hall, London. The program notes, prepared by Felix Aprahamian, read in part as follows:

> The Third Concerto begins with an orchestral *ritornello* of exceptional length. Its bold initial theme in C minor is announced *alla breve* by the strings and answered by the wind. The succeeding transitional theme is equally uncompromising in the way it moves to the relative E flat major, the key in which the initial theme is restated and expanded and followed by the second subject . . . The piano then leads the musical argument, arriving by way of E flat minor to the second subject, again in E flat major. A high piano trill and downward scale ends the exposition. The relatively short development section soon veers from E flat major to G minor and thence, by means of another downward scale, to C minor for the recapitulation section. Here the second subject returns in the tonic major, in which key

the initial theme is heard just before the cadenza. But, after it, the coda, in which the piano, unusually, plays an important role, ends firmly in the minor.

Again unusually, the slow movement is in the quite unexpected key of E major . . . after a brief cadenza, the movement concludes with an eight-bar coda based on the first subject.

The G sharp in the final E major chord of the *Largo*, becomes A flat in the prominent second note when the soloist announces the jaunty principal theme of Beethoven's brisk rondo-finale. It drops immediately to B natural, the leading note of the tonic C minor but also the dominant of the key of the previous movement, an ingenious and undoubtedly intentional link on Beethoven's part . . . Beethoven again exploits the ambivalence of A flat by slipping into E major before the rondo theme returns in the tonic C minor. The second subject returns in the tonic major and with a look at previous elements, the movement reaches the final cadenza and a precipitous coda, *Presto* in C major.[1]

I read that, and find to my paradoxical astonishment that the very act of reading it determines my illiteracy. I cannot understand what is being said. I do not know what I might say as a response. I have been excluded from discussion. And yet this is a concerto I listen to often, which I love dearly, which I know well enough to hum from beginning to end, and which I thought I could discuss with some authority and confidence.

My problem is that Aprahamian has set his commentary on the concerto within a field of discourse that is beyond my informed understanding. The discourse is not totally foreign to me, or meaningless. If it were I could more easily ignore it, just as I can shrug off a nearby conversation in Sanskrit or Old Icelandic of which I do not understand a single word. No: the problem is that the discourse is being conducted in terms which I at least recognize, and which, more importantly, I recognize to be legitimate. I know that music is written in keys from A to G, with sharps and flats thrown in; and I know that Italian terms are used to name sections of total works, as well as to indicate the timing, pace, and volume at which the music should be played. Thus I know that the statement "The G sharp in the final E major chord of the *Largo*, becomes A flat in the prominent second note" makes sense. But it does not make sense to me. Thus I am ignorant. Worse; I am ignorant, illiterate, and consequently impotent—and all because I have not been sufficiently initiated into a field of discourse which I recognize, and which I concede to be legitimate.

In the face of Aprahamian's program notes, or indeed any text, I have three options open to me. I can *ignore* the field of discourse employed and let it pass, but at the cost of remaining ignorant, illiterate, and impotent whenever it holds sway. I can *accept* and learn it in order to become sufficiently literate to enter into it. Or I can *challenge* the discourse, and thus engage in the exercise of critical literacy.

It should be made clear right here at the beginning that which option ought to be adopted is never immediately given. Making an adequate choice would require at least serious consideration of the substance of the text, the historical circumstances in which the text is being produced and presented, and equally serious consideration of the purposes, overt or otherwise, the text seeks to accomplish. It is thus by no means the case that *challenge* is always the 'given' best alternative; nor is it necessarily the case that *challenge* should foreclose *acceptance* as an alternative and instead lead inexorably to the more ambitious enterprises of attempting either to delegitimate a discourse or else to legitimate an alternative one. What is more the case, however, is that the implications for the historical development and political force of a discourse will depend considerably on whether challenge takes place, and if it does, then whether it takes place as an intervention with the discourse in its moment, as the history is being made, or whether it is mounted from a position of distance and hindsight.

The point has now been reached where an unsuspecting critic's text on a Beethoven concerto has led this discussion into waters in which that particular text is almost certainly out of its depth. So let us therefore now consider a more substantial variation.

Variation 2

First movement (slowly and hesitatingly)

> Placed at the door of learning, youth to guide,
> We never suffer it to stand too wide.
> To ask, to guess, to know as they commence,
> As fancy opens the quick springs of sense,
> We ply the memory, we load the brain,
> Bind rebel wit, and double chain on chain;
> Confine the thought, to exercize the breath;
> And keep them in the pale of words till death.
>   Alexander Pope

My confrontation with Felix Aprahamian's program notes was a minor, if enlightening, incident in my life. Of far greater import, to me, was my simultaneous confrontation with analytic philosophy of education, Professor R.S. Peters (which accounts for my presence in London at that time), and that which I shall take for my central subject—my engagement with Peters's book *Ethics and Education*. Aspects of that experience which relate to the control of discourse shall now be stated and elaborated.

It is commonly known that what passed generally for philosophy of education up until the early 1960s was a fairly confused, ill-defined field of discourse. History of ideas masqueraded as theory, theory pretended to be philosophy, and disputants often tended to talk past each other in uninteresting debate. It was into this scene that R.S. Peters arrived, not from education, but from the field of philosophy itself, a field which had recently experienced revolutionary rumblings of an analytic sort. Peters described much of what he encountered in education as "undifferentiated mush," and he set about to replace that "mush" with a distinct form of discourse, with clear rules and procedures which he, along with many others both in the United Kingdom and the United States considered more appropriate for rigorous debate on matters educational.

It thus fell historically to Peters to give birth to what had been gestating for some time, and then to nurture and engineer the process of legitimating what was to become known initially as a "postrevolutionary" analytic philosophy of education. The birth occurred, appropriately, in the form of the delivery of Peters's inaugural lecture on taking up the Chair of Philosophy of Education at the University of London Institute of Education in 1963. The legitimation process began at the Institute almost immediately, and in the course of a decade spread far beyond that site.

A central feature of the legitimation process was what might be called "instititionalizing" the new discipline. Societies, such as the Philosophy of Education Society of Great Britain, were established. Publications were controlled through the creation and editing of journals and series. (The journal *Proceedings of the Philosophy of Education Society of Great Britain* was edited by Peters and consisted of a selection of papers originally accepted for reading to the above Society, of which, incidentally, Peters was President: Peters was also General Editor of Routledge's series, the "International Library of the Philosophy of Education".) Content was controlled through hiring teaching staff (Peters, as the Professor in the Department, sat on Selection Committees), as well as through devising, teaching, and assessing courses which were prescribed as part of a credentialing process for wide audiences. For instance, in the late 1960s literally thousands of students in London were compelled to study Peters-inspired courses as part of their professional preservice training as teachers.

A second feature of the legitimation process was the "establishment" of epistemic privilege for the newborn discipline, and the consequent provision of a form of immunity for its practitioners. Here it was decreed that the proper task of philosophy of education was to lead to clarification rather than to engage in prescription, and that "real" philosophy of education had to be more rigorous, tougher, and concern itself centrally with conceptual analysis and asking "second-order" questions. It was then assumed that only those who forsook pursuing "first-order" issues and who sought clarification through asking "second-order" questions were able to probe educational issues in a philosophically respectable way. A closed school was thus created wherein to query details in a colleague's substance was considered legitimate, but to query the worth of the practice of producing the substance was to risk being charged with failing to understand philosophy. Only a philosopher of the right persuasion, who was judged competent by others of that persuasion, could legitimately engage in philosophical debate on educational issues and criticize other philosophers constituting the debate. Thus particular activities, unable to be joined, judged, or criticized by people neither competent in nor desirous of performing them, were marked out and bestowed with epistemic privilege. For instance, Peters and others dismissed certain issues, such as seeking to change the world, or even the "first-order" question of what schools actually do in a society, as being beyond the concern of philosophers; and not surprisingly philosophers tended to eschew such concerns and concentrate mainly on linguistic and conceptual issues. A related closed school was simultaneously built up on the precept that one had to be initiated as a liberal-rational "educated man" (sic.) of a particular type before one could properly engage in discourse about liberalism, rationality, and education. To enter the fold meant accepting and embracing the principles in question: to remain outside illustrated one's very illiberalism, irrationality, and lack of proper education.

This is by no means the full story of how a particular discourse came to be legitimated, and a proper understanding would require attention to, at least, Jim Walker's important tone poem, "The Evolution of the Ape"[2] (which will be recalled later). But it is enough for present purposes. The theme of legitimation, having now been stated, will be elaborated through consideration of certain aspects of the development of the new philosophy of education, and especially my engagement with Peters's *Ethics and Education*.

By 1966 only a limited number of courses in the "new" philosophy of education were operating, and these were led almost exclusively by colleagues and/or former students of Peters. A small body of literature, mainly in the form of "Readings," had built up; and then, into this almost vacuous situation, the long, comprehensive *Ethics and Education* was launched.[3] It thus came to pass that those seeking to study what had been introduced and announced as "real" philosophy of education would, almost inevitably, end up at the feet of one of Peters's disciples, work through the lesser readings (many by Peters), and then have to tangle with the complexities of *Ethics and Education*, written by the very Professor of Philosophy of Education at the University of London Institute of Education who, so his followers proclaimed, was leading us from the wilderness of confusion into a sea of clarity.

I was no exception. Eager to put aside the old and move with the changes, I worked my way through the lesser readings, and I then spent two years engaging with *Ethics and Education*. It seemed only right to do that.

My teachers recommended the book, and set it as our text; it was written by a famous professor; and as a postgraduate student I still held the beliefs that expensive texts in shiny covers are, ipso facto, good (publishers surely have their standards), and that one doesn't criticize what one doesn't understand. So I tried to understand the book and its approach, and put off thoughts of criticism while I tried harder to understand it better. Basically, I went for the second of the options indicated above: acceptance. I gave myself to, or allowed myself, even if tentatively, to be appropriated by, the new discourse.

But it was not as simple as that. There were other factors which also helped dampen my critical tendencies; and most of these are found embedded in the two-and-a-half-page Preface—in a real sense Peters's own "Program Notes"—to *Ethics and Education*. The Preface begins by outlining the dual purposes of the book. We are told that it was written for both hard-headed teachers and students of philosophy, the former of whom might complain that it is too abstract, and the latter of whom might decry the insufficient detail in philosophic argumentation. The book is admitted as a compromise which cannot satisfy both camps. This confession, however, serves to shield the book against criticism of its abstraction from the teaching situation, and also defuses shots aimed at the holes in the philosophic arguments. To attack in either way would be to reproach the book for not being what it clearly says it sets out not to be. Thus right from the beginning certain means of otherwise legitimate forms of criticism are being closed off. But that is not the end of the foreclosing and disarming.

Peters next states that the book was written too soon, and too quickly, taking three years to write instead of the five years really required, and that it was published prematurely in order to "provide a few signposts for others and to map the contours of the field for others to explore in a more leisurely and detailed manner."[4] That may not totally foreclose criticism, but it does establish the grounds for a defense that an early critique might not consider the book carefully enough, or with as much care as that with which the book itself had been produced.[5] So, how long should common decency and academic honesty keep one from challenging *Ethics and Education?* Well, even five years might not really be enough, for, as Peters says, the book is only a premature statement to be considered in a more leisurely manner. This also raises the problem that, no matter how long one waits, one will hardly make telling points against something premature by pointing out that it is under-weight and malformed. Again I was temporarily disarmed.

But as if that were not enough, a further aspect of the Preface not only put me in an even more defensive position, but also made me far more amenable to accept the book as it stood, along with what it stood for. Peters states that Part 3 of the book owes much to five years of prior collaboration with Stanley Benn, a professor at the Australian National University, who also commented on Part 2. The sections on ethics and philosophy of mind grew from work with Ruth Saw, David Hamlyn, and A. Phillips Griffiths. Griffiths, Professor of Philosophy at the University of Warwick, helped with "continuous discussion" "over a period of years," collaborated in a joint article which provided the springboard for Chapter 5, and commented in detail on Part 2. Hamlyn, also a professor, commented on Chapter 8. Paul Hirst, Professor of Education at King's College, Cambridge, chipped in with "vigorous discussions" over three years, the influence of which is reflected in Part 1. Basil Bernstein, another professor at the Institute of Education, discussed many sociological issues and made detailed comments on Chapter 9. Lionel Elvin, Director of the Institute, commented on Chapter 4, and Professor Israel Scheffler, of the Harvard Graduate School of Education, contributed significantly to the published version of Part 1. Finally, Professor A.C.F. Beales of King's College; Professor W.R. Niblett, Dean of the Institute of Education; and Professor L.A. Reid, former Professor of Philosophy of Education at the Institute, all commented on the completed manuscript prior to publication.

That is an impressive list of institutionally legitimated experts! And none of them, it seems, in their readings of the text, had been troubled sufficiently to seek amendments regarding a myriad of things that I found disconcerting in the published version of the book. I suspected that the book contained literally hundreds of errors, ranging from minor details to major substantive contradictions.[6] But I also felt it unlikely that I alone could find so much wrong, and so initially I accepted that the faults had to be with me. At this period it was common for Peters to state that his critics simply didn't understand him: if he could say that about the likes of the world-renowned Professor W.H. Dray,[7] then where would a mere student like myself stand?

Ethics and Education thus emerged largely closed off from challenge, at least from the likes of me and others new to or outside the discipline it heralded. Not only did it offer new tools for exploration and new fields to explore, not only had years of concerted effort gone into it, and not only did it admit its compromising and premature nature, but added to that it bore an imprimatur signed by a host of the biggest names in the business. Faced with all of that, what could a newcomer or an outsider, let alone a poor student, do? The situation was like that of the confrontation with the program notes: the discourse was being conducted in terms I recognized, which I conceded to be legitimate, but into which I felt unqualified (as yet) to enter.

But if the cases were similar in one sense, they also differed on at least one major dimension. Despite my love of Beethoven's concerto, I had no desire, aspiration, or intention of entering the field of musical analysis or criticism. Thus, with ignorance not a worry and challenge not an issue, I felt no need to engage with Aprahamian's type of key-shift analysis, or indeed any other form. I did, however, wish to continue with philosophy of education, and so had to engage in and with its discourse. Here the easy option would have been to accept the newly legitimated form of discourse, to master and practice that form, and thus to further legitimize the discourse myself.[8]

But what if one was not satisfied with what passed for the legitimated discourse, or if, try as one might, one simply could not hack it? Although I did not know, at first, that many others felt the same way, I came to realize that my own case was not an instance of perversity or of ignorance. There were problems with *Ethics and Education,* and with the whole "analytic school." But there were also problems in getting at those problems. As I began wrestling with those latter problems, I also began to understand that to try to mount opposition was not just an intellectual exercise: it was also a *political* exercise in challenging legitimation, naturalization, and power.

Interestingly, the key to beginning that task was actually sitting within the very Preface that had otherwise been so disarming. The modest claims about "premature publication" and "providing a few signposts" are quite gone in the sentence which immediately follows them. Peters says, "The important thing in the philosophy of education is that something should be there to indicate what it is and to provide a determinate structure on which students can train their critical faculties." Philosophy of education, we are then told, "will only develop as a rigorous field of study if a few more philosophers are prepared to plough premature furrows which run more or less in the right direction." There Peters quite categorically claims to have indicated *what philosophy of education is,* on what people should train their critical faculties, and that his furrows head pretty much in the *right* direction. This sort of declaration, bolstered by the legitimation process, helped to ensure that a decade after the premature furrows were ploughed most within the field were still following them, and that philosophy of education in the United Kingdom and initially, at least, in Australasia, sought to advance largely by exploring Peters's field, with Peters's tools, under the directions of Peters's signposts.

The 1966 Preface describes and sets the agenda thus: "Philosophy is essentially a cooperative enterprise. Advances are made when two or three are gathered together *who speak more or less the same language* and can meet frequently for the purpose of hitting each other politely on the head." Here, however, the statement serving to legitimate one cooperative activity also provides the clue to mounting oppositional activity: in neat dialectical fashion the negation is found within the thesis itself. In stating that advances in philosophy require a gathering of people "who speak more or less the same language," Peters has linked "advances" (it is hard to tell whether the link is proposed as logical or contingent, or both)[9] to sharing a common discourse. Peters's argument then appears to proceed in the fallacious form of "asserting the consequent," for it is strongly suggested that sharing a discourse will result in advances. But this, of course, is not necessarily the case. A discourse, although widely shared, may be regressive, stupid, useless, mistaken, interest serving, or any combination of the above; the fact that a discourse is shared does not in itself establish the epistemic privilege of that discourse. It now became clear that what in fact had happened in the process of marking out, cultivating, and developing the field of discourse known as analytic philosophy of education was that what was touted as "epistemic privilege" was really nothing more than an extension of professional privilege, or a stipulation made by those in power. Inspection of the literature revealed that, although rules and procedures had been laid down, no objective tests for competence in the discourse had been devised, nor had competency requirements been spelled out. Rather, the whole thing reduced to judgments made by the practicing professionals, and the legitimacy and inevitable superiority of certain philosophic activities was ensured simply through definition of the philosophic process and its parameters. And as for the imprimatur that read so impressively—well, it might just be possible that a bunch of professors in English universities in the sixties were speaking more or less the same language, and yet talking nonsense. The Academy of Lagado has many times come down to earth, and central England is as accommodating a landing field as any.

The recognition that the "epistemic privilege" of analytic philosophy of education was nothing more than a disguised extension of professional privilege allowed those of us who had moved from ignorance to acceptance, but who still remained dissatisfied, to now move from acceptance to challenge. It provided the initial opening for developing an alternative discourse. It revealed that the development and legitimation of analytic philosophy of education was not a neutral intellectual academic exercise but rather the setting of a political agenda. All those professors talking the same language to each other, and to students via classes and publications, did not reveal what philosophy of education is. Rather, their discourse resulted in a barren field being mapped and safaris being undertaken in detailed explorations for academic mirages.[10] Students, encouraged to sow in furrows ploughed in oblique directions across wastelands where no seed could grow, were not being escorted out of the wilderness; we were all being led up the creek.

But even when it had finally become clear to me and others that, at least on epistemic grounds, we didn't have to follow and accept, and that we were free to challenge, the question remained as to how, realistically, we might challenge the legitimated discourse.

Second movement (with much gusto)

The recognition that the development and legitimation of analytic philosophy of education was the setting of a political agenda rather than a neutral intellectual academic exercise had more to it than first appeared. The critical process underlying and driving this recognition revealed also that the very basis on which the entire substance of analytic philosophy had been built— namely, the belief that language, discourse, and philosophy were themselves neutral, detached, second-order activities—was false. It further revealed that the discourse which promised clarification and the hope of reaching a position of neutral clear-sightedness was leading instead to an ideological rationalization for passive liberal conservatism. And thus the agenda for those like me who wished to stop being led that way became set. The task before us was not to debate substantive points within the legitimated game. Rather, we had to establish an opposing discourse, engage in, and confess to engaging in, setting our own political agenda. There were a number of steps in this procedure, and varied levels of success.

The first phase, given our lack of institutional powers, was to produce alternative literature; and interestingly, when that was done, our products were immediately branded "political" by those who still claimed theirs to be the outcome of the neutral application of rational processes. The production of the alternative literature certainly was a concrete political task. Study groups had to be formed among those dissatisfied with analytic philosophy of education; drafts had to be prepared, circulated and discussed; and ongoing debate had to be literally instituted somewhere outside of the mainstream. In our own particular case at Sydney University, a fluid group of people, who had initially been brought together through shared revulsion to apartheid in South Africa and a particular desire to plan oppositional activities against a visiting (white) South African football team, began to meet weekly for a three-hour session, in an office deep in the bowels of the library, to produce an alternative discourse in philosophy of education. In doing this we soon learned that we were doing more than producing alternative literature. We were politicizing ourselves as well. We were changing ourselves and our modes of operation and our relation to the mainstream, not alongside but actually within the very act of challenging the legitimate discourse. In hindsight it is clear that we were working as much on ourselves as we were on the literature. We were practicing reading and writing in a critical way while engaging in political activities at a number of different levels in the educational arena. In short, we were engaging in and living through a period of critical literacy.

There quickly came a time when this production of alternative discourse grew in confidence but also became unsatisfactory in itself. This now seemed the point where the "establishment" had to be confronted within its own legitimated parameters. The first venue for attack was the less formal one of conferences, and in that arena it quickly became clear that a real battle was emerging. At this point a number of our group quit. Politicized, empowered, and either sufficiently sure of themselves or sufficiently disenchanted, they left philosophy of education for other struggles within the educational arena, or else left the educational and academic arenas altogether, some to struggle on elsewhere. But our group also grew, as people heard at conferences things they hadn't been reading in the literature. There followed an exciting time in which a marked difference existed between what was being said in the corridors of philosophy of education and what was being published and read.

The second site for attack was the legitimated publication channels, and here very solid resistance was met. The establishment might have allowed radical papers offering alternative perspectives to be read at symposia and conferences, but while they controlled the journals and publishing houses they were hardly keen to have that sort of stuff appear in print. For instance, Walker's paper referred to earlier, and undoubtably a major landmark work in philosophy of education, was not only rejected by the Editor of a mainstream journal, but was rejected almost instantaneously without due process of being sent to referees, whereas my own paper, "Peters on Schooling" (which has kindly been referred to as a form of landmark by others),[11] was less abruptly but just as conclusively rejected by a number of similar "legitimate" journals.

At this point a split in tactics occurred. Some kept confronting the legitimated channels, hoping that the growing pressure behind them, along with changing historical circumstances, might be enough to drive the beginnings of a wedge into the literature. In some cases it was. For instance, a severely edited version of "Peters on Schooling" was eventually published in the legitimate literature,[12] and Routledge and Kegan Paul did publish my *Education and Knowledge*, but only after requesting major deletions of criticisms of Peters, which I refused to comply with. Routledge, however, did not include the book in the International Library of the Philosophy of Education, and they even chose not to list it in the "philosophy of education" section of their catalogues. Other people made different interventions by founding their own publishing sources and launching journals more sympathetic to the emerging radical literature: this too being both a political exercise and an example of the practice of critical literacy. Some of these journals, as with

Radical Philosophy, ran in close parallel to the existing traditional ones, targeting the same audience with different material (it was one such journal, *Access,* which published Walker's paper, along with a number of other worthy pieces rejected elsewhere). Other journals, such as *Radical Education* in the United Kingdom and *Radical Education Dossier* in Australia, were directed largely (although by no means entirely) to a different audience—teachers. The thinking behind this move was that, although teachers had been constrained in what they were exposed to as students during their training period, the opportunity could at least be made available to them to confront an alternative discourse as practitioners. These journals similarly provided an outlet for a large amount of material which was otherwise failing to meet with the approval of editors and panels of referees of more traditional journals.

Thus struggle for control of the discourse went on, and in developing forms has continued until the present. But with that chord sounded and ringing, we can here turn to introduce a different subject.

Variation 3 (at first energetically; then gravely, and with a dying fall)

And the LORD said, Behold, the people is one, and they have all one language; and this they begin to do: and now nothing will be restrained from them, which they have imagined to do.

Go to, let us go down, and there confound their language . . .
Genesis 11:6–7

The struggle for control of the discourse of philosophy of education was part of a larger, enduring enlightenment, and yet it might ultimately have turned out to be of little specific substantive importance. The struggle for the control of public contemporary educational policy discourse, which is so much broader in scope and reaches into so many areas and corners, has potentially far more significance. Let me illustrate this struggle and elaborate on its significance through two examples. One comes from New Zealand and the other from Australia, although, given current tendencies, I suspect that broadly similar examples could have been supplied from comparable discourse and situations within at least the United States and the United Kingdom.

In New Zealand in 1987 the Treasury took the unprecedented step of producing a major document on education for the incoming government.[13] This nearly three-hundred-page document, not surprisingly, has been the focus of much debate; but rather than summarize and/or analyze that debate here, I want instead to consider one significant though hardly isolated reaction—namely, that made by Gerald Grace.[14] In his analysis of the Treasury document, Grace identifies four major moves. First, a new language for thinking about education—one dealing with inputs, outputs, and production functions—is introduced. Second, it is noted that applying this language to education involves difficulties. Third, the need to surmount these difficulties and apply this language to education to produce corresponding benefits is stressed. And fourth, regret is expressed that this approach hasn't been followed before. Grace comments: "Language is not neutral without a special effort to make it so. The language of inputs, outputs and production functions in education is being introduced to us as an analytically more robust way of thinking about education and we are being encouraged to engage in research which utilizes these more analytically robust categories."[15] Grace argues that Treasury's constant use of a particular form of language, put forward as natural common sense, is a classic example of a strategy leading to the establishment of an ideological position, that is, "a set of ideas and propositions which are related to a particular interest group in a contested situation. Such a position attempts to establish itself as the most authoritative explanation in the particular field of discourse. Characteristically it represents itself as expertness or disinterestedness set against vested interests or the propositions of sector groups." Grace notes further that once the "language is accepted, taken up and used without question, an important part of that ideological position has already been assimilated."[16]

Here, then, a new discourse is being presented and promoted as disinterested expertise and, although difficult, more analytically robust than what went before. We are assured (as part of a process of both legitimation and declaration of epistemic privilege) that if we take the trouble to accept, master, and utilize this discourse, we will be able to see more clearly, and in a better light. Through having this difficult-to-gain but privileged view of education we will then be able to move forward in new and valuable ways.

Interestingly, not only is Treasury's tactical approach extremely similar to that which was adopted by the purveyors of analytic philosophy of education, but also Grace's responses clearly echo those which some of us tried (with difficulty) to make back in the 1960s and early 1970s. The response that Treasury is involved in an ideological maneuver is precisely what I said about Peters in "Peters on Schooling"; it is also what Adelstein said a number of years earlier.[17] And the insistence that language, and with it conceptual analysis, is not neutral, is the very point at which most of the fundamental challenges to analytic philosophy of education gathered.

Clearly, some lessons had been learned in the historical changes that had occurred between 1966 and 1988.[18] Grace was able to confront his target document in a way in which it was difficult to confront the documents of analytic philosophy of education. He was able to challenge the discourse as it was being made, and intervene directly in the history of the developing discourse rather than attack an established mode from a position of hindsight, distance, and weakness. Grace was able to move directly to challenge and to confidently claim entitlements in an area in which we were struggling our hardest merely to gain a hearing. Grace says, "We are entitled to ask why we should use this language and we are entitled to ask where such language and its associated modes of thinking is leading us."[19] Why, he continues to question, in the current historical circumstances is an ideological maneuver being employed to legitimate the necessity of applying a rigorous form of economic and quantitative analysis to the whole of the educational system?

Grace suggests that accepting the necessity of the New Zealand Treasury's form of analysis, (and it is, of course, by no means theirs alone) would lead inexorably to, and legitimate, the view that education is a commodity in the marketplace, that this in turn fundamentally affects the relation of Government to education, and that forces in the marketplace can be relied on to provide optimal solutions to educational issues and policy. Having "established" this position, Government can then ease itself into new relations with education; and with its ideological maneuver having legitimated its position, along with the discourse that served to establish that position, opportunities for effective and legitimate opposing discourse become neatly and progressively closed off. Political programs can then be brought into operation with little fear of challenge through the practice of critical literacy. And if there is challenge, it can more easily be put down as the misinformed or outdated product of the disenchanted or of those with sectarian political interests.

For my example from Australia, let me consider broadly the conference "Taking Charge of Change: Restructuring the Education Industry," sponsored by the National Board of Employment, Education and Training (NBEET)[20] in February 1990, and more specifically one paper delivered at that conference. In his Introduction to the *Proceedings* of the conference, the Conference Manager, Tim Baker, states, "The conference provided an opportunity for leading educators representing institutions from around Australia to meet and discuss key issues facing the education profession as it moves into the next century."[21] Baker is partly correct. The participants did have a chance to meet, but hardly to discuss. There were no spaces between papers, and addresses were given even at mealtimes. As Glen Postle notes later in the *Proceedings*, "We had been assembled to be presented with a 'not so hidden agenda.'" NBEET patently sought to control and naturalize a form of discourse, notwithstanding Baker's reference to the education *profession* rather than NBEET's preferred term *industry*.

Let me now look more specifically at one attempt to legitimate and claim epistemic privilege for a particular form of discourse, namely, the paper "Responses to Change" presented, at NBEET's invitation, by Helen Nugent, who, the *Proceedings* tell us, held a Ph.D. in history and lectured in history at the University of Queensland before she completed an M.B.A. (with Distinction) at Harvard and joined the management consultancy firm McKinsey and Company, of which she is now a principal. Nugent begins with three confessions: first, to having "embraced the world of economic rationalism"; second, to holding a strong belief "that a university environment that does not have its share of Sanskrit or Old Icelandic scholars, as examples of fields of more esoteric studies, would be a far poorer place"; and third, to her academic background as a lecturer and researcher in Asian History. Leading out of the first confession, she begins the major argument of her paper thus: "The approach I have adopted is the same which, as a management consultant, I would use to analyze and develop recommendations in industries as disparate as mining, banking or automobiles. The frameworks I have used are those, modified where appropriate, that I would use for a private or public sector client. For that I make no apology." The basic parameters of the discourse are thus established; the first suggestions are given that the approach employed has been widely legitimated and that the framework has its element of epistemic privilege; and education has already been "naturalized" as an industry within a broad set containing members such as mining magnesium, managing money, and manufacturing Mitsubishi Magnas.

Nugent then casts her discussion into the context of a contrast between the "old game" which universities were once engaged in and the "changing game"—a special term coined to indicate the current state of affairs. Here, in becoming totally ahistorical, Nugent dramatically ignores her third confession and indicates how clear her break from history has been. One might expect a historian to know better than most people that every era exists in a state of flux, and that the era of the "old game" was in all likelihood no more or less changing than the present situation is. But there is point (intended or otherwise) to this move; for through her categorization Nugent instantly brands that which "once was," the past, along with its way of looking at things, pejoratively. She is thus clearly engaging in the sort of thing Grace has pointed to as an ideological maneuver. With that noted, let us stay with Nugent's argument.

In the "changing game"—presented as the real existential state of affairs which has to be faced, and the language which we are invited (nay, urged) to take up and use if we are to survive and advance—Nugent indicates that educational institutions need to make greater efforts to create a distinct and different identity for themselves within a competitive ethos. By implication it also emerges very strongly that those playing the "old game," who wish either to ignore or not accept the discourse of the "education industry" with its "competitive market-edge-seeking practices," are out of touch, behind the times, and are courting impotence through their ignorance or nonacceptance of the difficult, "more robust," "epistemically privileged" analysis that is being offered.

Not surprisingly, the paper proceeds within the context of "supply" and "demand." We hear that academic researchers are in competition for industrial and venture capital, "like it or not"; that institutes of higher education must be competitive to attract students—*and in this regard they might well consider the standard of the on-campus golf courses that they can offer for the use of full fee-paying students;* that academic (as well as golf) courses should be market oriented; that institutions should learn how to "market" their academic courses; that attracting corporate funding or "being a first mover in locking up funds" is not just good for the attracting institution but has the added advantage of making it tougher for other institutions (these are now the competition or opposition) to attract funds in the same area; that we should seek to gain "first-mover advantages"; that we should "differentiate high-potential disciplines"; and that we must decide "how best to leverage the research output for the benefit of the institution as a whole."

A lot of this stirring stuff is then fleshed out by situating it within the "McKinsey 7S organizational framework," which is beautifully alliterative although, at least prima facie, somewhat lacking as an analytic vehicle (this judgment, I fear, reveals me as an "old game" player).[22] Then after a trip through the seven S's—the style, skills, systems, structure, staff, strategy, and shared values of the organization—those playing the "changing game" are advised "to build a competitive position based on being the low-cost or most efficient deliverer of an educational service" because "Being the low-cost producer might be particularly advantageous in marketing full fee-paying services, particularly to overseas students. It might enable your institution to price lower and hence gain a disproportionate number of students compared with competing Australian or overseas institutions. Alternatively, you could price at the same level and retain the surplus funds generated."

There, then, is the language of the "education industry": supply, demand, competitive edge, marketplace, and so on, with but three passing references to those concepts, such as standards, excellence, and pursuit of knowledge, that cluttered the "old game." And with the discourse comes a seductive self-legitimation. Since we cannot deny that times have changed, and since the "changing game" really is the "present game," it almost appears to follow that Nugent's discourse is a more realistic and more robust way of analyzing and clarifying things, and that there is no serious alternative to talking this way and acting in accord with this way of talking. It is strongly intimated that if we ask where this particular "changing game" discourse is leading us, the answer will be—to survival.

We should be clear as to what is involved here. Times have, of course, changed; and perhaps a more robust analysis, along with a new language, would serve us better to face the changes and meet the problems they present. But the fact that the discourse of economic rationalism is available and prevalent in the present conjuncture does not mean that it is epistemically privileged, or even that it is the one to do the job.

Let me indicate quickly, from inspecting Nugent's text and examining two of her particular suggestions, that the discourse hardly offers the most authoritative of explanations, that it is a poor analytic tool, and that it is leading neither to survival nor to a necessarily desirable state of affairs. Consider, first, the directive that institutes of higher education will have to adopt a differential salary structure and pay market rates to staff who are able to earn more externally; and second, the advice to "changing game" players to see that "scarce resources are directed to priority areas, as lower priorities are wound down." I would think that here Nugent has ignored certainly the second, and perhaps the first, of her confessions. As economic rationalism turns into economic irrationality, it signs an obsolescence warrant for the very people whose absence it admits would make universities far poorer places. These proposals would surely make things difficult for *present* staff who can earn little if anything plying their expertise outside of the university, as well as for those whose priority rating within the university is continually being redefined downward by the very rules and rhetoric of "changing game" discourse itself. I refer specifically to Sanskrit and Old Icelandic scholars, as well as to most philosophers, certain sociologists, many historians, and even philosophers of education.[23] Further, if Nugent's logic is followed through, then not only might staff who can earn more in industry and elsewhere desert a system of higher education that fails to pay market rates, but also potential staff would surely prepare for and line up at the higher-paying faculties. It is thus hard to conceive of *future* scholars pursuing Old Icelandic Studies, Sanskrit, Philosophy, or History, if a career in Business Management, either within or outside of the higher education system, were to pay more highly. Ironically, all of these, for whom it might be said that the university, at least in part, exists, face being "written out" of universities by "changing game discourse."

Clearly there are problems with both the logic and the analytic value of economic rationalism, problems which readily invite challenge. Economic rationalism may provide answers of a sort to particular questions, but those very answers themselves call forth other questions. Grace, it will be recalled, offered two that we might pose of any discourse: why should we use it, and where is it leading us? There would be value in following through with these questions directly; but instead I shall conclude this exercise by exploring what is implied in *not asking Grace's questions:* in not challenging the discourse of economic rationalism in this very moment of its historical development.

To refrain from asking Grace's questions, whether of a field of academic discourse, a single treasury document, or an entire economic-rationalist agenda, is not merely an academic failing—it is a political failing. And to refrain from asking them of an agenda presented by a government body as part of the orchestration of an ideological position is a much more significant failing.

We are not playing here with Program Notes that can be taken or left as one wishes. There is now a patent and particular need for those concerned with education to engage in the practice of critical literacy and to reestablish control of educational discourse. For some it might be their first conscious political engagement at this level (as was mine in the engagement with analytic philosophy of education), and it may take some effort and wrenching. To fail to do this in the present moment could be to allow those with narrow techno-rational interests, who have unapologetically embraced the nonneutral world of economic rationalism, and who analyze education with the same categories and within the same framework as they analyze the automobile industry, to create a discourse which—and here I recall Aprahamian's notes—effectively excludes those "outside" it from informed participation. To then legitimate such a discourse by silence or awe would be to acquiesce in bringing about one's own impotence. But in this particular case there is a further, deeper, and far more insidious aspect to consider.

In the novel *Nineteen Eighty-Four* George Orwell said of "Newspeak" that its purpose "was not only to provide a medium of expression for the world-view and mental habits proper to the devotees of Ingsoc, but to make all other modes of thought impossible. It was intended that when Newspeak had been adopted once and for all . . . a thought diverging from the principles of Ingsoc should be literally unthinkable."[24] We must be realistic. It is not being suggested that all the treasury documents and economic rationalists in the world will result in a form of "Newspeak" being adopted "once and for all," or that critical thoughts will ever be made "literally unthinkable." But in certain circumstances we could go backwards a long, long way. We cannot lose the entitlements Grace has spoken of, or at least not in an abstract sense. But we can certainly lose the platform from which to seriously exercise them, and if not actually be left with no one to articulate challenge, then (which is nearly as bad) be left articulating challenges from the equivalent of the bowels of the library, with no one listening.

There is dangerous potential within the categories and analysis of the discourse of economic rationalism to establish the ideological position of identifying certain studies, and academics, not simply as part of the "old game," but also as uncompetitive low-potential disciplines and units no longer seriously relevant to higher education. It would be wise for those concerned with education to neither remain ignorant of that potential nor to endorse or accept such a categorization, but rather to enter the political arena of practicing critical literacy, and to do so before the debating rooms are demolished to make way for the new fairways and putting greens.

This is far more than a matter of personal survival or preserving self-interests. If the discourse of economic rationalism is to guide the agenda for the reconstruction of the provision of education, it could bring about the progressive exclusion and silencing of those best able to subject that discourse to critical scrutiny. If we do not challenge this possibility, in the present, to protect the future, we shall have to live with the consequences at least until the forces of critical literacy are developed from hindsight and weakness, marshaled from afar and beyond, and are brought painstakingly back to the lists.

Notes

1. Program of the performance of 27 February 1977; published by the London Symphony Orchestra; Ranelagh Press, London: 1977.
2. *Access*, 3, 1, 1984, pp. 1–16.
3. It was first published by Allen and Unwin (London) in 1966. Reprints, at least annually, followed for almost two decades; and a special

American edition, omitting details of the British educational system, was also produced.

4. This, and all other quotations from the Preface, are from p. 8 of the 1966 edition. All emphases are added.

5. Although it is, of course, possible for more or less spontaneous critiques of deeply considered matters to go off half-cocked, it is also a very common and effective political ploy to defuse potentially explosive critiques on the grounds that the position under attack has been insufficiently considered.

6. Some of these are indicated in my "Peters on Schooling," *Educational Philosophy and Theory*, 9, 1, March 1977, pp. 33–48. At least as many again were excised by the editor. Only by acquiescing in this mutilation and bowdlerization was I able to have a critique of Peters published in the legitimated literature at that time.

7. See Peters's reactions to Dray and Professor Woods in *Philosophy and Education: Proceedings of the International Seminar*, March 23–25, 1966, OISE Press, 1966.

8. I would, as Bourdieu and Passeron were to spell out later, have been adding symbolic force to existing power relations, by imposing meanings and imposing them as legitimate, while failing to reveal the power relations which formed the basis for the legitimating force. See Bourdieu, P., and Passeron, J-C., *Reproduction: In Education, Society and Culture* (London: Sage, 1977), p. 4.

9. This looseness, as I show in "Peters on Schooling," *op. cit.*, is symptomatic of much of the argument in *Ethics and Education*.

10. A clear example of this was the literature built up debating the link between the concepts of 'teaching' and 'indoctrination'. For a summary and critique of this debate, see Harris, K., "Conceptual Analysis and the Concept of "Teaching," *Forum of Education*, 33, 1, March 1974, pp. 65–79.

11. See Marshall, J., *Positivism or Pragmatism?* NZARE Monograph, 2, 1987, p. 13, and other places; and Snook, I., "Contexts and Essences: Indoctrination Revisited," *Educational Philosophy and Theory*, 21, 1, 1989, p. 63.

12. See note 6.

13. *Government Management: Brief to the Incoming Government; Volume 2: Education Issues* (Wellington, Government Printer, 1987).

14. Grace, G., "Education: Commodity or Public Good?" Victoria University Inaugural Address, 1988. This address was subsequently developed into a chapter in Middleton, S., Codd, J., and Jones, A. (eds.), *New Zealand Education Policy Today* (Wellington: Allen and Unwin, 1990).

15. Grace, *ibid.*, p. 7. I would argue that language is never neutral.

16. *Ibid.*, p. 17.

17. Adelstein, D., "The Philosophy of Education, or the Wisdom and Wit of R.S. Peters," in Pateman, T. (ed.), *Countercourse* (Harmondsworth: Penguin, 1972), pp. 115–139. Adelstein's paper originally appeared in a University of London students' publication in 1971: neither source was strictly the legitimated literature. I have been able to find no other paper published before 1977 arguing that Peters's work is ideological.

18. I am not intimating that Grace learned from us. His own work in the 1970s was an important part of the overall challenges being mounted at that time.

19. Grace, *op. cit.*, pp. 7–8.

20. A government body charged with advising the Minister for Employment, Education and Training: and thus not too far removed in function from New Zealand's Treasury.

21. The *Proceedings'* pages are not numbered.

22. This analytical vehicle schematizes the organizational framework of institutions as a web interconnecting seven aspects, all beginning with S. No justification of the design of the web is given, let alone why the particular seven categories have been chosen. The contrivance to find categories beginning with S seems more obvious to me than why some of the categories have been included and why others have been excluded.

23. Not all that long after the heady days of Peters, John White reports that philosophers of education in the United Kingdom are just about "down to zero" (*The Times Educational Supplement,* 9 February 1990).

24. Harmondsworth: Penguin Books, 1974, p. 241.

2

Informing critical literacy with ethnography

Gary L. Anderson and
Patricia Irvine

Most literacy studies view literacy as the acquisition of decoding and writing skills, vocabulary development, or reading comprehension leading explicitly to meeting the requirements of a complex, technological society and implicitly to upward social mobility. In such studies, learning to read and write is viewed primarily as a cognitive process, and when students fail to perform, technical strategies are suggested to remediate problems presumably located within the student. Some of these studies are useful because some reading problems do originate in the student. Nevertheless, the disproportionately large number of marginally literate among poor and minority groups has led researchers to look for the origins of reading and writing problems in school-community relations and the cultural context of classroom interaction. Although research conducted in this framework recognizes the social context of literacy learning, it often fails to acknowledge the ideological context, or the relationships between language and power which play so prominent a role in the construction of human subjectivities.

Three primary perspectives are evident in literacy studies: functionalist, interpretivist, and critical. Studies which construe literacy as a technical skill and which focus on the individual are limited by a generally unarticulated functionalist perspective, that is, they assume the existence of a societal consensus of values, a social system reflecting meritocratic principles, and take a cultural assimilationist posture. The studies mentioned above which take social context into account but which do not address issues of unequal power relations are interpretivist in that they believe social reality is constructed through social interaction. Critical theorists, on the other hand, agree with interpretivists that social reality is a construction, but they focus on how current social constructions are the product of unequal social relations and conflicts of interest. A critical approach presumes that people are not poor because they're illiterate: they're illiterate because they are poor. A critical perspective views illiteracy, or marginal literacy, as a consequence of unequal social relations which limit access to economic opportunity, quality education, and thus uses for literacy.[1]

The notion of critical literacy has its roots in the work of Paulo Freire. Freire insisted that if teachers help students from oppressed communities to read the word but do not also teach them to read the world, students might become literate in a technical sense but will remain passive objects of history rather than active subjects. According to Freire, "subjects" are those who know and act: "objects" are those who are known and acted upon.[2] Critical literacy, then, is learning to read and write as part of the process of becoming conscious of one's experience as historically constructed within specific power relations. The goal of critical literacy, as we will further define it in this paper, is to challenge these unequal power relations.

This chapter will distinguish interpretivist literacy research from research with a critical perspective. After critiquing some current approaches to ethnography, the chapter will conclude with suggestions for a critical literacy project that integrates research and practice.

Why ethnography?

Although much has been written recently on the theory of critical pedagogy and critical literacy, little empirical work is available to guide practice. Ethnography, as a method of discovery that documents patterns in cultural behavior and knowledge, can further our understanding of the processes and effectiveness of critical pedagogies because it represents the "insider's" point of view. For the purposes of this chapter, ethnography will not be defined in terms of methodology or length of time in the field, but in terms of its ability to capture cultural norms.

One advantage of ethnographic research is that it provides the researcher with the opportunity to study outlier cases in depth. Rather than use research methods that seek generalizations and tend to aggregate cases on a distribution, ethnographers can select unique instances of a teaching method and submit them to intense scrutiny, thereby providing us with case study data of the processes and problems associated with various approaches to critical literacy. Another advantage of using ethnography to inform the practice of critical literacy is its ability to capture the unique configurations of any cultural or subcultural setting. According to the definition we will promote in this paper, critical literacy is context bound in the sense that what constitutes critical practice in one setting may not be critical in another. For example, whether it is more liberating to use mother-tongue or second-language literacy will vary depending on the historical, economic, and cultural configuration of each setting.[3] Ethnographic research is well suited to reveal the distribution of language varieties and social uses of literacy, among other factors, which could be used to determine what kind of literacy practice would be critical (that is, would best challenge norms of inequality) in a particular setting.

However, it must be cautioned that ethnography, whether interpretivist or critical, is being increasingly criticized for the same detachment and alienating object-subject relationships characteristic of more traditional positivistic research.[4] As the gap widens between the findings of academic ethnographers and the work of practitioners in the field, the need increases for a critical praxis which incorporates theory and practice. Therefore, in the following sections, the term *critical literacy project* will refer to issues of both research and practice. The implication is that not only academics engage in ethnography, but for critical praxis literacy practitioners and their students may need to become ethnographers as well.

Current ethnographic approaches to the study of literacy

Limitations of interpretive field studies of classrooms and communities

What interpretivist studies have in common, influenced as they are by sociolinguistics and the ethnography of communication, is a view of literacy as a social construction rather than merely a cognitive process. Interpretive studies of literacy have succeeded in shifting the onus of school failure from the student's linguistic code, home situation, and cultural practices to a lack of congruence between these characteristics and classroom processes such as participation structures and interaction styles. Some ethnographic studies of classroom interaction are aimed primarily at better understanding and improving the acquisition of technical literacy, or how students learn to read and write.[5] Other studies attempt to account for the reasons why some learn while others don't, attributing the difficulties to cross-cultural or subcultural differences in communication patterns.[6] Although the importance of these studies in illuminating interaction in classrooms and between schools and communities is beyond question, they have been criticized for not providing a sufficiently critical analysis of the macrostructural causes of social inequality.[7]

Moving to a broader level of analysis, interpretive ethnographers have begun to identify the ways in which institutional arrangements and policies can contribute to illiteracy and inequality.[8] Elaborating on this kind of institutional, mesolevel analysis, Mehan[9] sees inequality as resulting from "constitutive action" which "defines the meaning of objects and events through elaborate enactments of cultural conventions, institutional practices and constitutive rules." He concludes that "differential educational opportunity is, sometimes, at least, an unintended consequence of bureaucratic organization rather than a direct result of [sociopolitical] structural forces." McNeil arrived at the same conclusion in her study of the impact of institutional arrangements on classroom dynamics.[10]

Illiteracy and school failure are no doubt partly due to problems at the classroom, institutional, and community levels, and solutions are rightly being sought there. But in attempting to account for inequality in micro- and mesolevel interactions, these interpretive studies fail to address the structure of opportunities that await these children in the world of work. As Feinberg[11] points out, the current division of labor assures economic success for some and failure for others, and it is, at least partly, up to schools to mediate this allocation of success and failure.

Most interpretive studies betray an underlying belief that if schools and classrooms are "fixed," then the opportunity structures of an unequal division of labor will somehow change too. It is precisely how one defines the origins and constitutive processes of macrostructural forces that distinguishes critical ethnographic accounts of social reality from interpretive ethnography.

Although critical ethnographers might agree theoretically with interpretivists that social structures are ultimately the historically sedimented result of microinteractions, they believe that the material forces that maintain these structures are not abstractions, but have names and faces with concrete interests to defend. Deetz and Kersten express this difference in their comparison of hermeneutic (interpretivist) and Marxist approaches to social explanation: "Even though hermeneutics and Marxism might agree that existing social, economic, and political arrangements are constructions, hermeneutics would seek to explain how they were constructed and how their coherence is maintained; Marxism would seek to examine the conditions making the construction necessary and whose interests are served by their maintenance."[12] Our knowledge of the dynamics of literacy acquisition and its relation to social class is richer because of the interpretivist studies cited above. We would argue, however, that a parallel set of studies is needed that take into account more explicitly the socially structured and historical context of literacy.

Critical ethnography

Critical ethnography is explicitly ideological in its approach to research. Although its methodology is similar to that of interpretive ethnography, it insists that neutrality and scientific objectivity are, in fact, highly political since they tend to maintain the status quo by not raising questions of unequal power relations in their research. Unlike interpretive ethnographers, who seek to understand the webs of meaning that human agents construct, critical ethnographers attempt to "ascertain why a particular meaning system exists by examining the conditions that necessitate its social construction and the advantages afforded certain interests."[13] There have recently been a number of attempts to describe critical ethnography, in terms of both its epistemological implications and its substantive concerns.[14]

Early works in critical ethnography dealt directly with the documentation of the role of schools in the reproduction of the social order. Focusing on social-class differences, Anyon[15] studied the correspondence of the beliefs, values, and attitudes required for schoolwork with those of the workplace. Willis, focusing on the role of human agency in social reproduction, explored the forms of resistance engaged in by working-class males.[16] Subsequent ethnographic studies have explored the ways that race and gender intersect with social class to reproduce unequal social relations.[17]

If, as critical ethnographers argue, schools are sites of cultural production achieved through conflict and struggle, then the students' subjectivities and the practices that both facilitate and block the possibility of human agency must be documented. "One of the most important elements at work in the construction of experience and subjectivity in schools is language. In this case, language intersects with power in the way a particular linguistic form is used in schools to legitimate and structure the ideologies and modes of life of specific groups."[18] The intersection of language and power in schools makes language and literacy contested terrains, raising an important question for critical ethnographers of literacy: How and when is illiteracy a form of social resistance?[19]

Many critical ethnographers attempt to display the subjective world of the oppressed in order to challenge policies that maintain inequality.[20] For example, recent ethnographic studies of teen pregnancy indicate that lack of options in social roles and economic opportunities for poor female teens is a compelling reason for not postponing motherhood, which may be the only socially sanctioned role available to them for self-actualization. For many female and male teens, the lack of employment opportunities which pay above minimum wages precludes the economic stability necessary to raise a child in a family context. This finding contradicts assumptions underlying current policies that teens get pregnant because they lack information about contraceptives or access to them, or because of other factors that fail to address social and economic causes.[21]

Critical ethnographers study what is not said and done in educational settings as well as what actually occurs. Anderson[22] and Fine[23] have explored the ways ideological control and unequal relations are sustained in educational institutions through subtle forms of "silencing," a process which renders many of the mechanisms of oppression invisible. Finally, Wexler[24] has criticized critical ethnographers for limiting their focus to schooling. Critical ethnographic studies of popular culture[25] and media[26] are broadening our understanding of how individuals are constituted as subjects outside educational institutions.

Action research: Teachers as ethnographers

There has been a resurgence of interest among teachers in doing classroom research either in collaboration with university-based researchers or on their own.[27] Ethnographic methods are widely used by these teachers, and in some cases the difference between research and practice is blurred. Educators are increasingly arguing that action research and ethnographic methods should be part of teacher-training programs, and groups of teacher-researchers that meet to share their work are forming with more frequency.[28] Current work in collaborative action research, or "teachers as researchers," does not preclude critical approaches to literacy. Nevertheless, its emphasis tends to be technical in the sense that the aim is improvement of practice within a functionalist paradigm.[29] Because critical literacy emphasizes reading the world as well as the word, its substance is not only technical instruction, but also a critique of the organizational and social structures and the social relations which support them.

Carr and Kemmis[30] have provided the most complete account of how critical theory can inform action research. Their account also implies criticism of critical ethnographic accounts that retain a traditional researcher-centered approach. According to Carr and Kemmis, critical action research represents the only authentic educational science and must do the following:

1. Reject positivistic notions of rationality

2. Employ participants' interpretive categories

3. Be aware of how interpretations are often distorted by ideology

4. Identify and expose those aspects of the existing social order that frustrate rational change

5. Be practical in the sense that "findings" are grounded in the reality of participants

Although some of these criteria overlap with the interpretive tradition of action research, there is a greater emphasis in critical action research on unmasking the ideological aspects of schooling and on analyzing the impact on the classroom of asymmetrical power relations in the broader society.

Critical reflection

Many practitioners—primarily academics—are beginning to reflect critically upon their own practice. Not bound by the constraints of traditional research paradigms, this form of inquiry involves, in Berthoff's term, a RE-research of the practitioners' own experience.[31] Although these critical reflective accounts by practitioners might be dismissed by some as "thought pieces" or "merely anecdotal," it might be helpful to place them in historical context.

Although these writers do not engage in formal ethnography, they can be seen as part of a "preethnographic" tradition of cultural analysis. According to Van Maanen, "Only during the first third of this century did ethnography itself become a recognizable topical and literary genre set off from similar written products such as travel and adventure stories, fiction, biography, social history, journalism, statistical survey, and cultural speculation."[32] Adaptations of many of these quasi-ethnographic forms are being rediscovered by educational researchers as appropriate ways to provide accounts of critical literacy.

Although methodologically nonsystematic, reflective articles provide an antidote to the abstractness that has characterized so much of the writing in critical educational theory. In these examinations of their own teaching, practitioners try to make sense of critical literacy and critical pedagogy in general. Whether viewed as new journalism,[33] educational criticism,[34] portraiture,[35] experiential analysis,[36] or "impressionist tales,"[37] these anecdotal descriptions are helping educators understand the complex processes of critical literacy practices.

For example, Delpit has reflected on her early experience as a black teacher and the limitations of the whole-language instructional approach to literacy for poor black students.[38] Ellsworth describes her experiences with critical pedagogy, pointing out its conceptual and practical limitations.[39] Lewis has reflected on classroom events in the course of using feminist teaching.[40] Gitlin writes about his efforts to infuse a teacher education program with a practitioner-centered, question-posing approach to ethnographic research.[41] Bell and Schniedewind describe a fifth-grade classroom in which a teacher tries to implement an instructional model that combines humanistic and critical approaches to pedagogy.[42] And McLaren seeks to create a larger theoretical context for a journal he kept as an inner-city elementary school teacher.[43] These firsthand accounts of critical practitioners struggling with new and untested forms of teaching question the assumptions of critical pedagogy and raise issues often ignored in empirical research. As such, they offer valuable criticism of schools and classrooms and promise to contribute to our understanding of critical practice.

Ethnography as social action: Freirean participatory research

In some form, the work of Paulo Freire has influenced all critical ethnography and critically reflective accounts as well. However, because Freire and his followers have combined research and social action with the concept of literacy at the forefront of their work, a sketch of the evolution of this form of research-as-action may be helpful for those engaged in critical literacy studies. In Latin America, Freire's work in Chile and Brazil during the 1960s spawned a research tradition, variously named "thematic research," "militant research," and "participatory research." This tradition is little known to many North American researchers unfamiliar with Third World research paradigms.

Freire's notion of thematic research is a highly inductive process in which research is viewed as a form of social action. In this type of research, "generative themes," or issues important to the participants, are identified and studied together with researchers. According to Freire, "When carried out with a methodology of conscientização, the investigation of the generative theme contained in the minimum thematic universe (the generative themes in interaction) introduces or begins to introduce men (sic) to a critical form of thinking about their world."[44] Although methodological considerations depend on the context within which the study is undertaken, de Schutter describes the following as general characteristics of Freirean participatory research:

- The point of departure is a vision of social reality as a totality.
- Social processes and structures are understood within a historical context.
- Theory and practice are integrated.
- The subject-object relationship is transformed into a subject-subject relationship through dialogue.
- Research and action (including education itself) become a single process.
- The synchronic and quantitative nature of traditional research is replaced by a diachronic orientation and an integration of quantitative and qualitative elements.
- The community and researcher together produce critical knowledge aimed at social transformation.
- The results of research are immediately applied to a concrete situation.[45]

Although thematic research has a longer history in Latin America and other parts of the Third World, reports of North American researchers working to implement a Freirean approach to literacy are becoming more numerous.[46] Feminist researchers have been particularly successful in breaking down the subject-object relationship as a move toward transformative action.[47] Although he ignores the twenty-year tradition of Freire-inspired participatory research, Gitlin[48] offers a helpful description, similar to de Schutter's,[49] of how research and action can be wedded in what he calls "educative research."

Using ethnography to create a critical literacy project

As we stated at the beginning of this chapter, a critical literacy project strives to merge research and practice. For this reason we use *project* rather than *research program*. As we have seen, there is a strong movement in this direction within the traditions of participatory research,[50] feminist research,[51] action research,[52] critical ethnography,[53] and poststructural research.[54] In such a project, both critical researchers and literacy workers become researcher-activists, ideally working together with students to address the relationship between literacy and empowerment in a given context.

Ethnographic methods are particularly useful in analyzing which actions, curricula, or texts will lead to empowerment in different contexts. By definition, there can be no generic critical literacy curriculum in the style of the readymade "cultural literacy" curriculum proposed by Hirsch[55] because in each community the specific oppressive practices to be addressed and the distribution of language varieties (and values associated with oral and written language) differ. Instead, what students will write and read, in which language(s), for which audiences, and to what ends changes according to the setting and the needs of the participants.

In the remainder of this paper, we will raise the key questions which need to be addressed in critical literacy praxis: What is the appropriate content for critical literacy study? Which language variety (standard or vernacular) should be used for critical literacy? How can critical literacy lead to social action?[56]

What is the appropriate context for a critical literacy project?

Critical literacy is not just a clever approach to make literacy acquisition more topical for students; it "demands an ideological critique of the social situation in which students and educators find themselves."[57] Critical literacy analyzes how social texts and discourse practices are constituted to maintain inequality and how the consensus to maintain this inequality is achieved.[58]

Starting a critical literacy project

Because the social issues in each community differ, the ethnographer-practitioner must decide, with other participants, which school or community problem can provide a focus for the content of the critical literacy project. After choosing a generative theme,[59] students and teachers coinvestigate, or conduct research together. The theme needs to represent a conflict in the lives of all project members; a generative theme is not just a social problem students agree to discuss, such as "crime" or "the environment." If the theme is truly generative, it will yield many aspects of a problem to study. In one example from the University of the Virgin Islands, West Indian Creole speakers focused on their anger at being placed in a noncredit remedial English class. For the first assignment, the students wrote essays answering the question "Why do I lack college-level English skills?" Two reasons they identified were lack of preparation in high school and their belief that they spoke "broken English." The coinvestigation proceeded from there.[60]

Students and practitioners can become ethnographers as they investigate how the problem is manifested locally. In order to counteract oppressive norms, one must describe the norms as they currently operate. As part of the research, students can document their own experience as well as that of others in their community affected by the issue. In the example cited above, students in one group surveyed local high school teachers to find out what was actually taught in English classes. The entire class studied linguistics, learning that Creole is, in fact, a language. In addition to writing about their own negative attitudes toward their language, they surveyed the attitudes of their fellow students. Honors students investigating this theme conducted sociolinguistic research about code switching.

Connecting the personal and the social

Exploring students' personal experience is the first step in countering the idea that meaning exists only in structures external to the individual. It also brings into the classroom the culture of the community, not just that of the institution. But the process cannot stop there. A critical approach requires that students connect their experience to larger, oppressive social patterns. The West Indian students learned that the denigration of their language and the consequent negative effect on their self-esteem was a result of a number of sociohistorical factors, slavery and colonialism among them. In a different part of the Caribbean, a class of Bahamian women in a critical literacy project began by complaining about the physical and emotional abuse they suffered in their marriages and sexual relationships; by sharing personal stories, they learned that there was a pattern to their experiences. By reading about other women's experiences and analyzing texts, they learned to connect their experience to the wider phenomenon of sexism.[61]

Critiquing ideology: Reading the world

Since the theme will vary from setting to setting, the kinds of materials for study will also vary. In addition to the data generated by the kind of participatory research mentioned above, other texts, media, videos, cultural practices, or artifacts can be analyzed for nonsubjective information about the problem. However, no literacy text or activity is neutral because all knowledge addresses specific interests and is historically generated. Therefore, a crucial critical literacy process is discovering the ideology implicit in any cultural texts used as resources. All participants can problematize the knowledge in the resources they consult: What is considered knowledge about the topic by the school or other dominant institutions? Who creates it? Who has access to it? Who may challenge it and in what ways?

Similar questions must be asked about community resources, such as songs, stories, traditional practices, or oral history. How do the form and content of community and school knowledge differ and why? What relevance does the information have to the experience of the group members? What assumptions are implicit in "official" sources of information, and how do they differ from the assumptions of local sources? How do the assumptions of either support or subvert the status quo?

Just as text or other artifacts can be analyzed critically, so can any personal, community, or institutional practice. For example, we might explore how race, class, and gender barriers are maintained (or broken) in a typical classroom: Who talks? How much and under what circumstances? Lewis performed this kind of analysis when she articulated the subtle dynamics in a feminist theory class that reinforced the subordination of women.[62] As part of any investigation, we need to ask what the historical origins of the practices are and whose interests are served by them.

Although we advocate bringing the norms of the community into the classroom as a validation of students' reality and not just as a transition to dominant norms, there is a caveat: the cultural norms of the local community can be as limiting as the sanctioned norms of the dominant institutions or culture. Romanticizing the norms of either the dominant or the nondominant culture offers no vision for transformation. Instead, we need to ask how the cultural, political, and linguistic practices of both the dominant institutions and the local community can be reenvisioned to create a more equitable and humane society.

Which language variety should be used for critical literacy?

A key issue in critical literacy is the choice of language for writing. In light of the emphasis we have placed on critical literacy as a means for addressing social inequality, it can never be a given whether a critical literacy project will take place in the standard, the vernacular, or both.

Research in sociolinguistics and ethnography of communication has extensively documented how social meaning is signaled in variations in language use within and between language varieties. These variations signal sociohistorical differences in power relations between groups, and they serve to maintain those differences.[63] Given that the values associated with language use are socially constituted and thus value laden, the choice of language variety either challenges an oppressive status quo or reaffirms it.

A poignant example of the powerful role of language in critical literacy took place in the example cited earlier from the Virgin Islands. The students believed that they couldn't write because as speakers of "broken English" they "had no language." As part of the coinvestigation, the instructors invited a West Indian linguist who presented concepts legitimating Creole as a language. Energized, the students experimented with writing essays in Creole, discovering that composing an essay is difficult in any language. In the process they had to agree on which of their varieties of Creole would be the standard for creating an orthography, and discovered the reasons for conventions in standard English at the same time. Their sociolinguistic research documented which settings and topics called for Creole and which for standard English, revealing that Creole was appropriate for only "non-serious" functions. Their surveys revealed native speakers' negative attitudes toward Creole.

In much of the writing about the importance of literacy in maintaining a viable democracy, it seems implicit that what is meant is essayist (or standard language) literacy, the kind that enables people to do well in schools. The assumption is that the way to change the conditions of oppressed people is to teach standard English, the language of power. However, when literacy in the standard is presented to speakers from stigmatized speech communities, it implies assimilation in a group which openly rejects the language, and by implication the speakers, of the nonstandard variety. Those who choose assimilation and succeed do so at the expense of their identity as a member of their own group. Most critically, trying to make some students socially mobile fails to address the primary issue: challenging the inequality between groups which has resulted in stigmatized varieties in the first place.

People learn a language variety by being a member of a group—a speech community—and using it for the same purpose as other members.[64] Oppressed people speak stigmatized language varieties, signaling that they are not members of the group with the power to set the standard. When nonstandard speakers learn how language standardization operates (the West Indian students referred joyfully and often to Noam Chomsky's famous quip that a language is a dialect with an army and a navy to back it up), they can choose to learn the standard for certain functions without having to reject their own language, family, and community.

Research into how language varieties are distributed and valued in any community can be used to decide which language varieties are appropriate for critical literacy study. Students can be guided through an ethnographic description and analysis themselves.[65] If students create materials which challenge the norms in their community as well as in the institution, it is necessary to question which variety is appropriate to their audience and purposes. What values are associated with standard or vernacular usage? Which oral and written functions are allocated to the standard and to the vernacular language? What are rules of evidence in each language? Which community groups have or don't have access to written materials in the standard? Of course, the choice of the standard or the vernacular may shift as the audience, the political purpose of student writing or activities, and the students' goals for their own learning change.

Since the choice of language for reading and writing determines who produces knowledge and who has access to it, the critical literacy practitioner-ethnographer needs to ask a number of questions in deciding whether critical literacy should be practiced in the standard, the vernacular, or both. Choice of language includes not just the formal code but also the social uses and values associated with different forms (essays, letters, or songs) and the audiences and purposes for the intended critical products. Also, the choice depends on students' educational goals. The West Indian college students in honors and remedial classes wrote in a variety of genres: research papers, expository guest editorials and letters to the editor in standard English; fictional stories in Creole for other West Indians about issues such as teenage pregnancy and tenants' rights; and thank-you letters in Creole to guest speakers from the community, among others.

In investigating this issue, ethnographers-participants may ask how information is disseminated to the vernacular-speaking community. To what extent is it written? Which groups in the local community have access to written vernacular language? In addition, what forms and functions are already allocated to it? If it is not developed, to what extent can new forms and functions be developed through its use?

How can critical literacy result in social action?

Action which challenges social inequality is the ultimate goal of a critical literacy project. The central question is when and to what extent social action can be connected to learning to read and write. As the following quote by a literacy worker in India indicates, a critical literacy project may result in actions that have little to do with literacy work in its narrow sense of "reading the word."

> Women attended our literacy classes only as long as it took them to find work, anything to help them augment the family's meagre monthly income.

They bluntly told our teachers to go away, or stick to teaching children. Learning how to sign their names or write the alphabet would not help to fill empty bellies. So we stopped worrying about literacy as an end in itself, or as being central to our work. We began to work together with people in trying to understand their immediate and daily concerns and difficulties, learning together to analyze the problems and understand the root causes; then planning how we could, together, find answers and, above all, take action.[66]

Social, not individual, solutions

Critical literacy precludes viewing individual solutions as meaningful social action. Simply promoting more effective literacy practices to increase the upward mobility of individuals does not address the social forces which limited access to literacy in the first place. In the words of Zacharakis-Jutz:

> Individualization, as Foucault (1982) and Lasch (1979) warn, is a tool used by the dominant culture to foster utopian visions, riches, and glory, and personal freedom and power. Yet, in reality, focusing on the individual leaves most people in isolation and profoundly powerless relative to the state or dominant institution . . . Through individualization, resistance to institutions and values dissipates.[67]

Solutions which focus on individuals do not challenge the social conditions which promote and support illiteracy. Moreover, they simply do not work for more than the minority of individuals who succeed against all odds. If it were so easy to remediate years of undereducation, there wouldn't be the large numbers of marginally literate that now exist or the current interest in developing alternative approaches to literacy and education

Social action as a public challenge to oppressive norms

Most Freirean approaches to education acknowledge social action as the goal of critical literary praxis. However, it is much less clear how to define it. In much recent writing about critical literacy, positive changes in self-esteem, because they are personally empowering, are equated with social action. However, although increased self-esteem may be necessary for action, it is not sufficient, since it focuses on the individual and not on changing the conditions that contribute to the systematic denigration of groups. In this chapter, we offer a definition of social action as concrete social practice to confront social, political, or economic realities.[68]

Ways in which the praxis of equality can be accomplished through literacy acts will change according to setting. In what ways do literacy products, activities, or other "texts" such as video, film, performance, or visual art affect attitudes or result in changes in social practice inside or outside the classroom? In what ways do the products make legible the processes and structures that create oppressive ideology?

In the example from the remedial class at the University of the Virgin Islands, the students published a letter to the editor of the local paper reporting the results of their survey of high school English teachers. The survey revealed that essay writing was rarely assigned by local high school teachers. The curricular changes that students suggested received a hostile response from the president of the teachers' union, who reminded them that they were, after all, only remedial students. Subsequent letters from the school board and other community members pursued the issue in the newspaper. Honors students published articles in the Creole vernacular, challenging norms for language use in a formal education setting. In both instances, students publicly challenged norms and offered alternatives.

A critical literacy project in Albuquerque, New Mexico, offers another illustration of social action. Immigrant children in middle school whose dominant language was Spanish wrote books in Spanish and English for Nicaraguan children who had few educational materials because of the U.S. boycott. Over five thousand copies of these books have been sent to the town of Bluefields on the Atlantic coast and are being used in classrooms.[69]

How participants' lives (as well as community and school norms) are affected by action through critical literacy praxis is a question that needs to be part of the ethnographic coinvestigation. In these examples, students did not change the high school English curriculum, overturn norms for language use, or affect U.S. relations with Nicaragua. They did, however, publicly defy the rules for who may create knowledge and in which language varieties. They did not "practice" reading and writing for possible use later in their lives, but learned it in critical literacy praxis as subjects of their own reality.

Conclusion

In exploring how ethnographic methods have been used to study literacy, this chapter has discussed interpretive ethnography, critical ethnography, action research, "critical reflection," and participatory research. In search of an ethnographic approach to a critical literacy project we also offer questions that focus on content; on the role of language in conceptualizing, contextualizing, and implementing critical literacy; and on the goals of social action. Although we see the greatest promise for the use of ethnographic methods as forming part of a critical literacy project which is both critical and participatory, we do not wish to create some new "regime of truth" in which the only forms of inquiry that are valid collapse the dualism of research and activism. We do feel, however, that unless the problems with detached approaches to literacy research carried out by academics are addressed, we will have little impact on practice in either a technical or critical sense.

Notes

* We want to thank Michele Minnis and Nina Wallerstein for careful comments on an earlier draft of this paper.

1. When functionalists use terms like *critical thinking, critical literacy,* or *empowerment,* they are generally referring to individual processes and goals rather than social ones. These terms are currently being widely co-opted and used to promote a conservative political agenda. Witness the current Republican administration's use of *empowerment* to promote schools of choice.

2. Although all of Freire's written work is germane to this study, we will draw mainly here on his seminal book, *Pedagogy of the Oppressed* (New York: Herder and Herder, 1971).

3. Kerfoot, C., *Voice, Structure and Agency: Literacy in South Africa,* unpublished manuscript, 1990.

4. Gitlin, A., "Educative Research, Voice, and School Change," *Harvard Educational Review,* 60, 4, 1990, pp. 443–466.

5. See, for example, the following: Bloome, D., *Literacy and Schooling* (Norwood, N.J.: Ablex, 1987); Cazden, C., John, V., and Hymes, D., (eds.), *Functions of Language in the Classroom* (New York: Teachers College Press,

1972); and Cochran-Smith, M., *The Making of a Reader* (Norwood, N.J.: Ablex, 1984).

6. See Heath, S.B., *Ways with Words: Language, Life, and Work in Communities and Classrooms* (Cambridge: Cambridge University Press, 1983); McDermott, R., "Achieving School Failure: An Anthropological Approach to Illiteracy and Social Stratification," in Spindler, G. (ed.), *Education and Cultural Process: Anthropological Approaches*, 2nd ed. (Prospect Heights, Ill.: Waveland Press, 1987, pp. 173–209; Philips, S., *The Invisible Culture: Communication in Classroom and Community on the Warmsprings Indian Reservation* (New York: Longman, 1982); and Rist, R., *The Urban School: Factory for Failure* (Cambridge, Mass: MIT Press, 1973).

7. Anderson, G.L., "Critical Ethnography in Education: Origins, Current Status, and New Directions," *Review of Educational Research*, 59, 3, 1990, pp. 249-270; Everhart, R., review of *The Egalitarian Ideal and the American High School, Anthropology and Education Quarterly*, 16, 1985, pp. 73–77; Ogbu, J., "School Ethnography: A Multilevel Approach," *Anthropology and Education Quarterly*, 12, 1981, pp. 3–29.

8. McNeil, L., *Contradictions of Control* (London: Routledge, 1988).

9. Mehan, H., "Understanding Inequality in Schools: The Contribution of Interpretive Studies," invited address at the annual meeting of the American Sociological Association, 9 August 1989.

10. McNeil, *op. cit.*

11. Feinberg, W., *Understanding Education: Toward a Reconstruction of Educational Inquiry* (Cambridge: Cambridge University Press, 1983).

12. Deetz, S., and Kersten, A., "Critical Models of Interpretive Research," in Putnam, L., and Pacanowski, M. (eds.), *Communication and Organizations: An Interpretive Approach* (Beverly Hills: Sage, 1983), p. 150.

13. *Ibid.*, p. 160.

14. These include Anderson, *op. cit.*; Angus, L., "Developments in Ethnographic Research in Education: From Interpretive to Critical Ethnography," *Journal of Research and Development in Education*, 20, 1986, pp. 59–67; Gitlin, A., Siegel, M., and Boru, K., "The Politics of Method: From Leftist Ethnography to Educational Research," *Qualitative Studies in Education*, 2, 3, 1989, pp. 237–253; and Lather, P., "Research as Praxis," *Harvard Educational Review*, 56, 1986, pp. 257–277.

15. Anyon, J., "Social Class and the Hidden Curriculum of Work," *Journal of Education*, 161, 1980, pp. 67–72.

16. Willis, P., *Learning to Labor: How Working Class Kids Get Working Class Jobs* (New York: Columbia University Press, 1977).

17. See McLeod, J., *Ain't No Makin' It: Levelled Aspirations in a Low Income Neighbourhood* (San Diego: Westview Press, 1987); Weiler, K., *Wom-*

en Teaching for Change: Gender, Class and Power (South Hadley, Mass.: Bergin and Garvey, 1988).

18. Giroux, H., "Critical Pedagogy, Cultural Politics, and the Discourse of Experience," *Journal of Education*, 167, 2, 1985, pp. 22–41.

19. Gilmore, P., "Gimme Room: School Resistance, Attitude, and Access to Literacy," *Journal of Education*, 167, 1985, pp. 111–128.

20. Mischler, E., *Research Interviewing: Context and Narrative* (Cambridge, Mass.: Harvard University Press, 1986).

21. Herr, K., "Portrait of a Teen Mother," in Donmoyer, R., and Kos, R. (eds.), *At-Risk Students: Portraits, Policies, and Programs* (Albany: SUNY Press) (in press); Lesko, N., "Social Context and the problem of teen pregnancy," paper presented at the American Educational Research Association, Boston, 1990.

22. Anderson, G.L., "Toward a Critical Constructivist Approach to School Administration: Invisibility, Legitimation, and the Study of Non-Events," *Education Administration Quarterly*, 26, 1990, pp. 38–59.

23. Fine, M., "Silencing and Nurturing Voice in an Improbable Context: Urban Adolescents in Public School," in Giroux, H., and McLaren, P. (eds.), *Critical Pedagogy, the State, and Cultural Struggle* (Albany: SUNY Press, 1989).

24. Wexler, P., *Social Analysis of Education: After the New Sociology* (London: Routledge, 1987).

25. Roman, L.G., "Intimacy, Labor, and Class: Ideologies of Feminine Sexuality in the Punk Slam Dance," in Roman, L.G., Christian-Smith, L.K., and Ellsworth, E. (eds.), *Becoming Feminine: The Politics of Popular Culture* (London: Falmer Press, 1988), pp. 143–184.

26. Ellsworth, E., "Illicit Pleasures: Feminist Spectators and Personal Best," in Roman, L.G., Christian-Smith, L.K., and Ellsworth, E. (eds.), *Becoming Feminine: The Politics of Popular Culture* (London: Falmer Press), pp. 102–119.

27. Cochran-Smith, M., and Lytle, S., "Research on Teaching and Teacher Research: The Issues That Divide," *Educational Researcher*, 19, 2, 1990, pp. 2–11.

28. Mohr, M., and McLean, M., *Working Together: A Guide for Teacher Researchers* (Urbana, Ill.: National Council of Teachers of English, 1987).

29. Cochran-Smith and Lytle, *op. cit.*

30. Carr, W., and Kemmis, S., *Becoming Critical: Knowing through Action Research* (Victoria: Deakin University Press, 1983).

31. Berthoff, A., "The Teacher as Researcher," in Goswami, D., and Stillman, P. (eds.), *Reclaiming the Classroom: Teacher Research as an Agent for Change* (Upper Montclair, N.J.: Boynton, 1987).

32. Van Maanen, J., *Tales of the Field: On Ethnographic Writing* (Chicago: University of Chicago Press, 1987).

33. Barone, T., "Effectively Critiquing the Experienced Curriculum: Clues from the 'New Journalism,'" *Curriculum Inquiry*, 10, 1980, pp. 29–53.

34. Eisner, E., *The Educational Imagination* (New York: MacMillan, 1979).

35. Lightfoot, S., *The Good High School: Portraits of Character and Culture* (New York: Basic Books, 1983).

36. Reinharz, S., "Experiential Analysis: A Contribution to Feminist Research," in Bowles, G., and Duelli Klein, R. (eds.), *Theories of Women's Studies* (Boston: Routledge, 1983), pp. 162–191.

37. Van Maanen, *op. cit.*

38. Delpit, L., "Skills and Other Dilemmas of a Progressive Black Educator," *Harvard Educational Review*, 56, 4, 1986, pp. 379–385.

39. Ellsworth, E., "Why Doesn't This Feel Empowering? Working through the Repressive Myths of Critical Pedagogy," *Harvard Educational Review*, 59, 3, 1989, pp. 294–334.

40. Lewis, M., "Interrupting Patriarchy: Politics, Resistance, and Transformation in the Feminist Classroom," *Harvard Educational Review*, 60, 4, 1990, pp. 467–488.

41. Gitlin, *op. cit.*

42. Bell, L., and Schniedewind, N., "Reflective Minds/Intentional Hearts: Joining Humanistic Education and Critical Theory in Liberating Education," *Journal of Education*, 169, 2, 1987, pp. 55–78.

43. McLaren, P., *Life in Schools* (New York: Longman, 1989).

44. Freire, *op. cit.*, p. 95.

45. de Schutter, A., and Yopo, B., "Desarrollo y Perspectiva de la Investigación Participativa," in Vejarano, G. (ed.), *La Investigacíon Participativa en America Latina* (Patzcuaro, Michoacan, Mex: CREFAL, 1983), p. 68. The original is as follows:

- El punto de partida lo constituye la visión de la realidad como una totalidad.
- Los procesos y estructuras son comprendidos en su dimensión histórica.
- Teoriá y práctica se integran.
- La relación sujet-objeto se convierte en una relación sujeto-sujeto a traves del diálogo.
- La investigación y la acción (inclusive lo educativo), se convierten en un solo proceso.

• El carácter sincrónico y cuantitativo de la investigación tradicional es reemplazado por una orientación diacrónica y una integración de elementos cualitativos y cuantitativos.
• La comunidad y el investigador producen conjuntamente conocimientos críticos dirigidos a la transformación social.
• Los resultados de la investigación son aplicados de inmediato a la realidad concreta.

46. Sola, M., and Bennett, A.T., "The Struggle for Voice: Narrative, Literacy, and Consciousness in an East Harlem school," *Journal of Education*, 167, 1985, pp. 88–110; Finlay, L., and Faith, V., "Illiteracy and Alienation in American Colleges: Is Paulo Freire's Pedagogy Relevant?" *Radical Teacher*, 8, 1980, pp. 28–37; Fiore, K., and Elsasser, N., "Strangers No More: A Liberating Literacy Curriculum," *College English*, 44, 1982, pp. 169–181; Irvine, P., and Elsasser, N., "The Ecology of Literacy: Negotiating Writing Standards in a Caribbean Setting," in Rayfoth, B., and Rubin, D. (eds.), *The Social Construction of Written Communication* (Norwood, N.J.: Ablex, 1988), pp. 304–320; Solorzano, D., "Teaching and Social Change: Reflections of a Freirean Approach in a College Classroom," *Teaching Sociology*, 17, 1989, pp. 218–225.

47. Mies, M., "Towards a Methodology for Feminist Research," in Bowles, G., and Duelli Klein, R. (eds.), *Theories of Womens Studies* (Boston: Routledge, 1983). See also Roman, L., and Apple, M., "Is Naturalism a Move Away from Positivism? Materialist and Feminist Approaches to Subjectivity in Ethnographic Research," in Eisner, E., and Peshkin, A. (eds.), *Qualitative Inquiry in Education: The Continuing Debate* (New York: Teachers College Press, 1990).

48. Gitlin, *op. cit.*

49. De Schutter, *op cit.*

50. *Ibid.*

51. Mies, *op. cit.*

52. Carr and Kemmis, *op. cit.*

53. Gitlin, 1990, and Gitlin, Siegel, and Boru, 1989, both *op. cit.*

54. Lather, P., "Deconstructing/Deconstructive Inquiry: The Politics of Knowing and Being Known," paper presented at the annual conference of the New Zealand Association for Research in Education, Wellington, November 1989.

55. Hirsch, E.D., Jr., *Cultural Literacy: What Every American Needs to Know* (Boston: Houghton Mifflin, 1987).

56. Many of the ideas appearing in this definition of critical literacy

2 have been developed by Patricia Irvine and Nan Elsasser as part of their concept of the "New Speech Community."

57. Kretovics, J., "Critical Literacy: Challenging the Assumptions of Mainstream Educational Theory," *Journal of Education*, 167, 2, 1985, pp. 50–62.

58. Cherryholmes, C., *Power and Criticism: Poststructural Investigations in Education* (New York: Teachers College Press, 1988).

59. Freire, *op. cit.*

60. Elsasser, N., and Irvine, P., "English and Creole: The Dialectics of Choice in a College Writing Program," *Harvard Educational Review*, 55, 4, 1985, pp. 399–415.

61. Fiore and Elsasser, *op. cit.*

62. Lewis, M., *op. cit.*

63. Bennett, A. T., "Discourse of Power, the Dialectics of Understanding, the Power of Literacy," *Journal of Education*, 165, 1982, pp. 53–74; Collins, J., "Hegemonic Practice: Literacy and Standard Language in Public Education," *Journal of Education*, 171, 2, 1989, pp. 9–34; Woolard, K., "Language Variation and Cultural Hegemony: Toward an Integration of Sociolinguistic and Social Theory," *American Ethnologist*, 12, 1985, pp. 738–748.

64. Hymes, D., *Foundations in Sociolinguistics* (Philadelphia: University of Pennsylvania Press, 1974).

65. Elsasser and Irvine, 1985, *op. cit.*; Heath, *op. cit.*

66. Ramdas, L., "Literacy and Empowerment: A Definition for Literacy," *Viewpoints: A Series of Occasional Papers on Basic Education*, no. 9, 1989.

67. Zacharakis-Jutz, J., "Post-Freirean Adult Education: A Question of Empowerment and Power," *Adult Education Quarterly*, 39, 1988, p. 43. The references are to Foucault, M., "The Subject and Power," in Dreyfus, H., and Rabinow, P. (eds.), *Michel Foucault: Beyond Structuralism and Hermeneutics* (Chicago: University of Chicago Press, 1982), pp. 208–226; and Lasch, C., *The Culture of Narcissism* (New York: Warner Books, 1979).

68. Elsasser, N., and Irvine, P., "Literacy as a Commodity: A Plan to Redistribute the Goods," unpublished manuscript, 1990.

69. *Ibid.*

3

Critical literacy and the politics of gender

Barbara Bee

This chapter draws on a decade of work among socially and educationally disadvantaged women. During this time I have worked as an adult literacy teacher and author of literacy materials designed to enable women to develop their critical abilities through reading and writing. My underlying hope has been that through their development of critical literacy and critical thought, such women can enhance their personal and collective power and increase their status and opportunities within Australian society. Throughout, my work has been greatly influenced by Paulo Freire's pedagogical approach and by feminist insights into the workings of patriarchy (which condition my own status and social role along with those of women in general).[1] The following account reflects my understanding of the connection between critical literacy and the politics of gender, as informed by my literacy work with adult women.

I believe the key to genuine emancipation for women lies in economic independence and the subsequent loss of women's need to look to males for their care, protection, and approval. This, however, cannot be achieved unless women actively understand those structural arrangements within society which subjugate them and maintain their economic, political, and social inferiority. Unlike conventional approaches to functional literacy, critical literacy offers an approach by which to help women understand the root causes of their subordination and subservience and to enable them to turn individual powerlessness into collective struggle with the capacity to transform their lives and, ultimately, the wider social order.

The point of taking a critical approach to women's literacy' is to use reading and writing as a means for enabling women who have been conditioned to accept second-class status to affirm their aspirations as valid and their knowledge and views of life as genuine contributions to the net stock of human understanding. Merely enabling women to read and write without reference to their social and political inequality and its origins contributes materially to maintaining their oppression. As Wayne O'Neil has observed, proper literacy should extend people's control over their lives, enabling them "to construct coherence around experience, to deal in words and actions with their experience."[2]

Women need pedagogies and content which promote such a literacy, but all too often their needs are subordinated to short-term goals, often essentially determined by male policymakers and program planners. Lalita Ramdas[3] claims that most literacy programs do little to alert women to significant political and social factors which determine how they are treated within their society. Programs designed specifically for women typically serve to reinforce traditional female roles, thereby reinforcing the dependent status and mental perspective of girls and women.

Despite the fact that in 1987 the New South Wales state government eliminated eighteen Women's Access coordinator positions within its system of technical and further education, gains have certainly been made in improving the vocational status of women in several Australian states. Yet it remains common for women's literacy programs to identify "the raising of confidence and self-esteem through improved communications skills" as the key aim. This, of course, is a valid aim. But unless such programs also contain opportunities for women to analyze critically the social causes for so many of them lacking confidence in their own abilities—and especially the relationship between this state of mind and women's social conditioning within family, education, religion, and the state—there is little chance of women moving beyond enhanced personal attitudes to a *deeper awareness* of the need for structural change if women are collectively to achieve genuine and lasting equality of opportunity.

Teaching women to read and write through critical analysis of generative themes which reflect their lives and experience will not of itself bring about a "revolution" in attitudes toward women and the manner in which they are treated. Hopefully, however, it will enable women to travel with a different consciousness of their world, their place within it, and their personal and collective power to transform what is inhumane and unjust within their current circumstances. Any lesser view of the aims and purposes of literacy for women effectively promotes and prolongs their *domestication*—in Freire's sense of the word, and within his realms of word and world alike.[4]

A background to working with women in Australia

The women I have worked with since 1979 entered adult literacy because either they did not get literacy opportunities when they were children or they lacked confidence in their abilities to enter (or reenter) the world of work after having taken years out of mainstream employment to raise families. During this time I have also written three literacy programs specifically for women over the age of twenty-five[5] to help them explore social and political issues in relation to their status and position within daily life.

When I began literacy work, there was a dearth of material relating specifically to the experience, needs, and interests of women whose lives had been bounded by home and family. The quest for self-identity, particularly among economically impoverished women, the politics of house and paid work, the vocational and occupational status of women, and the issue of child care are vital themes in helping women understand why they lack power. Furthermore, I worked with immigrant women who had moved to Australia with their husbands and now sought educational opportunities to enable them to better understand their adopted country. I could find little material which matched their needs or experiences and had to adapt my own teaching to what migrant women saw as necessary for helping them gain greater awareness of and control over their lives in Australia, and to move toward developing appropriate programs for the entire range of women in classes like my own.

Early work

In 1979, after six years as a lecturer in a teachers' college, I began teaching women, mostly migrants, in a technical and further education college community outreach program located in an inner suburban area of Sydney. My first group attended a women's community and information center. The center coordinator explained that they were immigrants, although long-term residents in Australia, having arrived in the 1960s. They wanted to improve their speaking and reading skills.

Of the ten women, one had a part-time job. The rest were housebound and relatively isolated from their adopted country by what they saw as their language inadequacies. They visited each other's homes in the same street, went shopping together, and attended church on weekends. Beyond occasional visits by friends or relatives, the women appeared socially isolated. When they had to negotiate matters beyond the home, they did so through their children, who had been born in Australia and felt more at home with its culture than their parents (who felt powerless within it).

Most had accompanied husbands bound for Australia as immigrant workers. They had hoped to find a "promised land" of job opportunities and financial security. The men were unskilled workers, who gravitated to the lowest-paid jobs at the bottom of the employment ladder. Although this particular group of women were not in paid work outside the home, many immigrant women of their day were forced economically to find work. They, like the men, worked in the dirtiest, most menial, and repetitive jobs— detrimental to body and spirit. Yet there was a general silence surrounding their experiences of work and their contribution to Australian society.

Jeannie Martin[6] argues that immigrant women are not regarded as a distinct subgroup within the Australian working population, but merely as adjuncts to their husbands. Consequently, their needs received scant attention, and it was largely through their own efforts that they began to organize support for themselves through community health, legal, and social centers, such as the one to which I was assigned. Through such centers their struggles gradually began to improve the living and working conditions of immigrant women and to make these conditions more widely known.

Around the same time I was also asked to begin work at a community center serving a Housing Commission high-rise estate in Sydney's inner city. There too I found women who were largely overlooked or positively ignored by the social mainstream. Struggling to get by on inadequate pensions, cooped up with small children in boxlike rooms high above the ground and away from recreation areas, these women's lives were "cribbed, cabined and confined," and they received few if any opportunities to extend their lives, or encouragement to create opportunities for themselves.

Some were severely depressed, others displayed an air of resignation, and a few were cheerful and coped relatively well with their confinement. Most were poor. Few had gone beyond the earliest years of secondary education. Access to child care was limited, and, apart from sewing classes, little existed for those who sought educational chances. Not surprisingly, these women's lives were often lonely, isolated, and frustrating.

For the first time I became aware in an informed way of the existence within Australia of women whose abilities and potential were being ignored, who were not appearing on educational or political agendas, but instead were hidden away in homes and high-rise flats, literally confined to the role of housewife and/or mother. The immigrant and high-rise women alike were suffering economically, socially, and in their health. Short-term solutions included welfare support and pensions. Long-term solutions, however, called for creating vocational and educational opportunities with proper child-care support. To its credit, the New South Wales system of technical and further education began creating such opportunities through the establishment of its Women's Co-ordination Unit. This began to implement policies and develop strategies to give "mature age" women access—some for the first time, others for the second time after years of raising families—to prevocational and further studies schemes and programs.

I was not able to continue working with the women on the housing estate, but I spent eighteen months meeting with the immigrant women's group twice weekly, in what became a turning point in my understanding and practice of critical literacy. When I was first invited to work with the group, they stated they wanted to speak and read English more confidently and understand it more easily. Although I had previously been involved in teaching Freire's philosophy of education to tertiary students and recognized the importance of beginning from the social context of the learners, I failed to do this initially with the group of migrant women. Instead, I turned my attention to formal language schemes which, because they did not relate to the daily realities of my students' lives, only alienated and frustrated them. Although the language schemes were supposed to be based on "living English" situations, they bore little resemblance to how these particular women experienced life and were a long way from their comprehension. Instead of being in a situation where they could gain confidence in their own abilities through critical analysis of their particular situations, the students were forced into responding in stilted and unreal ways. They grew silent and withdrawn as I did most of the talking. My approach effectively alienated them from the educative process and divorced the act of learning from meaning and context. Where there should have been dialogue, discussion, analysis, and interchange, there was instead a one-sided discourse and explanation. I succeeded in silencing the women when I was aiming to do exactly the opposite.

Addressing pedagogy in context

Without being aware at the time of just what was happening, it is clear that I had begun to view the group as living on the fringes of knowledge and understanding, needing to be brought in from the "outside" and "joined" to the mainstream of knowledge. I was treating the class as passive learners, imposing on them ways to know better or more expertly—forgetting Freire's view of the oppressed as oppressed *from within* (as well as without) and needing to analyze *their* circumstances of oppression, as integral members of their society and culture and not as fringe members living on the outside.

I struggled along for some time with a growing sense of frustration and failure. The only occasions on which the women showed any genuine responsiveness were when they greeted each other before class or talked after it was over. Fortunately, I came upon a small book which changed completely my teaching direction. It was called *I Want to Write It Down*,[7] and detailed the lives of a group of women in a community literacy class in southeast London through a series of words and photographs. These women wrote about their lives at work and at home, as mothers, and as women from different cultures and parts of the world. They also wrote about their efforts to change their own lives and the world they inhabited. The prevailing message of the book was unequivocal: "the personal in women's lives is the political."

These women were in the process of examining their own lives in relation to women in history, while also learning how to create and take up new opportunities and move into what had always been viewed as "men only" jobs and positions of responsibility. I was transfixed by what I read and by the lively approach the book adopted—strip cartoons, poems, personal accounts, conversations, letters, and so on—to get the message across to women in a way that included rather than excluded their interest and enthusiasm. It contained a heady mixture of personal, historical, and sociological insights, of a kind which had been entirely absent from my own practice. Moreover, it reminded me of the necessity to begin with students' own lives as a backdrop against which to study and analyze the larger issues concerning the social and political context of women's lives.

On the next occasion I met with my own group I came armed only with three words: *wife, mother, woman*. I introduced these in turn as a stimulus to talking together about the work involved in each role, and how they felt about their personal experiences within each role. I wrote on the board a sentence from each woman dealing with each word, for example: "I am not a happy wife." "Sometimes I get angry with my children." "I work hard for my family." Although I helped the women formulate their sentences, the words and sentiments were their own.

When finished we read the sentences aloud: together, and then individually. There was neither lack of interest nor hesitancy until I introduced the word *woman* and asked students to say something positive about themselves in relation to this word and the role it denotes. They sat silently for a time and then began to speak about their function as wives and mothers all over again. I insisted I didn't want to hear any more about these, but required each member to say or describe something positive about herself as a woman. They found this very difficult, and a lot of prompting was necessary. Finally, we put a set of sentences on the board, each quite telling in its own way. "I like to drive a tractor" came from the shyest and least fluent woman in the class and referred to the time when, as a child in Greece on her father's farm,

MY WIFE DOESN'T WORK.

she had been allowed to drive the tractor when she worked the land. "I am a strong and happy woman," said the oldest woman in the class, who, in her early sixties, was divorcing her absent husband.

Already I was beginning to get more insight into the women's lives and was conscious of issuing a challenge to their traditional view of themselves as women whose principal roles were as wife or mother. In saying something about their experiences and feelings as women, they had to step outside their habitual view of themselves and respond as individuals in their own right, something they found hard to do. Moreover, I had required a positive response, and would not accept a self-denigratory or critical description. When asked what had made it difficult to say something positive about themselves, the women thought it was because they were rarely called upon to think or act in a capacity other than as caretaker of their husbands' or children's needs. "I don't get any time to think about myself," replied one.

The women were at last talking and taking part, and there was a genuine interchange between us. At the next class I handed out a copy of a cartoon strip, *My Wife Doesn't Work*, which came from *I Want to Write It Down*.[8] I knew the women would identify with its theme because they often came to the group commenting on how tired they were or how difficult it was to come to class because they were so busy. I asked them to look at each picture in turn and tell me what the woman was doing. Naming the woman Maria, we then made a sentence to go with each picture. It looked like this:

6 a.m.   Maria goes to get her baby.

7 a.m.   She feeds her family.

8 a.m.   Maria washes the dishes.

9 a.m.   She takes the children to school.

Together we compiled sentences for every picture until we had a complete description of a typical day's work in the life of a wife and mother. When I asked the women to read aloud the sentences they had suggested, they did so promptly and with few errors.

I then drew their attention to the 1 p.m. picture, showing the woman's husband in a bar commenting "My wife doesn't work." Next I asked the following questions:

Who said these words?

What does he mean?

What was he doing?

Do you agree with him?

Whose work is important?

Could he do his work if she didn't do hers?

Who gets paid?

Who doesn't? Why?

Who would do the housework and child care if this woman found paid work?

How could this woman's husband share the housework?

The cartoon theme provided an excellent pretext for linking the women's own personal experiences with the wider political issue of the value of women's unpaid and unacknowledged labor in the home. They understood firsthand the point of the story, and from it were able to extrapolate the exploitation of women through the lack of recognition of their domestic role and the low value accorded socially to housework. They were unanimous in their opinion that if the wife in the story took a paid job she would automatically assume the double burden of housework and paid labor, "fitting in" the household chores early in the morning, late at night, and during weekends. They could see many places where the husband could ease his wife's burden by helping her, but opined that in their experience this would be extremely unlikely. The 11 p.m. picture provoked a strong and heartfelt response. Everyone in the class assumed that, having worn herself out in her eighteen-hour day, Maria was now about to fulfill her final daily "duty" to her husband, when, in the women's view, she would much rather go to sleep!

Much was happening throughout these proceedings. The women were talking and inventing words for their sentences, reading aloud and improving their fluency. They were using their own experiences as a base from which to analyze the content and meaning of the story, as well as discovering its social and political context. At the next session we made a list together of all the jobs women do unpaid in the home, and set them against their professional designation and value in the public sector: for example, "child-care worker," $8–10 per hour. There were two aims in view. First, we wanted to see that women have and develop a great many skills in managing household members and economies. Second, if women were paid for housework, the national wages bill would rise considerably. The points were not lost.

After discussing the theme of women and housework, I handed out a short poem.

> I am a full-time housewife
> I work around the clock
> I get no pay for what I do

I wash, cook, clean, iron and shop.
I have no holidays
Sometimes I feel discouraged[9]

A few sessions after the class had read and discussed this poem, a student arrived late to class saying that her husband had told her she was to stay at home that morning on his day off to make his breakfast and serve him coffee. This person had a hostile and difficult marriage and had often required comforting in class. I was surprised, then, when she told the class how she had reacted to her husband's demand. Going to the door and opening it, she had paused to recite the poem at her husband, in its entirety, finishing with a definite emphasis on *discouraged*. "Then," she continued, "I *slam* the door and come to class. I like this word *discouraged*. I feel this way a lot."

Other students shared her response to the poem. It triggered discussion about why and how they often felt isolated and lonely at home, and even cut off from their children, who were identifying more with Australian culture than that of their parents, choosing Australian-born friends and schoolmates. This made the women fearful, particularly since they regarded standards of discipline in Australian schools as not being strict enough. Here, then, was another theme to explore in the process of these women coming to understand and take more control over their own lives.

Over the time we worked together these women slowly changed from being passive observers of their own circumstances to active participants in critically analyzing social expectations of women's roles. They would often bring to class a problem or issue which was making them fearful or anxious. This would generate discussion and critical analysis. If, for example, an adolescent daughter was angry with her mother for not allowing her to go on a supervised school camp and the mother came to class upset after an argument with the girl, the class would talk about the problem together. I would then extend the issue to include a discussion about the different treatment of boys and girls, or the culture clash which arises when parents find themselves at loggerheads with children raised in a different cultural context and holding very different cultural beliefs and norms from their own.

One day I read to the group a letter written by a girl who had been discovered in a relationship with a boy from a different religion. The girl had promptly been married by her parents to an older cousin and was desperately unhappy. What was she to do? The letter prompted a storm of response and discussion about women's right to choose their own partners, whose interests are served when young girls are traded as marriage partners to older men, and what this has to do with bride prices and dowry burnings in some countries.

I tried to follow a single set of principles with all the different themes and issues used to stimulate response among the students. The material had to be directly relevant to the students concerned, bearing on their subjective knowledge. It had to pose a problem of a kind which demanded critical analysis. It had to offer opportunities for deepening students' awareness of the wider social and political implications of the issue at hand. Finally, and importantly, what had to emerge from the final analysis was informed awareness that circumstances and situations are neither static nor immutable, and that change for the better is possible. An example will illustrate how this worked out in practice.

After being with the group for some time I realized that some of the women frequently used popular brands of analgesics for vague stomach complaints or indigestion. These bouts seemed to correspond with times of stress or tension associated with their families. Headaches were also common occurrences. The women complained that when they consulted their doctor about the pain he invariably was too busy to listen to them, or would diagnose nervous tension for which his only remedy would be tranquilizers: usually valium.

I felt the physical symptoms probably were to some extent the result of the women's isolation and loneliness in the home, where, in some cases, they were under even more rigid control and supervision by their husbands than they might have been in their home countries. I took the opportunity of raising the issue of headaches and their causes when one of the women had been absent, yet again, with a severe attack. How, I asked, do people treat headaches? They answered, "with headache powders or tablets." Research around this time revealed alarming numbers of women, in particular housebound women, addicted to a popular powder form of remedy. We then talked about and made a list of possible causes for head pain. These included physical damage, infection, period pain, eyestrain, poor diet, worry, tension, noise, and pollution. I asked if tablets or powders were the most appropriate treatment for all these conditions. What alternatives were there?

We came up with a range of seemingly viable alternatives, varying with the headache's cause: a warm bath, a visit to the optician, a walk in the park or by the sea, less sugar and cigarettes, a sympathetic neighbor or counselor in times of stress. I talked with the class about the dangers of substance poisoning and abuse, and suggested they might like to visit a women's health center where they could talk to health workers in their own language about medical and personal matters, and where we could all learn much about taking proper care of and control over our bodies.

The proposed visit eventuated and introduced the women to a service specifically tailored to their needs and providing services at a preventive rather than a pathology-model level. There were classes in women's health issues aimed at helping women develop greater autonomy in taking care of their bodies and minds. The visit provided insights into the politics of health, showing the women that they need not be powerless in addressing the needs of their bodies.

Developing materials for literacy work with women

When I designed a set of literacy and language materials based on issues we had investigated jointly in that group, it included a unit on "body talk." This contained materials and ideas designed to stimulate discussion, reading, and writing around issues of women's health and self-help. The material included an account by a migrant woman of what stress, isolation, and the language barrier did to her life.

Antonino's Story

Introduction

Antonino is Italian.
She came to Australia when she was seventeen and she married here.
She takes care of her family and works on a machine for a boss who brings
   her clothes to sew.

When her children have all grown up Antonino wants to study so she can go out of the house and find a job.

She wants to be with other people because sometimes staying at home is lonely for her.

Her friends talk to her on the telephone when they feel sick and she can help them a lot because she was sick a few years ago.

Now she is well again she takes good care of her body.

She does not take any pills and she prepares good food which keeps her and her family strong and healthy.

This is the story of her sickness and how she made herself better again.

Transcript. (I = Interviewer; A = Antonino)

I: Antonino, why did you go to the doctor?

A: I felt weak. I couldn't sleep.

I: What did the doctor say to you?

A: He said I was depressed and he gave me some tablets—valium, serapax.

I: How did the tablets make you feel?

A: At first I felt a little bit better. Then when I used to take them every day I felt really bad. I needed them more and more.

I: So as you felt worse you began to take more and more tablets. What happened then?

A: Then, one day, I couldn't get up in the morning. I started to be dizzy. I couldn't get up from the bed. I called my daughter to call my sister by telephone because I was very ill in the morning. I never want to remember (this day) any more. They called the doctor and the doctor sent me to hospital because I was very nervous with depression. Then they gave me a lot of tablets and they treated me and always I wanted to come home to see my children.

I: You had electric shocks in the hospital so you wanted to come home.

A: Yes, I wanted to come home.

I: When you were in the hospital did the doctor see you?

A: Yes, he came to see me and you know what he did? He always made me sign the Medibank forms and that's all and he never answered my questions.

I: So he never asked you what was wrong?

A: No, nothing about what was wrong.

I: When you came out of hospital why did you go to a women's health center?

A: My sister told me to go there in case they could help me.

I: And did they help you?

A: Oh yes! They helped me a lot! They told me not to take any more tablets or drugs because they would make me more sick. It was true. Because since I stopped taking the drugs and to take some chamomile (tea) to eat better and more natural foods, to take herbs—vitamins—not eat strong tablets but just chamomile I take. I started like this—a little bit each time and I started to feel *much much* better so that I took off all the tablets. Now for two and a half years I have used herbs and when I can't sleep I take a cup of chamomile and I felt much, much better. I was never better than now.

I: So you don't take any pills at all now?

A: Nothing at all. Not even disprin. When I've got a headache it goes by itself.

I: And does your family take natural foods?

A: Oh yes, because I teach my children and my husband not to take any tablets.

I: And now you feel so much better that you don't take any tablets?

A: Of course. I was never stronger.[10]

Antonino's Story is by no means uncommon. It offers an opportunity for women in language and literacy classes with similar problems or experiences to put them into political and social perspective.

The resource book *Women's Work, Women's Lives*[11] emerged from the time spent with the immigrant women's group. Besides "body talk," it includes activities around the issues of identity, the politics of housework, culture clash, women and the law, child care, women in the work force, and world issues. Although each unit was planned to be complete in itself, the work was conceived as a whole, moving gradually through issues of the individual self (the personal) to wider social issues (the political).

A constraining factor: The nuclear family

Most of the women I have worked with have been in nuclear families or have been sole parents from nuclear families. This form of social organization poses its own limitations on how far we can take women down a liberatory path in getting them to critically examine issues of patriarchal oppression and lack of personal opportunities. On many occasions I have been aware of raising issues of physical and mental violence, for example, when there have been women in the group who have been subjected to both. Because of their economic and emotional dependence (the two are closely linked) within destructive and painful situations, they have limited opportunities for escape or negotiation for change. Likewise, women who are trying to improve their vocational opportunities while at the same time conducting their households and taking full child-care responsibilities have little time or energy to question whether they are getting a fair deal in the nuclear family. Most are relieved simply to make it through each week intact, combining their home-based chores with study and assignment demands.

One immigrant student used to arrive twice weekly at class after delivering six children to various schools while her unemployed husband enjoyed his coffee. He would try to stop her practicing reading at night, telling her she had no need of literacy. She persisted. Although illiterate in her own language she had begun reading and writing in English and was proud of her success. She would say, "I feel different. I can understand things I didn't before. I can help my children. I don't feel ashamed now." She said her husband "would never stop me reading. I will divorce him first." She had recognized her increased understanding of her life and control over it, and went to great lengths to create time in her day to practice reading.

Although I have known many like her, it is difficult to expect women in general to secure significant lasting changes under patriarchy when they have so few spaces and opportunities to problematize the politics of gender in relation to their own lives. Critical literacy must deal with issues relating to women's work in the home as well as the work force, precisely so that women can see how demands made on them by their families serve a political and social function beyond the immediate domestic situation.

Lesley Adamson points to the special difficulty involved in addressing oppression specifically associated with the nuclear family. Within this structural arrangement, women are unable to unite and take action to change matters because their struggles for liberation are played out behind closed doors, away from the public gaze. Adamson also reminds us that

> the process of injustice toward women is set not only in the vast impersonal context of international economies or industrial relations. It is also set in the detailed context of home and family. And the relationship of oppression is characterized not only by careless brutality and callous disregard but also, in many cases, by love, tenderness and care.[12]

It is, argues Adamson, unthinkable for women in nuclear families to adopt as a revolutionary strategy against patriarchal oppression the nonfeeding or neglect of their children or families. It is, she goes on, women's very indispensability which prevents them from translating it so readily into power to bring about change:

> ironically women are less able
> to fight for their rights because
> they have so much responsibility . . .
> they are more exploited because they
> are more exploitable
> And to the classic cry of liberation
> —nothing to lose but your chains—
> women can only smile, for they
> know the chains must be broken with care[13]

Clearly, the process of consciousness raising and empowerment must proceed cautiously, and with respect and empathy for women who choose, or are forced, to stay within the nuclear family unit. It is one thing to attack patriarchal structures from a theoretical standpoint, but quite another when a teacher faces a group of women who must at the end of the session return to a home situation they feel powerless to leave—because they lack financial resources, or wonder what will happen to the children or to themselves— despite believing that it would be in their best interests to go.

Sensitivity requires that, as they relate to women, liberation themes and issues be presented with compassion and awareness of personal states and circumstances. The aim is to unite women in hopefulness and solidarity, not to alienate them or make them feel more worthless than they may already. Even so, it is imperative that literacy programs and materials designed for women present educational and political issues in a critical way. They should not be watered down or otherwise made palatable in order never to offend. Oppression, injustice, and human pain—and their internalization—should be dealt with in appropriate contexts, including the classroom, as they arise.

Writing about literacy and justice for women, Lalita Ramdas argues for an approach to women's literacy that is "consciously emancipatory" and that teaches women to recognize the social and political structures which oppress them. She claims that the subject matter of women's literacy should address the big issues of the social and sexual subjugation of women arising from structural arrangements. These include the division of labor in the home, removing institutionalized forms of gender discrimination, establishing political equality, freedom of choice over childbearing, and domestic violence and control of women.[14]

Ramdas insists that women's literacy programs be conceived as both educational and political projects, since the implications of patriarchy as a political ideology militate against women's quests for justice. She adds that "a truly women- and justice-oriented approach would mean a critical appraisal of attitudes, values, content and form."[15] I agree with Ramdas. Literacy programs which merely address immediate practical and functional problems of women, important though these are, neglect to take up questions concerning their structured subordination and control, and tacitly encourage women to locate the source of their problems within their personal selves and not to interrogate those socially structured processes, practices, and ideologies that impede women in realizing their potential.

Freire recognizes that education is an instrument of either liberation or domestication.[16] There can be no neutral territory. But he also reminds educators that they should not impose their own versions of liberation on students. Rather, they should take cues from the lives of their students as to what knowledge has most liberatory potential and worth. If the teacher prescribes the program content, students may adapt to it, but this will likely impede the development of critical consciousness and end up as paternalistic domination.

Critical literacy and historical perspective

In assisting women to become properly rather than merely functionally literate, we want them to be able to understand and interpret the world from their standpoint as subjects in and of it. Catherine MacKinnon refers here to the importance of "the collective critical reconstitution of the meaning of women's social experience, as women live through it."[17] The challenge is to provide literacy activities of a type that encourage women to locate their place in the world and talk about their lives in relation to the process of making history.[18] My own work has tried in various ways to stimulate critical awareness of history as a process, and to understand the political significance of "official" accounts of history. Literacy classes address such issues as the following: Are official accounts of history true (or accurate)? Who makes history? How is it made? How is women's version of history—her-story— different from men's? Why is it different? Why have women's stories been absent from history? Which or whose interests are served by denying certain groups a place in history?

Women and Work Literacy Resources[19] contains a unit of activities designed to activate women's interest in these questions. The unit was prompted by an extract from Herbert Kohl's book, *Reading: How To*, in which the following sequence appeared:

Nostory
history
herstory
blackstory
no more stories
no story[20]

Using the word *story*, and having women tell or write their own stories about childhood or their past in the form of time lines, I aim to get students to recall significant events for themselves and to explore these in relation to their status and treatment within their families. What expectations did their families have of them? How were they treated in relation to their brothers? Who made decisions in their families? Often women will relate how, especially in rural economies, girls were kept at home and denied opportunities for schooling and literacy, while boys were encouraged.

In encouraging women to look back and critically evaluate their pasts, I want them to consider the extent to which they are involved in making history. They are also invited to assess how far a view of history as the lives of "great" men or "great" women is an ideological construction which renders invisible the contribution of ordinary individuals, undermines a conception of ourselves as human *subjects*, and presents a distorted view of the past and present. We examine stories about the so-called founding of Australia from two different points of view: the white colonizers and the aboriginals. Questions are posed: Which story has been silenced? Why? To counter the notion that it was only men who built Australia, I have students read and talk about the women—convict and freeborn—who settled there.

A powerful means of linking women's present lives with women from the past involves having the class choose an imaginary female persona who lived in Australia in the early years of settlement. It could be a released female convict now married to a farmer in the bush remote from settlements, a prostitute, a domestic, and so on. With the help of books and pictures for building up a character role, the students then speak briefly at an imaginary inquiry into the status and conditions of women in the Australian colony. In this way, students become aware that in the past, as in the present, women have struggled to overcome oppressive economic and social conditions. They learn too that official accounts of Australian history were provided by, or on behalf of, those whose interests prevailed. Women and aboriginals, then, were generally absent or blotted out from official accounts. If an accurate story of the past and present is to be told and written, the gaps must be filled in by those who have been denied justice and voice by dominant elites.

M. McCormack's "Silence is Deafening" provides an excellent resource with which to challenge women students to fill in the gaps. The following segments capture its tone.

Silence Is Deafening

Silence is something women know a lot
about.
"Be silent you're a woman."
"Be silent you're a mother."
"Be silent you're a lesbian, a migrant
woman, disabled, working class."
"Be silent you're Black."
"Be silent you're not black enough."
"Be silent, we don't want to hear your
story. You don't count. You're not
important. Your story doesn't count."
"Be silent you're Aboriginal."
"Be silent you're not."

As I said silence is deafening, it makes
us sick, it makes us powerless and so we
speak. I encourage you to speak too—to
break the silences amongst us as women.[21]

When students have read and discussed the piece, they are asked to comment orally and to write briefly about the meaning and social context of such
phrases from the text as the following:

"Silence is something women know a lot about."
"Silence is deafening"
"I encourage you to speak too"
"I want to tell you that silence is a product of
colonization."

Of course, analyzing oppressive structures and relations can be daunt-
ing and depressing unless celebratory stories of action and change are included. To this end I include in the unit "Whose Story," an extract from a
book by an aboriginal writer and artist, Sally Morgan. This is the fragment
"Celebrating Her Black Story," a delightful passage with a deeply serious
message. Morgan grew up in 1950s Australia with a mother and grandmother
who had learned it was safer to deny their aboriginality—to silence it. One

day, as mother and daughter are having a relaxed conversation over a cup of tea, Morgan casually (but calculatingly) drops the question "We're Aboriginal, aren't we Mum?" "Yes dear," replies her mother without thinking. With her attention drawn to the secret she had just let slip, mother puts her cake back onto her plate, looking as if she would be sick.

> "All those years, Mum," I said, "how could you have
> lied to us all those years?"
> "It was only a little white lie," she replied sadly.
> I couldn't help laughing at her unintentional humor.
> In no time at all we were both giggling uncontrollably.
> It was as if a wall that had been between us suddenly
> crumbled away. I felt closer to Mum than I had for
> years.[22]

Morgan's dedication for her book reads:

> "How deprived we would have been
> if we had been willing
> to let things stay as they were.
> We would have survived,
> but not as a whole people.
> We would never have known our place.[23]

The fragment and the dedication both illustrate vividly what internalizing oppression means: in the lives of ordinary people and within a particular culture. Lines like "It was only a little white lie" and "We would never have known our place" can trigger rich critical discovery and evaluation when students investigate the silences and deceptions within the personal lives of women schooled and otherwise conditioned to "know their place." This is especially so when followed by the questions "And what happens to women who refuse to stay in their place?" and "If you do not like your place, what can you do to change it?"

Final words

In Australia the push for economic rationalization and a restructured work force has intensified the "commodification" of education.[24] Heavy cuts in public spending have impacted on educational access initiatives for women like those in the groups I teach. This undermines still further their prospects for vocational opportunities, economic improvement, and personal growth and independence, and pushes social recognition of their needs deeper into the background. When jobs are scarce and prioritized for men, boys, and young women, there is little perceived payoff in considering the bids of housebound women for a better standard of education and quality of life. Indeed, it is widely believed that such women should stay out of the work force, leaving the jobs that remain for "those in need." Since women are supported at home by the male wage, what need have they for economic self-sufficiency? Such ideological buttresses of patriarchy die hard.

Of course, the fact that literacy program goals are increasingly couched in pragmatic utilitarian terms—stressing acquisition of functional literacy skills to improve workplace performance by creating more "skilled" workers—undermines commitment to adult literacy and education for personal and collective empowerment of subordinate groups. This makes the need to create and preserve well-informed and effective programs of critical literacy all the more urgent.

While working recently on a project in Southeast Asia, I found myself sitting next to a woman in a hill tribe village in northern Thailand and making comparisons between her life and the lives of women I have taught in Australia. She looked to be in her midsixties but was, in fact, in her midforties: worn out by too many children, hard physical work in the fields, at risk from the introduction of fertilizers and pesticides, and responsible for feeding and caring for the family and maintaining the dwelling. It was difficult to see how her dignity and emancipation would be served by the attainment of merely *functional* literacy skills. A critical dimension addressing the social arrangements of village life, the impact of encroaching "civilization" as the highway reaches close to her village, and like themes seems indispensable.

Whether we are speaking of a hill tribe woman or an Australian woman worker overburdened with the multiple load of home, child care, and paid work, with little time or opportunity to invest in herself and her own development, there is no question that women's respective lives are presently governed by forces and circumstances which damage and inhibit—and which remain out of their control. This is the reality critical literacy is intended to address.

This chapter has rested on the view that critical literacy approaches depend crucially on appropriate pedagogy and a search for the "right" words to unlock students' capacities for critiquing and engaging in informed action, and for giving expression to their experiences of the everyday. I return briefly to these themes in concluding.

Frances Maher addresses women's pedagogy in the context of teaching women's studies courses at university. She espouses a pedagogical approach which

> draws on a rich tradition going back to Paulo Freire, John Dewey, and even Socrates, of involving students in constructing and evaluating their own education. It assumes that each student has legitimate rights and potential contributions to the subject matter. Its goal is to enable students to draw on their personal and intellectual experiences to build a satisfying version of the subject, one that they can use productively in their own lives.[25]

The same holds true for working with poor and disadvantaged women in Technical and Further Education colleges. Using women's own lives as subject matter for investigation and the classroom as a site for creating dialogue between teacher and students encourages the creation of new learning models which authenticate appropriate ways of knowing, experiencing, and negotiating the world. Women who initially enter classrooms with trepidation and doubts that they belong there gradually discover confidence and power within themselves as they come to understand that the social and political constraints that limit their lives are neither of their own making nor immutable.

For some the risks associated with claiming responsibility for one's own life become too threatening and they retreat to the "security" of their families, tightening the grip of dependency. Others, however, willing to pursue issues associated with economic insecurity and dissatisfaction with traditional roles and expectations, become transformed into subjects active in their own liberation: determined to renegotiate their relationships with family members and their wider society on a more equal footing.

Finally, there are some profound differences in the views of culture and knowledge of a radical educator like Paulo Freire and that icon of high culture, T. S. Eliot. Nonetheless, I have long admired Eliot's *Four Quartets*. In the first, Eliot writes

> Words strain,
> Crack and sometimes break,
> Under the burden,
> Under the tension, slip, slide, perish
> Decay with imprecision,
> Will not stay in place,
> Will not stay still.[26]

He is commenting on the poet's quest to find exactly the right word to match the thought or sentiment seeking expression. Critical literacy is not unlike this, as educators seek to assist women to give expression to thoughts, attitudes, feelings, and experiences surrounding their lives. Slowly, hesitantly, they speak the first words of question or comment about their knowledge of culture and society, and how they perceive their place within their world. As they grow confident that *their* issues and views of the world constitute valid knowledge bases, as much as "man-made" variants, their voices become stronger and their words more precise. Finally, having broken the silence of marginality, they speak evenly, and in measured tones, about the condition of the world and their commitment to *humanizing* it.[27] At this point "the world" and "the word" become one, and the purposes of critical literacy have been fulfilled.

Notes

1. See for example, Freire, P., *Education: The Practice of Freedom* (London: Writers and Readers, 1974); and *Pedagogy of the Oppressed* (Harmondsworth: Penguin) 1972. Influential feminists works include Firestone, S., *The Dialectic of Sex* (London: Paladin, 1973); Rogers, B., *52%: Getting Women's Power into Politics* (London: The Women's Press, 1983); Allen, S.,

Sanders, L., and Willis, J. (eds.), *Conditions of Illusion* (London: Feminist Books, 1973); Mitchell, J., *Women's Estate* (Harmondsworth: Penguin, 1973); Davies, M., *Third World, Second Sex* (London: Zed Press, 1983); Eisenstein, H., *Contemporary Feminist Thought* (London: Unwin, 1984); Spender, D., *Feminist Theorists* (London: The Women's Press, 1983); Rowbotham, S., *Hidden from History* (1973), *Woman's Consciousness, Man's World* (1974), *Women, Resistance and Revolution* (1974), all Harmondsworth: Penguin; Dixson, M., *The Real Matilda: Women and Identity in Australia 1788–1975* (Sydney: Penguin, 1976); Figes, E., *Patriarchal Attitudes* (London: Panther, 1972); Pocock, B., *Demanding Skill: Women and Technical Education in Australia* (Sydney: Allen and Unwin, 1988).

2. O'Neil, W., "Properly Literate," in Hoyles, M. (ed.), *The Politics of Literacy*, (London: Writers and Readers, 1974).

3. Ramdas, L., "Women and Literacy: A Quest for Justice," *Convergence*, vol. 23, 1990.

4. See Freire (1972) and (1974), *op. cit.*; also Freire, P. and Macedo, D., *Literacy: Reading the Word and the World* (South Hadley, Mass.: Bergin and Garvey, 1987).

5. Bee, B., *Women's Work, Women's Lives* (N.S.W. Department of TAFE, 1984); *Women and Work Literacy Resources* (N.S.W. Department of TAFE, 1989).

6. Martin, J., "Non English-Speaking Women: Production and Social Reproduction," in Bottomley, G., and de Lepervanche, M. (eds.), *Ethnicity, Class and Gender in Australia* (Sydney: Allen and Unwin, 1984).

7. Peckham Publishing Project, *I Want to Write It Down* (London: Carisbrooke Press, 1980).

8. *Ibid.*, p. 39.

9. E.C., in *ibid.*

10. In Bee (1984), *op. cit.*, session 7.

11. Bee, *ibid.*

12. Adamson, L., "More to Lose Than Their Chains," *The New Internationalist*, no. 84, July 1980.

13. *Ibid.*

14. Ramdas, *op. cit.*

15. *Ibid.*

16. Freire (1972) and (1974), *op. cit.*

17. MacKinnon, C., cited in Maher, F., "Classroom Pedagogy and the New Scholarship on Women," no source available, October 1985.

18. Mills, C. Wright, *The Sociological Imagination* (New York: Oxford University Press, 1959).

19. Bee (1989), *op. cit.*

20. Kohl, H., *Reading: How To* (Harmondsworth: Penguin, 1974).

21. McCormack, M., "Silence Is Deafening," *Education Links*, Autumn 1988, p. 14.

22. Morgan, Sally, cited in Bee (1989), *op. cit.*, p. 162.

23. *Ibid*.

24. For a discussion of the commodification of education, see Apple, M., *Education and Power* (London: Routledge, 1982).

25. Maher, *op. cit.*, p. 30.

26. Eliot, T. S., *Four Quartets* (London: Faber and Faber, 1944).

27. See Freire (1972), *op. cit.*

4

The challenge of popular education in the Grenada revolution

Didacus Jules

Of all of the achievements of the Grenada Revolution (1979–1983), the efforts at promoting critical literacy and institutionalizing adult education stand out as among the most notable. Among the Grenadian people, the adult education initiatives were seen as tangible evidence of the orientation of the revolutionary process in favor of the poor, women, youth, farmers, and workers, and were inseparable from the democratization process set in motion by the revolution. This perception was the result of the high priority accorded to the Center for Popular Education (CPE), the main adult education institution, and numerous affirmations from the highest levels of the People's Revolutionary Government (PRG) of their commitment to the emancipation of working people through education. The tragic internal events of 19 October 1983, in which the revolutionary party, the New Jewel Movement (NJM), attempted to impose its will in the face of popular discontent, pose problems for speaking about critical literacy and popular education as part of a democratic thrust within the revolution. However, it is indisputable that during the preceding four and a half years the Grenadian revolution was characterized by mass support and broad participation in political life on a scale unprecedented in the country's history.

The most impartial support for this claim is found in the survey of public opinion carried out by the University of the West Indies in 1984 (while the country was still under U.S. occupation). This revealed that

> in relation to the People's Revolutionary Government and its Prime Minister on the majority of indicators used, there was consistently positive evaluation from respondents. Seventy-seven point two percent (77.2%) said that the PRG always had popular support and 86.2% expressed admiration for Bishop's leadership. On eight of the ten specified indicators of Government policies well over one half of the respondents opined that conditions had improved, and in general 53.7% of respondents felt that life had improved under the PRG. But there was clearly a high level of disagreement with the PRG's refusal to hold elections, as indicated by responses of 70.1% of the sample on this issue.[1]

In the Grenadian historical process, as in many revolutions, a fundamental tension existed between democratization and centralization. The events of October 1983 were a tragic "resolution" of the contradiction between centralizing authoritarian tendencies inherent in the NJM's conception of itself as a Marxist-Leninist "vanguard" and the democratizing impulses created by the removal of the Gairy dictatorship and assertion of the people's jurisdiction within the transition state.

In Grenada, a small country of 264 square kilometers with a predominantly black population (estimated in 1981 to have been 91,000), the impact of these contradictions was sharply felt. With an essentially agricultural economy based on the production of cocoa, nutmeg, and bananas, Grenada had, comparatively speaking, the largest peasantry in the anglophone Caribbean. A dependent and underdeveloped economy in a small country with significant peasantry created unique problems for a process of revolutionary transformation. Given this political economy, a leading scholar on Grenada surmised that

> despite its short lifespan, the [Grenada] revolution deserves a prominent niche not only in Third World decolonization but also in Marxist theory and praxis. Grenada's very small size and population; strictly limited and underdeveloped resources; an entrenched class system with strong overtones of color; an independent peasantry to whom land ownership was a high

priority; a psychological dependency upon imported culture and values; and its strategic geo-political location: all combined to prompt a veteran West Indian Marxist, Richard Hart, to label the experience "the Improbable Revolution."[2]

Twenty-eight years of malevolent dictatorship under Eric Gairy had left a legacy of neglect, acute underdevelopment, and ignorance. The combined effects of British elitism, governmental disregard, and cultural colonization had debilitating effects on the education system. The 1970 population census revealed that 86 percent of the adult population had received no more than a primary school education and, of that segment, a staggering 92 percent had passed no examination. Functional illiteracy was estimated at approximately 40 to 45 percent of the adult population.

The NJM insisted that creating an alternative development strategy involved not simply the revitalization and structural transformation of the national economy and the social structure but, just as importantly, reconstituting political culture. From its formation in March 1973, the NJM called for the replacement of the Westminster system of parliamentary democracy with a more grass-roots system of participatory democracy involving the devolution of power to Assemblies of the People and the right to recall elected representatives. In such a revolutionary project, education was seen as an essential requirement for genuine people's control. It was believed that the economics and politics of Grenadian society had to be grasped and understood by the working people in such a manner that they could self-consciously become the active agents of its transformation. Educational transformation thus became one of the major items on the revolutionary agenda.

Defining popular education within the revolution

In an address to teachers early in 1980, Maurice Bishop outlined what the PRG considered to be the four main elements of a revolutionary education system:

> Firstly, it attempts to teach people a greater critical appreciation of their own reality in order for them to understand how to change it.

Secondly, it attempts to develop the innate abilities of the masses of the people and not just to entrench the privileges of the few.

Thirdly, it should seek to develop the productive capacity of our society since it is only through an expansion in production that the standard of living, including the education system, can be improved.

And fourthly, it tries to promote the democratization of our society— the process by which people are encouraged to take an active part in the education system itself and in all major decisions that affect our lives.

The process of educational transformation in the Grenada revolution was largely predicated on the achievement of these four goals. Popular education was defined as the new type of education which supported these aims. Within the formal education system, reform initiatives were necessarily slower because of systemic constraints. Ministry officials were acutely aware of the fact that although there was a general consensus for change within the system (which was reflected in the conclusions of two national education consultations), public expectations were still strongly conditioned by the former colonial educational traditions. For some elements of the national bourgeoisie and the church, educational change meant maintaining particular elements of the status quo (such as competitiveness, dual church-state control of schools, religious education) and the infusion of greater efficiency in administration and management. Their prescription merely involved a technocratic approach to the many existing problems.

Within the party, and among radical teachers and the local intelligentsia, the challenges were perceived to be primarily ideological. Educational transformation was seen as a historical imperative involving, on the one hand, removing the most pernicious elements of the neocolonial legacy and, on the other, asserting a more revolutionary and nationalist orientation. Constructing a more egalitarian system of educational opportunity for all and reconstructing knowledge to reflect indigenous values and realities were integral to this new logic. In complementary fashion, it was felt equally important to develop an internationalist perspective based on identification with the rest of the Third World. In the early stages, when the design of the adult education programs was under discussion, there was a strong contest between these two philosophical visions of adult education, which, as we shall see later, produced different outcomes at different stages.

The conception of popular education in the revolution was closely linked to the broader conception of a new democracy. As Bishop described it in declaring 1983 the "Year of Academic and Political Education," "Without education, no genuine people's democracy can be built since real democracy always assumes the informed, conscious and intelligent participation of the people. Without education, there can be no real worker participation, no substantial increase in production and productivity, no individual and collective growth, no true dignity, no genuine independence."[3] This very wording—"Year of Academic and Political Education"—reflected the preoccupation within the revolution with balancing academic and political education.

The process of revolution itself was seen as having intrinsically an educational dimension: it was an apprenticeship in history, with the working people becoming authors of their own history by studying their past, understanding and refashioning the conditions of their present existence, and collectively articulating their future. Critical reflection as a complement to revolutionary action constituted the essence of popular education within the revolution. Virtually every opportunity for popular participation in the revolution called for a learning process.[4] The village, women's, workers' and zonal councils were forums for discussing problems affecting particular social constituencies and for sharing solutions; the national budget preparation process, which involved multiple consultations on the country's economic performance and invited the suggestions of the people, required learning the arithmetic of the national economy. In every such instance, meaningful participation required some collective learning; knowledge was being created and shared so that life could be refashioned.

In theoretical terms the Grenada experience was deeply influenced by several Third World examples. The pedagogical insights of Paulo Freire, the organizational lessons of the Cuban literacy campaign, the inspiration of the JAMAL literacy campaign (initiated by the social-democratic Manley regime in Jamaica), and the experiences of the Study and Action Group in neighboring St. Lucia, which had attempted to apply Freirean approaches to the Caribbean context,[5] were the major influences. But other imperatives were also at work. There was the economic necessity of developing the productive capacity of the thousands of workers and youth in order to create the material basis for a better life, and the powerful expectations of the subeducated majority, who believed that new educational opportunity would be extended through the expansion of traditional forms. These influences and imperatives mediated popular education as much through the constraints they imposed as through the creative possibilities they opened.

Other significant aspects of popular education in Grenada were its continuous character and the emphasis on cultural liberation. Maurice Bishop put it succinctly:

> Every historical process which seeks to improve the condition of the working people must provide for their educational and cultural development. In Grenada our most precious resources are our people and the process of national development is not simply an economic one but also a question of the . . . liberation of the cultural energy of our people. And because the frontiers of human knowledge are forever expanding, because the horizons of the mind are ever widening, education should be a continuous process.[6]

In summary, then, popular education was aimed "at making the practice of reading and study permanent habits of an informed and conscious people." Reading the word was essential to reading the world, and the word to be read was generated from the reading of the world with its shifting conjunctures.

Literacy and participation

One of the first concrete actions of the revolution was the establishment of the Center for Popular Education (CPE) with a mandate to develop a comprehensive national approach to adult education. The broad goals of the CPE, as stated in the earliest concept paper (1979), were as follows:

1. To assist in the conscientization of our people

2. To consolidate the presence of the people in the revolutionary process through the development of a critical awareness

3. To consolidate the right of the people to be informed participants in development through the eradication of illiteracy, the understanding of the

nature of poverty and exploitation, and the acquisition of skills to build a new revolutionary society

4. To assist in the redefinition of education and the formulation of a dialogical and revolutionary pedagogy

Operationalizing these goals presented two fundamental challenges: organizational and pedagogical. In organizational terms the question was how to turn the country into a big school, providing structured opportunities for collective learning and interaction at a community level. This involved working out the logistics of mass education consistent with the human and cultural realities of the country. At the pedagogical level, the challenges related to creating new knowledge, finding the most appropriate methods of bringing people together to reflect on their situation, and making the lives, struggles, and aspirations of the people the subject of educational inquiry. Associated with this was a need to provide mastery of existing knowledge forms: skills training of various kinds, and building a strong base of scientific knowledge on which higher levels of indigenous inventiveness could be developed. Alongside this emphasis on creating indigenous knowledge was a concern to ensure that working people could appropriate cultural capital so that the educational opportunities provided by the revolution would compare in terms of "standards" to formerly privileged conformations of knowledge.

The educational objectives of the CPE were to be realized in three main phases:

1. A national literacy campaign (which ended in early March 1981)

2. A systematic program of basic adult education, involving a core curriculum of English, mathematics, geography, general science, and history to follow the literacy campaign

3. The provision of skills training in technical and vocational subjects, directed to upgrading the capacity of the Grenadian worker to be productively employed

Although *absolute* illiteracy was not a major social problem in Grenada, it existed mainly among the peasantry and agroproletariat. Those most affected by low educational levels were those who had traditionally been downtrodden and exploited yet who played a vital role in producing the nation's wealth: agricultural workers, fishermen, nutmeg pool and cocoa plant workers, rural women, and marginalized youth. Providing education for these sectors was a priority of the revolution, partly because education was seen as a basic right but also because, as the NJM motto "Let Those Who Labor Hold the Reins" put it, the needs of the working people were to be paramount. As Carnoy and Samoff point out, in many revolutions adult education gains priority status because it is a means of legitimating the social policy of the revolution and, by implication, the transition state itself.[7] The emphasis is on the needs of labor as distinct from the requirements of capital; adult education is directed to the social and cultural development of workers as well as to upgrading their technical capacity. During the Gairy era, adult education was limited to ad hoc training activities, and in the educational discourse of that period the term invariably referred to vocational training aimed at enhancing the employability of people: adult education then was limited to fulfilling private-sector labor needs. As the revolution sought to develop adult education, part of the contestation that occurred around its definition involved this issue. Conservative elements argued for the vocationalization of adult education, contending that it should train workers for self-employment and greater productivity in private enterprise. This was not a new debate. In the United States, as early as 1902 the great African American scholar W. E. B. Du Bois argued that "the ideals of education, whether men (sic) are taught to teach or to plow, to weave or to write must not be allowed to sink into sordid utilitarianism. Education must keep broad ideals before it and never forget that it is dealing with Souls and not with Dollars."[8]

In the Grenadian context, the great fear represented by conservatives concerned the impact of politicizing working people. So intense was the struggle over the definition of adult education that the CPE was portrayed, by these forces, as being the Center for Political Education, and every effort was made to make its content appear spurious and inferior to the traditional "official" knowledge. The position espoused by the NJM, however, asserted that the working people were entitled to a broad education that not only provided skills but that would also enhance their capacity for self-development, social participation, and cultural creation. The minister of education, George Louison, addressing a training seminar for literacy volunteers, affirmed the necessity of this approach:

Early on, some people were accusing us of being political. Is it political to teach people that the Revolution brings free milk for mothers and babies and that this milk builds strong bones and teeth?

If teaching people that the people of Grenada, Carriacou, and Petit Martinique are one people in a proud and free nation is political, then we should be political.

If teaching people that the people of the Caribbean are one, that we have a long, common history of struggle and that a new Grenada cannot be built overnight is political, then we are.

If teaching people that our youth can be what they want to be now because the Revolution brings more scholarships to our children is political, then we must be.

Who can deny the need for national unity? . . . Who can deny the principle that the Revolution has room for all of us and the reality that this new society of equal opportunity can only be built by hard work and sacrifice, with discipline and unity?[9]

From this early stage, popular education served as a focus for displacement politics. It became the oppositional arena of convenience for those having political and ideological concerns of a different nature.

The national literacy campaign

In the initial stage of the literacy campaign, the major preoccupations were questions of organization. The basic question was how to organize hundreds of volunteers to carry out the task of teaching in their villages, how to successfully undertake a task like this, which required some basic training, constant supervision and consultation, and consistent effort, self-sacrifice, and discipline.

As planning for the campaign progressed, it became increasingly evident that combating illiteracy on a national scale involved much more than simply implementing a program of instruction. It required overcoming shame and hesitation among the illiterate, reorienting the public mind on the nature and causes of illiteracy, and refashioning the public conscience on its social responsibility to assist in the successful achievement of an objective so vital to the nation's future. The undertaking then was nothing short of an attempt to shift from an understanding of illiteracy as the "fault" of the individual illiterate to an appreciation of the social construction of illiteracy.

Major effort was put into a massive national publicity and information initiative leading up to the launching of the literacy campaign. It was felt that if the public were sensitized to the societal bases of illiteracy and the challenge of literacy defined in patriotic terms, the stereotype of the "dunce" and the "stupid illiterate" could be negated. Illiteracy would be seen instead as another legacy of neocolonialism and an expression of the injustice and inequality of prerevolutionary society. The public awareness effort took many forms:

- Panel discussions in virtually all villages throughout the country organized by party cadres and volunteers (mainly teachers and senior students). Debates on the significance of literacy to the development of the country and the emancipation of the working people were conducted between people from the village, members of the revolutionary government, and CPE national personnel.
- Showing films and videos in the villages on adult education and literacy programs in other parts of the Third World.
- Sale and distribution of ten thousand T-shirts with the CPE symbol and slogans on education.
- Radio ads aimed at potential learners as well as volunteer teachers calling for maximum public support for the campaign. A five-minute daily CPE spot on the national radio providing news on the mobilization effort, including short interviews with workers and other potential participants.
- Distribution of ten thousand CPE posters in strategic public locations throughout the country by volunteer workers.
- Publication of features on the CPE by all the national newspapers, including human interest stories and interviews with national leaders of the campaign on the process that would be followed.

- Full media coverage of major preparatory events, including radio broadcasts by the prime minister and minister of education.
- Cultural promotion involving the use of poems, songs, and plays about literacy written by members of the public.

These public awareness initiatives were also the beginning of the process of creating and legitimating a new cultural capital. It was the first act of building a new knowledge base predicated on social conscience and collective responsibility for change.

At the first meeting of the National Technical Commission in June 1980 the structure of the literacy campaign was finally elaborated and the manual and literacy method were approved. At parish-level seminars the volunteers who were to play key roles were introduced to the materials and the method. The key organizational structure in the campaign was the Committee for Popular Education, the base-level structure of the literacy campaign where the real work of the program was carried out.

In every village requiring literacy work these committees were actively engaged in carrying it out. Made up of all the volunteer literacy teachers in that community, the Committee for Popular Education was headed by a village coordinator and technician and met weekly to discuss pedagogical and other difficulties which affected the progress of the campaign. The village coordinator was generally responsible for the literacy work in the village, and some of his or her specific tasks included recruiting volunteers, registering learners, organizing classes, organizing cultural activities (film shows, panel discussions) to mobilize villagers, and so on.

The village technician was invariably a professional teacher who had volunteered to work in the CPE and whose experience in teaching was used to provide guidance and orientation to the rest of the volunteers (most of whom had never taught before). The technician advised volunteers on resolving teaching difficulties and provided technical orientation. Selection of technicians was largely based on having had prior teaching experience and openness to innovative and participatory methods.

At the parish level (the state was divided into seven parishes or administrative districts), there was a parish coordinator and a technician who directed the work of the campaign locally. Parish coordinators were principally responsible for supervising mobilization and logistical preparations in their parish, and the parish technicians handled the pedagogical aspects: organizing training in the villages, providing technical guidance and orientation to village technicians, and supervising the teaching and learning process in the parish.

At the national level, an Advisory Committee, chaired by the minister of education, George Louison,[10] played an important role in drawing together the support and participation of the mass organizations and national service associations.

Some of the major bodies represented on the National Advisory Committee (NAC) included the Grenada Union of Teachers, the Grenada Chamber of Commerce, the Trade Union Council, the People's Armed Forces, the National Women's Organization, the National Youth Organization, the Grenada Conference of Churches, the Agricultural Workers' Union, Jaycees, and the Catholic Youth Organization. The participation of these social sectors in the campaign made it a democratic challenge of the Revolution, aptly expressed in one of the slogans of the CPE: "If you know, teach; if you don't, learn." Of these bodies, the unions and the national organizations of women and youth played an especially vital role in mobilizing volunteer teachers and learners. Each undertook to mobilize within its particular constituency and with varying degrees of success (almost indexical to their organizational strength) secured the participation of their membership. The presence of the more traditional civic organizations and interest groups, such as the Chamber of Commerce, the Council of Churches, and the Jaycees, was an important statement of the broad social and multiclass character of the literacy campaign.

To strengthen motivation and sustain participation, a system of emulation ceremonies at village and parish levels was introduced. During the course of the literacy campaign, three major national emulation periods were observed (September, October, and November) corresponding to the periods of most intensive literacy instruction. Emulation involved recognition of the "Example of the Best." Each month awards were given to the most outstanding learners and volunteers at public cultural celebrations at village, parish, and national levels. In this practice the National Technical Commission was concerned to find a way of recognizing disciplined effort without promoting individualistic competition, since cooperative endeavor was an organizational principle of the revolution. (Indeed, the CPE literacy reader, *Let Us Learn Together*, emphasized the collective nature of learning itself.) Participation, consistent effort, and creative initiative, more than actual achievement, were the measure of the best. The success of the emulation program was such that the mass organizations and other programs of the revolution began to implement the principle. A concept of excellence as the product of collective creative endeavor was promoted.

A six-member National Technical Commission (NTC) at the center was responsible for shaping pedagogy, preparing teaching material, and training parish-level trainers. Its specific tasks included preparing lesson plans (additional exercises for each lesson in the reader) and holding monthly seminars with parish technicians and coordinators, at which the campaign statistics were compiled and reports from the parishes were discussed and strategies recommended. The commission also visited private homes, community centers, and schools where literacy classes were conducted, and participated in meetings with literacy volunteers. At the height of the campaign the NTC published a periodic newsletter containing news of the campaign, technical tips, and a calendar of events. Innovative teaching strategies and unique ideas for strengthening the connection between literacy and community life which were developed in different villages were reported in the newsletter to stimulate creativity in other locations.

One of the NTC's central functions was to initiate the overall planning process in the CPE. During the literacy campaign, work plans were part of the NTC's modus operandi, and in January 1981 literacy volunteers contributed for the first time to elaborating a national plan during a refresher seminar. Thereafter the NTC utilized the CPE structure to ensure broad participation among literacy workers, and in many cases learners, in preparing its plans. Six-month plans were developed in collaboration with village and parish personnel. These plans identified the main objectives of the period as well as the specific ways and means by which they were to be realized.

The first texts produced were the literacy reader *Let Us Learn Together* and a corresponding teacher's manual, *Forward Ever!* Prepared within months of the overthrow of Gairy, it contained fourteen reading themes aimed at reinforcing the dominant sentiment of that period, for example: "Let us learn together," "We build our communities," "The land must produce more," "Our international airport," "Our history of struggle," and "Education is a must."[11] Many of the sentences used were those that had been written spontaneously on walls in the communities by the people. They were selected by the NTC precisely because they represented the people's own linguistic universe. They expressed the lived experience and values of the people, and their inclusion in the literacy text signaled the arrival and validity of popular experience as official educational knowledge and also helped legitimate the text itself by speaking in the language of the people. Because the NTC considered the literacy campaign essentially a political task with pedagogical implications, the content of this reader embodied values of national unity, social commitment, and cooperation. As a first step in working people appropriating educational opportunity, the acquisition of literacy skills had to address the new historical reality by affirming new values.

In preparation for writing the reader and manual, the NTC reviewed and critiqued several literacy readers developed within the Caribbean and abroad. Small teams drafted several different models of what could be an appropriate literacy reader. These were then subjected to intense scrutiny and criticism. In preliminary debate, the commission drew on regional experiences such as the JAMAL program in Jamaica; the Cuban literacy experience; experiments in St. Lucia by the Study and Action Group during the late 1970s, which used Paulo Freire's methodology; and the advice of Freire himself (who twice visited Grenada) and of Angel Arrechea Funtes, a Cuban who provided insights and directions based on the Cuban experience.

The generative themes finally selected emerged from intense discussion within the NTC about the political stances implicit in the "technical rationality" of different literacy methods and approaches. This debate occurred after members of the NTC had traveled throughout the country speaking with groups of prospective learners about their aspirations and researching their vocabulary. Two primary considerations were the technical effectiveness of the methodology and its capacity for eliciting critical participation of the learner in the learning process. The generative themes covered education (of adults and children); national development priorities of the revolution; and the values of the new political culture (popular participation, unity, regional identity).

The literacy reader *Let Us Learn Together* was designed to promote and affirm new values and a more humanist ideology. It tried to promote a patriotic vision of Grenada as a birthright of the working people to be claimed by them. Revolutionary nationalism and patriotism were promoted by emphasizing a collective sense of belonging and of responsibility for the country. Themes such as "We build our communities" and "Grenada, Carriacou, and Petit Martinique" stressed ownership of country; others solicited pride in major national projects and institutions ("Our international airport", "NCB—the bank of our people").

Recognition by Grenadian people of their Caribbean identity and their internationalist responsibilities formed an intrinsic dimension of revolutionary patriotism. The fifth lesson in the reader was entitled "One Caribbean" and summarized the perspective of the revolution on Caribbean identity.

One Caribbean

> I am from Grenada, Carriacou and Petit Martinique
> You are from Martinique.
> He is from Cuba.
> She is from Aruba.
>
> We are from the Caribbean.
>
> We are one people.
> We are one Caribbean.

Each of the countries mentioned represents a different linguistic and political dimension of the Caribbean: anglophone and revolutionary Grenada, francophone and colonized Martinique, Spanish-speaking and socialist Cuba, and Dutch Aruba. Within this lesson, the technical requirements of literacy are interwoven with a vital political message grounded in the historical condition of the region. The message of unity across the linguistic barriers historically imposed by Western European colonialism and the contemporary imperative of cultural and political pluralism was carried in a lesson structure intended to present the phonics of the "A" sound (GrenAdA,

ArubA, CubA) and to demonstrate the conjugation of the copula (a structure absent from Caribbean Creoles but essential to standard English). The political and the pedagogical reached their most organic fusion in such a lesson.

Promoting positive and indigenous cultural values formed a further dimension of the literacy reader. Some inherited values were to be explicitly challenged, and certain traditional values were to be reasserted.

Given that the political base of the Gairy dictatorship comprised mainly elderly agricultural workers, and given the political tribalism that characterized the multiparty Westminster system, political sectarianism had to be openly confronted. The NJM leadership was concerned that the triumph over Gairy should not provide an opportunity to settle old scores. They set an example here by not prosecuting members of the police force and "Mongoose Gang" (terror squad) who had beaten key NJM leaders almost to death in an incident (known as Bloody Sunday) on 18 November 1973. To this end, the final lesson of the literacy reader was entitled "The Revolution has room for all of us."

Cooperation was a traditional value reiterated among the generative themes of the campaign. Grenada had a long history of communal collaboration in the folk tradition of the "maroon." Maroons involved the provision of voluntary labor for some communal (or individual) benefit with the benefactor providing food, music, and the required material. After the triumph of the revolution, people throughout the country spontaneously undertook repair and beautification projects in their communities. In the literacy reader, the values of cooperation, voluntary effort, and self-reliance were emphasized to reinforce the resurgence of that spirit.

The reader was accompanied by a teacher's guide, *Forward Ever!* This provided a general orientation to teaching adults, explained the method used in the reader, and discussed each theme covered in the reader. The orientation section identified the development of a mutually respectful and sharing relationship between teacher and learner as of paramount importance. In addition, the use of a reader's word list was advanced as an important generative aspect of the teaching method. This list contained key words (whether in standard English or Grenadian English) used by the reader himself or herself in discussing the lesson themes. It formed the basis for building a personal sight vocabulary and helping learners master words which were already an active part of their own linguistic universe.

The reader and manual made up the main orientation material used in the initial training sessions for volunteer teachers. In July 1980 "base-level seminars" were held in every parish in Grenada to introduce volunteer teachers to the campaign methodology and use of materials. These seminars were conducted by village and parish technicians, who had been involved in reviewing the materials and approaches. A total of 1,473 persons participated in this event, the largest decentralized yet coordinated national seminar hitherto held in Grenada.

Throughout the literacy campaign, training was systematic and regular at the village, parish, and national levels. Wherever and whenever successful methodological innovations emerged they were incorporated into these training sessions. Weaknesses noted from field observation of classes by parish and NTC technicians indicated areas for additional training.

The work of the CPE reflected commitment to participatory evaluation exemplified in the Midway Evaluation Congress, held halfway through the literacy campaign. This was attended by all parish and village coordinators and technicians. It focused on the weaknesses (rather than the achievements) of the campaign to that point in an effort to strengthen the campaign and to intensify work. This process of critical reflection was structured around three commissions: The Commission for Technical and Pedagogical Issues; The Commission on Statistics, Control, and Logistical Support; The Commission on Mass Organizations.

The commissions discussed the major problems being experienced in the various areas and proposed solutions. Problems affecting regular attendance, transport difficulties, dropouts, and inconsistent levels of support from mass organizations were among those discussed. The congress infused the campaign with a new vitality: volunteer teachers taught with renewed vigor, and general enthusiasm for the campaign was heightened. Evidence of the value of open, participatory, critical reflection on its work by those most actively engaged in it presented an important "lesson" to the CPE.

The literacy campaign concluded in February 1981. Its results were not dramatic in statistical terms compared with the mass campaigns of countries like Cuba and Nicaragua. With a relatively low percentage of absolute illiteracy in Grenada, some three thousand people went through the campaign. Throughout, the sister island of Carriacou remained the leading parish, with 86 percent of its illiterate population in consistent study. At its height the campaign reached 130 out of the 135 villages in Grenada.

One immediate observable outcome was a tremendous upsurge of cultural activity based on educational themes: in poems, songs, and plays on illiteracy produced by CPE volunteers and learners alike.

Lessons learned about organization and the effect of sustained voluntary participation by hundreds of Grenadians—old and young—in the demanding tasks of the campaign had an impact on the process of democratization far beyond the numbers formally involved. As the chairperson remarked at the Midway Evaluation Congress, besides the objective of eradicating illiteracy, the campaign was also about "the gathering of organizational experience [and] the formulation of pedagogical principles based on the local reality so that we [could] be prepared for the continuous task of adult education."[12]

Many people became committed to the revolution through their participation in literacy work. And the direct outcomes spread beyond Grenada itself. Two outstanding volunteer teachers were sent to Nicaragua's Atlantic Coast region to participate in the English language component of the literacy campaign in that country. The involvement helped open cultural communication between the two revolutionary societies. Thirty Grenadian youth subsequently took part in the Atlantic Coast "Follow-Up" campaign. Technical exchanges were arranged between the two countries, and the twinning of Carriacou and Bluefields was planned.[13]

Centers for popular education

After the literacy campaign the CPE prepared to move into phase 2: the establishment of a structured countrywide system of adult education. The shape of this system was largely influenced by recommendations and feedback from teachers and learners during the campaign and from other consultative fora (such as the National Conferences on Education held in 1980). Strong preferences had been expressed for structured learning opportunities which could provide adults with the chance to "move on from where they left off" or gain certification in specific areas.

Accordingly, the CPE adopted as its slogan for phase 2 "CPE—taking you from where you are to where you want to be!" Five dimensions to adult education were identified:

1. Intellectual formation—helping to develop the capacity for independent acquisition of knowledge

2. Scientific and technical education—exposure to the fundamentals of the sciences and relating these to the socioeconomic condition of the country

3. Political-ideological formation—through strengthening participation in national events and programs of the revolution

4. Moral education—contributing to reshaping and reaffirming positive social values in peoples' habits of daily conduct

5. Aesthetic education—promotion of artistic appreciation and expression

The specific objectives of phase 2 were stated as follows:

a) To raise the cultural level, political and ideological consciousness of all our people generally, and in particular to create a deeper awareness of the need and importance of education in the revolutionary process of building a new society

b) To provide primary education for all the adults in our country who need it, in a two year course

c) To provide avenues for our communities to develop organizational skills and a deeper understanding of the need for cooperative effort to solve the common problems faced by the people

d) To assist other departments, ministries, national programs, etc. in popular education of the masses on issues relevant to the particular program, project or institution.[14]

Structure and organization

Since phase 2 involved the establishment of Centers for Popular Education in the villages, the structure of the adult education program was revised. Virtually every community in which the literacy campaign had taken place was linked into the adult education network. Centers for Popular Education were established in every community in which there was a primary or secondary school or some suitable infrastructure (like a community center).

At a local level, the structure of the program involved four structures:

- *A Learners' Council,* comprising all of the adult learners attending the center. They elected a representative from each class to an Executive Committee. The functions of the Learners' Council included organizing center recreational activities, encouraging and stimulating emulation between groups, promoting punctuality and regular attendance, and providing support to learners experiencing domestic difficulties which affected their studies.

- *A Center Committee,* consisting of the center director, staff, and representative(s) of the Learners' Council. It was responsible for the collective management of the center, including organization of center activities and timetabling.

- *A Zonal Committee* which comprised all center directors in a particular zone. This met fortnightly to review the work accomplished, plan major activities (including fund-raising, cultural events, emulations, and intrazonal indoor and outdoor sporting events), and coordinate the work and activities of centers in the zone. The committee was chaired by a zonal coordinator elected from its members.

- *Parish Committees* performed essentially the same functions as the Zonal Committee but at a parish level, and were chaired by full-time parish coordinators responsible for the day-to-day execution of all of the logistical and mobilization work. Each committee comprised zonal coordinators from within the parish. An additional responsibility involved liaising with the NJM's parish coordinating bodies (PCBs), the umbrella body of party organizations within the parish. Through this contact, the support of the party and mass organizations for adult education in the parish was to be ensured. In practice, however, this relationship worked only where the PCBs were effectively organized and actively functioning. In many cases the CPE structure was more functional and more systematically in contact with the masses than the PCBs. This led to intense debate within the subcommittee of the political bureau responsible for overseeing the CPE about the strategic prioritization of these structures.

One line of argument sought to promote the full development of the CPE as an educational program to which the people were favorably disposed and through which their historical and civic awareness could be developed. The other viewpoint sought to place greater emphasis on the strengthening of the PCB as a priority of party members within which promotion of CPE was simply another task. The following views typified the debate.

Cde. Jules said on the question of other activities in the various parishes that these activities should be incorporated into CPE so as to expand the curriculum activities of the program. He said that the party must decide whether the mass organizations will help to strengthen the CPE or the CPE will help strengthen the mass organizations. He suggested the formation of mass organization groups in the CPE centers.

Cde. Bartholomew said that the program cannot move forward until the activities of the mass organizations are scaled down, because these activities, such as sport etc. are major attractions to the people.

Cde. Strachan said that the danger is that in scaling down the activities of the mass organizations they can soon lose their identity. He agreed that if more time is given to CPE it will strengthen the mass organizations, but he feels that the activities of the mass organizations should be directed towards strengthening the CPE.[15]

This issue went well beyond the question of time and activity management in the communities, involving also a conception of the Centers for Popular Education as integrated loci of village life, as places where learning and doing became praxis.

At the national level, the structure of the program included many of those structures which had guided the literacy campaign. Hence the National Advisory Committee continued to function as it had during the literacy campaign as a broad-based advisory body chaired by the minister of education, and the National Technical Commission assumed a considerably larger role than before. It continued to be responsible for production of instructional programs and material, training of adult education teachers, and national record keeping. But in addition it took on curriculum development, supervision of the centers, and the production of a wide range and volume of instructional and supplementary material.

Training of adult education teachers was organized into three main types of activity:

1. Initial induction seminars—induction of new adult education teachers into the program philosophy and methodology, introduction to the textbooks, and orientation in the organization of the adult education program

2. Regular refresher seminars—orientation in the teaching of different subject areas, analysis of difficulties experienced in teaching specific lessons, exchange of ideas and experiences among teachers in a zone, and preparation of lesson outlines for the upcoming period

3. Annual evaluation and planning seminars—analysis of the work accomplished in the year under review, and planning of the main activities and calendar for an upcoming year (this activity involved not only the center teachers but also members of the Learners' Council)

The adult education program involved thirty-six weeks of instruction divided into two semesters. The course of study covered six levels:

Literacy

1. Basic literacy—for those who had not participated in the literacy campaign

2. Postliteracy—for consolidating newly acquired literacy skills and stressing the development of independent reading habits as a foundation for acquiring knowledge

Primary education

3. Level 1—involving English language (reading, writing, grammar), mathematics, and natural science

4. Level 2—with geography added from this level on

5. Level 3—at which English language, mathematics, natural science, and geography (including elements of the economy and the demography of Grenada) were taught

6. Level 4—at which the history of Grenada was added to the academic subjects and plans were being developed to include an option in two technical skill areas

Content

It was expected that a learner could achieve the equivalent of a primary school education within two years of study. The curriculum for phase 2, although structured in some respects like a formal school, was designed with integrated subject areas, cross-disciplinary reinforcement, and practical application of knowledge. The subject areas selected were considered core areas which afforded the best opportunities for redefining content (along the lines of greater relevance) and for providing a "solid" academic foundation, opening paths to ongoing personal development. Field and community assignments to be undertaken by CPE classes were introduced alongside exercises in grammar, writing, science, and geography. These activities were not simply *prescribed* (in the curriculum). There was provision for learners to determine activities and ways in which the knowledge gained could be applied in a practical context. The goal of the CPE syllabi went beyond the mastery of "traditional, academic" knowledge to include discovery and creation of new knowledge by learners and deeper involvement in the revolutionary process.

The general principles underlying the curriculum content in the CPE involved the following:

- Deconstruction of neocolonial ideology and construction of revolutionary perspectives
- Promotion of revolutionary nationalism and patriotism
- Advancement of Caribbean identity and internationalism
- Promotion of positive and indigenous cultural values
- Democratization of science and knowledge
- Reconstruction of gender
- Reclamation of language

Beyond the curriculum, a strong emphasis was placed on extracurricular activities, to be determined entirely by the Learners' Councils. The most common types of extracurricular activity included voluntary community work, holding of minicouncils (in which members of the community were invited to the center to discuss some vital community issue or view some audiovisual presentation), panel discussions, sporting activities, domino competitions, intra- and intercenter knowledge quizzes, and the like. Even "traditionalists" had to acknowledge the creative pedagogical possibilities within the CPE, but the political and ideological impact of the CPEs was strongly feared and opposed by critics of the revolutionary process.

A CPE Emulation Program was established to promote even greater initiative and to strengthen the work of the CPEs. This was a means for recognizing the effort of the most consistent learners and teachers— "Recognizing the Example of the Best"—and was geared to promoting collective initiative within centers. Emulation occurred at class, center, parish, and national levels. Emulation criteria for learners included class attendance, participation in the center's cultural, sporting, or social activities, and involvement in community work. The criteria for teachers included class attendance, punctuality, participation in technical and training seminars, and involvement in community work.

A further mechanism developed as part of the strategy to improve the quality of instruction within the CPEs was the formation of an Audiovisual Production Unit for preparation of slide-tape programs to complement textbook content. Slide-tape packages for each of the major themes and topics in the consolidated texts were developed to make the content more interesting and visual. Experience had shown that learner interest and community participation was boosted whenever audiovisuals were used in classes. Requiring relatively cheap technology, slide-tape packages encouraged more specialized discussion of the themes and drew on the expertise of people from different sectors. For example, a series devoted to the national economy was developed. This provided general overviews of the vital sectors of the Grenadian economy, using simple language and domestic analogies to explain its operation, problems, and prospects. Here the CPE drew on the expertise of leading Grenadian economists.

These innovations helped to strengthen links with other sectors such as health, women's affairs, crafts, trade unions, and so forth. Given positive responses from the centers, numerous requests for assistance with disseminating public education materials were being made of the CPE by various agencies and ministries by 1983. It was decided that conditions were appropriate for rationalizing adult and popular education on a national scale and for revising the adult education texts in the light of insightful feedback from teachers, learners, and technical personnel. In March 1983, the Ministry of

Education held a workshop on nonformal education in Grenada under the sponsorship of UNESCO.[16]

This was attended by almost all public and private voluntary agencies which were either engaged in some form of public education or were interested in having input into the popular education process (nineteen agencies). Its objectives included sharing information on the public education mandates of participating agencies, critically reviewing the CPE curriculum and formulating concrete recommendations for improvement, and identifying areas of interagency collaboration.

The workshop resulted in a detailed critique of the adult education texts and a plan for interagency collaboration in the preparation of print and audiovisual material for public education. Revision of texts was the first priority agreed upon, with various agencies assuming responsibility for providing information on specific topics. The NTC also devised a plan for receiving submissions (reading material, learners' writings, activity ideas, pedagogical recommendations) from the Centers for Popular Education throughout the country to inform revisions.

Worker education classes

Although the CPE was the largest and most successful of the popular education programs of the revolution, there were other more specialized initiatives. One was the Worker Education Program. This was a political education program run directly by the party and limited to workers within the public sector. All ministries and public enterprises were closed one afternoon a week for about three hours for these classes. Since the classes were conducted during the regular working hours, attendance was compulsory.

The rationale for holding such classes was valid and convincing, but the manner in which the program was designed and delivered undermined its good intent. Since the program had inherited a bureaucracy which, after twenty-eight years of Gairyism, had been "demotivated" and permeated by patronage (the revolutionary government did not make a policy of mass purging from the state sector), it was felt that such classes would provide an opportunity for workers to gain better insights into the development policies of the revolution and to become politicized and motivated.

A party committee was given responsibility for designing the program to be taught by party members. With pressure from the higher organs of the NJM to introduce the program, it was hastily designed and poorly conceived, notwithstanding several recommendations made by representatives of the Curriculum Development Unit of the National In-Service Teacher Education Program and the CPE. The committee identified forty-eight concepts,[17] nine of which were deemed priority concepts: imperialism, capitalism, class struggle, the state, internationalism, people's democracy, economic goals and development, and socialism. While paying lip service to the need for "grounding" these, the committee proceeded to elaborate them as largely theoretical concepts. The popular educators on the committee argued that the approach to workers' education should begin from whatever issues and perspectives prevailed among the workers, and that concepts should be dealt with as they emerge from self-critical reflection on workers' views. It was further suggested that tutors be provided with basic training in more participatory pedagogies.

This recommendation was ignored in the rush to implement the program. In the view of the higher bodies of the party, the "low level" of political consciousness was proving an impediment to efficiency and performance in the public sector. The difficulties of implementation were further aggravated by the zealousness and, in some cases, the intellectual arrogance of the party cadres leading the classes.

The result was resistance by workers and the emergence of general disillusionment and cynicism. As a French researcher reported: "A number of people I spoke to said these classes were not very successful; they were too ideological and too divorced from Grenadian reality. 'I would have liked to learn more about my future as a worker in Grenada,' one woman told me, 'I don't care about that fellow Marx.' She and a colleague laughed as they recalled how people slept through the compulsory classes."[18]

There were, however, some inspired moments in some classes, but these invariably occurred when tutors departed from the prescribed agenda to deal with matters of current interest to workers. In the Ministry of Education class, for example, workers read and critiqued a *Time* magazine article on Grenada; the famous West Indian novelist, George Lamming, gave a talk on the meaning of Christmas; the Grenadian historian, George Brizan, made a presentation on the history of the Grenadian peasantry; working sessions were held on the national budget; and a review of the work of the Ministry of Education and its five-year indicative plan was undertaken.

Literacy and economic justice

Two other initiatives bear mention since they are relevant to the concept of popular education in the Grenadian process: the Agricultural Workers' Education Program and the National Budget Preparation Process.

Agricultural workers' education program

With appropriation of lands belonging to the Gairy dictatorship, the state acquired several agricultural farms which were incorporated into plans for revitalizing the agricultural sector. One of the big challenges faced by the Ministry of Agriculture was to make the state farms economically viable and productive. By 1982 it had become evident that the absence of management and technical skills was a major constraint to achieving this goal.

In its commitment to worker participation and maximizing human resource potential, the Ministry of Agriculture, in collaboration with the CPE, began preparations for an Agricultural Workers' Education Program for 911 workers on the twenty-six state farms constituting the Grenada Farms Corporation. The program was to be a sixteen-week course in five subject areas: general education (literacy/numeracy), political education, general principles of crop production, agricultural engineering, and management and farm organization. It was to be launched with 280 workers in three centers: Boulogne (100), Bocage (80), and La Sagesse (100)—and taught by fourteen tutors who were CPE facilitators and graduates of the Mirabeau Agricultural School.

From 23 May to 4 June 1983 a two-week initial training workshop for tutors was held in Bocage. A diagnostic test was then given to workers for grading them into classes. Tutor training covered three basic areas:

1. Political education
2. Agricultural science (basic crop science, farm planning and layout,

cropping systems, plant propagation, farm management, chemical usage, tree crop production, agricultural development issues)

3. Principles of adult education, basic English and math, history and geography of Grenada, and unit planning

To assist in instruction, a modular approach was proposed and three technical advisory panels (Agricultural Engineering, Farm Organization and Management, and Crop Production) comprising specialists from the Ministry of Agriculture were formed. Classes had just started when the political crisis of October 1983 (culminating in the assassination of Maurice Bishop and several others and the self-destruction of the revolution) ended the initiative.

National budget process

The process of preparing and presenting the national budget represented a further endeavor with significant implications for popular education.

> The budget exercise was regarded by the PRG as being one of its most pioneering innovations and involved quite an extended procedure. First, expenditure requests from all government departments were studied by the Ministry of Finance . . . A preliminary draft was then submitted to the PRG Cabinet for discussion. This was followed by a period during which officials from the Ministry went before the trade unions, mass organizations, [and] zonal and parish councils to discuss the draft with them. The high point of the exercise was the national conference on the economy, which was attended by delegates from all the mass organizations. Breaking up into workshops devoted to specific areas of the economy, the delegates made detailed comments and criticisms on the draft proposals. The budget then went back to the Ministry of Finance for final revisions and then to the Cabinet for approval. Finally, a detailed report was made to the people by the ministry and an explanation was given as to which recommendations had been rejected and why.[19]

The entire process challenged the technicians of the Ministry of Finance to make the national economy intelligible to the masses. Discussions and consultations were like huge economics classes, except that the people had to consider real opportunity costs and to think about the acceptable options that served their interests. As its contribution to the consolidation of this process, the CPE incorporated issues arising from the national budget in its curriculum. In mathematics, for example, problems centered around the mathematics of the budget and national development were included, and in the geography section of the adult education texts (Book 3), an introduction to Grenadian economy was presented.

The lessons: Problems, difficulties, and constraints

What lessons are to be learned from the Grenada experience? The main historical constraints and problems were of two kinds: political and pedagogical.

The major political issue had to do with the most appropriate mobilization focus and strategy. There was a recurring debate within the NJM Central Committee on the role of the party in building the CPE and the priority between the mass organizations and the CPE. On this issue there were two distinct approaches: one was to build the mass organizations and then through them strengthen the CPE; the other was to concentrate on the CPE as a means of developing the capacity for self-organization and informed participation and to use it for building the mass organizations. The comments frequently heard on the streets during the mass demonstrations against the Central Committee in October 1983 (about the people's capacity to make decisions affecting their future and the fact that CPE had helped them achieve this) and Coard's hindsight analysis of the mass organizations show clearly how this dilemma was part of the more global tension between centralized authority and democratization within the revolution: "It is my considered view, in hindsight, that the greatest mistake that the entire leadership of the NJM made during our party crisis of September/October 1983, was our failure to even think of, not to mention submit to, the Assemblies, all the facts (and factors) affecting our internal party crisis, and lean on the people in such organized, structured fora, as the basis for resolving our grave difficulties."[20]

Programs like the CPE and the other popular education initiatives contributed cumulatively to the political awakening of the Grenadian people and to legitimating the social and political agenda of the revolution. To what extent critical perspectives and a capacity for independent action by the masses were nurtured through them is a matter for historical speculation.

At the pedagogical level, the Grenadian programs differed from the more "Freirean" forms used in oppositional contexts. Although the Grenada model was influenced by Freirean perspectives, it was felt that the success of such popular education approaches was highly dependent on the quality of facilitation provided. Popular education as the practice of critical education requires a cadre of highly committed, politically and technically developed teachers. Mass education programs in revolutionary contexts, on the other hand, are faced with the necessity of nurturing critical perspectives where the quality of facilitation is limited. As a democratic task of revolution, adult education cannot afford to be overly selective (in terms of the ideal balance of political and technical skills) in the process of forming teachers.

Associated with this dilemma is the question of methodology: the selection of generative approaches versus structured and more formal curricula. Popular education programming is invariably opposed to highly structured curricula, and many advocates shun the use of tests. The Grenada approach sought to achieve a compromise between the expectations of learners predicated on traditional forms and the imperative of being open to the experiences of learners and the sociopolitical context. From the early stages of the literacy campaign, CPE learners insisted on the provision of certification for their achievements and emphasized the importance to them of being able to continue their formal education. In a revolutionary situation, working people recognize the legitimation of knowledge as a proper function of the state. Although learners in Grenada valued the fact that their lives, their history, and their geography constituted the basis of new knowledge, they still called for its legitimation in the form of examinations and certification. The organizational forms developed by the CPE proved useful, not only in responding to these demands, but also as a mechanism for exerting pressures for change on the inherited formal education system. Parents who attended CPE classes and teachers who also taught in the CPE program were at the forefront of the efforts to reform the school curriculum, to reorganize the system of national examinations, and to bring the schools closer to the community.

Perhaps the most important conclusion from the Grenada experience is that in the organization of popular education and critical literacy programs educators should be sensitive to the needs and expectations of learners. While recognizing that particular organizational forms imply particular pedagogies and philosophies, one must not overlook the possibilities of evolving new forms or turning old forms to new use.

Notes

*I wish to acknowledge the helpful critical comments of my colleague Jim Ladwig in the preparation of this chapter.

1. Barriteau, E., Brathwaite, F., and Emmanuel, P., *Political Change and Public Opinion in Grenada 1979–1984* (Barbados: UWI-ISER, 1986), p. 37.

2. Thorndike, T., *Grenada: Politics, Economics and Society* (London: Frances Pinter, 1985), p. 1.

3. Marcus, B., and Taber, M. (eds.), *Maurice Bishop Speaks* (New York: Pathfinder Press, 1983), p. 278.

4. For lengthier discussions of popular participation in the Grenada revolution, see Hodge, M., and Searle, C., *Is Freedom We Making—The New Democracy in Grenada* (St. Georges: GIS, 1981); EPICA Task Force, *Grenada: The Peaceful Revolution* (Washington: EPICA, 1982); and Thorndike, T., *op. cit.*

5. The Study and Action Group was a Catholic youth group influenced by liberation theology and struggling for social change. One of these attempts is documented in Jules, D., *Education for Conscientization: The Prison Literacy Project in St. Lucia* (Castries: Folk Research Center, 1978).

6. Bishop, M., "Emulation Is the Seed That Brings the Fruit of Excellence," in Jules, D., and Rojas, D., *Maurice Bishop—Selected Speeches 1979–81* (Havana: Casa De Las Americas, 1982).

7. Carnoy, M., and Samoff, J., *Education and Social Transition in the Third World* (Princeton, N.J.: Princeton University Press, 1990).

8. W. E. B. Du Bois, "The Negro Artisan," Atlanta, Ga.: Atlanta University Press, 1902), quoted in Kliebard, H., *The Struggle for the American Curriculum 1893–1958* (New York: Routledge, 1987), p. 134.

9. In the *Free West Indian*, Saturday, 28 February 1981, p. 12.

10. Later succeeded by Jacqueline Creft as minister of education.

11. The contents of the literacy reader, *Let Us Learn Together*, included the following themes:

Topic	Theme
1. Let us learn from each other	Learning as a cooperative activity
2. We build our communities	Working together to build Grenada
3. Grenada, Carriacou, and Petit Martinique	National pride and unity
4. The land must produce more	Agricultural self-reliance/productivity
5. One Caribbean	Caribbean unity, linguistic and ideological pluralism
6. Free milk for mothers and babies	Better nutrition, awareness of milk distribution program
7. The Revolution brings more doctors	Prioritization of health care by the revolution
8. Our international airport	The international airport as a national development priority
9. NCB—the bank of our people	Promotion of the National Commercial Bank/savings habits
10. Building a new Grenada	Need for unity, discipline and hard work for new society
11. Vigilance in our villages	Building the militia
12. Our history of struggle	History as collective struggle
13. Education is a must	Awareness of the importance of educating the youth
14. The revolution has room for all of us	Promotion of popular participation, against sectarianism

12. Report of the CPE Evaluation Congress, "Comments by Congress Chairman Cde. Didacus Jules," p. 4.

13. The twinning idea was considered especially important at the time since the Sandinista government was just beginning to experience difficulty in dealing with the Atlantic Coast and it was felt that cultural tours, exchange

visits, and other opportunities for interaction between Carriacou and the Coast could strengthen the identification of the anglophone Atlantic Coast people with the revolution.

14. *Education for True Liberation and Independence—A Handbook of Norms and Guidelines for the Primary Education Programme*, CPE/Ministry of Education, 1982, p. 5.

15. "Minutes of the Meeting of the NJM Political Bureau" (undated), DSI-83-C-371.7.

16. See *Final Report on the Workshop on Non-Formal Education in Grenada* (St. Georges: UNESCO/CPE/Ministry of Education, 1983).

17. The concepts selected were as follows:

1. Political education
2. Academic education
3. Capitalist crisis
4. Capitalism
5. Socialism
6. Imperialism/anti-imperialism
7. The state
8. Class
9. Class struggle
10. Economic growth
11. Economic development
13. Planning
14. Political independence
15. Unemployment
16. People's democracy
17. Means of production
18. Mode of production
19. Inflation
20. Productivity
21. Emulation
22. Capital expenditure
23. Recurrent expenditure
24. Internationalism
25. Consumption/investment
26. Infrastructure
27. Colonialism
28. Neocolonialism
29. Exploitation
30. Trade (export/import)
31. Agricultural diversification
32. Private sector
33. Mixed economy
34. Open economy
35. Working class
36. National Liberation Movement
37. Industrialization/modernization
38. Patriotism
39. Peace
40. Detente/disarmament
41. Revolution
42. Progressive
43. Nonalignment
44. Ideological pluralism
45. Caribbean integration
46. Trade unionism
47. Human rights
48. Social wage

18. Lesser, L., "Education in Grenada: Before, During and After the Revolution," Paris: unpublished paper, June 1984, p. 23.

19. Ambursley, F., and Dunkerley, J., *Grenada: Whose Freedom?* (London: Latin American Bureau, 1984), pp. 38–39.

20. Coard, B., *Village and Workers, Women, Farmers and Youth Assemblies during the Grenada Revolution—Their Genesis, Evolution and Significance* (London: Karia Press, 1989).

5

Words to a life-land:
Literacy, the imagination, and Palestine

Chris Searle

It was a normal day
A normal morning
And a normal unhappy feeling.

I went to a market
To buy all I can afford
For my family,
When a man dressed
In a green suit
A cap
And carrying a rifle
(And that made him a soldier,
And that gave him the right to order me around!)
Suddenly stopped me with his rifle.
He pointed it at me,
Asking me where is my identity card?
Identity? We are the Palestinians!
We were born free
In our fathers' and grandfathers' land called Palestine
—The Holy Land.

We have our identity
Not just in Palestine but through the whole world,
And it destroys the happiness and the joy which
is in our hearts
And it destroys our children too!
Children who don't have freedom any more
They don't have a future to enjoy
They don't have a future to finish their education.
They want to build their future

But deep, deep inside
They know the Israelis won't give them a chance.
It is all right for the Israeli children,
They have the right
Yes, they have the right to be free
And to have a bright future—
Because they have a life-land,
A land which is not taken over by other people.

Our children
As soon as they learn to walk,
They need to learn how to carry a weapon!
They have to
Our children,
They would love to go to school
And to hold a pen and pencil like other children
around the world.
After all we are all the same
But nobody, nobody will give them a chance.

And we cry
Cry for all the world
Cry for the Israeli government
To give us our freedom and our country.
You know the Israeli system—
Why, why do they treat us like this?

Democracy, democracy is just for Israelis—
Palestinians are not included.
In the name of *Allah*,
We don't ask much from the Israeli government,
But we ask for all the Palestinians
To be free and to live like everyone else in the world,
To be with our families
To sleep in our homes in peace
And to hope for a glorious morning!
Nadia Saleh (fourteen-year-old Sheffield school student)

The word *literacy* is not commonly used within the context of British schools. As a term it has been much more widely adopted by adult educators than by schoolteachers. And yet, at almost any period in the history of modern education worldwide—except in those areas of revolutionary upheaval in nations of vast populations which have been mobilized for large-scale campaigns of mass adult literacy, such as in the Soviet Union, China, or Ethiopia—the majority of people learning how to read and write in the world have been children studying in their schools.

It is important to remember this; otherwise we shall see literacy generally as a process in which adults involve themselves, while children are engaged in a different form of learning about language and experience—something which certainly involves them in learning how to read and write, but something which cannot be called "literacy" because it happens early in life, as if it happens "when it should," as part of the sequence of civilized and "normal" human social development. To be part of a literacy program or process is almost certainly to be seen as working in an adult context, learning in a compensatory mode, making up for that which was either lost or not offered when the student was of school age—as something exceptional and special, rather than as a routine activity that corresponds to a phase of "natural" development.

There may be many reasons for these misconceptions, but one of them certainly is the value that "literacy" (if we mean mass and campaigning approaches to adult literacy, such as those initiatives connected with radical educators like Paulo Freire[1] or national liberation movements and anti-imperialist governments such as those in Cuba, Vietnam, Guinea-Bissau, Chile, or Nicaragua) puts upon transforming *consciousness*, and in particular social and political consciousness. For whereas such consciousness may be seen as part and parcel of progressive, modern literacy processes involving adults, "teaching children to read and write"—whatever the method being used, from phonetic approaches, "look and say," and the use of reading schemes to the so-called real books method—is still largely viewed as a routine, unpolitical, non-consciousness-raising process, just a phase of learning (albeit a vital one, since there is so much controversy and heat about what is the "best" method) of a child's state-organized primary education.

So there is "literacy," which adult students do (although ironically, in mass campaigns as in Nicaragua and Ethiopia, schoolchildren are often the *teachers*[2]), and "learning how to read and write," which child students do every day in their schools throughout the "developed" world. The discomfort many schoolteachers of language may feel in considering what they do as teaching "literacy" may well be connected to the implication that whereas "teaching reading and writing" is simply and mechanically teaching the decontextualized skills to achieve just and only that with a child, *literacy* means going completely against the accepted grain of school life and culture, abandoning curriculum "neutrality" and "objectivity" and concerning oneself with the "adults only" ingredient of raising consciousness through the selection of "provocative" or "propagandist" content or contexts.

Literacy and school

As a teacher of English in the British state school system of education, I, and many other teachers, have always challenged this apparent consensus on the "neutrality" of language teaching and curriculum. In other state systems of education where I have taught and contributed—such as those in Mozambique, Grenada, and Ethiopia—there have been foundations based upon revolutionary transformations in state power and the subsequent reordering of state educational provision. In such contexts, this neutrality concept, bogus as it has always proved to be in Britain, has been swiftly or progressively abandoned and replaced by an alternative structure and a declared ideological and practical determination to support the cause and advancement of the working people and the peasantry.

In 1975, in the introduction to my book *Classrooms of Resistance*,[3] I wrote as a young teacher from a classroom in East London that "working class children should learn to read, write, spell, punctuate, to develop the word as a weapon and tool in the inevitable struggles for improvement and liberation for them, and the rest of their class all over the world." To me, this was what literacy was all about. Nothing in my subsequent educational experiences, from teaching in postindependence Mozambique, to leading an innovative teacher education program in revolutionary Grenada, to now being a head teacher in a British inner-city comprehensive school, has made me change my mind on that statement and all its implications. The imperative task facing the language teacher, of ensuring that his or her students fully develop a knowledge, understanding, and ability to use to their full the language resources they will need in their lives, still holds primacy over all the other tasks, and has, indeed, never been so important as it is now.

Yet to detach the social and political context of working-class children's literacy from the skills that it involves for reasons of a spurious "neutrality" has always been and continues to be as pedagogically crippling as it is politically and morally wrong. That children, like adults—as shown millions of times over by Freire in Brazil or by the literacy processes in Guinea-Bissau, Nicaragua, Ethiopia, Grenada, or the struggling barrios of Mexico City or La Paz[4]—learn best when they read their own worlds as well as their own words, has also been demonstrated in the *schools* of those same countries countless times and continues to be the truth in British inner-city classrooms, or those holding children from oppressed and exploited sections of the population anywhere in the world where they learn. This is why the insights of mass literacy campaigns have always been as relevant to schoolchildren and their teachers as they are to adult learners and educators. Children can never be too young to use their skills-in-acquisition of literacy to confront, criticize, or question, as well as to form their own rational attitudes to issues arising from their own world, whether it be the state of their school or street, the taxes or rents paid by their parents, the suffering or struggles of other human beings or life anywhere on their planet, or current questions of peace, war, consent, or resistance. In all these areas and contexts of learning and teaching, skills and consciousness go hand in hand.

The third dimension

Yet there is another vital dimension, and that is the *imagination,* which can turn a moribund and static form of language teaching into a vibrant, living literacy. In the poem that follows, a ten-year-old boy from a Sheffield primary school considers literacy—and in particular the tool of writing and language, the pencil—from the imaginative perspective of an Ethiopian school student who has taken part in his nation's mass literacy campaign by teaching illiterate adults within his own family.[5] By this act of learning about learning through imaginative empathy, he brings forward new insights about the functions of literacy in his own life, as well as in another life thousands of miles away, and expands his own burgeoning use of words and ideas:

It's only a pencil

Here I am looking at something that holds my whole life.
If I let it go my life will be gone.
Not only my life, but my family's as well.
But who cares? After all, it's only a pencil.

It's only a pencil, but look what I can do with it.
I can write a letter for help with it.
I can learn at school with it.
I can teach my family with it—
If only we had more pencils and less guns.

Joe Carlisle

"More pencils and less guns": within that new and discovered combination of reflection and words are unexpected meanings which stretch the poetry of a Yorkshire child writing in a Sheffield classroom to the crux of political tensions and inequalities across the entire world. Thus his achievement has centered upon the exercise of three developing areas of his education: skills, consciousness, and the imagination—all essential components of a school literacy process and, in his case, all in balance and working in cooperation.

At this point we should consider what happens when these components get out of balance or become divorced from each other, or when undue emphasis is taken off one and put onto another. As I have already argued, the teaching of "reading and writing" in schools, as opposed to the teaching of *literacy* in schools, has only rarely been concerned with the development of a critical consciousness among children. It was certainly a vehicle for teaching children to imbibe approved and establishment attitudes and consciousness, the ways of thinking and acting that were licensed and approved by the ruling interests in the state and the economy. These involved support for the status quo, for Empire, for King or Queen and country, and for its prevailing social, cultural, and economic systems. The dozens of reading schemes and early childhood reading books give unending testimony to this unquestioning, consenting, and uncritical child's reading universe, a cosmos of Empire and Britain that was implanted in the mind of the colonized child too, all over the world, as well as deeply into the psyche of the child of the British working class. This is what this child found herself in for generations through the books she had to read at school: the settled, cuddly middle-class life of Janet and John, Peter and Jane, their families, cozy streets, holidays by the seaside, their large gardens and dogs and cats. It was this world, always white and comfortable, that she was projected into by her school, no matter how little her actual life resembled this read and distant version of reality. It was this world that she had to exchange for her own when she entered the doors of the school reading curriculum.

Much of this stereotyped and regulated approach in Britain changed with the liberal and child-centered ideas of primary school signaled by the 1967 Plowden Report.[6] This put the individual *child*, rather than children and their *communities*, at the focal point of school life and curriculum. "At the heart of the educational process is the child," declared the report in its introductory passages. One result of this shift as manifested in the teaching of reading and writing was a move from an emphasis on "sheer skills" toward "sheer creativity" and self-expression, which often damaged further the opportunities for working-class children to become proficient readers and writers. For those children coming from homes or whole communities where parents were illiterate in English or spoke a language other than English, the deemphasising of the *skills* dimension of literacy was even more serious and handicapping, particularly because throughout the seventies and much of the eighties there was a devaluation of standard English as a common language currency. It became fashionable among some "progressive" educationists to portray standard English as solely the language of suburbia and therefore not applicable to the language needs of working-class and black children, and much more stress was put on the validity of regional and Creole dialects, "mother tongues," and working-class varieties of English as vehicles for language learning. Although much of this emphasis was valuable, according new recognition to the strength and founding power of the underlying first language, it too often threw the kernel of proficiency in the standard language out with the reactionary cultural content it was wrapped inside.[7]

A new complexity

The growing presence in the British inner-city classrooms throughout the seventies and eighties of potentially bilingual children of primary and secondary school age who were categorized as ESL (English as a second language) learners also caused more overall effort to be put toward "literacy" teaching, although the very low number of bilingual teachers in schools made bilingual language teaching a rare, even though much wished for, phenomenon. But this new situation throughout British inner cities raised some key questions which questioning and radical teachers strove to answer for the sake of *all* their students, including those from the white working class who were also experiencing a lack of success in the learning of literacy— questions which went to the very heart of their pedagogy. Where does "literacy" teaching stop (if it ever stops) and English, language arts, humanities, or whatever it happened to be called in particular schools, begin? Can there be a line of demarcation? And what about the situation, now increasingly *usual* (rather than uncommon or exceptional) in working-class or inner-city schools, where those who are literate in basics as native English users, but have a very limited knowledge of the standard language, share classrooms and curriculum with those who are illiterate or semiliterate in the standard language or *any* variety of English? And how is a unified language strategy to be developed where the historical language complexities are governed by class difference, whereby children with dialectal and regional variants of English who have always had difficulties in coming to terms with standard English share school and learning with children with underlaid languages like Punjabi, Hindi, Bengali, Arabic, Somali, Turkish, Greek, or the Caribbean Creole languages? And where these same speakers pass through an informal peer learning phase of language during which they speak the English of East London, Sheffield, Glasgow, or Liverpool before they come to grips with the standard English of their school curriculum (now increasingly taking the form of a narrow and uniform national curriculum[8]), how can the question of literacy in school be simply resolved by "teaching them how to read and write" in the early years of primary education?

In such a complexity of language and learning situations, can teachers of language ever be free of the need and responsibility to teach literacy, as an integral part of language teaching itself? Then literacy, like education itself, becomes more than a school-long process; it becomes a lifelong process too, and across the entire curriculum of the school, not just in "language" or

"English" lessons. A part of the answer to such questions must be to envisage the advance of literacy in the British inner-city classroom as a dialogue, a communal learning act, not only in the sense of a cooperative, life-exchanging process between teacher and student, but even more importantly a communion among the student body, among the minds, skills, and imaginations that make up the cohort of the classroom in all "subject" areas. These individuals add up to a combination of separate communities, interweaving histories and interdependent cultures and nations all gathered for the tasks of learning, yet all starting from variously and pointedly different points of arrival—linguistically, as in many other dimensions. Thus schools must take a central responsibility to bring cohesion and unity to a heterogeneous community: to move away from the context of solely serving the individual child to serving the entire community of learners. And to change the maxim quoted earlier from the Plowden Report: "At the centre of the educational process is the school: at the heart of the school is the community."

A communality of peace

The spinal cord of this communal dialogue must be a commitment to *peace*, in both its detailed affirmation in questions of human activity between individuals from different communities learning together in the same school, and its wider and principled application to social justice, cooperation, and friendship throughout the world, between all peoples and nations. Certainly in British inner-city classrooms, and following the horrific watershed of the racist playground murder of Ahmed Ullah at Burnage High School in Manchester in September 1986,[9] the words once coined by Fidel Castro have never been more apt: "The cause of peace and the cause of the working class march side by side." In the learning and teaching context of literacy that is described in the pages that follow, *peace* is certainly the overall theme of the material being considered and developed, and during a period when, as a twelve-year-old Greek Cypriot expressed it once in an East London classroom, it was at its most stretched and fragile:

> Peace is trembling
> Like a tooth just about to pop.
> Peace should always be with us.

I am referring to December 1990 and the critical period leading up to the expiry of the United Nations deadline ordering the Iraqi troops of President Saddam Hussein to withdraw from Kuwait, which had been invaded the previous August and later annexed. There had been a continuous hectoring by both sides throughout this confrontation, as U.S. troops and their commanders, supported enthusiastically by those of Britain and less so by other nations, had assembled in Saudi Arabia to the south of Kuwait and in a standoff with the Iraqi armies had built up their Operation Desert Shield in readiness to attack the Iraqis if they did not withdraw from Kuwait. With the day-to-day stoking up of war fever by the British tabloid press and Tory and Labor politicians, the moral and religious all clear to begin the conflict being given by church leaders, and the warmongering and buffoonery of U.S. President George Bush and Secretary of State James Baker using the fig leaf of U.N. resolutions against Iraq but with their minds fixed on Kuwaiti oil and on preserving the client leadership of the expelled Sabah Kuwaiti ruling dynasty, the chances of a peaceful solution to the Gulf conflict were fast receding, as from the other side came the strident and uncompromising vows that "Americans would swim in their own blood" if there were war.

From Sheffield to Palestine

This was the broader world context of the work which follows. The much more local context was of a group of thirteen-year-old students from various communities studying in a Sheffield comprehensive school and working to improve their command of English literacy by focusing on the key to lasting and genuine peace in the Middle East: the resolution to the question of Palestine, and in particular to the Israeli occupation of the territories of the West Bank, this at a time when anti-Arab racism in Britain was at its most virulent for many years largely because of the tabloid reaction to the depredations in Kuwait provoked by Saddam Hussein's armies. Newspapers like Rupert Murdoch's *Sun* have a long and shameful history of attacking Arabs and Muslims generally, sparked by their hatred of such leaders as Gaddafi or

Khomeini in the Middle East and of Muslims struggling against the effects of racism in Britain.[10] Certainly this tabloid hype was contributing to anti-Arab feeling in Sheffield, and being directed toward the local community of Yemenis, many of whose children attended the school. During this same period Yemenis living in the neighborhood of the school had felt this increased level of racism, and their community center close to the school had been daubed with racist slogans.

Thus a combination of the enemies of peace near and far—the threat of armed conflict, hostile propaganda and attacks by a reactionary media, racism, and ignorance—all contributed to the setting for the classroom work on Palestine. The significant Arab presence in the school (there were students from Syrian, Jordanian, Saudi Arabian, and Libyan families also attending, plus an Iraqi teacher who was a refugee from the Saddam Hussein regime) gave this project an additional resonance. The strong Yemeni community association, composed of the families of the Yemeni arrivants who had come to work as unskilled laborers in Sheffield's steel industry in the fifties and sixties, held its Arabic language school three evenings a week in the school buildings and organized a community literacy campaign (in both Arabic and English) in a base in a nearby primary school. The students in the classes concerned were a cross-section of students from the local Yemeni, Pakistani, Somali, and white communities. So at least four languages were at work, including the Sheffield variety of English. The school itself was involved in preparations to create a link with a secondary school in the city of Ramallah on the West Bank as a part of its commitment to internationalism, and the Sheffield students were being encouraged to write letters in both English and Arabic to school students there, in order to consolidate some of this exchange work and to get to know the Palestinian students as pen pals.

The project began with a study of Palestine's recent history, the creation of the state of Israel, the wars against Israel's Arab neighbors, and the 1967 occupation of the West Bank. The television film *Children of Fire*,[11] telling of experiences of the young people of the West Bank city of Nablus in their *Intifada* against the Israeli occupation, was shown and made a deep impression, particularly upon the Arabic-speaking students, who needed no recourse to subtitles. Discussions of the content of this film were followed up by reading a series of poems about Palestine mostly by Palestinian writers. There was also "Lullabye to a Palestinian Child" (translated from the Urdu) by the outstanding Pakistani poet Faiz Ahmad Faiz, which had a very strong impact, especially since so many of the students were of Pakistani origin. Poems by Mahmoud Darwish,[12] such as "Identity Card," "Victim Number 18," "Weddings," and "The First Date," communicated with a simple power the thoughts and feelings of the Palestinian people, as did some of the short and pithy poems of another Palestinian, Samih al-Qasim.[13] Since we had the poems in their original Arabic available, we were able to have bilingual readings in the classroom: first the poems in Arabic, read out loud by one of the Arabic speakers, and then the English translation.

The linking imagination

The first response of the students was to the Faiz poem. A Pakistani girl, Sufarah, wrote as if she were a child responding to the soothing lullabye of her mother, but with words of indignation and struggle:

Child of Palestine

Please don't cry Mum,
When I grow up I'll fight the soldiers with a gun.
They can break my flesh and bones
But the only weapons I have are stones.
With my friends and families too
I will fight these soldiers for you.
Don't cry Mum,
I always dreamed I could play out without fear,
But every time I do, the soldiers appear.
When I grip those stones
I feel that I could break their bones.

Don't cry Mum,
When I grow up, one day,
I'll make those soldiers regret and pay.
They have closed our schools and relationships—
Don't cry Mum,
Now I am part of the *Intifada* Mum.
Don't cry Mum,

I had a dream that we defeated the soldiers
And had our country back with us in peace.
Don't cry Mum!

Sufurah Bibi

Another young Pakistani poet, Faheem, composed his couplets in a determined appeal for peace and justice:

Intifada

Why does it have to be this way,
Bullying at night and fighting all day?
I throw stones and rocks with my own bare hands,
Remembering my brother who lay dead in the sands.
Shot by the army and the police—
We don't want a war, we want peace!
Why does it have to be like this,
Losing your family without a bless or a kiss?
I'm losing a part of my life everyday,
Why can't we just throw war away?
I walk the streets in fear of a soldier,
My fist clenched, and within it a boulder.
We all fight as one under the sun,
Yet this war has not been won.
We throw stones, they pull the trigger,
What falls to the ground is a tall, dark figure.
"Ayman Jamous! Ayman Jamous!"
Why can't we call this war to a truce?

Faheem Khan

There was no doubt that the film *Children of Fire* had strongly moved the students. The footage and vivid images of the Palestinian children stoning the Israeli soldiers, the long hours of the curfew, the death of the young *shebab* Ayman Jamous and the Israeli's refusal to allow his body to be released after his killing, the day-by-day disruption to the schooling of Palestinian children—all prompted the viewers to raise these issues in their letters to the students of Ramallah, as if they were asking for confirmation in words of what they had seen so starkly on the screen:

I was very sad because I saw soldiers beat up very small children, and kill some children. I felt very sad when I heard about a young boy who got

killed called Ayman Jamous and the soldiers would not hand his body to his
family, and they only allowed ten people to come and bury him at night.

And when I saw those little children throwing stones at those big
soldiers who have got guns, my heart felt for them and those little babies
who have got shot and killed. How do those soldiers do it, breaking into
schools and homes and slapping children and closing the schools down?
How do they do it? I wonder how it feels being there with all those soldiers
around you and you can't do anything about it? This has never happened in
England.

Or again, from another Pakistani girl:

At school we watched a programme about the sort of life a Palestinian
child leads. It differs very much from ours. Ours is very simple whereas
yours is to fight for your rights. In the programme very young children were
fighting the soldiers back with stones. They promised themselves they
would win. After the programme I had knowledge about your lives, how you
risk them. What with the soldiers carrying guns and all you have is stones.
It was very painful for us to watch that programme. I know that we children
in Britain would not have the same courage that you carry in your hearts.

The communal language was extending beyond the classroom, beyond the
nation: now between Sheffield and Ramallah, but also through the pain and
resistance of the children of Nablus, as the young people asked their questions and sought authentic answers from those across the world who, alone,
know.

Other poems were now emerging about the *Intifada*, as young Shef-
fielders took on, through their living imaginations, the struggles of the young
Palestinians:

A Child of Palestine

No school today
No school tomorrow,
Soldiers closed it down.
We fight today
We fight tomorrow,
Then sleep a sleepless night.

Life is a nightmare
That the *Intifada* is trying to change.
Maybe soon
Maybe too late
Maybe today
Or maybe tomorrow—
Soon, we hope and pray

Stones in hand
Ready to throw,
maybe now
And forever more!

Dreams of the future
In our minds.
Peace will never come too soon,
We've waited long enough.

Why don't they go?
And leave us alone.
Give us back our land
And leave us in peace—
Because we'll never leave,
Here we'll stay.

Tricks and games
They play,
leave us bombs
Wrapped like chocolate
For little children killed this way.

We children are
Beaten and hit
By soldiers that should be far away.
Our homes are wrecked
And yet we have to stay inside.
Curfew times we have—
They're not worthy to live and laugh.

Soon we hope that peace will come,
I hope that war's not just begun!

We play games
As we live,
Play—fight

Then fight for real,
No weapons but stones.

Even babies
Are shot and killed,
Families grow very close.

We wish
For peace and tranquillity,
We've lived like this
For too long.

Yet we'll never give up without a fight!
We have the right!

Marie Howe

Child of Palestine

Fighting for my rights,
Risking my life.
Me and my friends playing with stones,
Then going out and fighting with stones.
Small or big it's just the same—
Get caught by the soldiers, get beaten or shot,
Lighting fires on the streets so the soldiers won't get us.
Close the school, take the children and beat them,
Make you stay at home all day and night in the curfew.
But we will still make our flag stay in the air!

Mumtaz Ali

Intifada

As the last stones of freedom slip through my fingers, hate
    and anger run through my body.
Why doesn't my country belong to me? Why do I feel like
    a prisoner in my own home?
Our family were never so close, but the fighting has
    brought us closer. We all seem to be one,
fighting for the same thing.

My brother and I used to fight side by side in the streets,
    until one day there was a loud noise

and my brother fell to the ground just like a ripe apple
would.

My brother to me will always be a hero, a martyr who died
for his beliefs.

I just hope it ends soon, so my brother's soul can rest like
the others.

And Palestine can be one again.

Corin Ovendale

And a Somali boy looked beyond Israel, toward the weapons suppliers and
profiteers of Israeli repression beyond the Atlantic.

Intifada

Life in Palestine is unbearable. I call it Palestine because it's my
country, not theirs. It's a Muslim country, not a Jewish country. In our
school it's another day, another death. They come and kill. Why, I ask
myself, why oh Allah, do they kill us and beat us up? Our playground, it's
pure blood red. Boys and girls with their brains beaten out. We do not
believe in guns or bombs or making them die. We just want them to leave
us, our families, our friends, our houses and our homeland.

We throw stones, they pull the trigger. What is their hobby, murder?
Or is it the enjoyment of seeing us suffer with pain and sorrow? When we
throw, they get grazed. When they shoot, we die. How can they sleep,
knowing they've killed someone's loved one? Old women, men, children
and babies? They will not rest until they've wiped us out. In the West
people have freedom and love, but the Israelis do not know the word *love*,
nor loyalty. All they know is murder and violence.

Every night for two years I wept for my family who were killed for
swearing at the soldiers. I was out shopping and when I came back I saw the
blood of my family. I want my Mum to wipe my eyes and cuddle me, and my
father to pick me up and swing me, my brother to play games with me like
football and my only sister to love me like her baby. But alas, they've gone

now. I live in the mountains at night and throw stones in the light. One day we shall live as people and not as hostages in our homes.

For every Palestinian that dies, the days get closer when we will rule our country. Until that time we wait until Allah gives us our birthright back, and then we won't shoot the Israelis. We'll let their consciences sort out what's wrong or right. America can help us by stopping their supply of weapons. But to them, money is more precious than life.

Musa Ibrahim

These passages were in their own way, through the power of their imaginative empathy, recreating Palestine in the minds of the students. This process of imaginative fire, entering the lives of others, was expressed very nakedly by one of the Pakistani girls, who wrote: "Don't just think about yourself, think about other people in the world. They may be in the war, while we are in England." The same point was made by another girl writing about the young people of South Africa, struggling in the townships against the effects of apartheid:

Immortal

They'll live forever,
And never die.
They're joined to us,
More than ever.

We breathe for them.
Fight for them,
Live for them.
We *are* them.

Sallie Higgins[14]

Now it was Palestine, and Sajid, another Pakistani boy, directly provoked by the lyrics of Mahmoud Darwish, imagined himself as the lover of a Palestinian patriot who leaves to carry on a struggle from exile:

Love in Palestine

Now you go to fight,
How do I know if you will return?
You have gone now,
The time has passed and you're not back.
Oh my love, your children cry!
I hope you will be here to see them live.
For a year now I have been waiting
For you to walk through that door!

Sajid Mustafa

And Leanne, after reading some testimonies describing the daily routine of patrolling Israeli soldiers who were ordered to harass Palestinian school students, disrupt their classes, and close their schools,[15] decided to set down her version of such a soldier's experiences, and the shame and tension racking his brain:

The Side of the Soldiers

A Palestinian child started throwing stones at me. Some of them come very close to hitting me. It hurts me deep down inside to see that all the children hate me. I can understand why the *adults* hate me but why does it have to be a child? Some of them are only three to five years of age. It gives me pain to see the children hating me so much and them being so young. I know I shouldn't, but I keep a diary of what happens day by day. If anyone finds out I would be punished and the diary would be destroyed.

These are some of the days in the diary, some of the worst days, that is.

Monday 15th November

Today we made a scene in the school and all the kids stopped what they were doing and looked at me with anger and hatred in their faces. The teacher was stood there looking very timid, frightened and frozen stiff with fear. The children started throwing paper at us. A piece of paper hit one of the soldiers and it made him mad. He walked very boldly up to the child and started hitting him. He hit the boy across the face with the end of his gun. Blood gushed from the boy's face. The soldier then kicked him and threw him against a wall. There was blood everywhere.

Only three of us went into that school and yet we caused so much pain towards that child. Silence broke, and we left, feeling guilt and rage inside us.

Friday 19th November

Today we walked the streets angry. A woman was trying to hurry up and get inside her house. She was pregnant. She was scared of losing her baby, you could tell by the look on her face. It said *fear* all over.

She swore at us, so one of the soldiers came up to her and kicked her in the stomach. She swore at us and fell to the ground with pain. I turned away in disgust. I went up to her and with pain inside me, hit her across the face with the end of my gun. We took her away with us. All the people came out of their doors, screaming for her. I also felt their pain.

Some of the soldiers started trying to kiss her. She turned away, so they shot her for her rejection. I just stood there watching.

Nearly every day was like this. Either some one got hurt, or they were killed by us. I am not proud of what I have done but it is too late now because I am a part of the hate and pain. I am now destroying my diary in fear of someone finding it.

Leanne Carter

Among the many poems, letters, and prose passages coming directly from these students' engagement with Palestine and its people's striving for peace with justice was this poem, which, in the week after it was written, was read out loud by its author to the assembled parents, students, and school governors at the school's Presentation Evening. The poem followed closely upon the event of October 1990, when twenty-one young Palestinians were killed by Israeli soldiers in Jerusalem, as they demonstrated to defend the Temple Mount mosque. A national black newspaper[16] had published a harrowing photograph in the aftermath of these events, depicting the father of one of the victims praying on the flagstones at the exact place where his son had been shot down. Nadia, a Yemeni girl, tried to express with her poem the terrible grief of this father, the loss and denials that were deep in his mind— and which in the final line turn into his stolen country itself.

My Son

My son
Who I loved dearly,
Who protected the Holy House

My son,
Of all the sons in the world,
Who got shot and killed
And who loved his family

My son
Who I protected all my life
Brought up
And bred,
Who I lived my life for.
Now I don't care
Whether I live or die.

My son,
I pray on your blood,
Hoping you would come back—
Why couldn't it be me instead?
I'll do anything to get you back!

When I saw him
Lying there
On the stones,
Helpless and cold
I did not want to believe it.
He was dead.
When my son fell down dead on the stones
I felt I could weep forever!
So everyone in the world could hear me.
People asked "Why, why do you weep?"
I told them if you take a knife
And cut part of yourself—
You would feel pain and cry.
That's why I weep—
Because I feel the pain!

The saddest thing is, he was so young,
Like a flower
Just bloomed within Spring

And suddenly, just died
In front of my eyes!

I felt the life just slip from my body,
And this pain is shared
With every Palestinian—
Young and old!

My son
What have you done to deserve this?
I was just looking forward
To carry your first-born!

My son,
It was not so long ago
That I held you in my arms with joy and pride—
The first moment you were born.

Now my son
I hold you
Dead in my arms,
My heart filled with sorrow,
My eyes filled with tears
And all this for you, my Palestine!

Nadia Saleh

Literacy, the imagination, and peace

The twin hopes of peace and justice were never far from these children's
words. Yet all around them, in the newspapers their parents read, in the
television screens that dominated their living rooms, and in the sounds from
their radios, were reports and images of the relentless training and maneu-
vers of the thousands of troops, tanks, aircraft, and warships being primed in
Saudi Arabia and readied for attack. Prophecies of chemical, biological, and
nuclear warfare, together with the endless burning of oilfields and environmental disasters, were being declared day after day. Even one of their own
schoolmates, a local boy with a Saudi Arabian father, who had been on an
extended visit to his family in the Gulf, had been called up for military
service by the Saudi army, and the school was writing letters to the authorities of that country, petitioning for him to be released so he could

return to England and continue his studies at the school. Sick, warmongering humor was the order of the day, featuring so-called comedians like Jim Davidson—the favorite comedian of the British Armed Forces—whose answer to his own question: "What have Baghdad and Hiroshima got in common?" was "Nothing—yet!" To be building up their own language, together—with such a growing understanding of the injustices behind the tension and violence in a critical region of the world, and using their imaginations to reach into the consciousness of those truly involved, to achieve that understanding—all this was not easy in the heart of such unpromising and bellicose surroundings.

Yet such work, a part of a curriculum of extended literacy for young people that fuses the abilities to develop new skills with words, to sharpen human consciousness and stretch the imagination to enter the lives of others in a shared world, creating new, communal forms of expression, becomes more and more essential in our schools, even as the stranglehold of the state's "national curriculum" seeks to squeeze out such human solidarity and breadth of understanding.[17] Certainly the young Sheffield students recognized very quickly the bond that the Palestinian people felt with their own country—their "life-land," as one girl expressed it. Their understanding had already traveled a long distance. And as I write this, on the third day of the war against Iraq (19/1/91), I am reading an essay written spontaneously by one of our Yemeni students who has been learning English only a few months. She set down these words on the day war broke out and allied planes and missiles fell upon Baghdad.

Why the War?

I don't know what I can say about this problem. Really it is a big problem because we do not know what will happen.

I really don't like the war and everyone I know doesn't like the war. Why the war, why?

I get in my head more questions about this problem . . . why when Israel went to Palestine did no one do anything, it's just all countries said "It's not my problem, it is a Palestine problem."

Why does no country care about the Palestine problem? . . . I want to ask America, England and all the countries why in an Arab area have these countries come to help Kuwait?

I know some people from America and England don't like the war and don't want to go to Kuwait to fight because it is not their country . . . but the heads of state want to help Kuwait not because they love Kuwait, not all this, it's because they want oil. I am sorry if I said this . . . but this is all in my head.

I don't like the war so please leave the Arabic countries to solve this problem themselves. I really want to see all Arabic countries working together, not as like they do now.

Notes

1. See Freire, P., *Pedagogy of the Oppressed* (London: Penguin, 1972), *Education: the Practice of Freedom* (London: Writers and Readers, 1974), *Pedagogy in Process* (London: Writers and Readers, 1978), and *Literacy: Reading the Word and the World* (London: Routledge, 1987).

2. See Hirshon, S., *And Also Teach Them to Read* (Westport, Conn.: Lawrence Hill, 1983); and Lankshear, C., with Lawler, M., *Literacy, Schooling and Revolution* (Sussex: Falmer Press, 1987), for excellent accounts of the literacy campaign in Nicaragua.

Searle, C., *A Blindfold Removed: Ethiopia's Struggle for Literacy* (London: Karia, 1991), describes the literacy campaign in Ethiopia.

3. Searle, C., *Classrooms of Resistance* (London: Writers and Readers, 1975). See also *The World in a Classroom* (London: Writers and Readers, 1977).

4. For an account of the literacy campaign in Grenada, see Searle, C., *Words Unchained: Language and Revolution in Grenada* (London: Zed Press, 1984). For descriptions of literacy processes in Bolivia and Mexico, read *Literacy and Power: The Latin American Battleground*, by David Archer and Patrick Costello (London: Earthscan, 1990).

5. See Searle (1991), *op. cit.*

6. *Children and Their Primary Schools: A Report of the Central Council for Education*, vol. 1, part 2: *The Growth of the Child*, London, 1967.

7. See Searle, C., "A Common Language," *Race and Class*, 25, Autumn 1983, Institute of Race Relations, London.

8. See Searle, C., "From Foster to Baker: The New Struggle for

Education," *Race and Class*, 30, April–June 1989, Institute of Race Relations, London.

9. See *Murder in the Playground: The Report of the MacDonald Inquiry into Racism and Racial Violence in Manchester Schools* (London: Longsight Press, 1989).

10. See Searle, C., *Your Daily Dose: Racism and the 'Sun'*, Campaign for Press and Broadcasting Freedom, London, 1989.

11. *Children of Fire*, a film by Mai Masri: MTC Productions, London, 1990.

12. See Darwish, M., *The Music of Human Flesh* (London: Heinemann, 1980), and *Victims of a Map* (London: Al Saqi, 1984).

13. See Darwish (1984), *ibid*.

14. See *Freedom Children: A tribute in Poetry to the Young People of South Africa from the Young People of Sheffield*, Sheffield City Council, 1990.

15. See Israeli soldiers' accounts in Aronson, G., *Israel, Palestinians and the Intifada* (London: Kegan Paul International, 1990).

16. *Caribbean Times*, London, 27 October 1990.

17. *Morning Star*, London, 4 January 1991.

6

Between moral regulation and democracy: The cultural contradictions of the text

Michael W. Apple

For most people, literacy has a nonpolitical function. It is there supposedly to help form the intellectual character of a person and to provide paths to upward mobility. Yet the process of defining both what counts as literacy and how it should be gained has always had links to particular regimes of morality as well. Literacy was often there to produce economic skills and a shared system of beliefs and values, to help create a "national culture." As the author of a recent volume on newly emerging redefinitions of literacy in education has put it, it served as something of a "moral technology of the soul."[1]

An emphasis on literacy as both "moral technology" and economically driven skills is of course not the only way one could and should approach the issue. The value of writing, speaking, and listening should not be seen as access to "refined culture" or to "life skills" for our allotted (by whom?) places in the paid and unpaid labor market, but as a crucial means to gain power and control over our entire lives. Our aim should be to create not "functional literacy," but *critical* literacy, *powerful* literacy, *political* literacy which enables the growth of genuine understanding and control of all of the spheres of social life in which we participate.[2]

Take the word *culture*. Culture—the way of life of a people, the constant and complex process by which meanings are made and shared—does not

193

grow out of the pregiven unity of a society. Rather, in many ways, it grows out of its divisions. It has to *work* to construct any unity it has. The idea of culture should not be used to "celebrate an achieved or natural harmony." Culture is instead "a producer and reproducer of value systems and power relations."[3]

The same is true for the way we think about knowledge. Speaking theoretically, John Fiske reminds us of this.

> Knowledge is never neutral, it never exists in an empiricist, objective relationship to the real. Knowledge is power, and the circulation of knowledge is part of the social distribution of power. The discursive power to construct a commonsense reality that can be inserted into cultural and political life is central in the social relationship of power. The power of knowledge has to struggle to exert itself in two dimensions. The first is to control the "real," to reduce reality to the knowable, which entails producing it as a discursive construct whose arbitrariness and inadequacy are disguised as far as possible. The second struggle is to have this discursively (and therefore sociopolitically) constructed reality accepted as truth by those whose interests may not necessarily be served by accepting it. Discursive power involves a struggle both to construct (a sense of) reality and to circulate that reality as widely and smoothly as possible throughout society.[4]

Now Fiske's language may perhaps be a bit too abstract here, but his points are essential. They point to the relationship among what counts as knowledge, who has power and how power actually functions in our daily lives, and, finally, how this determines what we see as "real" and important in our institutions in general and in education in particular. In this chapter, I want to focus on one particular aspect of education that helps define what "reality" is and how it is connected to critical, powerful, and political literacy in contradictory ways.

Whose knowledge is of most worth?

Reality, then, doesn't stalk around with a label. What something is, what it does, one's evaluation of it—all this is not naturally preordained. It is socially constructed. This is the case even when we talk about the institutions that organize a good deal of our lives. Take schools, for example. For some groups of people, schooling is seen as a vast engine of democracy—opening horizons, ensuring mobility, and so on. For others, the reality of schooling is strikingly different. It is seen as a form of social control, or perhaps as the embodiment of cultural dangers, effected within institutions whose curricula and teaching practices threaten the moral universe of the students who attend them. Although not all of us may agree with this diagnosis of what schools do, this latter position contains a very important insight. It recognizes that behind Spencer's famous question, "What knowledge is of most worth?" there lies another even more contentious question, "*Whose* knowledge is of most worth?"

During the past two decades, a good deal of progress has been made in answering the question of whose knowledge becomes socially legitimate in schools.[5] Although much still remains to be understood, we are now much closer to having an adequate understanding of the relationship between school knowledge and the larger society than before. Yet little attention has actually been paid to that one artifact that plays such a major role in defining whose culture is taught: *the textbook*. Of course, there have been literally thousands of studies of textbooks over the years.[6] But, by and large, until relatively recently, most of these remained unconcerned with the politics of culture. All too many researchers could still be characterized by the phrase coined years ago by C. Wright Mills, "abstract empiricists." These "hunters and gatherers of social numbers" remain unconnected to the relations of inequality that surround them.[7]

This is a distinct problem, since texts are not simply "delivery systems" of "facts." They are at once the results of political, economic, and cultural activities, battles, and compromises. They are conceived, designed, and authored by real people with real interests. They are published within the political and economic constraints of markets, resources, and power.[8] And what texts mean and how they are used are fought over by communities with distinctly different commitments and by teachers and students as well.

As I have argued in a series of volumes, it is naive to think of the school curriculum as neutral knowledge.[9] Rather, what counts as legitimate knowledge is the result of complex power relations and struggles among identifiable class, race, gender, and religious groups. Thus *education* and *power* are terms of an indissoluble couplet. It is at times of social upheaval that this relationship between education and power becomes most visible. Such a relationship was and continues to be made manifest in the struggles by women, people of color, and others to have their history and knowledge included in the curriculum. Driven by an economic crisis and a crisis in ideology and authority relations, it has become even more visible in the past decade or so in the resurgent conservative attacks on schooling. "Authoritarian populism" is in the air, and the New Right has been more than a little successful in bringing its own power to bear on the goals, content, and process of schooling.[10]

The movement to the right has not stopped outside the schoolroom door, as you well know. Current plans for the centralization of authority over teaching and curriculum, often cleverly disguised as "democratic" reforms, are hardly off the drawing board before new management proposals or privatization initiatives are introduced. In the United States, evidence for such offensives abounds with the introduction of mandatory competency testing for students and teachers, the calls for a return to a (romanticized) common curriculum, the reduction of educational goals to those primarily of business and industry, the proposals for voucher or "choice" plans, the pressure to legislate morality and values from the right, and the introduction of state-mandated content on "free enterprise" and the like. Similar tendencies are more than evident in Britain and in some cases are even more advanced.

All of this has brought about countervailing movements in the schools. The slower but still interesting growth of more democratically run schools, of practices and policies that give community groups and teachers considerably more authority in text selection and curriculum determination, in teaching strategy, in the use of funds, in administration, and in developing more flexible and less authoritarian evaluation schemes, is providing some cause for optimism in the midst of the conservative restoration.[11]

Even with these positive signs, however, it is clear that the New Right has been able to rearticulate traditional political and cultural themes. In so doing, it has often effectively mobilized a mass base of adherents. Among its most powerful causes and effects has been the growing feeling of disaffection about public schooling among conservative groups. Large numbers of parents and other people no longer trust either the institutions or the teachers and administrators in them to make "correct" decisions about what should be taught and how to teach it. The rapid growth of evangelical schooling, of censorship, and of textbook controversies and the emerging tendency of many parents to teach their children at home rather than send them to state-supported schools are clear indications of this loss of legitimacy.[12]

The ideology that stands behind this is often very complex. It combines a commitment to both the "traditional family" and clear gender roles with a commitment to "traditional values" and literal religiosity. Also often packed into this is a defense of capitalist economics, patriotism, the "Western tradition," anticommunism, and a deep mistrust of the "welfare state."[13] When this ideology is applied to schooling, the result can be as simple as dissatisfaction with an occasional book or assignment. On the other hand, the result can be a major conflict that threatens to go well beyond the boundaries of our usual debates about schooling.

Few places in the United States are more well known in this latter context than Kanawha County, West Virginia. In the mid-1970s, it became the scene of one of the most explosive controversies over what schools should teach, who should decide, and what beliefs should guide our educational programs. What began as a protest by a small group of conservative parents, religious leaders, and business people over the content and design of the textbooks that had been approved for use in local schools soon spread to include school boycotts, violence, and a wrenching split within the community that in many ways has yet to heal.

There were a number of important contributing factors that heightened tensions in West Virginia. Schools in rural areas had been recently consolidated. Class relations and relations between the country and the city were increasingly tense. The lack of participation by rural parents (or many parents at all, for that matter) in text selection or in educational decision making in general also led to increasing alienation. Furthermore, the cultural history of the region, with its fierce independence, its fundamentalist religious traditions, and its history of economic depression, helped create conditions for serious unrest. Finally, Kanawha County became a cause célèbre for national right-wing groups who offered moral, legal, and organizational support to the conservative activists there.[14]

It is important to realize, then, that controversies over "official knowledge" that usually center around what is included and excluded in textbooks really signify more profound political, economic, and cultural relations and histories. Conflicts over texts are often proxies for wider questions of power relations. They involve what people hold most dear. And, as in the case of Kanawha County, they can quickly escalate into conflicts over these deeper issues.

Yet, textbooks are surely important in and of themselves. They signify, through their content *and* form, particular constructions of reality, particular ways of selecting and organizing that vast universe of possible knowledge. They embody what Raymond Williams called the *selective tradition:* someone's selection, someone's vision of legitimate knowledge and culture, one that in the process of enfranchising one group's cultural capital disenfranchises another's.[15]

Texts are really messages to and about the future. As part of a curriculum, they participate in no less than the organized knowledge system of society. They participate in creating what a society has recognized as legitimate and truthful. They help set the canons of truthfulness and, as such, also help recreate a major reference point for what knowledge, culture, belief, and morality really *are*.[16] Yet such a statement, even with its recognition that texts participate in constructing ideologies and ontologies, is basically misleading in many important ways. For it is not a "society" that has created such texts, but specific groups of people. "We" haven't built such curriculum artifacts in the simple sense that there is universal agreement among all of us and therefore this is what gets to be official knowledge. In fact, the very use of the pronoun *we* simplifies matters all too much. As Fred Inglis so cogently argues, the pronoun *we* "smooths over the deep corrugations and ruptures caused precisely by struggle over how that authoritative and editorial 'we' is going to be used. The (text), it is not melodramatic to declare, really is the battleground for an intellectual civil war, and the battle for cultural authority is a wayward, intermittingly fierce, always protracted and fervent one."[17]

Let us give one example. In the 1930s, conservative groups in the United States mounted a campaign against one of the progressive textbook series in use in schools. *Man and His Changing World* by Harold Rugg and his colleagues became the subject of a concerted attack by the National Association of Manufacturers, the American Legion, the Advertizing Federation of America, and other "neutral" groups. They charged that Rugg's books were socialist, anti-American, antibusiness, and so forth. The conservative campaign was more than a little successful in forcing school districts to withdraw Rugg's series from classrooms and libraries. So successful were they that sales fell from nearly three hundred thousand copies in 1938 to only approximately twenty thousand in 1944.[18]

We, of course, may have reservations about such texts today, not least of which would be the sexist title. But one thing that the Rugg case makes clear is that the *politics* of the textbook is not something new by any means. Current issues surrounding texts—their ideology, their very status as central definers of what we should teach, even their very effectiveness and their design—echo the past moments of these concerns that have had such a long history in so many countries.

Few aspects of schooling currently have been subject to more intense scrutiny and criticism than the text. Perhaps one of the most graphic descriptions is provided by A. Graham Down of the Council for Basic Education.

> Textbooks, for better or worse, dominate what students learn. They set the curriculum, and often the facts learned, in most subjects. For many students, textbooks are their first and sometimes only early exposure to books and to reading. The public regards textbooks as authoritative, accurate and necessary. And teachers rely on them to organize lessons and structure subject matters. But the current system of textbook adoption has filled our schools with Trojan horses—glossily covered blocks of paper whose words emerge to deaden the minds of our nation's youth, and make them enemies of learning.[19]

This statement is made just as powerfully by the author of a recent study of what she has called "America's textbook fiasco":

> Imagine a public policy system that is perfectly designed to produce textbooks that confuse, mislead, and profoundly bore students, while at the same time making all of the adults involved in the process look good, not only in their own eyes, but in the eyes of others. Although there are some good textbooks on the market, publishers and editors are virtually compelled by public policies and practices to create textbooks that confuse

students with non sequiturs, that mislead them with misinformation, and that profoundly bore them with pointlessly arid writing.[20]

Regulation or liberation and the text

In order to understand these criticisms and to understand both some of the reasons why texts look the way they do and why they contain some groups' perspectives and not others', we also need to realize that the world of the books has not been cut off from the world of commerce. Books are not only cultural artifacts; they are economic commodities as well. Even though texts may be vehicles of ideas, they still have to be "peddled on a market."[21] This is a market, however, that—especially in the national and international world of textbook marketing—is politically volatile, as the Kanawha County experience so clearly documented.

Texts are caught up in a complicated set of political and economic dynamics. Text publishing often is highly competitive. In the United States, where text production is a commercial enterprise situated within the vicissitudes of a capitalist market, decisions about the "bottom line" determine what books are published and for how long. Yet this situation is not just controlled by the "invisible hand" of the market. It is also largely determined by the highly visible "political" hand of state textbook adoption policies.[22] Nearly half of the states, most of them in the southern tier and the Sun Belt, have state textbook adoption committees that by and large choose what texts will be purchased by the schools in that state. The economics of profit and loss of this situation makes it imperative that publishers devote nearly all of their efforts to guaranteeing a place on these lists of approved texts. Because of this, the texts made available to the entire nation, and the knowledge considered legitimate in them, are determined by what will sell in Texas, California, Florida, and so forth. There can be no doubt that the political and ideological controversies over content in these states, controversies that were often very similar to those that surfaced in Kanawha County, have had a very real impact on what and whose knowledge is made available. It is also clear that Kanawha County was affected by and had an impact on these larger battles over legitimate knowledge.

Economic and political realities structure text publishing not only internally, however. On an international level, the major text-publishing conglomerates control the market of much of the material not only in the capitalist centers, but in many other nations as well. Cultural domination is a facet of life for millions of students throughout the world, in part because of the economic control of communication and publishing by multinational firms, in part because of the ideologies and systems of political and cultural control of new elites within former colonial countries.[23] All of this, too, has led to complicated relations and struggles over official knowledge and the text, between "center" and "periphery," and within these areas as well.

I want to stress that all of this is not simply, as in the case of newly emerging nations, Kanawha County, or the Rugg textbooks, of historical interest. The controversies over the form and content of the textbook have not diminished. In fact, they have become even more heated, particularly in the United States. The changing ideological climate has had a major impact on debates over what should be taught in schools and on how it should be taught and evaluated. There is considerable pressure to raise the standards of texts, make them more "difficult," standardize their content, make certain that they place more stress on "American" themes of patriotism, free enterprise, and the "Western tradition," and link their content to statewide and national tests of educational achievement. These kinds of pressures are not only felt in the United States. The text has become the center of ideological and educational conflict in a number of other countries as well. In Japan, for instance, the government approval of a right-wing history textbook that retells the story of the brutal Japanese invasion and occupation of China and Korea in a more positive light has stimulated widespread international antagonism and has led to considerable controversy in Japan as well.

Along these same lines, at the very time that the text has become a source of contention for conservative movements, it has stood at the center of controversy for not being progressive enough. Class, gender, and race bias has been widespread in the materials. All too often, "legitimate" knowledge does not include the historical experiences and cultural expressions of labor, women, people of color, and others who have been less powerful.[24]

All of these controversies are not "simply" about the content of the books students find—or don't find—in their schools, though obviously they are about that as well. The issues also involve profoundly different definitions of the common good,[25] about our society and where it should be heading, about cultural visions, and about our children's future. To quote from Inglis again, the entire curriculum, in which the text plays so large a part, is "both the text and context in which production and values intersect; it is the twistpoint of imagination and power."[26] In the context of the politics of the textbook, it is the issue of power that should concern us the most.

The concept of power merely connotes the capacity to act and to do so effectively. However, in the ways we use the idea of power in our daily discourse, "the word comes on strongly and menacingly, and its presence is duly fearful."[27] This "dark side" of power is, of course, complemented by a more positive vision. Here power is seen as connected to a people acting democratically and collectively, in the open, for the best ideals.[28] It is this dual concept of power that concerns us here, at the level of both theory (how we think about the relationship between legitimate knowledge and power) and practice (how texts actually embody this relationship). Both the positive and the negative senses of power are essential for us to understand these relationships. Taken together, they signify that arguments about textbooks are really a form of *cultural politics*. They involve the very nature of the connections between cultural visions and differential power.

This, of course, is not new to anyone who has been interested in the history of the relationship among books, literacy, and popular movements. Books, and one's ability to read them, have themselves been inherently caught up in cultural politics. Take the case of Voltaire, that leader of the Enlightenment who so wanted to become a member of the nobility. For him, the Enlightenment should begin with the "grands." Only when it had captured the hearts and minds of society's commanding heights—only then could it concern itself with the masses below. But, for Voltaire and many of his followers, one caution should be taken very seriously. One should take care to prevent the masses from learning to read.[29]

For others, teaching "the masses" to read could have a more "beneficial" effect. It could promote a "civilizing" process, in which dominated groups would be made more moral, more obedient, more influenced by "real culture."[30] And for still others, such literacy could bring social transformation in its wake. It could lead to a "critical literacy," one that would be part of a larger movement for a more democratic culture, economy, and polity.[31] The dual sense of the power of the text emerges clearly here.

Thus activities that we now ask students to engage in every day, activities as "simple" and basic as reading and writing, can be at one and the same time forms of regulation and exploitation *and* potential modes of resistance, celebration, and solidarity. Here I am reminded of Caliban's cry, "You taught me language; and my profit on't is, I know how to curse."[32]

This contradictory sense of the politics of the book is made clearer if we go into the classrooms of the past. For example, texts have often been related to forms of bureaucratic regulation of both teachers' lives and those of students. One teacher in Boston in 1899 relates a story of what happened in her first year of teaching during an observation by the school principal. As the teacher rather proudly watched one of her children read aloud an assigned lesson from the text, the principal was less than pleased with the performance of the teacher or her pupil. In the words of the teacher:

> The proper way to read in the public school in 1899 was to say, "page 35, chapter 4" and holding the book in the right hand, with the toes pointing at an angle of forty-five degrees, the head held straight and high, the eyes looking directly ahead, the pupil would lift up his voice and struggle in loud, unnatural tones. Now, I had attended to the position of the toes, the right arm, and the nose, but had failed to enforce the mentioning of page and chapter.[33]

Here the text participates in both bodily and ideological regulation. The textbook in this instance is part of a system of enforcing a sense of duty, morality, and cultural correctness. Yet historically, the standardized text was struggled *for* as well as against by many teachers. Faced with large classes, difficult working conditions, insufficient training, and, even more importantly, little time to prepare lessons for the vast array of subjects and students they were responsible for, teachers often looked upon texts not necessarily as impositions but as essential tools. For young women elementary school teachers, the text helped prevent exploitation.[34] It solved a multitude of practical problems. It led not only to deskilling, but also to time to become more skilled as a teacher.[35] Thus, there were demands for standardized texts by teachers even in the face of what happened to that teacher in Boston and to so many others.

This struggle over texts was linked to broader concerns about who should control the curriculum in schools. Teachers, especially those most politically active, constantly sought to have a say in what they taught. This was seen as part of a larger fight for democratic rights. Margaret Haley, for instance, one of the leaders of the first teachers' union in the United States, saw a great need for teachers to work against the tendency toward making the teacher "a mere factory hand, whose duty it is to carry out mechanically and unquestioningly the ideas and orders of those clothed with authority of position."[36] Teachers had to fight against the deskilling or, as she called it, "factoryizing" methods of control being sponsored by administrative and industrial leaders. One of the reasons she was so strongly in favor of teachers' councils as mechanisms of control of schools was that this would considerably reduce the immense power over teaching and texts that administrators then possessed. Quoting John Dewey approvingly, Haley wrote, "If there is a single public-school system in the United States where there is official and constitutional provision made for submitting questions of methods, of discipline and teaching, and the questions of curriculum, textbooks, etc. to the discussion of those actually engaged in the work of teaching, that fact has escaped my notice."[37]

In this instance, teacher control over the choice of textbooks and how they were to be used was part of a more extensive movement to enhance the democratic rights of teachers on the job. Without such teacher control, teachers would be the equivalent of factory workers whose every move was determined by management.

These points about the contradictory relationships teachers have had with texts and the way such books depower and empower at different moments (and perhaps at the same time) documents something of importance. It is too easy to see a cultural practice or a book as totally carrying its politics around with it, "as if written on its brow for ever and a day." Rather, its political functioning "depends on the network of social and ideological relations" in which it participates.[38] Text writing, reading, and use can be retrogressive or progressive (and sometimes some combination of both) depending on the social context. Textbooks can be fought against because they are part of a system of moral regulation. They can be fought for because they provide essential assistance in the labor of teaching or because they are part of a larger strategy of democratization.

What textbooks do, the social roles they play for different groups, is then *very complicated*. This has important implications not only for the politics of how and by whom textbooks are used, but for the politics of the internal qualities, the content and organization, of the text. Just as crucially, it also has an immense bearing on how people actually read and interpret the text. It is to these issues that I now want to turn.

The politics of cultural incorporation

We cannot assume that because so much of education has been linked to processes of class, gender, and race stratification[39] that all of the knowledge chosen to be included in texts simply represents relations of, say, cultural domination or only includes the knowledge of dominant groups. This point requires that I speak theoretically and politically in this section of my argument, for all too many critical analyses of school knowledge, of what is included and excluded in the overt and hidden curricula of the school, take the easy way out. Reductive analysis comes cheap. Reality, however, is complex. Let us look at this in more detail.

It has been argued in considerable detail elsewhere that the selection and organization of knowledge for schools is an ideological process, one that serves the interests of particular classes and social groups.[40] However, as I just noted, this does not mean that the entire corpus of school knowledge is "a mirror reflection of ruling class ideas, imposed in an unmediated and coercive manner." Instead, "the processes of cultural incorporation are dynamic, reflecting both continuities and contradictions of that dominant culture and the continual remaking and relegitimation of that culture's plausibility system."[41] Curricula aren't imposed in countries like the United States. Rather, they are the products of often intense conflicts, negotiations, and attempts at rebuilding hegemonic control by actually incorporating the knowledge and perspectives of the less powerful under the umbrella of the discourse of dominant groups.

This is clear in the case of the textbook. As disenfranchised groups have fought to have their knowledge take center stage in the debates over cultural legitimacy, one trend has dominated in text production. In essence, little is usually dropped from textbooks. Major ideological frameworks do not get markedly changed. Textbook publishers are under considerable and constant pressure to include *more* in their books. Progressive *items* are perhaps mentioned, then, but not developed in depth.[42] Dominance is partly maintained here through compromise and the process of "mentioning." Tony Bennett's discussion of the process by which dominant cultures actually become dominant is worth quoting at length here.

> Dominant culture gains a purchase not in being imposed, as an alien external force, on to the cultures of subordinate groups, but by reaching into these cultures, reshaping them, hooking them and, with them, the people whose consciousness and experience is defined in their terms, into an association with the values and ideologies of the ruling groups in society. Such processes neither erase the cultures of subordinate groups, nor do they rob "the people" of their "true culture": what they do do is shuffle those cultures on to an ideological and cultural terrain in which they can be disconnected from whatever radical impulses which may (but need not) have fuelled them and be connected to more conservative or, often, downright reactionary cultural and ideological tendencies.[43]

In some cases, "mentioning" may operate in exactly this way, integrating selective elements into the dominant tradition by bringing them into close association with the values of powerful groups. There will be times, however, when such a strategy will not be successful. Oppositional cultures may at times use elements of the dominant culture against such groups. Bennett goes on, describing how oppositional cultures also operate.

> Similarly, resistance to the dominant culture does not take the form of launching against it a ready-formed, constantly simmering oppositional culture—always there, but in need of being turned up from time to time. Oppositional cultural values are formed and take shape only in the context of their struggle with the dominant culture, a struggle which may borrow some of its resources from that culture and which must concede some

ground to it if it is to be able to connect with it—and thereby with those whose consciousness and experience is partly shaped by it—in order, by turning it back upon itself, to peel it away, to create a space within and against it in which contradictory values can echo, reverberate and be heard.[44]

Some texts may, in fact, have such progressive "echoes" within them. There are some victories in the politics of official knowledge, not only defeats.

Sometimes, of course, not only are people successful in creating some space where such contradictory values can indeed "echo, reverberate, and be heard," but they transform the entire social space. They create entirely new kinds of governments, new possibilities for democratic political, economic, and cultural arrangements. In these situations, the role of education takes on even more importance, since new knowledge, new ethics, and a new reality seek to replace the old. This is one of the reasons that those of us committed to more participatory and democratic cultures inside and outside of schools must give serious attention to changes in official knowledge in those nations that have sought to overthrow their colonial or elitist heritage. Here, the politics of the text takes on special importance, since the textbook often represents an overt attempt to help create a new cultural reality.[45]

New social contexts, new processes of text creation, a new cultural politics, the transformation of authority relations, and new ways of reading texts—all of this can evolve and help usher in a positive rather than a negative sense of the power of the text. Less regulatory and more emancipatory relations of texts to real people can begin to evolve, a possibility made real in many of the programs of critical literacy that have had such a positive impact in nations throughout the world. Here people help create their own "texts," ones that signify their emerging power in the control of their own destinies.

However, we should not be overly romantic here. Such transformations of cultural authority and mechanisms of control and incorporation will not be easy. For example, certainly the ideas and values of a people are not directly prescribed by the conceptions of the world of dominant groups, and just as certainly there will be many instances when people are successful in creating realistic and workable alternatives to the culture and texts in dominance. Yet we do need to acknowledge that the social distribution of what is considered legitimate knowledge *is* skewed in many nations. The social institutions directly concerned with the "transmission" of this knowledge, such as schools and the media, *are* grounded in and structured by the class, gender, and race inequalities that organize the society in which we live. The area of symbolic production is not divorced from the unequal relations of power that structure other spheres.[46] Speaking only of class relations (but much the same could be said about race and gender), Stuart Hall, one of the most insightful analysts of cultural politics, puts it this way.

> Ruling or dominant conceptions of the world do not directly prescribe the mental content of the illusions that supposedly fill the heads of dominated classes. But the circle of dominant ideas *does* accumulate the symbolic power to map or classify the world for others; its classifications do acquire not only the constraining power of dominance over other modes of thought but also the initial authority of habit and instinct. It becomes the horizon of the taken-for-granted; what the world is and how it works, for all practical purposes. Ruling ideas may dominate other conceptions of the social world by setting the limit on what will appear as rational, reasonable, credible, indeed sayable or thinkable within the given vocabularies of motive and action available to us. Their dominance lies precisely in the power they have to contain within their limits, to frame within their circumference of thought, the reasoning and calculation of other social groups.[47]

In the United States, there has been a movement of exactly this kind. Dominant groups—really a coalition of economic modernizers, what have been called the old humanists, and neoconservative intellectuals—have attempted to create an ideological consensus around the return to traditional knowledge. The "great books" and "great ideas" of the "Western tradition" will preserve democracy. By returning to the common culture that has made this nation great, schools will increase student achievement and discipline, increase our international competitiveness, and ultimately reduce unemployment and poverty.

Mirrored in the problematic educational and cultural visions of volumes such as Bloom's *The Closing of the American Mind* and Hirsch's *Cultural*

Literacy,[48] this position is probably best represented in quotes from former Secretary of Education William Bennett. In his view, we are finally emerging out of a crisis in which "we neglected and denied much of the best in American education." For a period, "we simply stopped doing the right things (and) allowed an assault on intellectual and moral standards." This assault on the current state of education has led schools to fall away from "the principles of our tradition."[49]

Yet, for Bennett, "the people" have now risen up. "The 1980's gave birth to a grass roots movement for educational reform that has generated a renewed commitment to excellence, character, and fundamentals." Because of this, "we have reason for optimism."[50] Why? Because "the national debate on education is now focused on truly important matters: mastering the basics; . . . insisting on high standards and expectations; ensuring discipline in the classrooms; conveying a grasp of our moral and political principles; and nurturing the character of our young."[51] Notice Bennett's use of "we" and "the people." Notice as well the assumed consensus on "basics" and "fundamentals" and the romanticization of the past both in schools and the larger society. The use of these terms, the attempt to bring people in under the ideological umbrella of the conservative restoration, is very clever rhetorically. As many people in the United States, Britain, and elsewhere—where rightist governments have been very active in transforming what education is about—have begun to realize, however, this ideological incorporation is having no small measure of success at the level of policy and at the level of whose knowledge and values are to be taught.[52]

If this movement has its way, the texts made available and the knowledge included in them will surely represent a major loss for many of the groups who have had successes in bringing their knowledge and culture more directly into the body of legitimate content in schools. Just as surely, the ideologies that will dominate the official knowledge will represent a considerably more elitist orientation than what we have now.

Yet perhaps *surely* is not the correct word here. The situation is actually more complex than that, something we have learned from many of the newer methods of interpreting how social messages are actually "found" in texts. Allan Luke has dealt with such issues very persuasively. It would be best to quote him at length here.

A major pitfall of research in the sociology of curriculum has been its willingness to accept text form as a mere adjunct means for the delivery of ideological content; the former described in terms of dominant metaphors, images, or key ideas; the latter described in terms of the sum total of values, beliefs, and ideas which might be seen to constitute a false consciousness. For much content analysis presumes that text mirrors or reflects a particular ideological position, which in turn can be connected to specific class interests . . . It is predicated on the possibility of a one-to-one identification of school knowledge with textually represented ideas of the dominant classes. Even those critics who have recognized that the ideology encoded in curricular texts may reflect the internally contradictory character of a dominant culture have tended to neglect the need for a more complex model of text analysis, one that does not suppose that texts are simply readable, literal representations of "someone else's" version of social reality, objective knowledge and human relations. For texts do not always mean or communicate what they say.[53]

These are important points, for they imply that we need more sophisticated and nuanced models of textual analysis. Although we should certainly *not* be at all sanguine about the effects of the conservative restoration on texts and the curriculum, if texts don't simply represent dominant beliefs in some straightforward way and if dominant cultures contain contradictions, fissures, and even elements of the culture of the popular groups, then our readings of what knowledge is "in" text cannot be done by the application of a simple formula.

We can claim, for instance, that the meaning of a text is not necessarily intrinsic to it. As poststructuralist theories would have it, meaning is "the product of a system of differences into which the text is articulated." Thus there is not "one text," but many. Any text is open to multiple readings. This puts into doubt any claim that one can determine the meanings and politics of a text "by a straightforward encounter with the text itself." It also raises serious questions about whether one can fully understand the text by mechanically applying any interpretive procedure. Meanings, then, can be and are multiple and contradictory, and we must always be willing to "read" our own readings of a text, to interpret our own interpretations of what it means.[54] Answering the question of "whose knowledge?" is in a text is not at all simple, it seems, though clearly the right would very much like to reduce the range of meanings one might find.

This is true of our own interpretations of what is in textbooks. But it is also just as true for the students who sit in schools and at home and read (or in many cases don't read) their texts. I want to stress this point, not only at the level of theory and politics as I have been stressing here, but also at the level of practice. We cannot assume that what is "in" the text is actually taught. Nor can we assume that what is taught is actually learned. Teachers have a long history of mediating and transforming text material when they employ it in classrooms. Students bring their own classed, raced, and gendered biographies with them as well. They too accept, reinterpret, and reject what counts as legitimate knowledge selectively. As critical ethnographies of schools have shown, students (and teachers) are not empty vessels into which knowledge is poured. What Freire has called "banking" education is not actually going on;[55] rather, students are active constructors of the meanings of the education they encounter.[56]

We can talk about three ways in which people can potentially respond to a text: in a dominated, negotiated, or oppositional way. In the dominant reading of a text, one accepts the messages at face value. In a negotiated response, the reader may dispute a particular claim but accept the overall tendencies or interpretations of a text. Finally, an oppositional response rejects these dominant tendencies and interpretations. The reader "repositions" herself or himself in relation to the text and takes on the position of the oppressed.[57] These are, of course, no more than ideal types, and many responses will be a contradictory combination of all three. But the point is that not only do texts themselves have contradictory elements; audiences *construct* their own responses to texts. They do not passively receive texts, but actively read them on the basis of their own class, race, gender, and religious experiences.

An immense amount of work needs to be done on student acceptance, interpretation, reinterpretation, and partial and/or total rejection of texts. Although there is a tradition of such research, much of it quite good, most of this in education is done in an overly psychologized manner. It is more concerned with questions of learning and achievement than it is with the equally important and prior issues of whose knowledge it is that students are learning, negotiating, or opposing and what the sociocultural roots and effects are of such processes. Yet we simply cannot fully understand the power of the text, what it does ideologically and politically (or educationally, for that matter), unless we take very seriously the way students actually read texts, not only as individuals but also as members of social groups with their own particular cultures and histories. [58] For every textbook, then, there are multiple texts: contradictions within it, multiple readings of it, and different uses to which it will be put. Texts—be they the standardized, grade-level specific books so beloved by school systems or the novels, trade books, and alternative materials that teachers either use to supplement these books or simply to replace them—are part of a complex story of cultural politics. They can signify authority (not always legitimate) or freedom.

To recognize this, then, is also to recognize that our task as critically and democratically minded educators is itself a political one. We must acknowledge and understand the tremendous capacity of dominant institutions to regenerate themselves "not only in their material foundations and structures but in the hearts and minds of people." Yet, at the very same time, we need to never lose sight of the power of popular organizations, of real people, to struggle, resist, and transform them. [59] Cultural authority, what counts as legitimate knowledge, what norms and values are represented in the officially sponsored curriculum of the school—all of these serve as important arenas in which the positive and negative relations of power surrounding the text will work themselves out. And all of them involve the hopes and dreams of real people in real institutions, in real relations of inequality.

From all that I have said here, it should be clear that I oppose the idea that there can be one textual authority, one definitive set of "facts" that is divorced from its context of power relations. A "common culture" can never be an extension to everyone of what a minority mean and believe. Rather, and crucially, it requires not the stipulation and incorporation within textbooks of lists and concepts that make us all "culturally literate," *but the creation of the conditions necessary for all people to participate in the creation and recreation of meanings and values*. It requires a democratic process in which all people, not simply those who see themselves as the intellectual guardians of the "Western tradition," can be involved in the deliberation of what is important.[60] It should go without saying that this necessitates the removal of the very real material obstacles—unequal power, wealth, time for reflection—that stand in the way of such participation.[61]

The very idea that there is one set of values that must guide the "selective tradition" can be a great danger, especially in contexts of differential power. Take, as one example, a famous line that was printed on an equally famous public building. It read, "There is one road to freedom. Its milestones are obedience, diligence, honesty, order, cleanliness, temperance, truth, sacrifice, and love of country." Many people may perhaps agree with much of the sentiment represented by these words. It may be of some interest that the building on which they appeared was in the administration block of the concentration camp at Dachau.[62]

We must ask, then, Are we in the business of creating dead texts and dead minds? If we accept the title of educator, with all of the ethical and political commitments this entails, I think we already know what our answer should be. Critical literacy demands no less.

Notes

*A more extensive version of this essay appears in Michael W. Apple and Linda Christian-Smith (eds.), *The Politics of the Textbook* (New York: Routledge, 1991).

1. See John Willinsky, *The New Literacy* (New York: Routledge, 1990).

2. Janet Batsleer, Tony Davies, Rebecca O'Rourke, and Chris Weedon, *Rewriting English: Cultural Politics of Gender and Class* (New York: Methuen, 1985), pp. 164–165. For an exceptional treatment of "political literacy" in theory and practice, see Colin Lankshear with Moira Lawler, *Literacy, Schooling and Revolution* (Philadelphia: Falmer Press, 1988).

3. John Fiske, Bob Hodge, and Graeme Turner, *Myths of Oz: Reading Australian Popular Culture* (Boston: Allen and Unwin, 1987), p. x.

4. John Fiske, *Reading the Popular* (Boston: Unwin Hyman, 1989), pp. 149–150.

5. See, for example, Michael W. Apple and Lois Weis (eds.), *Ideology and Practice in Schooling* (Philadelphia: Temple University Press, 1983).

6. For a current representative sample of the varied kinds of studies being done on the textbook, see Arthur Woodward, David L. Elliot, and Kathleen Carter Nagel (eds.), *Textbooks in School and Society* (New York: Garland, 1988).

7. Fred Inglis, *Popular Culture and Political Power* (New York: St. Martin's Press, 1988), p. 9.

8. Allan Luke, *Literacy, Textbooks and Ideology* (Philadelphia: Falmer Press, 1988), pp. 27–29.

9. Michael W. Apple, *Ideology and Curriculum* (New York: Routledge, 2nd edition, 1990); Michael W. Apple, *Education and Power* (New York: Routledge, 1985); and Michael W. Apple, *Teacher and Texts: A Political Economy of Class and Gender Relations in Education* (New York: Routledge, 1986).

10. Michael W. Apple, "Redefining Equality: Authoritarian Populism and the Conservative Restoration," *Teachers College Record*, 90, Winter 1988, pp. 167–184.

11. Ann Bastian, Norm Fruchter, Marilyn Gittell, Colin Greer, and Kenneth Haskins, *Choosing Equality: The Case for Democratic Schooling* (Philadelphia: Temple University Press, 1986).

12. See, for example, Susan Rose, *Keeping Them Out of the Hands of Satan* (New York: Routledge, 1988).

13. Allen Hunter, *Children in the Service of Conservation* (Madison: University of Wisconsin Institute for Legal Studies, 1988).

14. James Moffett, *Storm in the Mountains* (Carbondale: Southern Illinois University Press, 1988).

15. Raymond Williams, *The Long Revolution* (London: Chatto and Windus, 1961). See also Apple, *Ideology and Curriculum*.

16. Fred Inglis, *The Management of Ignorance: A Political Theory of the Curriculum* (New York: Basil Blackwell, 1985), pp. 22–23.

17. *Ibid.*, p. 23.

18. Miriam Schipper, "Textbook Controversy: Past and Present," *New York University Education Quarterly*, 14, Spring–Summer 1983, pp. 31–36.

19. A. Graham Down, "Preface" to Harriet Tyson-Bernstein, *A Conspiracy of Good Intentions: America's Textbook Fiasco* (Washington: The Council for Basic Education, 1988), p. viii.

20. Harriet Tyson-Bernstein, *A Conspiracy of Good Intentions*, p. 3.

21. Robert Darnton, *The Literacy Underground of the Old Regime* (Cambridge: Harvard University Press, 1982), p. 199.

22. For a history of the social roots of such adoption policies, see Michael W. Apple, "Regulating the Text: The Socio/Historical Roots of State Control," *Educational Policy*, 3, June 1989, pp. 107–123.

23. The issues surrounding cultural imperialism and colonialism are nicely laid out in Philip Altbach and Gail Kelly (eds.), *Education and the Colonial Experience* (New York: Transaction Books, 1984). For an excellent

discussion of international relations over texts and knowledge, see Philip Altbach, *The Knowledge Context* (Albany: State University of New York Press, 1988).

24. For some of the most elegant discussion of how we need to think about these "cultural silences," see Leslie Roman and Linda Christian-Smith with Elizabeth Ellsworth (eds.), *Becoming Feminine: The Politics of Popular Culture* (Philadelphia: Falmer Press, 1988).

25. Marcus Raskin, *The Common Good* (New York: Routledge, 1986).

26. Inglis, *The Management of Ignorance*, p. 142.

27. Inglis, *Popular Culture and Political Power*, p. 4.

28. *Ibid*.

29. Darnton, *The Literacy Underground of the Old Regime*, p. 13.

30. Batsleer et al., *Rewriting English*.

31. Lankshear with Lawler, *Literacy, Schooling and Revolution*.

32. Batsleer et al., *Rewriting English*, p. 5.

33. James W. Fraser, "Agents of Democracy: Urban Elementary School Teachers and the Conditions of Teaching," in Donald Warren (ed.), *American Teachers: Histories of a Profession at Work* (New York: Macmillan, 1989), p. 128.

34. Apple, *Teachers and Texts*.

35. For further discussion of deskilling and reskilling, see Apple, *Education and Power*.

36. Margaret Haley, quoted in Fraser, "Agents of Democracy," p. 128.

37. Haley, quoted in *ibid*., p. 138.

38. Tony Bennett, "Introduction: Popular Culture and 'The Turn to Gramsci'," in Tony Bennett, Colin Mercer, and Janet Woollacott (eds.), *Popular Culture and Social Relations* (Philadelphia: Open University Press, 1986), p. xvi.

39. The literature here is voluminous. For a more extended treatment, see Apple, *Education and Power*, and Cameron McCarthy and Michael W. Apple, "Race, Class and Gender in American Educational Research," in Lois Weis (ed.), *Class, Race and Gender in American Education* (Albany: State University of New York Press, 1989).

40. See Apple, *Ideology and Curriculum*, and Linda Christian-Smith, *Becoming a Woman through Romance* (New York: Routledge, 1990).

41. Luke, *Literacy, Textbooks and Ideology*, p. 24.

42. Tyson-Bernstein, *A Conspiracy of Good Intentions*, p. 18.

43. Tony Bennett, "The Politics of the 'Popular' and Popular Culture," in Bennett, Mercer, and Woollacott (eds.), *Popular Culture and Social Relations*, p. 19.

44. *Ibid*.

45. See Didacus Jules, "Building Democracy," in Michael W. Apple and Linda Christian-Smith (eds.), *The Politics of the Textbook* (New York: Routledge, 1991), pp. 259–287.

46. Stuart Hall, "The Toad in the Garden: Thatcherism among the Theorists," in Gary Nelson and Lawrence Grossberg (eds.), *Marxism and the Interpretation of Culture* (Urbana: University of Illinois Press, 1988), p. 44.

47. *Ibid.*

48. Allan Bloom, *The Closing of the American Mind* (New York: Simon and Schuster, 1987), and E. D. Hirsch, Jr., *Cultural Literacy* (New York: Houghton-Mifflin, 1986).

49. William Bennett, *Our Children and Our Country* (New York: Simon and Schuster, 1988), p. 9.

50. *Ibid.*, p. 10.

51. *Ibid.*

52. Apple, "Redefining Equality."

53. Luke, *Literacy, Textbooks and Ideology*, pp. 29–30.

54. Lawrence Grossberg and Gary Nelson, "Introduction: The Territory of Marxism," in Nelson and Grossberg (eds.), *Marxism and the Interpretation of Culture*, p. 8.

55. Paulo Freire, *Pedagogy of the Oppressed* (New York: Herder and Herder, 1973).

56. See, for example, Paul Willis, *Learning to Labor* (New York: Columbia University Press, 1981); Angela McRobbie, "Working Class Girls and the Culture of Femininity," in Women's Study Group (ed.), *Women Take Issue* (London: Hutchinson, 1978), pp. 96–108; Robert Everhart, *Reading, Writing and Resistance* (Boston: Routledge, 1983); Lois Weis, *Between Two Worlds* (Boston: Routledge, 1985); Bonnie Trudell, *Doing Sex Education* (New York: Routledge, in press); and Christian-Smith, *Becoming a Woman through Romance*.

57. Tania Modleski, "Introduction," *Studies in Entertainment* (Bloomington: Indiana University Press, 1986), p. xi.

58. See Elizabeth Ellsworth, "Illicit Pleasures: Feminist Spectators and *Personal Best*," in Roman, Christian-Smith, with Ellsworth (eds.), *Becoming Feminine*, pp. 102–119; Elizabeth Ellsworth, "Why Doesn't This Feel Empowering?" *Harvard Educational Review*, 59, August 1989, pp. 297–324; and Christian-Smith, *Becoming a Woman through Romance*.

59. Batsleer et al., *Rewriting English*, p. 5.

60. This is discussed in more detail in the new preface to the second edition of Apple, *Ideology and Curriculum*.

61. Raymond Williams, *Resources of Hope* (New York: Verso, 1989), pp. 37–38.

62. David Horne, *The Public Culture* (Dover, N.H.: Pluto Press, 1986). p. 76.

7

Literacy and urban school reform: Beyond vulgar pragmatism

Dennis Carlson

In curriculum policy-making, the resurgence of the "end of ideology" thesis over the past several decades has been associated with widespread acceptance by professional educators, state education officials, and a broad spectrum of the public that curricular issues are reducible to questions about how to more "effectively" instruct students in the literacy skills they "need" to become productive workers and responsible citizens and to advance themselves socially. This depoliticized, means-ends perspective on the curriculum—what Cleo Cherryholmes calls "vulgar pragmatism"—actually has served (wittingly or unwittingly) to extend a conservative corporate and bureaucratic state project of restructuring education that has been profoundly undemocratic.[1] In urban schools in particular, vulgar pragmatism has been associated with a "basic skills" focus and state-mandated minimum competency testing, supposedly designed to ensure that students disadvantaged by class and race leave school with the minimum competencies they will need to succeed in life. Yet the effect of two decades of "basic skills" reforms in urban schools has been to further accentuate the school's role in reproducing and maintaining socioeconomic inequalities. The "basic skills" reform movement has resulted in an urban school curriculum that steers students away from college and "sets up" most for entry-level jobs in the new, postindustrial work force. It has also increased centralized, bureaucratic

217

state "steerage" of urban schools, and in doing so it has deprofessionalized teachers and disenfranchised urban (increasingly poor African American and Hispanic) communities in regard to the education of their children.

The curriculum is thus much more than a corpus of knowledge deemed essential or worth knowing. It also is involved in the constitution of power relations, since it prepares students for a particular world of work and citizenry, structures teachers' work and their relations with students, and implies a particular organization and governance of the schools. All of these levels of power relations have been organized around and through the "basic skills" reform movement in urban education. In what follows I examine this conservative, bureaucratic state reform movement in terms of those power relations in which it is inextricably embedded. I also want to point to some of the contradictions, dilemmas, and crisis tendencies associated with conservative bureaucratic state discourse on the "basic skills" curriculum and "effective" urban schools. These have to do with legitimation problems, a failure to address the underlying structural roots of crisis, the further alienation of students and teachers from a reductionistic and disempowering conception of learning and teaching, and the dilemmas of raising student achievement levels through more top-down bureaucratic regulation of the schools.

Although I devote much of my attention to conservative state discourse, I also want to examine several other curriculum discourses that have emerged over the past decade or so that challenge some of the underlying assumptions of the "basic skills" reform movement and that have distinctly different implications for the kinds of work for which we should be preparing urban students, the restructuring of teaching, and the organization and governance of urban schools. The first and most influential of these is associated with American political liberalism, as represented in education during the 1980s by such groups as the Carnegie Foundation for the Advancement of Teaching, Theodore Sizer's "Coalition of Essential Schools," and the Holmes Group of major universities engaged in teacher education. Liberal discourse has emphasized "higher-order" literacy skills that prepare urban students for college and the new high-tech, professional, and managerial jobs, and they have linked "excellence" to "equity." To promote "higher-order" learning and "excellence" in urban schools, liberal groups have called for further decentralization of educational decision making to the local school level and the professionalization of teaching. I argue that although the liberal discourse on "higher-order" literacy and urban school reform offers important advances over the conservative, bureaucratic state discourse and although some of its specific proposals are worthy of support, it continues to support an economically functional view of education, ignores "hard" economic and social realities, and ultimately fails to offer a serious way out of the "literacy crisis."

A second oppositional discourse on the curricular "needs" of urban students may be associated with a democratic left political project. Although to this point this discourse has remained largely marginalized, it has begun to reassert the need to link up with broader social movements and projects. Consequently, it may be expected to influence public debate on educational issues in the decade ahead, as the crisis in urban schools and communities deepens and the current state reform movement fails to deliver on its promises. While building upon the more democratic aspects of liberal reform agendas, this discourse shifts our attention to notions of "critical literacy" and "critical pedagogy," student identity formation within struggles of class, race, and gender, and the restructuring of urban schools and teachers' work consistent with notions of workplace democratization.

"Functional literacy" and the conservative reform movement

Over the past two decades, the state tier of government has been controlled, for the most part, by political conservatives (of both major political parties). It has been an era of economic restructuring and political realignments and new definitions of equity; and conservative political groups have been most successful in articulating these developments in terms of a new "public philosophy," with the state and private enterprise viewed as working cooperatively to manage various institutions in the public interest.[2] In public education, this has implied an emphasis upon a "human capital" rationale for the curriculum, in which economic progress, increased productivity, and higher profits (the "bottom line") are believed to be causally linked to the preskilling and socializing of future workers in schools.[3] From this human capital perspective, if entry-level workers are more literate—if they possess more or better language coding and decoding skills—they will be more productive in their work. The decline of American industrial productivity in recent years is thus linked to a supposed decline in literacy skills among American workers. In urban education in particular, these skills have been defined through reference to the notion of "functional literacy," which has implied several things. First, it has implied that a functional relationship should exist between the organization of curriculum and instruction in urban schools and the skill "needs" of various sectors of the labor force. Reform is then aimed at bringing the schools into closer functional alignment with changes in the economy. Second, it has implied that the particular skill "needs" of urban students are related to the minimum language usage skills workers need to function effectively in the entry-level job market for high school graduates. Somewhat ironically, although critical theorists of education have often been accused of advancing a functionalist and deterministic theory of public schooling, based on a "correspondence principle" which explains the linkages between the organization of work in schools and in the work force in overly mechanistic and causal ways, the conservative discourse on urban school reform actually has done far more to advance an economically determinist and functionalist rationale.[4] The relative autonomy of educational sites, which leftist analysts have viewed as providing some hope for oppositional discursive practices within schools, is viewed within the mainstream conservative discourse as something that needs to be overcome, so that what is learned in school has a more direct and functional relationship to economic "needs" and so that the schools do not "lag behind" developments in the economy.

The changing character of work in postindustrial America was already becoming apparent by the 1960s, when business and state leaders began to talk of a growing mismatch between the literacy skills of high school graduates and the literacy requirements of the new jobs. Enrollments in vocational education programs and tracks were still relatively high, but graduates of these programs found fewer and fewer jobs waiting for them that required their particular skills.[5] Most of the new clerical, data-processing, janitorial, and service industry jobs being created in industry did not require much in the way of technical training in advance, but they increasingly required more in the way of basic reading (word and sentence decoding), comprehension, and direction-following skills.[6] As D. W. Livingstone has observed, education for this new, semiskilled labor force "entails instruction in general preparatory skills that are open-ended and can be built upon or refined in a range of work settings. In other words, it means the creation of labor market entrants who will be increasingly technically adaptable and capable of mobility among work settings in response to rapidly changing workplace technologies."[7] These general preparatory skills include the ability to follow written instructions and operating procedures to carry out various standardized tasks, and also to decode and recode data for entry into management information systems or computer programs. Beyond this, they include the capacity to produce quantitative output data on job performance. Many of the new jobs in the 1960s did not require ongoing supervision by management because employees were evaluated on the basis of data fed into computers or tabulated on charts. Finally, because these new working-class jobs did not pay as well as the old working-class industrial jobs did, and were also nonunionized and less secure, they initially were taken primarily by the new underclass of African American and Hispanic peoples, who were in the 1960s reclaiming America's inner cities, in many cases drawn there by the new jobs.

The Johnson administration's "war on poverty" in the 1960s represented the first attempt by the state to realign public education with changes in the labor market, particularly through its emphasis upon generalizable "basic" literacy skills for urban students rather than the more specific vocational skills that had been emphasized during earlier eras. For example, most of the Title 1 programs for disadvantaged students, funded under the Elementary and Secondary Education Act of 1965, were "compensatory" or "remedial" education programs which employed programmed instructional materials, drill sheets, and workbooks to teach "targeted" learning objectives, and programs were required to produce quantitative output data on "mastery" of instructional objectives to meet federal budgeting and program evaluation requirements.[8] This package of urban school reforms was new and different in some important ways, although the "cult of efficiency" and the adoption of industrial productivity models in education have been influential at least since the turn of the century.[9] However, by the late 1960s, technological advances in curriculum design, along with the organization of instruction consistent with new "systems theory" models of production, allowed state officials and local bureaucratic elites to come much closer than ever before to "targeting" instruction to the functional literacy skill "deficits" of urban students and thus waging effective "war" on illiteracy. When the Republicans took over management of the "literacy crisis" under the Nixon administration, the output-based planning and reporting requirements and the skill-based curricular emphasis of the "war on poverty" programs were maintained, although Democratic administration requirements for local community involvement in planning and overseeing Title 1 and other state programs were slowly eliminated. The conservative state reform agenda would involve a top-down, bureaucratic restructuring of urban education with few if any claims to involve the community in the policy-making process. Shortly after American astronauts first walked on the moon, the U.S. commissioner of education proclaimed that the achievement of universal literacy was to be the "moonshot for the seventies," and this suggested the need for a highly centralized plan of action. It *did not* imply, however, that, as in the manned space program, billions of dollars would be funnelled into fighting the "war against illiteracy."[10]

The adoption of minimum competency tests for high school graduation in many states by the late 1980s consolidated the urban school reform package and transformed urban schools, more than ever before, into an apparatus of the bureaucratic state, with state officials "steering" the schools in line with the interests and worldviews of the economic sector. Many disadvantaged students were enrolled in up to three or four basic skills classes or "communication skills" classes each day, with instruction targeting the particular skill "deficits" of each student. Teachers were expected to "teach to the test" using performance-based curriculum materials that prepared students for achievement tests and to keep students "on task" with their skill-based curricular materials. As enrollments in vocational educational programs plummeted in the 1980s, as extracurricular activities were cut, as liberal arts and humanities courses were gutted from the instructional program, the basic skills curriculum continued to grow.

I have argued to this point that the functional literacy reform movement in urban education can be understood as part of the effort by corporate elites, in cooperation with bureaucratic state officials, to realign public schools consistent with the rapidly developing changes in postindustrial America, to create a new semiskilled, entry-level work force. But the transformation of the urban school curriculum around "basic" or "functional" literacy skills also served the somewhat independent interests of bureaucratic state elites and dominant cultural groups, so that the basic skills reform movement is not to be explained simply as a case of economic realignment, with state officials bowing to corporate pressure. To at least some extent the "crisis of literacy" provided a convenient opportunity for bureaucratic elites and state education officials to intervene in urban schools, to bring them under much tighter top-down bureaucratic control and thus override formal democratic controls at the local district level; and this intervention was facilitated by a fiscal crisis in urban school districts which made them much more dependent upon state and federal monies. Ironically, the era of the "conservative restoration" in American politics has been associated with increasingly centralized, bureau-cratic regulation and control of urban schools, even if controls have been imposed more by states than by the federal government and even if conserva-tive political discourse continues to support the notion that the public school "monopoly" should be replaced with a free enterprise "voucher system" of education to provide consumers with educational choice. In fact, conserva-tive politicians have appealed persuasively to a "middle American" and New Right concern with reducing the size of government and decentralizing deci-sion making; but in positions of state power, conservatives have worked to extend elite bureaucratic state and corporate control of the schools. Once more, that control has been exercised increasingly at the state rather than the federal level of government and has been accompanied by a relative decline in overall public spending on education. This has also been the era during which poor and working-class African American and Hispanic peoples have been able to appropriate an urban, inner-city "space" within the dominant culture, albeit a space kept in a state of economic depression and exploita-tion.[11] The conservative state-sponsored "basic skills" reform movement therefore had the effect of overriding local control of the schools at a time when poor African American and Hispanic peoples were becoming the nu-merical majority in urban America, returning control to dominant cultural interests. This has ensured that the dominant culture maintains its grip upon schools when, at least formally, it might have slipped into the hands of marginalized groups.

Along with the disempowerment of local urban communities, teachers' work has been restructured during the basic skills era in ways that have further subordinated teachers within the bureaucratic chain of command. Teachers have been reconceptualized as "classroom managers" of a relatively self-guided, predetermined, standardized instructional process, and are evaluated on their abilities to "teach to the test" and keep students "on task." Compounding this disempowerment, teachers have been locked out of curricular and instructional decision making by state-mandated collective bargaining laws that rigidly separate labor and management roles in the schools. Without such a rigid bifurcation of roles in urban schools, current basic skills models of reform would not be possible. Finally, as teaching has been deskilled and routinized (as much as possible), urban school systems have found that they can "make do" with uncertified teachers, teacher aides, and "permanent substitutes" and can thereby lower labor costs in a time of fiscal crisis.[12]

How has a reform movement that has been more consistent with an elite than a democratic social project been "sold" or legitimated politically? A number of interrelated factors must be considered in responding to the issue of legitimation of state educational policy in urban education. First, state discourse on urban school reform generally has not couched support for a "functional" literacy curriculum solely or even primarily in economic terms, even if the business community has. "Functional" literacy skills have been presented more broadly as "real life" skills that everyone needs to participate successfully in political, social, and economic life in modern America. For example, the federally sponsored National Assessment of Educational Progress defined functional literacy in the mid-1980s as "the ability to perform reading and writing tasks needed to function adequately in everyday life (filling out a driver's license application, reading a train schedule, writing a check, applying for a job, or reading an article in the newspaper)."[13] Granted, these are hardly activities that require much active decision making by individuals, and one might even argue that they envision rather passive citizens; but the state cannot, on the face of it, be accused of emphasizing economic functionalism in such a definition.

Second, state officials have been successful in convincing many Americans that because there is a "literacy crisis" in urban schools, the state *must* intervene in far-reaching new ways to respond to the literacy crisis. In the mid-1970s the U.S. Office of Education, applying standards from studies of functional literacy (such as the Adult Performance Level study conducted at the University of Texas), estimated that 57 million American adults were functionally or marginally illiterate, or almost one-third of the entire adult population. This number included 44 percent of all African Americans and 56 percent of Hispanic Americans.[14] These alarming statistics were used to imply that drastic measures would be needed to combat this crisis. They were, to a large extent, arbitrary figures, since they were based on various samples of minimum competency testing, which could not automatically be taken as indicators of anything other than test-taking skills. Consequently, although there was some reason to be alarmed at the "functional literacy" skills of urban students, since those skills were defined by corporate and state officials, the "war" against illiteracy also provided a primary legitimating rationale for the extension of elite "steerage" of urban schools.

A related "selling point" of the conservative state reform movement emphasized by state officials, particularly with urban educators, community leaders, and students and their parents, is that only by focusing on "basic skills" can socioeconomically disadvantaged urban youth have a "fighting chance" to "get ahead." Supposedly all postsecondary education, and all "higher-order" literacy and thinking skills, are grounded in certain literacy "basics": identifiable language comprehension and usage skills that one can "build upon." Because disadvantaged students are presumed not to get these cultural capital "basics" in their "deprived" home environments, urban schools must focus on the "basics." Once students are certified as possessing these literacy skills (through minimum competency testing), it is the responsibility of each individual to decide whether to pursue his or her education in college or to enter directly into the job market after high school graduation. In either case, it is maintained, students have the "basics" they need. All of this may sound quite convincing, and it has a grain of truth to it. In truth, disadvantaged students remain disadvantaged partly because they do not acquire in their homes and communities certain forms of literacy that "pay off" for advancement into the dominant culture.[15] However, a focus upon a basic skills or functional literacy curriculum taught in a regimented manner that emphasizes following directions may actually have the effect of "setting up" most urban students for jobs that solidify their subordinate position within the existent socioeconomic order. Aside from the fact that students are learning the literacy skills and work routines associated with the entry-level work force, once students are "tracked" in basic skills classes, the possibility of a college education recedes quickly for most, since they lack the required college preparatory courses to consider four-year colleges. To some extent, dominant groups have been able to mask the reality of basic skills tracking in urban schools by maintaining that instruction is "individualized": that is to say, it is tailored to the individualized skills "deficits" and learning "needs" of the urban student. In fact, this individualization is within the context of a standardized curricular program and educational experience. Still, by claiming to treat each student as an individual and by setting minimum standards for student achievement, the bureaucratic state discourse has sought to position the state as the champion of equal opportunity in education and society and as a defender of the interests of disadvantaged students.

State officials also have sought to link basic skills legitimation claims to widespread public sentiment regarding a decline in educational and product-quality standards, and a corresponding desire to return to the "good old days" when people allegedly earned their diplomas and paychecks and took pride in their work. In the romanticized and idealized past depicted in this ideology of *authoritarian populism* (inhabited by "hardworking" and "God-fearing" students whose parents were European immigrants), young people studied hard, showed respect for teachers and other authority figures, earned their high school diplomas, and "pulled themselves up by their boot-straps."[16] State-mandated minimum competency testing for high school graduation is thus legitimated as a way of bringing back the good old days by restoring the credential value to the high school diploma. Those who cannot make the grade, it is argued, do not deserve to receive a state-endorsed diploma. Consider, for example, the Middle Atlantic state ("Midstate") where I conducted a longitudinal study of urban school reform during the 1970s and 1980s. In the mid-1980s Midstate's educational commissioner supported a high school diploma exam before various audiences around the state by reference to a then-popular television commercial for an investment banking firm in which an aging and austere Hollywood actor claimed that "at [name of investment firm] we make money the old-fashioned way, we earn it." The educational commissioner, paraphrasing the commercial, said that "every student who graduates from high school in Midstate will be able to say proudly that they got their diploma the old-fashioned way, they earned it."[17] In much the same way that advertisers recognized that the public could be sold a mass-produced, standardized product through appeals to homemade goodness and old-fashioned taste, conservative state discourse manipulated these cultural signs to sell its own package of school reforms: a package which was anything but traditional. In fact, it was a reform agenda meant to challenge a long tradition of local control of urban schools and to impose a new, highly technical curriculum.

Finally, functional literacy reforms have been legitimated among professional educators (and to a lesser degree within the general public) through claims that they represent outgrowths of scientific and managerial research on "effective schools," much of which has been state sponsored. The conservative state has thus attempted to direct educational discourse on the crisis of literacy around one technical question: How can urban schools be more effectively organized and managed to increase their effectiveness in teaching functional literacy skills, as measured by standardized achievement test scores? This question leads to an almost inevitable set of answers and reform proposals, inevitable in the sense that the answers and the question are part of a common discourse which unifies them. The "effective schools" discourse in urban education is based on the proposition that the attributes of effective urban schools (those in which student test scores are higher than expected given the socioeconomic mix of the student body) can be identified through scientific study, and that once these attributes are identified they can be replicated in schools which are less effective. Under the Reagan administration, effective schools research provided a basis for arguing that urban schools could "heal themselves" and respond to the literacy crisis without a massive infusion of new funds. The problem was identified as one of poor management at the local school level, calling for expert judgment based on the best research. In the introduction to a report on the findings of effective schools prepared by the U.S. Department of Education, Education Secretary

William Bennett wrote: "The first and most fundamental responsibility of the federal government in the field of education is to supply accurate and reliable information about education to the American people. The information in this volume is a distillation of a large body of scholarly research in the field of education . . . [We] now *know* certain things about teaching and learning as a result of the labors of the scholarly community."[18]

What, then, are we alleged to *know* about effective urban schools based on scientific research? Among the principles generally supported in the literature and endorsed by state officials are the importance of a clear school "mission" or ethos that focuses on mastery of basic literacy skills, commitment by the staff to this mission, and an organizational environment where all staff members know what they are expected to do to achieve.[19] The effective schools literature also emphasizes that school principals are particularly important in establishing "explicit operational goals regarding students' academic performance, which are clearly communicated to their staff members."[20] The principal is seen as analogous to the local plant manager who is made responsible by central office management for "running a tight ship" and achieving expected levels of productivity, with workers busily going about their assigned tasks.

The ideology behind this means-ends thinking is masked, albeit superficially, by presenting these principles as emerging in an unbiased way out of scientific research and management theory. Furthermore, aside from depoliticizing a state-sponsored urban school reform initiative through claims to scientific objectivity, the message of the effective schools movement is an optimistic and pragmatic one. This no doubt enhances its political appeal among a broad spectrum of educators who have grown tired of the despairing picture critics have painted of an oppressive, unresponsive, racist urban school system and citizens who do not want to see their taxes raised to pay for expensive new initiatives to "save" urban schools.[21] The effective schools research has helped state officials maintain the image that they have things under control, that progress is being made, that substantially more money is not needed to teach the basics effectively. All that is needed is a better application of the principles derived from unbiased scientific research.

Cleo Cherryholmes refers to this as *vulgar pragmatism*, a form of thinking about educational issues that "results when efficiency is pursued in the absence of criticism, when actions are privileged over thought, when practice is valued and theory disparaged, when practice is divorced from theory (as if that were possible) for the sake of making things work better."²² This unreflective acceptance of the existing structure of institutional power relations pervades bureaucratic state reform discourse, and the "end of ideology" thesis it celebrates depoliticizes (thereby legitimating) state intervention in education to support elite rather than democratic interests. The effective schools movement, of course, is correct in affirming that schools can make a difference and, in a few cases, actually do. However, by emphasizing the often slight or questionable statistical differences between "effective" and "ineffective" urban schools, it plays down the broader and more decisive uniformities in urban education.²³ Furthermore, minor statistical differences between urban schools may tell us something (although arguably little) about how to better organize schools to "teach to the test." But these differences tell us nothing about how to change urban schools in ways that empower students, teachers, and community, or about how to promote excellence—in the sense that implies striving to "be all you can be" (to borrow the army's own Madison Avenue appropriation).

Although the conservative, bureaucratic state discourse has been relatively successful in selling its response to the crisis of achievement in urban schools, the response itself has not solved the problems which generated the crisis in the first place. This may make for increasing legitimation problems in the years ahead. In fact, these delegitimation tendencies are already apparent on a number of fronts. For example, the latest federal statistics on student achievement in the nation's public schools indicate that state reform initiatives have failed to "turn around" the slow decline in urban education since *A Nation at Risk* warned of a rising tide of mediocrity in the schools in 1983.²⁴ It was still possible in 1989 for the *New York Times*, in a front-page story, to warn of an "impending U.S. jobs 'disaster'" with a "work force unqualified to work" and with "schools lagging far behind needs of employees." According to the article, based on reports from major corporations and interviews with corporate executives, "many of the students who are most at risk are children from minority groups, the same youngsters who the Labor Department says will fill 56 percent of the new jobs that will open up between 1986 and the year 2000."²⁵ Similarly, in its 1987 report, *An Imper-*

iled Generation: Saving Urban Schools, the Carnegie Foundation for the Advancement of Teaching argued that state-sponsored reforms had not altered certain fundamental facts of urban education: high school dropout rates, stagnant test scores, demoralized teachers, and a pervasive sense of failure.[26]

How can we account for this failure to win the war against illiteracy? In responding we must begin by questioning the notion that the corporate state reform initiative in urban education *has* failed, at least from the perspective of elite groups. As noted earlier, the state has been able to push through a major package of reforms which effectively transfers power upward within the bureaucratic state chain of command and thus brings urban schools under much greater centralized "steerage" by bureaucratic state and corporate elites; and in doing so it has kept poor, black, and Hispanic populations educationally disenfranchised. It has also stamped an economically functional curriculum and instructional process upon the schools which socializes students (however ineffectively) into the direction-following routines and work discipline of the new postindustrial, semiskilled work force. For these reasons, one may question whether corporate, state, and dominant culture groups really want to "win" the war against illiteracy, since it has been so convenient in the furtherance of dominant forms of institutional organization and social control. Still, one must assume that the literacy crisis has not been totally "manufactured" to serve these interests, and that the failure of the state war against illiteracy also requires an explanation which acknowledges the "reality" of the literacy crisis.

One of the reasons why the conservative state reform movement has not been as effective as its supporters hoped has to do with the accelerated growth during the past two decades of an American underclass which urban schools increasingly serve, along with the concurrent flight of white and middle-class groups from urban public schools. The nation's schools are continuing to become more "urban" each year as white and middle-class student enrollment continues to drop and poor African American and Hispanic enrollment rises. Already, approximately 60 percent of students currently enrolled in public schools come from low-income, single-parent families, with the parent most often the mother and a public welfare recipient.[27] Many of these students identify with a counterschool culture which does not value advancing into the dominant culture and does not take school knowledge or test taking seriously, and they speak and affirm a marginalized language rather than standard middle-class English. They also have lost faith in school credentials as a ticket to economic advancement and fulfillment of the "American dream." As "getting ahead" increasingly is perceived as an unrealistic option by most urban students, it becomes more difficult to convince them to stay in school, work hard, get their diploma, and graduate so they can get one of the new semiskilled, entry-level jobs. Quite aside from these socioeconomic factors (though related to them), the form and content of the functional literacy curriculum may be blamed for failing to engage or motivate students. Skill-based workbooks and drill sheets may provide a logical grounding for organizing the learning process to raise test scores, but they structure students' (and teachers') work in a manner which provides little if any opportunity for creativity, the expression of intrinsic interest, or variety in learning activities. Basic skills supporters argue that motivation can be supplied through an instrumental system of rewards for achievement. But as the curriculum becomes increasingly devoid of personal meaning, it seems doubtful whether a few rewards and praise for a job well done will adequately compensate for the loss of meaning. Finally, the functional literacy curriculum, by defining literacy in terms of minimum competency test passage, has encouraged an instrumental "teach to the test" perspective among school staff that may well be counterproductive to the actual achievement of functional literacy skills useful in "real-life" situations. Since administrators, teachers, and students are all urged to focus upon test passage and skill mastery, a form of institutional goal displacement is encouraged in which means increasingly become ends. Teachers are rewarded for going to almost any means (short of giving students the test in advance) in order to manufacture expected test scores. In this light, rising scores on high school diploma exams in some states may be attributed to the success of teaching to a specific test over a number of years, and these gains do not appear to be especially transferable to other standardized achievement tests for which students are not explicitly prepared, to say nothing of "real-life" situations.[28]

All of this suggests that the conservative state reform movement is undermined by deep-rooted contradictions and crisis tendencies which seem likely to catch up with it at some point. Its legitimating claims to meet the needs of socioeconomically disadvantaged students are increasingly hard to sustain. It fails to motivate students and teachers effectively, it encourages goal displacement (in the form of "teaching to the test"), and fails to deliver the literate, well-disciplined high school graduates that corporate supporters of reform expect. In these terms, the urban school reform initiative may be analyzed as a form of crisis management by dominant groups, aimed at maintaining elite "steerage" of urban schools by muddling through one crisis after another and trying to patch over contradictions.[29] In doing so, however, it generates its own dilemmas and contradictions. This is not meant to suggest that the collapse of the current system of urban schooling is imminent, since crisis management may continue indefinitely. To move beyond the conservative discourse and reform agenda in urban education will require articulating an alternative or oppositional discourse, one which expresses the public interest in new ways and builds a new coalition of support for a new reform agenda.

"Higher-order" literacy and liberal discourse

Although the conservative, bureaucratic state discourse on the literacy crisis has been by far the most influential in guiding reform initiatives in education during the past several decades, it has been challenged (although this challenge has been rather limited) by a liberal discourse constituted by various coalitions and groups operating for the most part outside the state. Theodore Sizer's "Coalition of Essential Schools," for example, is a loose federation of public schools in half a dozen states committed to "personalizing" education, lowering the teacher-student ratio, overcoming the fragmentation of the curriculum and school day by focusing on "essential" subjects (math and science, language skills, and social science and humanities), and giving teachers more control over their work. All students, whether in inner-city or suburban schools, are viewed as college preparatory students, and an emphasis is placed on the development of higher-order thinking skills, corresponding to the higher runs of Bloom's Taxonomy, through a rigorous liberal arts curriculum.[30]

Perhaps the most influential of the various liberal voices on school reform during the past decade has been the Carnegie Foundation for the

Advancement of Teaching, under the leadership of Ernest Boyer. I want to limit my comments in what follows to an analysis of its perspective on the urban school crisis. The foundation's 1986 report, *A Nation Prepared: Teachers for the 21st Century,* may be read as the liberal response to *A Nation at Risk,* the Reagan administration's 1983 blueprint for basic skills reforms.[31] Like that earlier federal report, the Carnegie report provided a general framework for analyzing the changing literacy "needs" of workers in postindustrial America and formulating an educational response. However, whereas *A Nation at Risk* called for more teacher accountability, more testing, and more emphasis on functional literacy skills to meet the "Japanese challenge" and improve worker productivity, the Carnegie report argued that such a reform agenda could actually deepen problems in the American economy rather than resolve them, since American workers would need higher-order literacy skills to adapt and respond creatively to the challenge of the new, highly competitive world economic order. It noted: "The skills needed now are not routine. Our economy will be increasingly dependent on people who have a good intuitive grasp of the ways in which all kinds of physical and social systems work. They must possess . . . an ability to see patterns of meaning where others see only confusion: a cultivated creativity that leads them to new problems, new products, and new services . . . ; and in many cases, the ability to work with other people in complex organizational environments where work groups must decide for themselves how to get the job done." The report was critical of an overemphasis upon functional literacy skills in state-sponsored reform, of regimented approaches to drilling and "teaching to the test," of an overenrollment of urban students in basic skills remedial courses that effectively locked them into semiskilled jobs, and of deskilling teachers through new instructional technologies. It warned that if urban schools continued to emphasize "the development of the routinized skills necessary for routinized work," then America's high school graduates would have to compete with Third World workers for low-pay, low-skill jobs.[32]

By arguing that urban students should have the same college preparatory, higher-order literacy curriculum that was currently available to students in America's better suburban schools, the Carnegie report reaffirmed the democratic conviction that educational excellence be linked to equity. This theme was taken up even more forcefully in a 1988 follow-up report by the

Carnegie Foundation entitled *An Imperiled Generation: Saving Urban Schools*. That report concluded that "urban America, regardless of its gleaming high rises and impressive skylines, is a place where education is neglected . . . The glittering signs of 'progress' remain a shameful facade."[33] In ominous terms, it warned that the division of America into "the two separate societies envisioned by the Kerner Commission two decades ago" was a "very real possibility" in the coming decade, and that the public schools were contributing to such a division.[34] Too many urban students were "academically restricted by the curriculum itself," which presumed that "students are divided between those who think and those who work," with most urban students relegated to the latter category.[35] The real "unfinished agenda for the nation's schools," the report argued, was "equality of opportunity, along with the support to make it real and not merely rhetorical . . . Clearly, equity and excellence cannot be divided."[36]

The Carnegie reports called for a major decentralization of power within the system and "freeing up" of teachers and principals from bureaucratic, centralized controls as a basis for teaching higher-order literacy skills and promoting excellence in urban schools. This supports both the heightened professionalization of teaching and site-based management. Of the importance of teachers, *A Nation Prepared* noted, "In schools where students are expected to master routine skills and acquire routine knowledge, the necessary skills and knowledge can, to a degree, be packaged in texts and teachers can be trained to deliver the material in the text to the students with reasonable efficiency. But a much higher order of skills is required to prepare students for the unexpected, the non-routine world they will face in the future." Thus, whereas bureaucratic state reformers had endorsed a model of teaching and learning that borrows heavily from industrial labor analogies, *A Nation Prepared* looked further up the labor hierarchy to borrow a model of teaching that draws upon craft and professional conceptions of work organization and control. Teachers had to be given the power to personalize instruction, to become facilitators, guides, coaches, and even counsellors to their students. "Textbooks cannot do it. Principals cannot do it. Directives from state authorities cannot do it. Only the people with whom the students come in contact every day can do it."[37] Similarly, *An Imperiled Generation* argued that site-based management is an essential prerequisite to promoting "excellent" education in urban schools and to overcoming the demoralization of local school staff. "Principals and teachers—those closest to the students— should be given more authority to run the schools." While recognizing that the state had an important role to play in overcoming financial inequalities between urban and suburban districts and in ensuring equality of opportunity, the report maintained that state and central office officials "must think of themselves primarily as providing services and resources to enable teachers and principals and parents to be successful."[38] Rather than top-down accountability through state-mandated minimum competency testing, the report called for the use of a wide range of qualitative and quantitative evaluation approaches adapted to local needs. Evaluation questions might include "What are the number and types of books being read by students? . . . Does the school have a core curriculum for all students? . . . Is the school organized into small units to overcome anonymity among students and provide a close relationship between each student and mentor [teacher]? . . . Does the school have connections with community institutions and outside agencies to enrich the learning possibilities of students?"[39] In these ways, the Carnegie reports called for an end to the bureaucratic state centralization of control of urban schools and a reempowerment of the actors immediately involved in the educative process in school and community sites as an essential prerequisite to the development of higher-order literacy among students.

In describing the crisis in urban schooling and teaching, in critiquing the bureaucratic state reform agenda of the 1980s and its consequences, in calling for the decentralization of power within the system, and in proposing a college preparatory, higher-order literacy curriculum for all students, *A Nation Prepared* and *An Imperiled Generation* provide a valuable contribution to the development of an alternative democratic response to the urban school crisis. But there are problems or limitations in this liberal discourse on reform that undermine its effectiveness as a combatant of the conservative, bureaucratic state discourse.

First, the central economic assumption that underlies the reasoning in both Carnegie reports is that the schools should prepare most if not all no American youth with higher-order thinking skills so that they can go on to college, and ultimately help build the high-quality, high-tech, professional-managerial labor force that American industry will need to compete effectively in the new economic world order. The most immediate problem with this scenario is that it assumes that schools play (or can play) a very important role in restructuring the economy by turning out new types of highly skilled workers. In fact, the schools respond to changes in the economy and the labor market much more than the other way around, and far more semi-skilled jobs have been created over the past decade than high-skill jobs requiring advanced or specialized training and on-the-job creativity and problem-solving skills. According to a recent report by the Labor Department, college graduates (who now make up 25 percent of the labor force— higher than in any other nation) are oversupplied on the labor market. This oversupply has significantly devalued the college degree during the 1980s, meaning that growing numbers of college graduates have had to settle for jobs that do not require degrees, thus making the job market more difficult for high school graduates.[40] Consequently, the liberal discourse proposes a system of public education designed to prepare everyone for college education and high-tech, professional-managerial jobs, when the hard reality is that the economic sector cannot, or will not, accommodate the aspirations of the vast majority. Although the idea of a common curriculum oriented around higher-order literacy skills, along with a commitment to "excellence for everyone," are ideas worthy of support, a serious proposal to implement such changes would need to address the continuing deskilling of American workers in the postindustrial economy. It would also need to shift the focus away from a primary concern with economic and job market "needs" (however they might be defined) to include personal, community, and democratic social "needs" as well. For example, *A Nation Prepared* viewed the development of higher-order literacy in terms of American economic competitiveness and the maintenance of a high standard of living for Americans. Not only are other values and concerns slighted, but the implicit assumption is that Third World countries should specialize in low-skill, low-paid, "functionally" literate workers, and that Americans (along with other First World countries such as Japan and Germany) should specialize in the development of "brainpower" to build new production technologies and develop new products and markets. The result is a form of *literacy colonialism* which ends up relegating Third World peoples to the status of exploitable labor power.

Beyond these economic considerations, a second set of problems in the liberal discourse has to do with its failure to account adequately for impediments that currently stand in the way of decentralizing power in urban schools consistent with teacher professionalism and site-based management. Reform efforts aimed at decentralizing power to local schools and classrooms as a means of freeing up administrators and teachers to pursue excellence are certainly worthy of support. However, a real decentralization of power to the local urban school sites would also threaten powerful interest groups. For example, the state could no longer guarantee that the urban school curriculum was organized in a manner consistent with corporate economic needs, and schools would begin to fall further out of alignment with the role that elite groups expect them to perform. This, consequently, would lead to pressure upon the state to intervene once more to reestablish centralized "steerage" of the schools through a network of bureaucratic and technical controls, even though this would also mean more bureaucratic inefficiency and "red tape," along with a lowering of morale and effort on the part of teachers and school administrators. The last movement for decentralization of authority in New York City in the 1960s, for example, was designed to overcome the dysfunctions associated with bureaucratic insularity and rigidity, to remotivate local teachers and school administrators, and to contain rising discontent with inner-city communities; and although it might have been somewhat effective in these aims, it was quickly followed by the reassertion of bureaucratic hierarchical control in the 1970s after elite groups began to realize that decentralization meant they could no longer "call the shots."[41] By failing to properly analyze this structurally generated "vicious cycle" of control in urban education or to challenge the interests that lie behind it, liberal discourse offers little basis for believing that current proposals for decentralization can be achieved, at least to any substantial degree or over a sustained time frame. In fact, although site-based management has been popularized in some urban school districts over the past few years, it has generally been consistent with a conservative rather than liberal reform agenda. Local principals and teachers are supposedly "freed up" to develop more creative ways of teaching to the test mandated by the state. In this form, site-based management paradoxically goes hand in hand with a project of extending central office and bureaucratic state control over urban schools. To decentralize power effectively within public education—to make schools more responsive to the needs of students and their communities, and to reempower local teachers and administrators to pursue excellence—will require moving beyond the limitations of the liberal discourse without abandoning its basic insights and commitments.

Critical literacy and the democratic left

At this juncture, the democratic left discourse on literacy and the urban school crisis remains fragmented and politically marginalized. Nevertheless, it is possible to identify a number of elements of a comprehensive democratic left response within existing critical theory and practice, elements related to notions like workplace democratization and socioeconomic justice, critical literacy and pedagogy, and student identity formation around class, race, and gender positions and struggles. Let me briefly suggest what each of these notions implies for moving the discourse on urban school crisis beyond its current limitations and elitist tendencies.

Although a democratic left discourse would need to go beyond an economically functional analysis of the curriculum, with its presumption that what is learned in schools must bear a rather direct relationship to economic needs, this does not imply a complete rejection of economic or workplace considerations in curriculum decision making. On the contrary, some relationship *should* exist between schoolwork and work in other important institutional sites in society, since education serves to initiate individuals into the productive work of building culture and objectifying experience. Marx argued that people make themselves and culture through work: "What they [humans] are, therefore, coincides with their production, both with *what* they produce and *how* they produce."[42] A democratic left reconceptualization of the literacy curriculum would thus entail preparing students with the discursive skills and capacities they would need for workplace democratization. Specifically, workplace democratization implies enhancing workers' participation in decisions affecting the organization and control of their particular work tasks, including the definition of procedures and outcomes, along with greater worker involvement in a wide scope of substantive rather than merely technical or procedural decisions at the workplace through representation on governing boards and councils.[43] Finally, it implies changes in the content and complexity of job tasks and the demands that work places on the individual, as with job rotation and sharing schemes. The literacy curriculum organized around such a conception of work would, following Ira Shor, be one that emphasizes *cointentionality* (involving joint teacher-student determination of learning activities and outcomes) and *dialogue* (involving problem-solving discourse about both the process and product of learning activities).[44] It also implies real (rather than pseudo) democratic involvement by student councils and other representative student committees in making decisions about specific learning objectives, activities, and outcomes. Reconceived in this way, the curriculum would still serve an important role in preparing young people to be more "productive" in their work once they leave school. However, in doing so, the schools would not function to meet economic needs *in opposition* to human needs for rewarding work experiences.

Beyond these job and workplace considerations, critical literacy implies more generally a capacity for discursive reflection on self-identity formation and on the culture within which one is positioned as a classed, raced, and gendered subject. According to Peter McLaren, "the purpose behind acquiring this type of literacy is to create a citizenry critical enough to both analyze and challenge the oppressive characteristics of the larger society so that a more just, equitable, and democratic society can be created."[45] This certainly implies helping urban students decode class and race power relations and practices that keep them subordinated. It also, however, implies helping them critique the ideology of gender domination. For example, in urban communities the dominant ideology most often blames the single-parent, fatherless, welfare-dependent family for the "cycle of poverty," and it also positions women at the bottom of the entry-level labor hierarchy. What the democratic left needs to support, then, is not simply or even primarily a more effective means of teaching economically functional literacy skills, but rather a new understanding of literacy as a form of discursive practice by students actively involved in constructing meaning and subjectivity within a context of struggle over democratic values and social goals of equity, respect for cultural difference and diversity, and socioeconomic justice. Questions posed by a critical literacy curriculum include the following: How can students be made aware of and call into question the construction of their subordinate positions in society? How can students resist subordination in ways that are not self-defeating and encapsulating? How can students begin to reshape their own cultural identity in positive and empowering ways?[46] For teachers, critical literacy education implies a reconceptualization of their pedagogic roles. Henry Giroux writes that teachers need "to undertake social criticism not as outsiders but as public intellectuals who address the social and political issues of their neighborhood, their nation, and the wider global world."[47] They must engage themselves as well in the struggles of their students to articulate their own voices and construct identities. Obviously, in applying these principles of critical or transformative pedagogy, teachers cannot rely upon any prescribed, standardized curriculum; and rather than provide students with answers and solutions, teachers will be called upon to confront students with important questions and choices.

Beyond reconceptualizing the role of students and teachers, education for critical literacy implies drastic changes in the way schools are organized and educational decisions are made: changes that shift power from bureaucratic state officials to local communities, schools, and classrooms. Like the liberal discourse, a democratic left discourse would imply increased decentralization of decision making within the public school system. However, it would emphasize issues of community control and workplace democratization within the school rather than site-based management and other forms of administrative decentralization which do not challenge the overall "steerage" of the system by bureaucratic elites. Local schools need to be made accountable to their student and community "clients" in a much more direct sense through (for example) local school governing boards composed of representatives of a number of affected groups, including administrators, teachers, students, and various neighborhood and community groups. These boards could be given substantial power to formulate learning activities and evaluate outcomes, consistent with general guidelines established by the state designed to ensure maximum democratic participation, equality of opportunity, and so on. Teachers' special expertise and job control rights would also need to be respected within this local decision-making process, although how much discretionary power is reserved for teachers as individual professional practitioners and as a professional occupational group would have to be resolved in concrete situations. Teachers, after all, are just one of the involved parties in the educational process, albeit an essential one, so that teachers' professional rights should not imply the exclusion of "nonprofessionals" from decision-making processes.

Finally, to institutionalize this package of reforms associated with critical literacy education will require that we look beyond the schools and redefine the role of the state. A democratic left politics implies greater involvement by the state in establishing an overall development strategy for the economy based on democratic goals and commitments, in guaranteeing minimum levels of economic well-being and security to all citizens, in promoting a fairer distribution of income, wealth, and power, in building a sense of community that respects difference, and in controlling the destructive side effects of profit making on the environment and the workplace.[48] This entails greatly reducing bureaucratic, top-down control of public education by predetermining outputs and by enforcing rigid accountability to state regulations and guidelines. Only when an agenda for democratic school reform is articulated within the context of a political movement prepared to undertake such interventions and changes can we seriously discuss moving beyond the current "mismanagement" of urban school crisis to a resolution of crisis tendencies. Even given the limitations and contradictions of the conservative and liberal discourses on urban education and the deepening crisis tendencies in the schools and the economy in late twentieth-century America, it may yet be possible to build a new democratic political movement that rearticulates the interests of the democratic majority around fundamentally new reform agendas.

Notes

1. Cherryholmes, Cleo, *Power and Criticism: Poststructural Investigations in Education* (New York: Teachers College Press, 1988).

2. See Giroux, Henry, "Public Philosophy and the Crisis in Education," *Harvard Educational Review*, 54, 2, 1984, pp. 186–194.

3. See Luke, Allan, *Literacy, Textbooks and Ideology: Postwar Literacy Instruction and the Mythology of Dick and Jane* (New York: Falmer, 1988); and Apple, Michael, *Education and Power* (Boston: Routledge, 1982), pp. 42–44.

4. The leftist "correspondence principle" is most associated with Samual Bowles and Herbert Gintis, *Schooling in Capitalist America* (Boston: Routledge, 1976). For a recent appraisal of both its usefulness and its limitations in leftist analysis, see Gintis and Bowles, "Contradiction and Reproduction in Educational Theory," in Cole, Mike (ed.), *Bowles and Gintis Revisited: Correspondence and Contradiction in Educational Theory* (New York: Falmer Press, 1988), pp. 16–32.

5. See Gray, Kenneth, "Vocational Education in High School: A Modern Phoenix?" *Phi Delta Kappan*, 72, 6, 1991, pp. 437–445.

6. See Levin, Henry, and Rumberger, Russell, *Educational Requirements for New Technologies* (Palo Alto: Stanford Center for Educational Research, 1986).

7. Livingstone, D. W., "Class, Educational ideologies, and mass opinion in capitalist crisis," *Sociology of Education*, 58 (January, 1985), p. 8.

8. I discuss these developments in Carlson, Dennis, "Curriculum Planning and the State: The Dynamics of Control in Education," in Michael Apple and Landon Beyer (eds.), *The Curriculum: Problems, Politics, and Possibilities* (Albany: SUNY Press, 1988), pp. 98–118.

9. See Callahan, Raymond, *Education and the Cult of Efficiency* (Chicago: University of Chicago Press, 1962).

10. Cited in Harman, David, *Illiteracy: A National Dilemma* (New York: Cambridge University Press, 1987), p. 1.

11. For Henri Lefebvre, spatial conflict entails the appropriation of space by marginalized groups from its capitalist spatial organization. See Lefebvre, "Space: Social Product and Use Value," in J. W. Freiberg (ed.), *Critical Sociology: European Perspectives* (New York: Irvington Publications, 1979), p. 293.

12. I explore some of these developments in Carlson, Dennis, "Teachers as Political Actors: From Reproductive Theory to the Crisis of Schooling," *Harvard Educational Review*, 57, 2, 1987, pp. 283–307.

13. Quoted in Winterowd, W. Ross, *The Culture and Politics of Literacy* (New York: Oxford University Press, 1989), p. 5.

14. Cited in Kozol, Jonathan, *Illiterate America* (Garden City, N.Y.: Anchor Press, 1985), pp. 4–5.

15. The critical "cultural capital" argument is associated with the work of Basil Bernstein and his notion that working-class students speak a "restricted code" and with the work of Pierre Bourdeiu, who uses the notion of "cultural capital" in his structuralist model of how schools operate to reproduce cultural and economic inequalities. Although I acknowledge that this critical "cultural capital" argument has some validity, it also tends to end up "blaming the victim." See Bernstein, *Class, Codes and Control: Theoretical*

Studies towards a Sociology of Language (New York: Schocken Books, 1971); and Bourdieu, "Cultural Reproduction and Social Reproduction," in Jerome Karabel and A. H. Halsey (eds.), *Power and Ideology in Education* (New York: Oxford University Press, 1977), pp. 487–510. For a critique of the "cultural capital" research and more particularly the work of Bernstein and Bourdieu, see Bisseret, Noelle, *Education, Class Language and Ideology* (London: Routledge, 1979).

16. The notion of "authoritarian populism" has been used by Stuart Hall and (in educational analysis) Michael Apple. See Hall, "Popular Democratic versus Authoritarian Populism: Two Ways of Taking Democracy Seriously," in Alan Hunt (ed.), *Marxism and Democracy* (London: Lawrence and Wishart, 1980), pp. 190–191; and Apple, "Redefining Equity: Authoritarian Populism and the Conservative Restoration," *Teachers College Record*, 90, 2, Winter 1988, pp. 167–184.

17. See Carlson, Dennis, "Of Basic Skills Curriculum Restructuring and Crisis Tendencies in Urban Education," paper presented at the 1990 annual meeting of the American Educational Research Association in Boston, Massachusetts.

18. Bennett, William, *What Works* (Washington, D.C.: U.S. Department of Education, 1987), p. v.

19. The "effective schools" movement in urban education during the 1980s has been influenced by the conceptual framework developed by Brooker, Wilber, et al., *School Social Systems and Student Achievement: Schools Can Make a Difference* (New York: Praeger, 1979); and Ronald Edmonds and John Frederiksen, *Search for Effective Schools: The Identification and Analysis of City Schools That Are Instructionally Effective for Poor Children* (East Michigan: Michigan State University Institute on Teaching, 1979).

20. Rosenholtz, Susan, "Effective Schools: Interpreting the Evidence," *American Journal of Education*, 93, 1985, p. 361.

21. See Bicke, William, "Knowledge, Dissemination, Inquiry," *Educational Research*, special issue on Effective Schools, 12, 4, 1983, pp. 3–5.

22. Cherryholmes, p. 152.

23. See Jencks, Christopher, et al., *Inequality: A Reassessment of the Effect of Family and Schooling in America* (New York: Harper and Row, 1972). Nothing has fundamentally changed over the past two decades to alter the author's conclusion that "if all high schools were equally effective (or ineffective) inequality between twelfth graders would fall less than one percent" (p. 91). Differences between schools, they found, tended to "wash out" in accounting for student achievement when compared to the much more powerful influence of the socioeconomic mix of the student population.

24. See Johnson, J., "Nation's Schools Termed 'stagnant' in Federal Report," *New York Times*, 4 May 1989, p. 1+. The report referred to is from the National Assessment of Educational Progress.

25. Fiske, Edward, "Impending U.S. Jobs 'Disaster': Work Force Unqualified to Work," *New York Times*, 25 September 1989, p. 1+.

26. Carnegie Foundation for the Advancement of Teaching, *An Imperiled Generation: Saving Urban Schools* (Lawrenceville, N.J.: Princeton University Press, 1987).

27. Johnson, *New York Times*, p. 1.

28. I provide an ethnographic account of "teaching to the test" in Carlson, Dennis, "Updating Individualism and the Work Ethic: Corporate Logic in the Classroom," *Curriculum Inquiry*, 12, 2, 1982, pp. 125–160. For a discussion of "teaching to the test" and the phenomenon of rising scores on state-mandated minimum competency tests, see Sedlak, Michael, Pullin, C., and Cusick, P., *Selling Students Short: Classroom Bargains and Academic Reform in the American High School* (New York: Teachers College Press, 1986), p. 31. See also the *New York Times*, "Student Challenges Standardized Test Results" (28 November 1987) for an account of a report by the Friends for Education, Inc., which contends that apparently superior performance by students on the Iowa Test of Basic Skills, Metropolitan Achievement Test, and other standardized tests may merely indicate that school districts are doing more "teaching to the test."

29. See Habermas, Jürgen, *Legitimation Crisis* (Boston: Beacon Press, 1973), Part 2: "Crisis Tendencies in Advanced Capitalism," pp. 33–94. The term *muddling through* is associated with Charles Lindblom, *The Policy-Making Process* (Englewood Cliffs, N.J.: Prentice-Hall, 1980). Lindblom applies this notion in a noncritical fashion to explain decision making by state officials as they react to one crisis situation after another.

30. For a discussion of the principles associated with the Coalition of Essential Schools, see Hechinger, Fred, "A War is Shaping Up between Politicians and Professionals over Who Should Reform Schools," *New York Times*, 17 February 1988, p. B9; Cushman, Kathleen, "Schedules That Bind," *American Educator*, Summer 1989, pp. 35–39; and Sizer, Theodore, *Horace's Compromise: The Dilemma of the American High School* (New York: Harper and Row, 1985).

31. *A Nation Prepared: Teachers for the 21st Century* (New York: Carnegie Foundation for the Advancement of Teaching, Carnegie Forum Task Force on Teaching as a Profession, 1986). All citations are from excerpts from the report published in the *Chronicle of Higher Education*, 32, May 21, 1986, pp. 43–55. *A Nation at Risk* was issued by the National Commission for

Excellence in Education (Washington, D.C.: U.S. Government Printing Office, 1983).

32. *A Nation Prepared*, pp. 44–45.

33. *An Imperiled Generation*, p. xii.

34. *Ibid.*, p. xiv.

35. *Ibid.*, p. 3.

36. *Ibid.*, p. 4.

37. *A Nation Prepared*, pp. 45–46.

38. *An Imperiled Generation*, pp. 8–9.

39. *Ibid.*, pp. 11–12.

40. Uchitelle, Louis, "Surplus of College Graduates Dims Job Outlook for Others," *New York Times* 18 June 1990, p. 1+.

41. See Tyack, David, "'Restructuring' in Historical Perspective: Tinkering Toward Utopia," *Teachers College Record*, 92, Winter 1990, pp. 170–191.

42. Marx, Karl, and Engels, Frederick, *The German Ideology, Part One* (New York: International Publishers, 1974), p. 42.

43. See Davis, Ed, and Lansbury, Russell, "Democracy and Control in the Workplace: An Introduction," in their (eds.), *Democracy and Control in the Workplace* (Melbourne, Australia: Longman Cheshire, 1986), pp. 1–29; and Schuller, Tom, *Democracy at Work* (New York: Oxford University Press, 1985), p. 4.

44. Shor, Ira, *Culture Wars: School and Society in the Conservative Restoration, 1969–1984* (Boston: Routledge, 1986), p. 188.

45. McLaren, Peter, "Culture or Canon? Critical Pedagogy and the Politics of Literacy," *Harvard Educational Review*, 58, May 1988, p. 214.

46. See Grant, Carl, and Sleeter, Christine, "Race, Class, and Gender and Abandoned Dreams," *Teachers College Record*, 90, 1, 1988, pp. 19–40.

47. Giroux, Henry, "Rethinking the Boundaries of Educational Discourse: Modernism, Postmodernism, and Feminism," *College Literature* 17, 2/3, 1990, p. 42.

48. Pollin, Robert, and Cockburn, Alexander, "The World, the Free Market, and the Left," *The Nation*, 25 February 1991, pp. 224–236.

8

Literacy, pedagogy, and English studies: Postmodern connections

James A. Berlin

My title assembles some of the most contested terms in discussions of language and learning today, each one serving as a terrain of ideological battle for designation rights. Literacy, as most people would readily concede, stands for the ability to read and to write, but there are innumerable ways of reading and writing, as the recent theoretical battles in rhetoric and literature circles have underscored. Pedagogy has to do with classroom practices, and these are likewise being heatedly discussed, with each camp of literacy education forwarding its own unique set of procedures. In addition, English studies, a major site of literacy instruction, is itself in crisis, the uncertainties about literacy and pedagogy playing themselves out in debates about the college major, teacher preparation, and graduate study. Finally, these discussions have been historically situated within a context signaled by the *postmodern*, a term uncommonly diverse in its range of meanings.

Any attempt to deal with so complex and conflicted a range of signifiers must then clearly announce the compass of references to be invoked. I would like to begin this essay by briefly discussing the formulation of the postmodern that I think can best inform considerations of reading and writing instruction today. This will include a look at the concrete economic and political conditions of the postmodern as well as the accompanying cultural arrangements. I will then turn to the reading and writing practices that I think respond most appropriately to these historical conditions. Here I will look at the developments in English studies at both the school and college level that are related to the turn to cultural studies and critical literacy, invoking such politically progressive figures as Raymond Williams, Stuart Hall, and Henry Giroux and Peter McLaren. Finally, I will explore the kinds of democratic classroom practices this new version of literacy recommends, keeping in mind that the procedures of literacy education are as important as the methods of reading and writing they recommend. Another way of characterizing this essay, I might add, is to see it as a plea for a reconstituted English studies that situates literacy instruction within the concrete economic, social, and political conditions of late capitalism, doing so in the interests of serving egalitarian ends for education in a participatory democracy.

Postmodernism

Postmodernism has come to stand for a staggering array of contemporary developments in economic, social, political, and cultural conditions. These developments in turn have been interpreted from a variety of ideological perspectives. In this essay, I want to align myself with those voices who see in the postmodern a complex interaction with the modern, at some points fulfilling modernist projects, at others actively rejecting them. Most important, I wish to insist that the relation between the economic, on the one hand, and the social, political, and cultural, on the other, is a dialectical one, the two spheres interacting with each other in ways that can be analyzed and described in terms of larger historical narratives, although not timeless and totalizing ones.

Viewed from the economic perspective, the postmodern does represent a unique and specifiable set of concrete material conditions and activities that, as David Harvey explains, can be characterized as the superseding of the Fordist mode of production by the "regime of flexible accumulation." This shift involves a number of obvious developments: the internationalization of production through the compression of space and time made possible by rapid travel and communication; small-batch production techniques, quicker responses to market conditions, and quicker turnover time; the decentering and diffusion of money and markets across national borders; and the reorganization of cities to respond to these conditions. These changes in turn have dramatic consequences for the structure of the work force. Workers tend to fall into two categories. The first consists of higher-level managerial positions enjoying large salaries, benefits, and job security. The second group is made up of poorly paid, expendable slots that bear the brunt of the rapid shifts that corporations make in quickly responding to changing market conditions. The isolation of workers in smaller and less stable units, in addition, results in a significant reduction in the ability of workers to organize for better wages, benefits, and conditions.

Changes in production and labor organization are in turn related to patterns of consumption, patterns that have heightened capitalism's feverish consumerism. Flexible accumulation has meant intensification of need inducement in order to increase consumption, calling on the media to create desire and promise its satisfaction. The society of the image, with its emphasis on fashion and the spectacle, is largely the result of this process. Services, including the supply of information to keep up with the rapidly fluctuating markets and the far-flung international enterprises of production, also increase significantly. Information and communication become commodities to be bought and sold as markets are as much created as identified.

The changes occasioned by this new mode of production and consumption have in turn given rise to the dramatic transformation of the experiences of daily life for most citizens of the First World. Figures as diverse as Williams, Jameson, Habermas, Lyotard, and Baudrillard have attempted to account in theoretical and practical terms for this new mode of the quotidian. Despite their differences, all agree that postmodern experience is marked by fragmentation, incoherence, and the lack of a stable center or foundation for experience. Ours is the age of the sensational and the spectacular, as we are daily bombarded by sensory stimuli, most of which is committed to selling a product or service. These incoherent images are paralleled by the apparent lack of a nucleus to the spaces in which we live, as urban areas are dislocated to accommodate the new economic arrangements. Like cities, nations as unified geographical and linguistic units are similarly threatened. The media's quick supply of information at times makes our differences as prominent as our points of similarity, a process reproduced on the international scale with telecommunications putting us in daily contact with diverse cultures. The speed of communication is matched by the speed of our lives: fast foods, fast cars, and fast trends placing us constantly in flux. Shopping in the neighborhood supermarket represents this time and space compression, with products from across the world assembled for purchase. The same compression is reproduced historically as styles of the past in clothing, architecture, and art are appropriated indiscriminately, merging past and present into an eternally now "pastiche," to use Jameson's description. This jumbling together of past and present, local and international, has given rise to the culture of the simulacrum, as Baudrillard characterizes it, the image and expression together connected to reproduce vicarious experiences that seem to transgress space and time. For those with the necessary means, life is made up of one manufactured event after another, a simulated production of other places and times. The result is the detachment of life from the concrete material and social conditions of our own historical moment.

The responses of cultural critics to these complex economic and social conditions have been diverse, even among those who agree about the conditions of experience in the postmodern. The debates about their significance have revolved around three main areas of contestation: the possibility of human agency and discursive representation; the possibility of historical representation; and the possibility of a totalizing discourse or metanarrative of experience. The arguments involved in the debate over these issues are too complex to be reproduced here.[1] I will instead present the positions that inform my discussion of the nature of literacy, pedagogy, and English studies needed today.

Speculation about the nature of language arising out of poststructuralist and deconstructionist discussions has led to the realization of the central place of the sign in human activity. At its extreme, this argument maintains that the subject who experiences and the object experienced are the mere effect—by-products as it were—of the free play of signifiers. The subject, far from being the unified, coherent, sovereign self apart and above language, is itself a fragmented construction of signification. Signs then speak humans rather than humans speaking signs. Here I wish to argue with this extreme position without abandoning its insistence on the death of the unified, autonomous, independent, and self-present subject. To deny the absolute sovereignty of the subject, however, is not necessarily to deny agency altogether. Invoking the Bakhtin circle, I will argue that the subject occupies a position at the center of conflicting discourses, serving as both product and producer of language. Although the subject is not altogether free, neither is it altogether determined. The subject's relation to material conditions is then always mediated by signs, signs that never simply reflect external conditions. This does not mean, however, that material conditions are beyond representation so that we live only in the ideal realm of signifiers. Despite the indeterminacy of language, material conditions do impose limits on humans and signifying systems: some representations can be demonstrated to be more adequate to human conditions, needs, and desires than others, even if no representation is completely and finally adequate.

This leads us to a consideration of the possibility of historical explanations as well as the prospects for totalizing metanarratives of human events, issues obviously imbricated in each other. Both the fragmented, disconnected nature of postmodern experience and the use of poststructuralist and deconstructionist conceptions of language in considering these conditions have led to the denial of the adequacy of any metanarrative to account for contemporary economic and political events. If we cannot even explain the larger power relations of the present, this position continues, how can we ever begin to explain these relations over time? Thus, society is decentered and displaced, history is one damn thing after another without significance, and politics, philosophy, and even science are simply the products of arbitrary and temporary expedients divorced from external warrants. The hope of the Enlightenment project of progress and perfection is as dead as the Enlightenment subject who formulated it.

Against this plea for an abandonment of history and a denial of any larger significance to the myriad detail of the postmodern experience, I would agree with those who argue for the necessity of provisional and contingent metanarratives of both the past and present. Although history is without any inherent plan or process, it is the product of complex interactions of people, political and social institutions, ideologies, technological conditions, and material modes of production. To abandon the attempt to make sense of history is for the vast majority of people everywhere to accept being victimized by it. Meanwhile, those who have the most to gain from historical accounts that validate present economic, social, and political arrangements, the most recent winners of historical conflicts, will continue to write histories from their point of view, presenting master narratives that authorize their continued power and privilege. It is not hard, of course, to extend this argument for explanatory narratives to the present and the political. However provisional and contingent these comprehensive accounts must be, they are always preferable to the atomistic responses to experience that, in the words of Aronowitz and Giroux, "run the risk of being trapped in particularist theories that cannot explain how the various diverse relations that constitute larger social, political, and global systems interrelate or mutually determine and constrain each other."[2] Metanarratives then become heuristics that open up "mediations, interrelations, and interdependencies that give shape and power to larger political and social systems."[3] Once again, these narratives are provisional and contingent, always remaining open to revisions and change. They are, however, necessary if history and politics are to serve the interests of democracy, equality, and justice, and not simply the interests of a wealthy and powerful ruling class.

A central purpose of this essay is to insist that these narratives are inevitable in responding to the complex conditions of our experience, enabling us to make sense of the myriad and confusing details of the postmodern. One clear and present danger is that the stories we tell ourselves in order to account for the events of our historical moment will become oversimplified, resting secure in comforting platitudes that avoid the convolutions of the moment, even at our own peril. These narratives can reduce the dazzling details of postmodern culture to a set of elementary and manageable propositions that deny the role of the economic and political in favor of more simple and soothing accounts. One form that this impulse has taken most recently is a reactionary and hysterical clinging to the imaginary certainties of an equally imaginary past. In *The Condition of Postmodernity*, Harvey describes this response: "the blocking out of sensory stimuli, denial, and cultivation of the blase attitude, myopic specialization, reversion to images of a lost past (hence the importance of mementoes, museums, ruins), and excessive simplification (either in the presentation of self or in the interpretation of events)."[4] Harvey locates these dangerous oversimplifications in the narratives provided by Thatcher in England and Reagan in the United States as rationales for their reactionary political programs, including their military interventions. The result of this response is what Harvey calls the "aesthetic-ization of politics," a process involving the insertion of a myth to mediate between the realms of truth and ethical action. This myth is a highly clichéd narrative that nevertheless provides a coherent basis for action. The coher-ence, however, is purchased at the price of ignoring the contradictions posed by actual material conditions, providing a misguided and partial narrative, most commonly about a nation-state and its destiny. This narrative escapes critique since it is accepted without reflection, by its nature immune from self-analysis and investigation in its obliviousness to historical realities. This aestheticization of politics prevents us from forming mental or cognitive maps, to use Jameson's phrase, that represent economic, social, political, and cultural conditions in a manner more adequate to their complex actu-ality. In a passage that prefigures the current crisis in U.S. foreign and domestic policy, Harvey concludes:

> The serious diminution of the power of individual nation states over fiscal and monetary policies, for example, has not been matched by a parallel shift towards an internalization of politics. Indeed, there are abundant signs that localism and nationalism have become stronger precisely be-cause of the quest for the security that place always offers in the midst of all the shifting that flexible accumulation implies. The resurgence of geopoli-tics and of faith in charismatic politics (Thatcher's Falklands War, Reagan's invasion of Grenada) fits only too well with a world that is increasingly nourished intellectually and politically by a vast flux of ephemeral im-ages.[5]

And the same can be said, we might add, of Bush's insane destruction of Iraq.

Literacy and pedagogy

This essay is a plea for encouraging a set of reading and writing practices that avoids the dangerous simplicities of the aestheticization of politics. These practices, I argue, will enable narratives that, despite their contingent and provisional nature, will encourage a complex reading of the complex inter-relations of the historical conditions of our experience. I wish to emphasize in my method and in my classroom practices the dialectical interaction between the economic and political and the cultural, forwarding a program for the literacy classroom that will invoke the cultural politics recommended by Giroux, Aronowitz, McLaren, and Shor. Calling as they do on the work of Raymond Williams, Stuart Hall, Richard Johnson, Terry Eagleton, and others, I wish to explore the encounters between socialist thought and poststructuralist linguistic theory, situating both within concrete historical and material conditions. I will, as I have already indicated, take into account the effects of postmodernism in revising our conceptions of language, subject formation, history and politics, and culture in general. My specific recommendations, however, will forward a project suited to the explicit institutional constraints of contemporary English studies. It will simultaneously regard the teacher as a transformative intellectual, a figure committed to encouraging democratic practices in all areas of experience—the economic, the social, the political, and the cultural.

I wish to propose that English studies be refigured as cultural studies, a move that carries a number of consequences that I wish to explore. To understand what is new in my proposal, however, it is necessary to understand the way English studies is constituted today. In "Rhetoric, Poetics, and Culture: The Collapsing Boundaries of English Studies," I have traced the historical formation of the main concerns of contemporary English departments and current attempts to reform them. Here I would like to survey a part of that presentation, considering first the arguments put forth by Gerald Graff in *Literature Against Itself: Literary Ideas in Modern Society* and by Robert Scholes in *Textual Power: Literary Theory and the Teaching of English*. Both argue that English studies is organized around a set of key preoccupations and terms functioning in binary opposition to each other, terms that determine which texts and experiences will be considered and which excluded in teaching reading and writing.

Graff argues that literary studies in the United States is based on the privileging of the literary text and the devalorization of the nonliterary text, the latter identified with the discourse of rhetoric (although he does not use the term), that is, the discourses of science and politics. Literary discourse is identified with the imaginary, the aesthetic, and the disinterested appeal to taste and sensibility. The rhetorical is found in the scientific, objective, practical, and political, all regarded as inferior because they are interested appeals to the public intellect and reason. Graff demonstrates the institutionalization of these dichotomies in successive schools of criticism, from the New Criticism of I.A. Richards to the neo-Aristotelian criticism of R.S. Crane to the myth criticism of Northrop Frye to the deconstructionist criticism of Paul de Man. Graff's entire argument is meant to demonstrate a set of binary oppositions inscribed in the institutional arrangement of literary studies, with the literary privileged over its rhetorical counterpart in consistent terms: creation against representation; texts as open, indeterminate "invitations" against texts as determinate objects; voyages into the unforeseen against boundaries and constraints; risk against docility and habit; truth as invention and fiction against truth as correspondence; and meaning as "process" against meaning as "product."[6] Graff wants to displace this opposition, but does so by resituating it within the literary, in this way reinforcing the power relations he wishes to contest, once again privileging literature over all other discourse. Still, his discussion of the play of binaries is instructive.

Scholes's treatment of these binaries is more explicit. He starts by openly admitting the invidious distinctions that privilege the study of literary texts over the study of other texts and the privileging of text interpretation over text production. He traces them to the division between production and consumption in a capitalist society, with consumption consistently valorized. In the English department scheme, nonliterary texts are relegated to the field of reading and the lower schools, since they lack both complication and disinterestedness. The nonliterary, after all, is "grounded in the realities of existence, where it is produced in response to personal or socio-economic imperatives and therefore justifies itself functionally." In being useful, it "can be read but not interpreted, because it supposedly lacks those secret-hidden-deeper meanings so dear to our pedagogic hearts."[7] The production of these nonliterary texts, in addition, cannot be taught apart from the exigencies of real-life situations, so that writing instruction is regarded as "pseudo nonliterature." The attempt to teach creative writing is similarly regarded as an effort to produce "pseudo literature," a futile gesture at teaching what cannot be taught. Finally, Scholes uses this governing scheme of oppositions to characterize English department practices along the same lines found in Graff: the division between sacred and profane texts, the division between the priestly class and the menial class, and the placing of beauty and truth against the utilitarian and commonplace. His intention is to analyze these binaries in order to deconstruct them and to forward in their place a new set of reading and writing practices to serve as the ground of English studies.

Scholes's effort is suggestive. Using deconstructionist and Marxist formulations, he argues for the multiple rather than monologic determination of texts. Since texts are based on culturally sponsored semiotic codes, the role of the reader is to locate these various codes through a variety of reading strategies invoked in their consideration. In other words, both literary and rhetorical texts can mean many things depending on the codes applied to them as well as the codes that may be inscribed in them, the two acting dialogically. Meaning is thus the product of an interactive process and is polysemic, and this is true whether the text is a poem or a political treatise.

Although Scholes effectively deconstructs many of the binaries he finds in the reading and writing strategies found in English departments, there are a number of flaws in his method. The choice of interpretive strategies—the code preferred in a particular reading, whether political or aesthetic or historical, for example—seems arbitrary. No standard for preferring one over another is provided. This means that the political and ethical become just one more set of choices, in no way to be recommended over any other. Since neither choosing codes nor integrating them is considered, there finally seems a capriciousness in the method. Furthermore, Scholes's attempt to deconstruct the current rhetoric/poetic opposition and its invidious distinctions focuses exclusively on literary texts, once again reinforcing the conviction that they alone merit close analysis. Similarly, he mentions nothing about the production of rhetorical texts—that is, the teaching of writing— assuming in the manner of those he opposes that learning to interpret literature will automatically teach students to master the methods of producing nonliterary discourse. Finally, *Textual Power* displays a political timidity, a reluctance to fully explore the subversiveness of the charges leveled at English studies. Thus, any role that it plays in reinforcing the injustices of race, class, and gender bias is scrupulously avoided, even though it is not difficult to see that this is a part of Scholes's tacit agenda.

Before turning to a consideration of my own plan for displacing the invidious discursive binary oppositions on which literacy in the English establishment is based, I would like to articulate their effects. The poetic/rhetoric bifurcation found in colleges and high schools in the United States serves the interests of a privileged professional managerial class while discriminating against those who are outside of this class. It does so, furthermore, through cruelly clandestine devices, refusing the political in the service of an aesthetic experience that implicitly reinforces discriminatory economic and social divisions. All of this, furthermore, is occulted by its pretensions to disinterestedness. Thus, the abhorrence of the rhetorical, of political and scientific texts, in English studies does far more than create a permanent underclass of department members at the college level whose putative role is the remediation of the poorly prepared. More importantly, it works to exclude from the ranks of the privileged managerial class those students not socialized from birth in the ways of the aesthetic response, doing so by its influence on the materials and methods of reading and writing required for success in secondary schools, college admission tests, and the colleges themselves. Thus English studies serves an important exclusionary function. It also mystifies the role it plays in precluding reading and writing practices that might address inequalities in the existing social order. In other words, by refusing reading practices that might discover the political unconscious of literary texts, and by refusing to take seriously the production and interpretation of rhetorical texts that address political matters, English studies has served as a powerful conservative and antidemocratic force, all the while insisting on its transcendence of the political. Thus the English establishment's insistence on the division of the literary and the nonliterary with its invidious dichotomies has served to entitle the entitled and to disempower the disempowered, doing so in the name of the sacred literary text.

Cultural literary

I would like to consider a formulation for reconceiving the rhetoric/poetic opposition that is now being forwarded by those within rhetorical studies. I wish to continue the discussion begun elsewhere by Patricia Bizzell and John Trimbur, although I will not comment directly on their work. I want to organize my remarks around the formulation that I have discussed elsewhere under the rubric of social-epistemic rhetoric. As I have argued in "Rhetoric Programs after World War II: Ideology, Power and Conflict," this rhetoric has acted as a counterpart to the calls from literary theorists such as Graff, Scholes, Jameson, Eagleton, Spivak, and others for a reconstituted English studies conceived as cultural studies. Growing primarily out of the work of Kenneth Burke and, more recently, the Bakhtin circle, this rhetoric is one with these figures in addressing the challenges to traditional discourse study presented by socialist influences and the poststructuralist linguistic turn as represented by Derrida and Foucault. Social-epistemic rhetoric most notably insists on examining all reading and writing practices within their historical context, on examining the ways language serves as mediator in the negotiations of individuals within their economic, political, and cultural moment. This reformulation of literacy practices—what I will call, after Freire, Shor, Giroux, McLaren and others, *critical literacy*—has accordingly begun with the displacement and refiguring of the divisive oppositions inscribed in the rhetoric/poetic relationship occupying the center of English studies.

Critical literacy denies the inherent distinction between representational texts and creative texts, arguing that language in all its uses structures rather than reflects signifieds. Language thus never acts as a simple referent to an extralinguistically verifiable thing-in-itself. It serves instead as a terministic screen that forms and shapes experience. Since all language use is inherently interpretive, all texts are involved in invention, in the process of meaning formation. This structuring of experience, however, is not undertaken by a unified, coherent, and self-present subject who can transcend language. Language is a social construction that shapes the subject as much as the subject shapes it. Since language is a product of social relations, it is inevitably involved in power and politics. Language thus constitutes an arena in which ideological battles are constantly fought. The different language practices of social groups are inscribed with ideological interpretations of experience that reinforce versions of what really exists, what is really good, and what is politically possible. The discourse of each and every social group tacitly instructs its members in who they are and how they fit into this larger scheme, as well as providing an interpretation of the scheme itself. Economic, social, political, and cultural "realities" are designated by the various discourses in circulation at any given moment. These ideologically inscribed discourses, furthermore, are in continual conflict for hegemony, with the groups in power calling on all of their discursive and material resources to maintain dominance in the face of continual opposition and resistance. This conception of the constructive capacity of language thus completely negates the distinctions between creative and referential discourse and the binaries they have been made to enforce. All texts shape experience because all texts are imbricated in economic, social, political, and cultural considerations.

These realizations displace the opposition between the production and consumption of texts. Producing and consuming discourse are both interpretations that require a knowledge of semiotic codes in which are inscribed a version of economic and political predispositions. All language is interested, and the task of the political writer as well as of the poet, and of the reader of the political writer as well as of the poet, is a working out of semiotic codes. The codes, furthermore, are never simply in the writer or in the text or in the reader. Instead, they always require a dialectical relation of the three, a rhetorical exchange in which writer, reader, text, and material conditions are simultaneously interacting with each other through the medium of the semiotic code, the linguistic center of experience. This encounter, it should also be mentioned, is never entirely free, since semiotic codes are always already interpretations. Signifying practices in poetic as well as rhetoric are thus historically conditioned, are always responses to the material and social formations of a particular moment.

This conception of the production and consumption of texts displaces and reformulates the contraries of the rhetoric/poetic relation. The clear oppositions between disinterested and interested, private and public, and contemplative and creative are obliterated. There are simply no disinterested uses of language, since all signifying practices, in both writing and reading, are involved in ideological predispositions. As Pierre Bourdieu has demonstrated, aesthetic judgements are closely related to class distinctions, so that all texts are at some level interested in social judgments. Furthermore, the distinction between high culture and low culture, the cultivated and the popular, can be characterized as a validation of the class structure, a distinction based on a hierarchy of texts created by a class interested in securing its own interests. That language is thoroughly social and communal means, in addition, the disappearance of the sharp distinction between private and public. Individuals are constituted by public discourse, although, as the Bakhtin circle reminds us, each individual becomes a differentiated site of converging discourses that enables agency and action for change. The subject as discursive formation acts as well as reacts, the private and public interacting dialectically. The private and public are never totally separate, nor are they totally identical. The distinction between action and contemplation likewise collapses as we recall that all texts are involved in politics and power, all tacitly endorsing certain platforms of action. Language, as Kenneth Burke has demonstrated, is always a program for action.

The perspective offered here does not mean that all distinctions between rhetoric and poetic will be expunged. It does mean, however, that the aesthetic cannot be regarded as a category functioning apart and beyond all other considerations. The historically constructed aesthetic code is a central element in literary production and interpretation, but it can only function in relation to other codes: it is never isolated and innocent. I have in mind the sort of practice recommended by Bakhtin and Medvedev, who argue that literary study "is concerned with the concrete life of the literary work in the unity of the generating literary environment, the literary environment in the generating ideological environment, and the latter, finally, in the generating socioeconomic environment which permeates it."[8] We will, of course, continue to distinguish between rhetorical texts and poetic texts, but we will do so on the basis of the writing and reading practices involved in each: the semiotic, culturally indicated codes deemed appropriate to each. Both are rich and complex in their expression of significance, and both are necessary to the health of a society. The work of English studies will be to study the discursive practices involved in generating and interpreting each. The English classroom will then provide methods for revealing the semiotic codes enacted in the production and interpretation of texts, codes that cut across the aesthetic, the economic and political, and the philosophical and scientific, preparing students to engage critically in the variety of reading and writing practices required of them as citizens, as workers, and as individuals.

The pedagogy

English studies refigured as cultural studies in the service of critical literacy will then regard its province as the examination and teaching of reading and writing practices. Rather than organizing its activities around the preservation and maintenance of a sacred canon of literary texts, it will consider the production, distribution, exchange, and reception of textuality in the general and in the specific, in both the past and present. English studies will then explore the role of signifying practices in the ongoing life of societies—more specifically, in their relations to economic, social, political, and cultural arrangements. These signifying practices, furthermore, will be regarded in their concrete relations to subject formation, to the shaping of consciousness in lived experience. Here the subject is not the sovereign and free agent of traditional literary studies. Instead, the subject is considered the point of convergence of conflicted discourses: it is itself the product of discourse rather than the unencumbered initiator of it. English studies will then examine the textual practices of reading and writing in order to explore their roles in consciousness formation within concrete historical conditions. Signifying practices serve as the mediator between these larger historical conditions and the formation of historical agents. And the entire process is historical, is in flux over time. Finally, the response of the agent to these signifying practices is regarded as at least partly unpredictable, involving a process of accommodation, negotiation, and resistance. The individual is not altogether determined, but neither is she altogether free.

English courses must now become self-consciously committed to the study of reading and writing practices. Whatever literary texts are chosen (and more of this shortly), all must be considered in relation to their conditions of production, distribution, exchange, and reception. Students will examine both the variety of audiences for these texts and the variety of ways the texts were received in their own time as well as the corresponding audiences and reception strategies across time. This will involve a selection of texts, including cross-cultural texts, and responses to them that demonstrate a wide range of interpretive reading practices. Historical interpretations different from our own, however, are accessible—make sense—only to readers who understand the economic, social, political, and cultural stakes involved in different strategies. Different readings usually carry with them different assumptions about the relative distribution of wealth and power within a society. The conflicting receptions of Matthew Arnold in his own time, for example, were often the result of the conflicting political loyalties of the periodicals considering his work, loyalties thoroughly enmeshed in questions of class and religion. Students can learn to locate these ideological predispositions by considering rhetorical texts produced and read as part of the discursive network of the historical moment. Students can study firsthand the intersections of aesthetic codes—certain formal and thematic elements, for example—with the economic and political. They can also undertake an analysis of the changing responses to these texts as successive generations of critics treat them—or, as just as often happens, fail to treat them. In other words, examining the creation of a canon with its inclusions and exclusions becomes a part of this study. Through the examination of the literary text, the concern, once again, is to look at the work in its generating literary environment, the literary environment in the generating ideological environment, and the ideological environment in the generating socioeconomic environment. In so doing, furthermore, students are gaining access to the ways that signifying practices shaped the subjectivities of the figures read as well as their audiences, observing the interaction of discourse and subject formation.[9]

The relation of the teacher and student in the critical literacy course will also involve reformation, and here I would invoke again Freire, Shor, and Giroux and McLaren as instructive models. This classroom will not be a stage for the virtuoso performance of the teacher. The teacher has much to do and is never simply another member of the class: institutional power cannot that easily be redistributed. The teacher will, however, attempt at every turn to share authority in the selection of materials and activities. This means that the student-teacher relation will be marked by a democratic dialogue that is in moments both collaborative and disputatious. The objectives of English studies are many. The most significant of these is developing a measure of facility in reading and writing practices so as to be prepared for public discourse in a democratic political community. The student must also learn to read and write for personal and private pleasure. And of course reading and writing in the diverse methods advocated here will prepare students for communication in their careers. These objectives can be achieved, however, only by sharing authority in the classroom, by allowing students to make choices, encouraging them to take part in the selection and evaluation of materials. Students must somewhere in their experience have choices that extend beyond commodity consumption. The teacher should also share responsibility for the presentation of materials with the class, arranging for students to work together in groups in investigating selected texts, texts which they will then share in written and oral reports with other class members. At the beginning course level, the teacher will assign most of these materials, although the students can still choose which parts of them will be their special responsibility. At the upper levels, it is often enough to identify texts and dates and periodicals, allowing students to fashion their own course materials. These materials and their presentation, furthermore, will involve students in a variety of reading *and* writing practices, cutting across textual genres in both interpretation and production, the students becoming composers as well as cultural critics.

At this point, the teacher's most demanding, engaging, and creative acts begin: the teaching of complex reading and writing strategies and practices. Students must learn the signifying practices of text production—academic discourse, political discourse, poetic discourse, scientific discourse, media discourse—as well as the signifying practices of text reception. And both must be considered in their ideological context: writing and reading the academic essay, for example, is not an innocent act.

The first difficulty in addressing this responsibility is that there is no comprehensive set of terms for describing these acts. Prior to the triumph of the middle class in the nineteenth century, rhetoric provided this language. Consider, for example, the method of Aristotle, a method that influenced discourse productions and reception for centuries. In the *Rhetoric* and *Poetics*, Aristotle presented a set of strategies and terms for both generating and interpreting both rhetorical and poetic texts. Aristotle's terms are no longer adequate to the theory informing our understanding of language, although there are those who have attempted a revival of them in both rhetoric and poetic. Even if this were not the case, the triumph of the middle class in discourse studies has been to naturalize its own rhetorical practices, concealing its ideology by denying the role of language in structuring experience when utilized according to its recommendations. The impulse to universalize its own conception of what is "natural" in economics, politics, sociology, and psychology is extended to signifying practices. This is why literature teachers can ask students to write an essay about a literary text without saying anything about the methods of reading the student is to prefer, or the production process to be following in preparing the essay. Both text interpretation and production are effaced, made invisible, their procedures readily accessible to those of the right class, gender, and racial background, while of course remaining inaccessible to the wrong sorts. In this scheme, rhetoric becomes synonymous with falsity and distortion, to be opposed to scientific truth (language as transparent sign system) in one moment, to poetic truth (language as free play) in the next. There is no space for political discourse because the debate of public discussion is silenced in the acquiescence in "what everybody knows."

The work of cultural literacy and pedagogy is to return us to a realization of the place of discourse in shaping knowledge and consciousness, doing so within the contemporary context of theory in language, literature, and rhetoric. The teacher must call on recent discussions of discourse analysis to develop a terminology adequate to the complexity of signifying systems. Although the various uses of semiotic theory in the work of Barthes, Eco, Hall, Fiske, Hodge, Kress, and others have begun this work, it remains the central task of teachers to rethink theory through classroom practice and classroom practice through theory. The result will be methods of locating and naming the discursive acts that encourage unjust class, race, gender, and other power relations through the tacit endorsement of certain economic, social, and political arrangements. Attempts to negotiate and resist semiotically enforced cultural codes can take place only when these codes can be named and interrogated in reading and writing, and this is the central role of the teacher in the literacy classroom.

I have presented an example of this kind of classroom in an essay entitled "Composition and Cultural Studies." Students in a freshman composition class pursued a process approach to learning writing, engaging in prewriting heuristic strategies, drafting, and revising. In addition to learning the language and practices of composing, they were introduced to a set of terms that enabled them to locate semiotic codes in the texts they encountered as well as in their daily experience as members of an ongoing culture, interpretive terms and strategies found in Barthes' *Mythologies* and Fiske's *Introduction to Communication Studies*. They learned to look for key terms and the binary oppositions in which the terms were inscribed. These in turn were located within the race, class, and gender codes that were being encouraged, with the students learning to look for the contradictions in these culturally sanctioned ideological codes. These were then situated within the larger economic, social, and political narratives of which they formed a significant part. Students were learning a language that encouraged them to look for the coded nature of the texts they read and composed, as well as the coded nature of their daily experiences. In successive three-week units on advertising, education, work, play, and individuality, they read and wrote and reread and rewrote the cultural codes that were being enacted in their daily lives, arriving at a position from which they could negotiate the discursive conditions of their experience. They began to develop the capacity to become active agents of their own histories rather than unreflective products of the cultural codes that had shaped them. The process, I hasten to add, was at times uncomfortable, since students were, as might be expected, reluctant to critique the historically situated cultural codes they had thought represented eternal truths. And in the end most did not radically depart from their initial ideological positions. They did, however, develop a set of strategies for reading and writing—that is, interpreting and producing—their experience that made them more active critical agents of the conditions of their lives.

One of the most effective ways of tackling the difficult job of identifying culturally determined textual codes is to examine the contrasting semiotics of different media. Indeed, critical pedagogy must insist that students are given the devices to interpret and critique the signifying practices that schools have typically refused to take seriously, the discourse of radio and television and film. Studying the manner in which meaning is constructed within these media works to demystify their characteristic textual practices and inevitable ideological inscriptions. It also illuminates the textual practices of print, by contrast indicating the diverse semiotic strategies of the differing forms of communication. This multimedia study is especially effective, furthermore, when students are encouraged to engage in the production as well as the interpretation of various kinds of texts. Students ought to write poetry and fiction as well as read them, create magazine ads as well as interpret them, produce television situation comedies and newscasts as well as critique them. In this way the inevitable commitment of all of these textual forms to culturally coded ideological notions of race, class, and gender in the service of economic and political projects can become accessible.

This brings me back to a matter considered in the first section of this essay: the aestheticization of politics. Although Harvey is correct in deploring the use of simplistic and cruel narratives of national identity and destiny to justify unjust political programs, it should now be apparent that the use of larger cultural narratives is unavoidable. The purpose of critical literacy within English studies will have as a prime objective the cultivation of the students' ability to critique the cultural narratives of others and to construct in their place narratives more adequate to the complexities of their historical conditions. Learning to write as well as read rhetorical arguments and poetic texts and to produce as well as critique video advertisements and newscasts and dramas will enable students to write and read and to produce and critique the conditions of their own experience. They will be given guidance in becoming active agents of social and political change and improvement, learning that the world has been made and can thus be remade to serve more justly the interests of a democratic society.

Finally, it should now be obvious that in this formulation the classroom becomes a site of political activity and struggle. If the genuinely utopian and critical possibilities of art and rhetoric—whether in print, oral, or visual form—are to be realized, the student's position as a political agent in a democratic society must be foregrounded. The teacher must serve as a trans-formative intellectual—as, again, Shor and Aronowitz and Giroux have shown us—concerned with improving economic and social conditions in the larger society. She must realize that her students are the products of concrete histories that have brought them to their present political positions, positions which are often committed to denying the conflicts and contradictions in their experiences as well as in the signifying practices they daily encounter. More appropriate responses can come only in acknowledging and confronting this denial and in examining its material and social sources. Students who on one day rejoice over the magnificence of their country because its billion-dollar-a-day military budget enables it to crush small Third World nations at will, and then on the next admit their fear that they, like their parents, will be without a job upon graduation, need to come to terms with the contradictions of their experience, contradictions obviously not of their own making. The teacher's role inside the classroom then becomes an extension of her role as a force for progressive change at all levels of society.

Notes

1. See Aronowitz, S., and Giroux, H., *Education under Seige*, (South Hadley, Mass.: Bergin and Garvey, 1985), Chapter 5; and Giroux, H., and McLaren, P., "Language, Schooling and Subjectivity: Beyond a Pedagogy of Resistance and Reproduction," in Borman, K., Swami, P., and Wagstaff, L. (eds.), *Contemporary Issues in U.S. Education* (Norwood, N.J.: Ablex, 1991).
2. Aronowitz and Giroux, *ibid.*, p. 70.
3. *Ibid.*
4. Harvey, D., *The Condition of Postmodernity* (Oxford: Basil Blackwell, 1989), p. 286.
5. *Ibid.*, pp. 305–306.
6. Graff, G., *Literature against Itself: Literary Ideas in Modern Society* (Chicago: University of Chicago Press, 1979), p. 24.
7. Scholes, R., *Textual Power: Literary Theory and the Teaching of English* (New Haven: Yale, 1985), p. 6.
8. Bakhtin, M., and Medvedev, P., *The Formal Method in Literary Scholarship*, trans. Wehrle, A. (Cambridge, Mass.: Harvard University Press, 1985), p. 271.
9. See McCormick, K., and Waller, G., with Flower, L., *Reading Texts* (Lexington: D.C. Heath, 1987), for an introduction to this method.

References

Aronowitz, Stanley, and Henry A. Giroux. *Education under Seige*. South Hadley, Mass.: Bergin and Garvey, 1985.

———. *Postmodern Education: Politics, Culture, and Social Criticism*. Minneapolis: University of Minnesota Press, 1991.

Bakhtin, M. M. *The Dialogic Imagination: Four Essays*. Trans. Caryl Emerson. Ed. Michael Holquist. Austin: University of Texas Press, 1981.

Bakhtin, M. M., and P. N. Medvedev. *The Formal Method in Literary Scholarship*. Trans. Albert J. Wehrle. Cambridge: Harvard University Press, 1985.

Barthes, Roland. *Mythologies*. Trans. Annette Lavers. New York: Hill, 1972.

Baudrillard, Jean. *Selected Writings*. Ed. Mark Poster. Stanford: Stanford University Press, 1988.

Berlin, James A. "Composition and Cultural Studies." In *Composition and Resistance*. Ed. Mark Hurlbert and Michael Blitz. Portsmouth, N.H.: Boynton/Cook, 1991.

———. "Rhetoric, Poetics, and Culture: The Collapsing Boundaries of English Studies." In *The Politics of Composition*. Ed. John Trimbur and Richard Bullock. Portsmouth, N.H.: Boynton/Cook, 1991.

———. "Rhetoric Programs after World War II: Ideology, Power and Conflict." In *Rhetoric and Ideology: Compositions and Criticisms of Power*. Ed. Charles Kneupper. Arlington, Tex.: Rhetoric Society of America, 1989.

Bizzell, Patricia. "On the Possibility of a Unified Theory of Composition and Literature." *Rhetoric Review*, 4, 2, 1986, pp. 174–180.

Bourdieu, Pierre. *Distinction: A Social Critique of the Judgement of Taste*. Trans. Richard Nice. Cambridge: Harvard University Press, 1984.

Burke, Kenneth. *Language as Symbolic Action*. Berkeley: University of California Press, 1966.

Eagleton, Terry. *Walter Benjamin: Or Towards a Revolutionary Criticism*. London: Verson, 1981.

Eco, Umberto. *A Theory of Semiotics*. Bloomington: Indiana University Press, 1976.

Fiske, John. *Introduction to Communication Studies*. 2nd ed. London: Routledge, 1990.

Freire, Paulo. *Pedagogy of the Oppressed*. New York: Continuum, 1970.

Giroux, Henry. *Schooling and the Struggle for Public Life*. Minneapolis: University of Minnesota Press, 1988.

———. "Schooling as a Form of Cultural Politics: Towards Pedagogy of and for Difference." In *Critical Pedagogy, the State, and Cultural Struggle*. Ed. Henry A. Giroux and Peter L. McLaren. Albany: SUNY, 1989.

Giroux, Henry A., and Peter McLaren. "Language, Schooling, and Subjectivity: Beyond a Pedagogy of Resistance and Reproduction." In *Contemporary Issues in U.S. Education*. Ed. Kathryn M. Borman, Piyushi Swami, and Lonnie D. Wagstaff. Norwood, N.J.: Ablex, 1991.

Graff, Gerald. *Literature against Itself: Literary Ideas in Modern Society.* Chicago: University of Chicago Press, 1979.

Habermas, Jürgen. "Modernity—An Incomplete Project." In *The Anti-Aesthetic: Essays in Postmodern Culture.* Ed. Hal Foster. Port Townsend, Wash.: Bay Press.

Hall, Stuart, D. Hobson, A. Lowe, and P. Willis (eds.). *Culture, Media, Language.* London: Hutchinson, 1980.

Harvey, David. *The Condition of Postmodernity.* Oxford: Basil Blackwell, 1989.

Hodge, Robert, and Gunther Kress. *Social Semiotics.* Ithaca: Cornell University Press, 1988.

Jameson, Fredric. "Postmodernism or the Cultural Logic of Late Capitalism." *New Left Review,* 146, 1984, pp. 53–93.

Johnson, Richard. "What is Cultural Studies Anyway?" *Social Text,* 16, 1986–87, pp. 38–80.

Lyotard, Jacques. *The Postmodern Condition.* Minneapolis: University of Minnesota Press, 1984.

McCormick, Kathleen, and Gary Waller with Linda Flower. *Reading Texts.* Lexington: D.C. Heath, 1987.

McLaren, Peter. *Life in Schools.* New York: Longman, 1989.

————. "Postmodernism and the Death of Politics: A Brazilian Reprieve." *Educational Theory* 36.4 (1986): 389–401.

Scholes, Robert. *Textual Power: Literary Theory and the Teaching of English.* New Haven: Yale, 1985.

Shor, Ira. *Critical Teaching and Everyday Life.* 3rd printing. Chicago: University of Chicago Press, 1987.

————. *Culture Wars: School and Society in the Conservative Restoration, 1969–1984.* London: Methuen, 1986.

Spivak, Gayatri Chakravorty. *In Other Words: Essays in Cultural Politics.* London: Methuen, 1987.

Trimbur, John. "Culture Studies and Teaching Writing." *Focuses* 1, 2, 1988, pp. 5–18.

Williams, Raymond. *Marxism and Literature.* Oxford: Oxford University Press, 1977.

9

Postmodernism and literacies

James Paul Gee

This paper first offers, from the perspective of a linguist and discourse analyst, a "poststructuralist" and "postmodern" perspective on meaning, demonstrating how this perspective grows "logically" out of paradoxes inherent in "structuralism" and modernism. It then develops the implications of this postmodern perspective for the theory and practice of "literacies" in the schools. Finally, it closes with a consideration of how moral judgments and practices of resistance can be "validated" in the face of the pervasive postmodern rejection of claims to exclusivity and privilege on the part of any social practice.

Two views of meaning

What is the meaning of the word *bird?* One answer is that the meaning of the word *bird* is a *concept* in my mind or brain (an image or a mental description), a concept of birds out in the world. It is in virtue of my having this concept in my head and its being associated with the word *bird* that *bird* can be used to refer to birds. This is the view of meaning held by most people across the world for most of human time on earth, including both the "folk" and a good many scholars,[1] at least until relatively recently. Let us call it the "first" view of meaning.

In this view of meaning, the meaning of a word or any other sort of sign is fixed by what is in my head. When I communicate, I know what I mean in a rather special way, since I have a rather special and privileged access to what is in my head. On the other hand, the fact that two people can successfully communicate about birds is a happy "accident." There is no necessary reason why they both should have the same sort of thing in their heads associated with the sign *birds*. That they do is simply the contingent result of their shared human biology and shared culture.

This view of meaning need never get undermined, so long as people continue to communicate only with people from their own culture. However, it cannot survive the thoughtful experience of confronting another sign system, one significantly different from one's own. Consider, for example, the sign *red*. This seems to fit perfectly well with our first view of meaning. I have an image in my head of red which is associated with the sign *red*, and by virtue of this association I can use *red* to refer to red. However, even a brief consideration of signs for colors in other languages renders this view of meaning problematic.[2]

Languages differ in how many single color terms they have. Some have only two basic color terms. For example, in Dugum Dani, a language spoken in New Guinea, the terms *modla* and *mili*, which may be roughly translated as "light/bright" and "dark/dull," respectively, are the only words that can be identified as basic color terms. On the other hand, like several other languages, English has eleven basic color terms: *black, white, red, yellow, blue, green, orange, brown, purple, pink,* and *gray*. Between these two extremes are languages with many different color term systems.

Human beings (except those who are "color-blind") see the same colors. Color in the physical world is a spectrum of continuously graded shades running into each other with no discrete boundaries (we all have trouble telling where blue stops and purple begins, where red stops and orange begins, and so forth). Each language must choose where it will cut the color spectrum and how many times, with its discrete words. Dugum Dani divides the spectrum in half with two words, and English makes eleven cuts; other languages make different numbers of cuts between these two extremes.

In every language there is a *prototype* (or typical instance) associated with each basic color term. For example, in English, the word *blue* can be applied to all types and shades of blue, but most native speakers agree on what shade of blue constitutes the *most typical* or *best example* of blue. Such a prototype shade is called the "focus" of the term.

It turns out that there are for human beings only eleven possible color focuses, and all languages, regardless of how many basic color terms they have, choose terms which have as a focus one of these eleven colors. The focus of the Dugum Dani word that speakers of the language apply to all dark colors, for example, is the same as the focus for the English word *black*; the focus of the Dugum Dani word that speakers of the language apply to bright colors is the same as the focus of the English word *white*.

Actually, there is yet more order here. If speakers of a language have less than eleven basic color terms, which colors they will have is determined by a set of universal principles. All languages that have only two basic color terms have one term whose focus (prototypical example) is black and one term whose focus is white (though, of course, the two terms will commonly be used to refer to all dark colors and all light colors, respectively). In languages that have three basic color terms, the focus of one term is black, the focus of the second term is white, and the focus of the third term is red. All languages with four basic color terms have a term whose focus is black, another whose focus is white, a third whose focus is red, and a fourth whose focus is yellow, green, or blue (typically, in fact, these languages have a fourth single term with two foci, one of which is green, the other of which is blue; that is, they have a single word meaning *blue or green*). A language with five color terms will typically have basic color words whose foci are black, white, red, blue/green, and yellow. A language with six basic color terms will distinguish blue and green with different terms, one having the focus green and the other having the focus blue. A language with seven basic color terms adds a term whose focus is brown to the terms in a language with six basic color terms. A language with more than seven terms adds terms with focuses for one or more of the following: purple, pink, orange, and gray.

We humans see eleven focal colors in the continuously graded color spectrum. That's just the way the eye is made. Other creatures—whether bees or Martians—whose eyes are differently made see this spectrum differently. Languages pick some subset or all of these eleven focal colors, depending on the interests and needs of the culture. They then extend the color terms they have to apply to nonfocal shades (for example, a term whose focus is black is extended to talk about all dark and dull things; a term whose focus is blue is extended to talk about all shades of blue, many of them rather far from the prototype or focus). In this way they can all talk about all the continuously graded shades of color in the spectrum.

Now, we can ask: do people from cultures with four basic color terms see the world differently, or think about it differently, than people from cultures with seven basic color terms? If you ask people from a culture with four color terms to sort colored chips into piles, they will initially sort them into four piles. And someone from a culture with seven terms will initially sort them into seven piles. This result once led psychologists to think that people with different languages saw and thought about colors differently.[3] However, if you go on to tell these people to make more piles, they will eventually come up with much the same piles. At some stage in the proceedings they quit using their language as a guide and just use the human eye—which is everywhere the same—as a guide.

These color chips are a good guide to how language, culture, and brain interact. Languages cut up the world in different ways. These ways are constrained, however, by the nature of the human body, the human eye, and the human brain. The way a language cuts up the world will influence how we *initially* think about something, but it does not determine how we *finish* thinking about it. Under pressure we can think about things outside the categories of our language, thanks to the fact that we can find other people's ways of doing things senseful. And we find them senseful because, at least where language is concerned, they are all chosen from the inventory of ways allowed by the human brain, which is, like the eye, essentially the same across cultures.

This consideration of color terms leads to a different view of meaning. Let us call it the "second" view of meaning. On this view the meaning of a sign, like *red*, emanates from the *system of signs* and is not rooted in the single sign itself.[4] The sign *modla* in Dugum Dani means what it means thanks to the fact that it contrasts with only one other color term (*mili*). It would perforce change its meaning if Dugum Dani added another color word. The English word *red* means what it means thanks to the fact that it contrasts with ten other color terms. It would change its meaning if English lost several of its color terms.

It is as if we laid out in front of ourselves a surface to be covered by colored tiles. If I cover this space with twenty tiles, this is going to look radically different from the case where I cover the space with nine tiles. The tiles are going to be different shapes and sizes in each case. In reality, a sign system covers the "space" with many different "subsystems" (color terms, animal terms, emotion terms, and so on), each of which makes a different number of distinctions than other sign systems do.

But this analogy between sign systems and covering a space with tiles breaks down at one important point: in the case of sign systems there is no way to know what the space being covered is (or its extent) apart from looking at the signs "covering" it. We cannot "take up" the signs and stare at the space (the "world," "reality," or whatever we want to call it) with no signs at all. Our perceptual system won't do this, as we will see below. The perceptual system is itself, it turns out, just another sign system. A bee sees a very different world from a human, and there is no way to adjudicate which one is seeing the world "as it really is."

Every sign system (every language, each creature's perceptual system) cuts up the world differently. How any human sign system cuts up the world is a contingent result of the human mind or brain and the human body (for example, the eye) and the culture one happens to be in. In this view there is in principle no real translation between sign systems. If the meaning of *modla* is simply the result of its relation to the other signs available in Dugum Dani and the meaning of *red* is the result of its relation to the other signs available in English, then there is no way to equate these two systems, since they have different numbers, falling into different subsystems.

This second view of meaning privileges the *system* of signs and the structure of the mind or brain and body over the individual human being. Human individuals and the "sense" they make of the world and each other are simply products of their sign systems and the mind or brain or bodies that "control" them. I personally cannot make *red* mean anything other than what value it takes on in the sign system. When the sign system changes, the meaning of red changes, quite regardless of what is in my head. What happens to be in my head is, in fact, quite irrelevant to meaning. All that matters is what is in the system.

This second view of meaning is the foundation of intellectual movements that went loosely under the name of "structuralism."[5] It is also at the heart of artistic movements that went, equally loosely, under the name of "modernism." Many have also seen this view of meaning as the perfect ideological expression of "Fordism," the system of advanced smokestack industrial capitalism, whose waxing and waning (loosely) corresponds with the waxing and waning of structuralism and modernism.[6] In such an economic and social system, workers, consumers, and commodities are meaningless in and of themselves. Their meaning ("value") is determined by their place within systems of production and consumption.[7] In fact, both structuralism and Fordism stress *systems* that produce meanings (values) over the individuals who carry out the production.

Imagism in poetry

To see the relevance of this second view of meaning to spheres beyond language, let us consider for a moment the 1930s movement in poetry referred to as imagism, a more or less typical type of modernism in art.[8] In fact, I will concentrate just on William Carlos Williams, a leading member of imagism and later related movements in modern poetry.

Imagist poets like William Carlos Williams believed that our sign systems and our routine and taken-for-granted ways of seeing the world habitualized our experience of the world. Williams sought to break the hold of these systems, to make the world "strange" again, so that we would "really" see and feel it anew.[9]

Of course the idea that art ought to concentrate on the authentic rendering of the object in all its immediacy and particularity goes well beyond Williams and indeed well beyond poetry as an art form. The great Russian formalist critic and writer Victor Shklovsky[10] added to the importance of the perceived object in art his notion of *ostranenie* (defamiliarization, "making strange") and concluded that "art exists that one may recover the sensation of life; it exists to make one feel things, to make the stone *stony*."[11] Williams also wanted to make the stone *stony*. He too saw a crucial link between the object, perceived as "an arrangement of appearances, of planes," and supraindividual human emotional states and experiences. And Williams too added an additional notion to the importance of the perceived object in art: his famous concept of "local consciousness." Let me quote Bram Dijkstra on this point:

> Williams saw one's immediate environment, one's "locality," as the only source of that universal experience which, he thought, "great" art expresses. Such universal experience was communicable only on the basis of an authentic perception of the objects of the material world, which, he reasoned, could only stem from an accurate representation of the things we know, the things with which we are intimately familiar: the "sensual accidents" bred out of "the local conditions which confront us."[12]

Williams insisted upon the importance of the structural ("system-atic") organization of objects. The poem is a *thing*, and Williams insisted upon its structural and perceptual integrity. It was through attention to the structural organization of things in the world and of poems that the poet conveyed the meaning and aesthetic value in things. So too it is by attention to structure that the reader constructs the meaning and aesthetic value of the poem. Williams made this point clear in his discussion of his favorite painter, the great modernist Cezanne ("the father of modern art"):

> I was tremendously involved in an appreciation of Cezanne. He was a designer. He put it down on the canvas so that there would be a meaning without saying anything at all. Just the relation of the parts to themselves. In considering a poem, I don't care whether it is finished or not; if it is put down with a good relation to the parts, it becomes a poem. And the meaning of the poem can be grasped by attention to design.[13]

Remarks like this make Williams sound every bit the structuralist. Every part of a poem or painting and every part of reality takes on meaning not in and of itself, but only in *relation* to other things as part of a *structure* or *system*. What was meaningful was the "relation of the parts to themselves," not the things themselves. Structuralism and modernism are a *designer's* view of meaning and reality. For Williams, the creative genius of the artist creates (or really "finds" by "authentically" seeing) the design; for the structuralist design is the product of human biology, culture, and history.

To see Williams's aesthetics in action, consider his poem "The Great Figure":[14]

The Great Figure

Among the rain
and lights
I saw the figure 5
in gold
on a red
firetruck
moving
tense
unheeded
to gong clangs
siren howls
and wheels rumbling
through the dark city.

In this poem Williams "fractures" both traditional poetry and our routinized way of image-ing the scene he depicts. He simultaneously renders poetry and everyday perceptual experience "strange" and "new." In doing so he makes clear how traditional poetry and our routinized way of seeing things are themselves just sign systems to which we have become accustomed. They "cut us off" from "authentic" perception; the poet restores this authenticity.

Williams and photographers (such as Alfred Stieglitz) and painters (such as Charles Demuth) that he influenced and was influenced by[15] were taken by the images of modern industrial society (for example, the machines, the factory, and the modern city). They saw these as "new images" that rendered "strange" our previously taken-for-granted "reality" (that is, the reality of precapitalist and early capitalist society, though they did not use these terms). They painted, photographed, and wrote poetry about the machines, buildings, and places of Fordist society in such a way as to make of them imagist art.

In the act, of course, they rendered the structures (relations) of modern capitalism "aesthetic" and "acceptable," and eventually, as they became commonplaces of modernist art, these relations themselves ironically became "routine" and "taken for granted." Modernist art had an interestingly "complicit" role in the ascendancy of Fordism and colonialism, however hostile individual modernists were (or were not) to capitalism.

In rendering Fordist structures, as well as the emerging colonial societies in Africa and India, "strange" and "art-ful," modernists ultimately "naturalized" them. They removed their "strangeness" from the moral realm to the aesthetic realm, and, in the act, equated the artifacts of colonial societies (such as African art and craft), the articles of capitalism, and the art objects of modernism.[16] Of course, capitalism rendered all of these simply *commodities* in any case, their value a pure result of the economic systems they were in.

A third view of meaning

There is a great deal of debate today about whether we are in a "postmodern," "postindustrial," "postcolonial" era, or whether we are just seeing the logical culmination of modernism in the arts, in the media, in intellectual affairs, and in economic, political, and social affairs generally.[17] Fordist industrial capitalism, with its attendant nationalism and colonialism, is, it is argued, being rapidly replaced by economic structures based on information rather than goods,[18] services rather than manufacturing,[19] and the absence of borders rather than their presence (for example, "multinational" corporations).

Contemporary electronics and computers allow goods, services, and ideas to be mass-produced in such a fashion that they look like they were designed specially for well-defined small groups or even individual consumers.[20] This creates the illusion of uniqueness at the very time in which electronics and computers are causing time and space to collapse into each other and in the process eliminating local cultural differences.[21] Information takes next to no time to cross space, rendering the world a point and borders transitory and meaningless.

"The local conditions which confront us"—which Williams saw as the foundation of the "universal experience" that art expresses—are now global. There are no more local regions, exempt from the social, economic, and political affairs of the world at large. You can follow in real time a distant war as easily as you can catch up on your "local" gang warfare.

It has been argued that the Fordist industrial capitalist "modern" world already contained the seeds of the emerging postmodern world, that postmodern reality is simply the "runaway" culmination of modernism.[22] Others have argued that the postmodern world represents a real disjuncture, a truly new reality.[23] I believe that this argument can be settled (if it, in fact, can be settled) only through detailed arguments about economics and the possibility that a new "mode of accumulation" arose in the 1970s. I do not plan to enter into this debate here. What I do want to argue, though, is that modernism in the arts and in intellectual affairs (for example, structuralism) already harbored paradoxes and contradictions that once exposed became the leading intellectual underpinnings of a "postmodern" view of meaning and reality.

We can see a paradox in modernism if we reconsider Williams for a moment. I said the following about Williams's poem "The Great Figure": "He simultaneously renders poetry and everyday perceptual experience 'strange' and 'new.' In doing so he makes clear how traditional poetry and our routinized way of seeing things are themselves just sign systems to which we have become accustomed. They 'cut us off' from 'authentic' perception; the poet restores this authenticity." There is a paradox here. Our languages, as well as our ways of thinking and seeing, are sign systems. As they become habitualized and routinized, inaccessible to our conscious awareness, they render, for Williams and other imagists, our perception of the world inauthentic. However, the poet can only restore authenticity to our perception of the world by creating a new form of poetry and a new way of looking at the world. But these new ways are just new and alternative sign systems. They too, in use, will become routinized and habitualized. They too stand between us and the "stoniness" of the stone. There is no nonrepresentational unmediated access to "reality;" reality is a construct of our sign systems. There is no "true" contact with the "stoniness" of the stone apart from the rather ethereal and abstract reality of sign (representational, symbol) systems.

This paradox leads immediately to another. We saw that (on our second, sign-based view of meaning) a sign has meaning not because of some direct contact with the world, but through its relations to the other signs in its sign system. The meaning of a sign is "tied down" by its relations to the sign system as a whole. *But what "ties down" the sign system itself?* We concede, as it appears we must on our second view of meaning, that *red* in English means what it means thanks to the other ten color terms in the language (and the overall number and organization of all the other English signs) and that an analogous term in a language with seven color terms means something different. But then how do we choose between one sign system or the other (the eleven-term one, the seven-term one, or some other one)? Which one is a more accurate or veridical view of color in the world? For that matter, why isn't the way a bee's visual system cuts up the world just as good as ours (or better)?

All we have got are sign systems; we have no immediate access to a reality apart from a sign system. So what *licenses* any one of them? A given sign system (language, way of seeing the world, form of art, social theory, and so forth) can *claim* universality or authenticity or naturalness, but this is always a claim made from *within* the system itself. Outside the system, we are in another sign system that may well have different canons of universality or authenticity. Where do we stand to claim "authority" for ourselves and our sign systems? The postmodern answer is "nowhere."[24]

With this we reach one of the central points of postmodern perspectives. The point is put nicely by Kwame Anthony Appiah:

> There is now a rough consensus about the structure of the mod-ern/postmodern dichotomy in the many domains—from architecture to poetry to philosophy to rock music to the movies—in which it has been invoked. In each of these domains there is an antecedent practice that laid claim to a certain exclusivity of insight, and in each of them "postmoder-nism" is a name for the rejection of that claim to exclusivity, a rejection that is almost always more playful, though not necessarily less serious, than the practice it aims to replace.[25]

A sign system operates not because it is inherently natural or valid, nor because it is universal, but simply because some group of people have engaged in the past and continue to engage in the present in a particular set of *social practices* that incorporate that sign system.[26] Wearing a suit and a tie of a certain sort, and talking and acting in certain ways in an executive boardroom, have certain meanings, constitute a sign system, within the social practices of the corporate business world. But these things mean what they mean, and the system is what it is, simply because these practices evolved in history and are continued into the present.

It is important to realize that this view of meaning sees sign systems simply as the historically derived social practices of particular groups. These practices have often evolved in order to claim authority and privilege for one group against other groups. The sign system is a social and historical tool in terms of which groups of people carry out their desires and claim and contest power. It is not a disinterested reflection of an ahistorical and asocial reality.

In this view of meaning, meaning is not *in the head*, but rooted in the historical and social practices of groups of people. As the corporate executives' social practices are lived out, it does not matter much what is going on "privately" in the heads of the people involved in the practice. Wearing a certain sort of suit and standing behind a certain sort of desk at the "right" time and place means what it means quite apart from whatever mental events are transpiring in my head. And it has this meaning because of what has happened in the past and what is currently going on in the present, in terms of the practices of both the executives and of others (or executives themselves in other settings) who contest the executives' powers and desires by means of their own sign systems embedded in their own historically derived social practices.

Implications of the third view for literacy and education

This third view of meaning has important implications for how we characterize literacy and for educational practices in general.[27] Education is an area where this postmodern view of meaning receives some of its strongest support.[28]

I will exemplify the points I want to make here by juxtaposing two texts that I have discussed in a number of places.[29] The first is a story that an upper-middle-class five-year-old girl told at home. The second is a story that a lower-socioeconomic seven-year-old black girl told during "sharing time" ("show-and-tell time") at school. Together these texts can lead us to a version of a postmodern view of literacy and schooling.

Five-Year-Old's Story

STANZA 1 (Introduction)
1. This is a story
2. About some kids who were once friends
3. But got into a big fight
4. And were not

STANZA 2 (Frame: Signaling of Genre)
5. You can read along in your storybook
6. I'm gonna read aloud

STANZA 3 (Title)
7. "How the Friends Got Unfriend"

STANZA 4 (Setting: Introduction of Characters)
8. Once upon a time there was three boys 'n three girls
9. They were named Betty Lou, Pallis, and Parshin, were the girls
10. And Michael, Jason, and Aaron were the boys
11. They were friends

STANZA 5 (Problem: Sex Differences)
12. The boys would play Transformers
13. And the girls would play Cabbage Patches

STANZA 6 (Crisis: Fight)
14. But then one day they got into a fight on who would be each team
15. It was a very bad fight
16. They were punching
17. And they were pulling
18. And they were banging

STANZA 7 (Resolution 1: Storm)
19. Then all of a sudden the sky turned dark
20. The rain began to fall
21. There was lightning going on
22. And they were not friends

STANZA 8 (Resolution 2: Mothers Punish)
23. Then um the mothers came shooting out 'n saying
24. "What are you punching for?
25. You are going to be punished for a whole year"

STANZA 9 (Frame)
26. The end
27. Wasn't it fun reading together?
28. Let's do it again
29. Real soon!

Seven-Year-Old's Story

STANZA 1
1. Today
2. it's Friday the 13th
3. an' it's bad luck day
4. an' my grandmother's birthday is on bad luck day

STANZA 2
5. an' my mother's bakin' a cake
6. an' I went up my grandmother's house while my
   mother's bakin' a cake
7. an' my mother was bakin' a cheese cake
8. my grandmother was bakin' whipped cream cup cakes

STANZA 3
9. an' we bof went over my mother's house
10. an' then my grandmother had made a chocolate cake
11. an' then we went over my aunt's house
12. an' she had made a cake

STANZA 4
13. an' everybody had made a cake for nana
14. so we came out with six cakes

STANZA 5
15. last night
16. my grandmother snuck out
17. an' she ate all the cake
18. an' we hadda make more

STANZA 6
(she knew we was makin' cakes)
19. an' we was sleepin'
20. an' she went in the room
21. an' gobbled em up
22. an' we hadda bake a whole bunch more

STANZA 7

23. she said mmmm
24. she had all chocolate on her face/ cream/ strawberries/
25. she said mmmm
26. that was good

STANZA 8

27. an' then an' then all came out
28. an' my grandmother had ate all of it
29. she said "what's this cheese cake doin' here"—she
    didn't like cheese cakes
30. an' she told everybody that she didn't like cheese cakes

STANZA 9

31. an' we kept makin' cakes
32. an' she kept eatin' 'em
33. an' we finally got tired of makin' cakes
34. an' so we all ate 'em

STANZA 10

35. an' now
36. today's my grandmother's birthday
37. an' a lot o'people's makin' a cake again
38. but my grandmother is goin' t'get her own cake at her
    bakery
39. an' she's gonna come out with a cake
40. that we didn't make
41. cause she likes chocolate cream

STANZA 11

42. an' I went t'the bakery with her
43. an' my grandmother ate cup cakes
44. an' an' she finally got sick on today
45. an' she was growling like a dog cause she ate so many
    cakes

STANZA 12

46. an' I finally told her that it was
47. it was Friday the thirteenth bad luck day

The five-year-old's story arose when the child's mother was reading storybooks to her two young daughters. Her five-year-old had had a birthday party, which had had some problems. In the next few days the five-year-old had told several relatives about the birthday party, reporting the events in the typical "just the facts—this happened, then this happened" language of middle-class "reports." A few days later, when the mother was reading a storybook to her other daughter, the five-year-old said that she wanted to "read," though she could not yet decode print. She then picked up a book and *pretended* to be reading it, while telling a literary version of what happened at her birthday party. I have demarcated the text in terms of "lines" and "stanzas" to show how "poetic" and "literary" the text is, though of course these were marked in speech only by the stress and pitch of her voice.

The home-based book activities surrounding this five-year-old encode language that is part of several different sign systems. These include, of course, "children's literature," but also "literature" proper. It is clear that this child has mastered large parts of these systems, despite the fact that she cannot yet "read" (decode print).

Children's storybooks use linguistic devices that are simplified analogues of "literary" devices used in traditional, canonical "high literature." One such device is the so-called sympathetic fallacy, whereby a poem or story treats natural events (such as sunshine or storms) as if they reflected or were "in harmony" or "in step" with (sympathetic with) human events and emotions. Nature becomes a sign system referring to human affairs. This device was a hallmark of nineteenth-century romantic poetry, though it is common in more recent poetry as well.

Notice how in the five-year-old's story the sympathetic fallacy is not only used but is, in fact, the central organizing device in the construction of the story. The fight between the girls and boys in stanza 6 is immediately followed in stanza 7 by the sky turning dark, with lightning flashing, and thence in line 22: "and they were not friends." Finally, in stanza 8, the mothers come on the scene to punish the children for their transgression. The sky is "in tune" or "in step" with human happenings.

The function of the sympathetic fallacy in "high literature" is to equate the world of nature (the macrocosm) with the world of human affairs (the microcosm) as it is depicted in a particular work of art. It also suggests that these human affairs, as they are depicted in the work of literary art, are "natural," part of the logic of the universe, rather than conventional, historical, cultural, or class based. In the five-year-old's story, the sympathetic fallacy functions in much the same way as it does in "high literature." In particular, the story suggests that gender differences (stanza 4: boy versus girl) are associated with different interests (stanza 5: Transformers versus Cabbage Patches), and that these different interests inevitably lead to conflict when male and female try to be "equal" or sort themselves on other grounds than gender (stanza 6: "a fight on who would be which team"—the fight had been about mixing genders on the teams). The children are punished for transgressing gender lines (stanza 8), but *only after* the use of the sympathetic fallacy (in stanza 7) has suggested that *division by gender,* and the conflicts which transgressing this division lead to, are sanctioned by nature, are "natural" and "inevitable," not merely conventional or constructed in the very act of play itself.

Note how the little girl incorporates aspects of book-reading activities into her story. Note, for example, the introduction in stanza 1, the frame in stanza 2, the title in stanza 3, and then the start of the story proper in stanza 4. She closes the frame in stanza 9. This overall structure shapes the text into "storybook reading," though, in fact, there is no book and the child can't read. I cannot help but add that this little girl is most certainly "literate" in the genre of children's stories, though she can't decode print—thus, decoding print cannot be what literacy is.

It is pointless to ask of our five-year-old's story, "Did she really intend, or does she really know about, such meanings?" She is five: she cannot possibly be fully aware, in any sense, of the structures or meanings inherent in her sign systems and the social practices that establish them. The social practices to which she is apprenticed "speak *through her,* so she can, in fact, "speak" quite beyond herself (much like "speaking in tongues," I suppose).

Furthermore, the little girl ingests an ideology whole here, so to speak, and not in any way in which she could analyze it, verbalize it, or critique it. There is no real reason to assume that the situation is significantly different in the case of adults; in fact, there is good reason to believe (from evidence coming from both neuropsychology and social psychology) that adults simply have in their heads a number of "self-serving" beliefs about what they mean and its value, beliefs that are not uncommonly false.

This five-year-old, like many of her peers, was seen as "gifted." Stories like the one above are seen as "signs" of early talents and inherent abilities. These talents and abilities are then seen as indications that she "deserves" and has "earned" her later school success. After all, there are individual differences, and this little girl is simply "smart." Of course, her "giftedness" is an "artifact" of the many hours of home-based practice that have allowed her to imbibe a given sign system whose use is then seen as a "sign" of intelligence and giftedness by our schools and the groups who "own" and "control" them.

There are then a number of "morals" to be drawn from our five-year-old's story: there are many literacies, tied to specific social practices. This girl, despite the fact that she cannot "read" (decode) print, is quite literate in the social practice of "literary stories" (of a certain type). Any literacy must be defined as fluency in a given social practice, and cannot be defined in terms of "the ability to read and write."[30] Meaning is not in the head, but in the social practice. However, another moral emerges when we juxtapose this girl's text to the black girl's story above about cakes.

This black seven-year-old told stories like the cakes story at "sharing time" in the first and second grades. This story too is very "literary." It uses intricate rhythmical language, repetition, and syntactic parallelism, the hallmarks of poetry. Note, for instance, how every line in stanza 2 ends on the word *cake*, or how the first and third lines of stanza 3 end on "went over X's house," and the second and fourth lines end on "had made a cake" (giving this stanza an "abab" structure). Stanzas 5 and 6 are direct repeats of each other, line for line, with stylistic variation. Stanzas 7 and 8, equally stylistically, vary the scene of the grandmother being "caught in the act."

The story artfully plays on the theme of *birthday cakes*. Note that the grandmother eats lots of full-size cakes at home and all that happens is that the family makes her more. Yet when she goes to the bakery to get a cake her family didn't make, she gets sick on little cakes (cup cakes) and loses her human status, growling like a dog. The grandmother has, in her greed, mistook the material base of the cake (its "cakeness"—the "*cakiness* of the cake," we might say) for its meaning. A birthday cake is not just food; it is also a sign. A birthday cake made in the home is a sign of belonging and kinship; a cake made by a bakery only looks the same, but it is a commodity for sale. The bakery cake is a sign whose meaning is established within the sign system of capitalist economy; the home cakes are signs whose meaning is established within the sign system of the home and black culture (in this case). Mistaking the meaning of signs turns the grandmother into an "eater" (a dog), not the taker and giver of meaning (a human).

This child's story is not so much "literary" in the "bookish" sense as "literary" in the sense of a dramatic *performance* of the spoken voice, like theater and (in its origins) poetry. Now what did the school make of stories like this one? Despite the fact that it is, like our five-year-old's story, "literary," it was not validated and rewarded by the school. This little girl was not seen as intelligent or gifted. She was repeatedly told during her stories to sit down because she was "not talking about one important thing"; she was simply rambling on. The only reason she finished the story, in fact, is that the teacher left the room and she ended up telling the story to her classroom peers (who enjoyed it immensely).

Here we see clearly that the value accredited to two texts does not appear to have anything to do with their "inherent" properties. So what determines this difference of reception? The sharing time literature[31] has indicated that at sharing time teachers are often looking, not for literary or oral language, but for "fact-by-fact" reports that use explicit and literal language typical of essayist writing (even when the children cannot yet write). Teachers are, often without full conscious awareness, treating sharing time as early "essayist literacy" training. They want the children to talk without relying on the shared knowledge of the audience, building overtly into their language as much of their meaning as they can. Of course, this "violates" the oral, participatory, face-to-face nature of the encounter, but such "violations" are not untypical of schools. Sharing time, in fact, has a bias against the voice, against performance, and against the active (physical or mental) participation of the audience (as against their passive reception of overt language to which they need add little).

The little black girl takes sharing time at "face value," assuming that she is supposed to really share a *story* (elaborated plot) in a participatory and entertaining way with her peers. She is never overtly told otherwise, because even the teacher is not fully aware what the "rules" are. The more middle-class children "catch on" to the rules, thanks to other home-based practices they have been engaged in from an early age. For example, many middle-class homes, but few lower socioeconomic homes, repeatedly engage children in practices that require them to tell adults what both the child and adult fully know the adult already knows. The child becomes well aware that adults are not primarily interested in what the child has to say, but in how explicitly and "booklike" the child will say it. Our five-year-old would never have told her "birthday story," in its literary version, as a sharing time story. She would have told the "fact-by-fact" report version.

What we see, then, is that texts of certain types are situated within social practices of certain sorts. Our five-year-old has a school practice at home connected to "children's literature." This practice is continuous (historically and today) with some of the school's practices, though not with sharing time. She has other practices at home that connect with sharing time. The little black girl has a home-based practice of telling oral stories that is connected to thousands of years of cultural history. It does not "translate" (resituate) to sharing time.

But neither does the school successfully resituate the black girl's story to its more literary practices, though it will do so for our five-year-old. Even when the school, in other activities, validates "literary" practices, it will validate our five-year-old's story, thanks to its "bookishness," and not the black child's, which is rooted in voice, performance, and participation. There is, however, nothing in the black girl's text that renders this latter failure on the school's part inevitable. After all, all literature had its origin in voice, performance, and participation. It is simply the case that "literary" language coming out of the middle-class girl's home-based social practices translates into a "foundation for literary literacy," and the "literary" language coming out of the lower-class girl's home-based social practices doesn't. This fact is rooted in the history and "desires" of the groups who have power in—are empowered by—our schools, not in any "reality" outside these desires and the practices that instantiate them.

The moral, then, is this: the meaning and value that these texts take on is a product of various social practices and their specific histories and contestations over power. The form of these texts, and what is going on inside these little girls' heads, have no inherent relationship with value, meaning, ability, intelligence, giftedness, or anything else. These latter are all simply social constructions of various social practices, carried out so as to privilege members of the practice ("insiders") and to contest entry to the practice on the part of "outsiders."

There is one final moral of this perspective for education. If meaning is not rooted in the signs and texts themselves, or in what is "in" people's heads, then education cannot be seen as the overt teaching of facts or skills. Education is always and everywhere the initiation of students as apprentices into various historically situated social practices so that they become "insiders."[32] Or it is the exclusion of children from these apprenticeships. Of course, this implies that schools can only expect opposition from those children and their families whom they either exclude or seek to apprentice to practices that are "owned" and "operated" by groups who otherwise oppose and oppress them in the wider society outside school.

A problem

Our third view of meaning leaves us with a major problem. If no sign system can be validated as against any other, if all sign systems are rooted simply in historically derived social practices instantiating the desires and claims to power of various groups, then how can we *morally* condemn the school's (and society's) treatment of the black child whose story we have seen above? How, indeed, can this black child—and her group—come to form a viable theory and practice of resistance?

We saw above that modernism removed the relations of modern industrial capitalism (and its attendant colonialism) from the moral realm to the aesthetic realm. Postmodernism often removes the relations of postindustrial capitalism from the moral realm to the *ludic:* it views these relations as simply the *play* of signs, desire, and power through history and society.[33] Indeed, much postmodernist literature[34] celebrates the creation of sign systems (as in television commercials) that "simulate" a "reality" that, in fact, doesn't exist (such as the connection between a dish soap and the "good" life).

However, whereas school and elite society do indeed "simulate" the deficits they find in the black child, her hurt and oppression are real indeed, and in no sense ludic. But how, given that this judgment itself is rooted in a sign system that like all sign systems cannot be validated from outside itself or outside the history and social practices it is rooted in, can this judgment be established?

There is no simple answer to this question. But the answer I would offer is as follows:[35] In our daily lives, the beliefs we have and the claims we make on the basis of these beliefs have, intentionally or not, consciously or not, and in tandem with others' beliefs and the institutions in our society, *effects* on other people, sometimes harmful, sometimes beneficial, sometimes a bit of both, and sometimes neither. There are, I believe, two conceptual principles that serve as the basis of *ethical human discourse* (talk and interaction). These principles are grounded in no further ones (save that the second relies on the first), and, if one fails to accept them, argument has "run out." The first principle is as follows:[36]

First Conceptual Principle Governing Ethical Human Discourse

That something would *harm* someone else (deprive them of what they or the society they are in view as "goods") is *always* a good reason (though perhaps not a sufficient reason) *not* to do it.

What this principle says is that when we consider whether to believe, claim, or do anything, then it is always a good reason *not to* if we believe that our believing, claiming, or doing this would harm someone else. This does not mean that there may not be other reasons that override this one, reasons that lead us to do the harmful thing nonetheless. There are, of course, other (and culturally variable) principles to ethics besides this one.

As I have said, I have (and can have, I believe) no *argument* for this principle (in particular, for well-known reasons, utilitarian arguments for it won't work.)[37] All I or anyone can say is that if people do not accept (and/or act as though they do not accept) the above principle, then I and most others are simply not going to interact with them, and we have come to a point at which one must simply offer *resistance*, not argument, if one must so interact.

The second conceptual principle is yet more specific:[38]

Second Conceptual Principle Governing Ethical Human Discourse

One always has the ethical obligation to try to explicate (render overt and conscious) any social practice that there is reason to believe advantages oneself or one's group over other people or other groups.

By "advantage" in this second principle I simply mean "bring to oneself or one's group more of what counts, in the society one is in, as *goods* (whether this be status, wealth, power, control, or whatever)." Once again, I do not argue that there is any "transcendental" argument for this principle, only that if one fails to accept it, argument has "run out" and all that one can do is fail to interact with such people and offer them resistance if one must so interact. This second principle is, I would claim, also the *ethical* basis (and main rationale) of education.

It would follow from this second principle that the information I have given about school sharing time would render it an obligation of teachers to think and argue about sharing time in an explicit manner. They would have to make clear to themselves and their students what the "rules" are. This "making clear" might, given our first principle, make them change the practice in various ways.

I believe that any human being would—provided he or she understood them—accept these conceptual principles, and so, if failing to live up to them, would (for consistency's sake) have to morally condemn his or her own behavior. However, I readily admit that, should people emerge who, understanding these principles, denied them (and/or acted as though they did), I would not give up the principles, but would withhold the term *human*—in its honorific, not its biological, sense—from such people.

In the end we run out of words, and meaning is rooted finally in judgment and action.

Notes

1. See, for example, Ogden, C., and Richards, I., *The Meaning of Meaning* (London: Routledge, 1923).

2. Compare, Berlin, B., and Kay, P., *Basic Color Terms: Their Universality and Evolution* (Berkeley: University of California Press, 1969); Fin-

negan, E., and Besnier, N., *Language: Its Structure and Use* (San Diego: Harcourt, Brace Jovanovich, 1989).

3. See Cole, M., and Scribner, S., *Culture and Thought: A Psychological Perspective* (New York: John Wiley, 1974).

4. De Saussure, F., *Course in General Linguistics*, trans. from 1917 French edition by Wade Baskin (New York: Philosophical Library, 1959); Levi-Strauss, C., *Structural Anthropology* (New York: Basic Books, 1963); Culler, J., *Structuralist Poetics: Structuralism, Linguistics, and the Study of Literature* (Ithaca, N.Y.: Cornell University Press, 1975).

5. Compare Culler, De Saussure, and Levi-Strauss, all *ibid*. See also Levi-Strauss, C., *The Savage Mind* (Chicago: University of Chicago Press, 1966); Scholes, R., *Structuralism in Literature: An Introduction* (New Haven, Conn.: Yale University Press, 1974).

6. Connor, S., *Postmodern Culture: An Introduction to the Theories of the Contemporary* (Oxford: Basil Blackwell, 1989); Harvey, D., *The Condition of Modernity* (Oxford: Basil Blackwell, 1989).

7. Taussig, M., *The Devil and Commodity Fetishism in South America* (Chapel Hill: University of North Carolina Press, 1980).

8. Perkins, D., *A History of Modern Poetry: From the 1890s to the High Modernist Mode* (Cambridge, Mass.: Harvard University Press, 1976).

9. Gee, J., "The Structure of Perception in the Poetry of William Carlos Williams," *Poetics Today*, 6, 3, 1985, pp. 375–397.

10. Stacy, R., *Defamiliarization in Language and Literature* (Syracuse, N.Y.: Syracuse University Press, 1977).

11. Lemon, L., and Reis, M. (trans.), *Russian Formalist Criticism: Four Essays* (Lincoln: University of Nebraska Press, 1965).

12. Dijkstra, B., Introduction to Bram Dijkstra (ed.), *A Recognizable Image: William Carlos Williams on Art and Artists* (New York: New Directions, 1978).

13. Sutton, W., "A Visit with William Carlos Williams," *The Minnesota Review*, 1, 3, April 1963, pp. 309–324.

14. This poem comes from Williams's 1921 collection, *Sour Grapes*. The American painter Charles Demuth painted a famous version of this poem.

15. See Dijkstra, B., *Cubism, Stieglitz and the early Poetry of William Carlos Williams: The Hieraglyphics of a New Speech* (Princeton: Princeton University Press, 1969); Sayre, H., *The Visual Text of William Carlos Williams* (Urbana: University of Illinois Press, 1983).

16. Eagleton, T., *The Ideology of the Aesthetic* (Oxford: Basil Blackwell, 1990); Clifford, J., *The Predicament of Culture: Twentieth-Century Ethnography, Literature and Art* (Cambridge: Mass.: Harvard University Press, 1988).

17. For discussion on both sides of the issue, see the following: Callinicos, A., *Against Postmodernism: A Marxist Critique* (New York: St. Martin's Press, 1990); Connor, *op. cit.*; Giddens, A., *The Consequences of Modernity* (Stanford: Stanford University Press, 1990); and Harvey, *op. cit.*

18. Poster, M., *The Mode of Information: Poststructuralism and Social Context* (Chicago: University of Chicago Press, 1990).

19. Toffler, A., *Powershift: Knowledge, Power, and Violence at the Edge of the 21st Century* (New York: Bantam, 1990).

20. Compare *ibid.*

21. See Giddens, *op. cit.*

22. Compare Callinicos and Giddens, both *op. cit.*

23. See Harvey, *op. cit.*, for the best argument.

24. See Culler, J., *On Deconstruction: Theory and Criticism after Structuralism* (Ithaca, N.Y.: Cornell University Press, 1982); Foucault, M., *Power/Knowledge: Selected Interviews and Other Writings 1972–77*, ed. C. Gordon, L. Marshall, J. Meplam, and K. Soper, Brighton (Sussex: The Harvester Press, 1980); Macdonnell, D., *Theories of Discourse: An Introduction* (Oxford: Basil Blackwell, 1986); Poster, *op. cit.*; and Smith, B., *Contingencies of Value: Alternative Perspectives for Critical Theory* (Cambridge, Mass.: Harvard University Press, 1988).

25. Appiah, K. A., "Is the post- in postmodernism the same as the post- in postcolonial?" *Critical Inquiry*, 17, 2, 1991, pp. 336–357.

26. Compare the following: Bourdieu, P., *Outline of a Theory of Practice* (Cambridge: Cambridge University Press, 1977); Bourdieu, P., *Distinction: A Social Critique of the Judgment of Taste* (Cambridge, Mass.: Harvard University Press); Bourdieu, P., *In Other Words: Essays Towards a Reflexive Sociology* (Stanford: Stanford University Press, 1990); Hodge, R., and Kress, G., *Social Semiotics* (Oxford: Polity Press, 1988); Gee, J., *Social Linguistics and Literacies: Ideologies in Discourse* (London: Falmer Press, 1991).

27. See Gee, J., *ibid.*, and *Literacy, Discourse and Linguistics: Essays by James Paul Gee*, special issue of the *Journal of Education*, 171, 1989.

28. Scholes, *op. cit.*

29. Gee (1989, 1991), *op. cit.*

30. *Ibid.*

31. Cazden, C., *Classroom Discourse: The Language of Teaching and Learning* (Portsmouth, N.H.: Heinemann, 1988; Michaels, S., "'Sharing Time': Children's Narrative Styles and Differential Access to Literacy," *Language in Society*, 10, 1981, pp. 423–442.

32. Gee (1991), *op. cit.*

10

Reading and writing the media: Critical media literacy and postmodernism

David Sholle and Stan Denski

> I believe that the system of meanings and values which a capitalist society has generated has to be defeated in general and in detail by the most sustained kinds of intellectual and educational work.
>
> —Raymond Williams[1]

As media teachers, practitioners, and critics we hope to offer a vision of a critical media practice linking the shared concerns of critical pedagogy, critical literacy, and media studies. Like critical pedagogy, a critical literacy of *media* must focus its energies toward opening up new spaces from within which traditionally marginalized and excluded voices may speak. Our approach to both the contemporary mass media and media education is, we believe, rather straightforward; the structures of media production, and the corresponding educational structures within which the creators of media products are trained, may be approached as sets of complex social practices which to varying degrees either serve to reproduce existing social inequalities or serve to overcome these inequalities in support of an emancipatory democracy. Our task here is to map those areas within the practices of contemporary media and media education which work either toward the continued exclusion of voices which challenge the status quo, or to offer possibilities for empowerment and the potential defeat of the dominant hegemony, to create a fleeting glimpse of a *promisse de bonheure*.[2]

The media (including their structures of production, distribution, economics, policy, technologies, and so forth), media education at all levels, and critical literacy exist as sites of struggle across the terrain of contemporary cultural politics in the United States. Further, each contributes pieces toward what we will offer as a new theorization of critical media literacy, offered in the context of the accumulation of media in the postmodern condition. This particular historical moment of postmodern late capitalism is embroiled in various sets of hegemonic practices in which the media play a central and complex part in everyday life.

Pedagogy, schizophrenia, and practice

Schizophrenia and media education

Contemporary media education is characterized by a condition most closely resembling that of schizophrenia. Media educators, trained not as educators but as theorists, live categorically distinct separate lives. These are lives led at desks and in libraries, as producers of media theory; lives engaged in the analysis and criticism of the mechanisms of mass-mediated hegemony, describing the intricacies of processes through which dominant cultural values are reproduced, maintained, supported, and resisted; and lives led envisioning an "other" future, not simply the extension of present conditions. And they are lives led at the lectern in the media production classroom: lives engaged, at least partially, in the reproduction of dominant culture and dominant practice.

This metaphor of schizophrenia is particularly useful in examining the "split personality" character of the contemporary media educator, a phenomenon engendered by the various *distancing dichotomies* caught up in the practice of "teaching the media." These dichotomies are "distancing," both in impeding the project of cultural democracy and in creating a rupture, an unbridgeable gap between theories and practices which may actually be aligned. These dichotomies appear and reappear throughout the various structures and processes of contemporary education, and our lives as educators sometimes seem to be lived out in the tensions generated between these various oppositional poles of teaching versus research, teacher versus scholar, teacher versus student, the library (where knowledge is produced) versus the lectern (where knowledge is reproduced), "the ivory tower" versus "the real world," and what seems to us to be the root of all of these: *theory versus practice*.

These dichotomies, however, have become increasingly problematized by both critical education theory's focused and expansive theorization of pedagogy and by various aspects of the postmodern condition. This is why it seems to us also, from our positions as media educators/schizophrenics, that the most important contribution of critical pedagogical theory to media studies lies in its potential role as figurative psychoanalyst in the treatment of our metaphorical schizophrenia: that is, the power of a properly theorized pedagogy is in its capacity to disrupt the operations of the distancing dichotomies which lurk at center of our disease.

This metaphor of schizophrenia is also multileveled. Henry S. Kariel suggests this notion of an underlying psychological disorder in commenting as follows:

> Making us aware of our distinctive interests, the knowledge of our impending end alerts us to the way we are needlessly submissive, pathologically distracted and preoccupied. It alerts us to the imposition of autonomous abstractions such as Success, of indispensable ideals and ontologies. It is this knowledge of our finitude which moves me to decenter the optimism and rationalism of the Enlightenment by installing a counter-progressive structure, a map for coping under contemporary conditions.[3]

This is the second level of our schizophrenia: the postmodern condition, the uneasy alliance (or perhaps split personality) of modernity and postmodernity. Centering around questions of authority and loss of authority in the project of critique within the public sphere, postmodernism seems to ask: From what position do we speak? What is our project? Indeed, can we have a project in modernism's sense—can we speak with authority without silencing others? And so on. Finally, we are faced with the question: How can we construct a nontotalizing politics based in postmodernism's concerns for difference and the other, without altogether erasing the possibility of a vital political project?

The first manifestation of our schizophrenia in the practice of media education and its reappearance in the practice of postmodern cultural politics is part and parcel of a third level of schizophrenia—that of late capitalism and the work of hegemony. In the postmodern, hegemony is won not simply through the transmission of ideas and the control of the population through centralization and homogenization; it operates also through the *abundance of choice* and the resultant increased fragmentation of the populace.

In capitalist representation, signs are not part of a central code that unifies their meaning and connects them with expression. Rather, as Deleuze and Guattari have described it, the deterritorialized flows of content/expression escape the rigid circuits of capitalist production, at which point they become "schizophrenic flux-signs of desire."[4] Put another way, meaning and affect no longer connect through a system of values unified in a coherent narrative (such as a theology or national myth). Instead, redundant and asignifying images mobilize affect without the need for ideological commitment.[5]

Again, another set of distancing dichotomies is evidenced in these schizophrenic moments: modern versus postmodern, centralization versus fragmentation, meaning versus affect, content versus expression, and so on. Overcoming these dichotomies will depend on the formation of a pedagogical practice that can link the critical project of modernity to possibilities opened up by the new theoretical ground of postmodernity.

Praxis and agency

At the center of critical pedagogy is the reconstruction of media theory and practice into media *praxis:* the praxis of media education. Critical pedagogy's disruption of the theory/practice dichotomy leads us toward this emerging notion of media praxis. We believe that any meaningful conceptualization of critical media literacy can only exist within a properly theorized notion of praxis.

Praxis, in the sense which adds most to this discussion, refers to self-creative activity through which men and women create (make, produce) and change (shape) the historical, human world and themselves. Praxis includes an element of critique of existing historical conditions and an element of possibility for reworking those conditions. In addition, the concept of praxis attempts to link or loop together theory and practice—in its strongest sense of *"practice as action."* The notion of a loop or circuit in rotation is crucial in describing the relationship between theory and practice. In the loop, theory and practice are in a transductive relationship, circulating back upon each other without canceling each other out. This is not a simple unity of theory and practice, but neither are theory and practice separate activities that merely connect or attach to each other at certain chosen moments.

It is in this sense, then, that praxis expresses human potentialities, something different both from what simply is and what merely ought to be. Media praxis suggests, in this specific context, a curricular approach directed at possibilities contained within the mass media: possibilities to counter the soporific and alienating results of both a traditional focus on technology and a fundamental misrepresentation of the inexorable bond between theory and practice. In the context of a critical media pedagogy, it is through a pedagogy of praxis (one of critique and possibility) that the debilitating effects of distancing dichotomies and a schizophrenic existence are broken down. In the circuit of theory and practice the stance of *professional* and *theorist* as two separate positions can no longer make sense. At the same time, the dichotomy of reading and writing so central to theorizations of literacy projects is itself *transformed* as existing notions of what it is to read and what it is to write are released from the sterile sphere of technical skills.

Context and practice

Any pedagogical practice must be formulated in the context of its specific historical location. Media must be examined in the context of their accumulation in the postmodern condition, in terms of the saturation of everyday life by the hegemonic practices of late capitalism and its subsumption of practice under the rubric of *consumerism*, in the erasure of the marginal and the exclusion of the other, and in the light of the place of media in the everyday lives of students who bring this background to every pedagogical encounter. We want to examine the goals of a critical media literacy project in these terms. In its greater location within the projects of critical theory and critical pedagogy, it must seek out silenced voices, address the terror and terrorism of the other, and employ practices directed at the opening of new space for new voices. Where does all this lead? What are the specific elements which inscribe a coherent theorization of a critical media literacy?

Past models of media literacy

In looking at past models of media literacy, the idea is again reinforced that the distancing dichotomy of the theoretical versus the practical (resulting, in part, from the disparate undertheorization of pedagogy) has set up structures within which current existing approaches to critical media literacy operate. Once these inadequacies in present approaches are uncovered, other theorizations of critical media literacy become possible in the spaces opened up by the disruption of these distancing dichotomies—a disruption resulting from critical pedagogy's interrogations and postmodern culture's assault upon the grand narratives.

Any adequate approach to media literacy must work within and against these disruptions, particularly in coming to terms with the recent historical conjuncture named and renamed by a number of diverse theorists as "the postmodern." We will rely on Peter McLaren's broad definition of the postmodern "as among other things, the rupturing of the unitary fixity and homogenizing logic of the grand narratives of Western European thought."[6] For our purposes, this condition includes the related phenomenon of the dissolution of the opposition of *high art* to *popular culture*, the construction of subjectivities through consumer myths and images, the construction of lifestyles as affective conditions, and the deintensifying of media production of ideology in favor of the production of difference for difference's sake. We want to explore what media literacy means today in light of these phenomena, but also in light of that other side of the postmodern—its theoretical work in delineating the politics of difference and identity.

First, we must be clear about what media literacy is *not*. Early versions of media literacy were constructed on a model of the media acting as a creator of messages that imposed meaning on the audience. These programs of media literacy simply cannot account for the phenomenon of contemporary postmodernism. The simplest version of media literacy recommends a process of parents monitoring their children's viewing and discussing programs with them. An extension of this view proposes the development of "critical viewing skills"—understanding the grammar of television, the types of genres, and the "meanings" that it produces. These approaches are limited by their reliance on a theory of the media-audience link as one of activity-passivity, and on their assumption of familial relationships as nurturing/authoritarian. These approaches face the further limitation imposed by liberal undertheorizations of "critical thinking" in which all politics are removed from the concept of "critical," reducing it to the level of the banal and unproblematic discussion of "cognitive thinking skills."[7]

A second and similar attempt at a media literacy program is based in the notion of "visual literacy." Again, this is a skills-based approach rooted in developing visual competence: an understanding of spatial construction, movement, film grammar, and so on. All of these approaches also rely on a notion of *discrimination;* that is, media literacy involves judging what is *good* and *bad* in media content. This discrimination may pertain to judging the political correctness of media or its status as "art." Such judgments are foreordained by a preselected canon of standards.

Critical approaches to media literacy differ from these other approaches by focusing on the production and consumption of media in the context of their existence as ideological texts. However, this text-based approach again relies on a communication model of encoding and decoding. Grossberg explains why the difference between encoding (production) and decoding (consumption) must be abandoned or at least severely amended. This dichotomy between encoding and decoding "divides interpretation into the search for intended or preferred meanings and received or effective meanings." But if one considers the context of communication, these two moments are never wholly separable. "Encoding is a continuous force and decoding is already active in the efforts to decode."[8]

Accordingly, the notion that ideology functions as an imposition of meaning (often hidden from decoders) upon a passive receptacle ignores the fact that meaning is produced on both sides of the communication situation. Further, placing the practice of ideological production within the context of the postmodern calls into question the notion that the primary and only effectivity of modern communication media is in the production of "meanings" as discrete knowledges. If there is any validity to the shift to a post-modern condition—a condition in which signifiers float, in which stable "truths" no longer function as foundations, and in which meaning and affect are separated—then any media literacy program focused upon ideological demystification must be rearticulated.

It is not that the production of meaning in the broad sense of ideology does not exist; rather, it is that *no adequate theory of media literacy can remain simply at this level*. We will argue that media literacy must be theorized through and within the context of postmodernism. But how seriously need we take the proposition that postmodernism has fundamentally changed the conditions of media production and consumption? Most important, however, is the question of whether we must abandon the entire ideology project of modernist theory. And, if we do so, do we risk abandoning politics altogether?

Media literacy and a critical postmodernism

Postmodernism, as a form of cultural criticism and as a historical condition, directly challenges the project of modernism. We believe that it rightly questions modernism's reliance on the notion of the autonomous individual, the emphasis on the linearity of thought, the aesthetic of rationality and order, the rationality of science in the process of progress, the preeminence of Western European thought, and history as the process of the progress of Western culture. However, we cannot accept the postmodernist stance without question; we cannot simply accept its critique of modernism as total and final, nor can we simply meld the various "posts" together into a sweeping theory.[9]

Postmodern theory makes us aware of how our subjectivity and experiences are constructed, how the meaning we attempt to grasp slips away in our failure to affectively commit to it, how our institutions and discursive formations lead us to erase difference and stand against the "other," and how the production of information and symbols has weakened the link between images and reality. Although such a breaking down of our present condition can lead us to question that condition and resist it, there is also the very real potential within postmodern theory for it to lead to *fatal strategies,* wherein resistance is replaced by refusal, and critique by play.

This regressive postmodernism is most evident in Baudrillard's[10] burned-out space of hyperconformity, and the further aestheticization of his position by Kroker,[11] in which the masses celebrate their own extermination in the black hole of television. Lost in this regressive version of postmodernism is any sense of how people struggle with the images and codes that confront them. Likewise, the affirmation of difference is disconnected from any account of how cultural, political, and economic constraints position various groups in asymmetrical power relations. In short, a postmodernism that endlessly plays with literary texts, or maps out a world of simulations in which there is no place from which to speak, erases any critical sense of history or politics.[12] Media literacy cannot exist under this view of the postmodern, for within the Baudrillardian space of the electronic simulation of reality the only strategy left for the subject is self-parody.

The bleak nihilism of postmodernist deconstruction must be connected to critical pedagogy's project of reconstruction (from out of the ashes looking back at the end of the world). The pessimism and despair which characterizes the postmodernism of Jameson, Lyotard, and Baudrillard must be understood as emanating from the context of their own individual subject positions. For those whose lives have benefited through occupying a position of privilege within these various "grand narratives," the collapse of these structures, the unmasking of the once absolute and eternal as now arbitrary and transient, the retransformation of the natural back into the cultural, the collapse of the mythic back into the arena of the human and the political—all of this will most certainly find a response in words like *crisis, the end of meaning, the end of history,* and so on. However, from the subject positions of those who have been excluded by these narratives, whose won voices have been silenced and marginalized, *such a collapse may be experienced as liberatory and empowering.* In other words, the response to these "collapses" may range from despair to celebration depending upon your location within a given set of asymmetrical power relations.[13] And this opens up the possibility of a *critical postmodernism.*

It is in this sense that Hebdige has argued that theories of the "post" have *"no intrinsic political belonging in themselves."*[14] Whereas for Baudrillard postmodernity is characterized by the utter annihilation of difference and the end of history and politics, a *critical postmodernism* is "identified with diversity and difference, a politics of contestation and change."[15] We must seek to connect postmodernism's notions of culture, difference, and subjectivity with the modernist concerns for the language of public life, thus reaffirming "a public philosophy" that broadens and deepens individual liberties and rights through rather than against a radical notion of democracy. By drawing upon this politicized notion of the postmodern, the practice of media literacy can be seen still to offer "vital strategies."

If media literacy is to be advanced within a critical pedagogy, it must be conceived as a political, social, and cultural practice. Thus a critical theory of media literacy must propose it as an arena of practices that still offers strategies that can be taken seriously as "vital." It is crucial then to distinguish between those postmodern positions that lead either to an aestheticization of politics or to a cultural pessimism, and that of a critical postmodernism offered by Giroux: "At its best, a critical postmodernism wants to redraw the map of modernism so as to effect a shift in power from the privileged and the powerful to those groups struggling to gain a measure of control over their lives in what is increasingly becoming a world marked by a logic of disintegration."[16]

As such, a critical postmodernism integrates the elements of the modernist political project with the resistant strategies of postmodernism. As theoretical projects, both modernism and postmodernism are flawed in certain respects, and each needs to be examined for its strengths and weaknesses. In particular, the elements of modernism which link memory, agency, and reason to the construction of a democratic public sphere need to be retained in the construction of a theory of media literacy for the present conditions of the postmodern world.[17]

The context of critical media literacy

Given the above discussion, how can a critical media literacy be developed? The location of these matters within the terrain of postmodern cultural theory may help to further flesh out the character of our media literacy theory. In postmodern late capitalist America, our efforts to describe a critical theory of media literacy are caught up in an initial paradox. On the one hand, the increasing development of science and technology provides the possibility of freeing humans from dehumanizing and backbreaking labor. In turn, this freedom offers humanity new opportunities for the development of, and access to, a culture that promotes a more critical and discriminatory sensibility in all modes of communication and experience. On the other hand, the development of technology and science, constructed according to the laws of capitalist rationality, has ushered in forms of domination and control that appear to thwart rather than extend the possibilities of human emancipation.

Given the existing social formation, the modes of communication are operated predominantly in the interests of oppression. This is not a simple mechanical operation but is tied to the hegemonic conjuncture of market, military, and political interests. Within this grouping of interests the media serve to construct consensus and dissensus, to reconfigure the relationship of meaning and affect in the construction of a narrative of nation, to surveil the population and in so doing create systems of normalization and subjectification. However, this operation of the media is not a seamless operation closing off all possibilities of alternative use. The media constitute a leaky system that is struggled over in its production and reception.

Popular culture as background

Our discussion here is grounded in the assertion that *educational theory must engage with the popular as the background that informs students' engagement with any pedagogical encounter.* In this, however, the distancing dichotomy of "high" culture versus "low" culture must be avoided. This is not simply a matter of either criticizing popular culture for the purpose of devalorizing student experience or, obversely, celebrating the popular in an acritical acceptance.[18] Rather, as Giroux and Simon suggest, we must consider popular culture as the background of knowledge forms and affective instruments which ground student "voice."[19]

Attending to the popular in student experiences involves not simply valorizing that experience, but working with (and on) that experience. Such a pedagogy must allow students to speak from their own experience at the same time that it encourages them to identify and unravel the codes of popular culture that may work to construct subject relations that serve to silence and disempower them. Popular culture must be viewed as a complex and contradictory sphere in which dominant culture attempts to structure experience through the production of meaning, and which at the same time may provide possibilities for more open democratic formations.

Student knowledge

It has long struck us as odd that the vast majority of students leave school from age sixteen on with extremely hazy levels of knowledge about matters which will concern them most in their lives. We are referring to their "knowledge" of (1) personal health, nutrition, and medical matters; (2) social and sexual interaction between individuals and groups; and (3) the structure and operation of the state, political organizations, local government, welfare benefits, housing, and so on—in short, the economic and institutional underpinning of society.[20]

Currently, however, the popular media work more toward both erasing these knowledge forms and supporting the regressive postmodern definition of "freedom" as the broad choice of consumption objects. The contemporary popular media fragment, create dissensus, and threaten, and erase the practical base of knowledge that marginal or powerless groups need in order to take hold of their everyday lives and work toward changing their historical conditions. And the state of media education within the contemporary U.S. university tends to function more as an acritical training ground complicit (at the very least) in an ongoing program of mediated cultural reproduction than as the kind of linking and bridging within a critical pedagogy of media praxis imagined by Alvarado:

> For our purposes today, such distinctions [as those drawn between "theoretical" and "practical"] don't help our understanding of "The Place and Purpose of Media Education" . . . What I am indicating here is that, at its best, Media Education involves work on the *symbolic*, media *content*, and *practical work*, together with work on areas which I initially identified as being important, i.e. work on the personal, the social, the economic, the political, the institutional and the contemporary.[21]

We are again confronted with the operations of the distancing dichotomy of theory versus practice and the concomitant undertheorization of pedagogy. What other understandings of critical media literacy become possible in the new spaces opened up by the disruption of these dichotomies? What new imaginings of a media pedagogy within a critical theory of the postmodern emerge from these spaces?

The media schoolhouse

In the light of these concerns, television can be looked at as a *pedagogical machine*, constructing discourses that function primarily in the locus of a mode of transmission where "culture becomes defined solely by markets for culture."[22] If we are to educate students to become media literate, we must attend to the multiple references and codes that position them. This means paying attention to the manner in which popular culture texts are constructed by and construct various discursive codes, but also how such texts express various contradictory ideological interests and how these texts might be taken up in a way that creates possibilities for different constructions of cultural and political life.

Critical media literacy: Three counterhegemonic practices

One: Rereading the media

Contemporary media are themselves pedagogical in function; they contribute to constructions of knowledge and the subject of knowledge. Thus a first step in a critical media literacy program involves the practice of ideology critique in a confrontation with the text. In the context of postmodernism, this means educating students to become media literate in a world of changing representations. This entails reworking the traditional practice of ideology critique, which tends to locate meaning in the text as an *isolated object* of interpretation. Instead, the practice of critique must involve a number of considerations: (1) the critical reading of how cultural texts are regulated by various discursive codes; (2) how such texts express and represent different ideological interests; and (3) how they might be taken up differently by various subjects in different contexts.

In this process of literacy acquisition, ideological criticism is an important first stage in the initial task of taking apart or breaking down the "natural" and "eternal" and replacing it with the *cultural* and the *historical*. It is here also where *hegemony* as the mechanism of ideology is introduced. It is in this introduction to media hegemony that a full array of rupturing practices, the processes of demythologizing and denaturalizing—that is, the processes of *making the invisible visible*—are undertaken. And it is here also where the contributions of contemporary structuralist and poststructuralist literary theory can be examined through the power of its critique in the disintegration of the traditional source-centered "transmission" models of mass communication. And it is here where we might begin to consider critical pedagogy's corresponding disruption of "transmission" models of education and examine the collapse of the distancing dichotomies of, among others, "reader/writer" and "teacher/student" necessary for the potential of both media and media education to be realized.

Media as a pedagogical machine is not simply a producer of meanings (an encoding of truths to be appropriated by the "minds" of the audience); it also produces "subjectivity." Certainly, students need to engage media representations as constructive of meanings which discursively set the boundaries of how reality may be approached, but they need to also look at how these meanings are mobilized in everyday life, how they hook up with emotional, affective commitments that are historically situated. Mark Poster succinctly characterizes these processes of the media in contemporary conditions in a manner worth quoting at length:

> For the subject in electronically mediated communication, the object tends to become not the material world as represented in language but the flow of signifiers itself. In the mode of information it becomes increasingly difficult, or even pointless, for the subject to distinguish a "real" existing "behind" the flow of signifiers, and as a consequence social life in part becomes a practice of positioning subjects to receive and interpret messages . . . Media language—contextless, monologic, self-referential— invites the recipient to play with the process of self-constitution, continuously to remake the self in "conversation" with differing modes of dis-

course . . . The subject has no defined identity as a pole of a conversation.[23]

At the level of critique the project of media literacy is to break down this practice by reconstituting the context of media communication and the material identity and agency of the reader or writer. Ideology critique is not disconnected from institutional, legal, cultural, political, and economic factors. The *contexts* of the text are both crucial to the reading of its historical construction and the gateway to further questions: Who produces images? For whose consumption? For what purposes? What alternative images are thereby excluded?

Most important to this project of a postmodern critical media literacy, this context *must* include the relationship of the reader to the text and the manner in which multiple identities are produced and reworked in the reader-text relationship through diverse modes of address, closure, identification, and reinscription. Literacy (in its traditional form of learning a language) is a bipolar practice, one involving developing skills of reading the language as well as speaking it. Media literacy has been treated differently, typically as simply the ability to read or decode media messages. This separation of reading from writing, unwittingly or not, buys into models of communication that foreclose the *very possibility* of an active media literacy.

In terms of a critical media literacy, it is also significant that this source-centered paradigm informed not only early mass communication research, but also the emergence of television itself into its current form. We have known no other norm for the operation of the TV industries in the United States. However, an important facet of media illiteracy lies in the popular affective "common-sense" understanding of the way television is as somehow normal and natural (how could it be other than this?). Emerging as a source-centered medium and industry, television cares little for the reactions of its audiences, other than in the form of quantifiable data which may be used as a basis for advertising rates.

Revised and expansive conceptualizations of *reading* and *authorship* offered by literary theory seem an important component in describing a basis for critical reading of mediated messages. In, for example, Barthes' notion of the oppositional relationship between two kinds of pleasure, *plaisir* and *jouissance*, we find this distinction between reading as *reading* and reading as *writing*. In a more concrete politics of reading, Freire has also proposed such a reconceptualization of literacy: "Reading is re-writing what we are reading. Reading is to discover the connections between the text and the context of the text, and also how to connect the text/context with my context, the context of the reader."[24] A practice of reading as writing must address the material context of everyday life in both of these dimensions: Freire's concern with moral and political agency, and Barthes' concern with the politics of pleasure (affective commitment).

The media must be "deconstructed where it hurts;" that is, we need to connect this critique to everyday life and those areas of student experience to which they are actively committed. Ideology critique is counterproductive at best when it simply draws upon an academic jargon to find various myths, and so on. Instead, we must question naturalized knowledge, pinpoint areas of ideology that students connect to and that make a difference in their lives. We must take seriously the experiences through which students constitute their identities and draw upon them as means for criticizing the dominant culture.[25] This leads us to consider the second area of counterhegemonic practice in critical media literacy.

Two: Affective reflexivity; remapping subject positions

Denaturalizing the text is not an isolated practice. If we know and can see that MTV is sexist in its representation, what implications follow? Do we then still watch MTV? The idea is not to batter and condemn popular forms. (The lesson is not "Ok, now don't watch television.") Instead, we must attend to the *affective investments* that students bring to the text: why do they watch what they watch, who do they watch it with, and what do they do with it? Again, we must question the communication model of examining the media. As Heath has pointed out:

> We need to understand the institution (of television) in respect of its funda-
> mental universalizing function, universalizing not in the sense of the cre-
> ation of some one coherent subject, some representative reason for its
> orders, but in that, more basically, of the universalization of the function of
> reception. The hierarchy of message and medium on which notions of

communication habitually depend here shifts: what is transmitted is important, but it is the realization and maintenance of the function of reception
that is all-important.[26]

Examining the reception of texts does not simply consist in cataloguing
the plurality of responses to the media, as if "audiences making meaning"
assures an activity of producing critical or resistant readings. The reading-
as-resistance approach leaves untouched television's role in constructing the
reality in which readings are offered.[27] The point is not that readers do not on
occasion make critical readings, but that an approach which simply valorizes
the reader as resistant is still trapped in the active-passive dichotomy.

Ideology does not directly create action or belief or investment. In fact,
perhaps one of the conditions of postmodern representation and appropriation is that we see the meaning, we don't believe it, but we go on watching it
anyway. We must attend to the possibility that media construct identity and
social position not by centralizing and homogenizing, but by fragmenting
viewpoints, creating a condition where *difference can make no difference,*
creating the postmodern condition. We still need to attend to how it is that
current forms of media representation invite acquiescence to subject positions defined within prevailing social conditions, and how it is that media
knowledge limits the range of possible interpretations of social relations.
Students need then to be media literate not just in the sense of being able to
decipher the meanings offered by the media, but also by attending to their
own modes of affective investment and consumption of the media.

Grossberg's notion of affect is crucial here—that is, in everyday life we
base our decisions not just on rational meanings, but through *emotional and
bodily* commitments, commitments understood as falling between "libidinal
economies of desire and affective economies of mood as two different planes
on which psychic energy is always dispersed."[28] In late capitalism these
affective dimensions may be used for tactics that mobilize affective alliances
through displacement, naturalization, normalization, and so on. They may
also, however, be reclaimed by audiences for the purposes of constructing
different forms of empowerment that cut through these tactics. The question
is: How can we become different kinds of consumers? Perhaps more elab-
orately, this asks: Is there the potential for a meaningfully conceptualized

counterhegemonic consumption within a properly theorized postmodern critical media literacy?

Perhaps the means toward a counterhegemonic consumption lies in the increased effort to integrate notions of affect within the context of critical discourse (which has historically been hostile to them). Whereas Jameson locates his own melancholy, in part, in "the waning of affect" in postmodern culture,[29] we might be much more inclined to agree with Woodward's response that "the emotions are not dead, they are simply not present in academic discourse."[30] It may be that two things (subprojects, if you will) need to be done as part of this project of critical media literacy. Both have to do with the idea that any understanding of a "counterhegemonic consumption" must be structured in such a manner that directly confronts notions of *desire*, and desire's problematic relationship with both "consumption" and "agency" in the context of postmodern culture. It seems that we need to both expand the discourse, that is, increase the ways in which we talk about the politics of consumption and desire, and, as part of this expansion of existing discursive locations, open up new discursive territories in which a language of the emotions might take root.

Critical media literacy must offer a practice of dialogue with students so that commitments, styles of consumption, and investments in the media can be foregrounded, questioned, and understood. Students must question the text and what "they" do with the text. Teachers must take seriously students' commitments to and affective investments in various forms of popular culture in order to both critically interrogate self-production and to draw out student "activity" that opens up possibilities for counterhegemonic practices. Media literacy must draw out these responses in the context of the historically bounded meanings available in media production, the interpretive assets available to the reader, and the reading formations that readers bring to acts of reception.

This literacy of reading and rewriting involves asking "Who am I when I see this?" Here the theoretical contribution of postmodern theory in tracing how the subject is constituted in multiple subjectivities is crucial in cutting through the banal theory of the individual framed by liberal pluralism. Television, particularly in advertisements, depends, first of all, on creating a dependent spectator: it constitutes the subject as consumer at the same time that it constitutes the subject as judge and validator of the meaning of the ad.[31] The monologic framing of the subject as consumer depends at the same time on the fragmentation of individual subjects into meaning producers who validate the ad and their own "freedom" in relation to it by regarding themselves as free-floating self-"constituters." In asking students to examine their multiple subjectivity in relation to media constructions, media literacy must turn the focus back onto the specificity of subject positions generated in media reading.

The media function by fragmenting the subject in order to produce a "knowing, cynical, self-constituting" viewer who nevertheless goes on consuming works by actually eliminating self-reflection. The practice of media literacy needs to retrieve the moment of self-reflexivity by encouraging students to directly attend to their own identifications and investments in the act of consumption. In Shor and Freire's terms, this is a reinvigoration of the act of critical consciousness as "gaining reflective distance on one's own thoughts, actions and social community."[32]

Finally, being media literate means both having a voice and giving the other a voice—seeing one's subjectivity in the threat of the other and then overcoming that threat in the recognition of the partiality of one's own perspective. Media literacy is not a practice that takes place in isolation. In order to understand the media, one's self, and one's relation to it, one must be able to speak with a voice and be able to recognize who is speaking in the media and who is not speaking. By recognizing the other, the difference that exists in a positive sense, we break down the dichotomies that structure capitalist hegemony: core/periphery, majority/minority, First World/Third World, and so on. Knowledge must be reinvented and reconstructed by inviting students to be *border crossers*.[33] Such a pedagogy defines itself as a project of educating students to take the stand of the other, to practice an analysis of their own conditions, and to believe that they *can* make a difference.

Three: Rewriting and the vital strategy of authorship

Finally, a critical media literacy produces a transformative alternative practice. A mode of problematizing, this course of action produces, "against the grain," an alternative attack and creation of representation. Students need to be encouraged to invent counterrepresentations and counterforms of organization and evaluation. First of all, active reading should itself be seen as a form of production, a form of countermemory that produces a reinscription that counters our present forms of truth and justice.

Add to this an active writing, an alternative practice, a direct handling of the tools and processes of media practice. In this way the concepts of reader and writer within the emergence of a critical media literacy are connected to notions of *audience* and *producer*. To return to our initial paradox: given the technologies available and their potential for the democratization of the media, how can the oppositional potential of these media be so easily thwarted? Further, and more specifically to our purposes here, how can these new technologies be used in the creation of a counterhegemony in support of the *long revolution?*

Both television (or, in its expanded sense, "video") and the classroom possess a potential to represent two democratic public spheres. As such, they also represent two crucial sites in the formation of subjectivities. Access to both (by "access" we refer to all levels of operations, programming, and ownership) are fundamental aspects of the ongoing struggle over the sociocultural status quo, and all which that entails. Both the classroom and the contemporary entertainment and news media are sites of struggle over the creation, recreation, and maintenance of our individual understanding of the values and relations which arise from our collective understanding of past, present, and future—the way things are and the way things could be—and struggles over the celebration of difference and voices critical of the way things are, or their continued exclusion and suppression.

Recent theory and practice have suggested a variety of approaches which erase the distance between these various dichotomized concepts and open up new space for new voices. In a manner which simultaneously suggests the contributions and problematics of literary theory, Gregory Ulmer[34] offers a vision of a "pedagogy of invention" in his notion of the "mystory" and "mystorical" writing, in which the traditional categories of theory and practice, the expert, the popular, and the personal all collapse into a poststructuralist language play of autobiography and theory.

Teaching TV, a recent exhibition at New York City's Artists' Space featured forty videotapes made by or with young people. Critical educators have, in light of dominant structures, always faced problems of isolation and related lack of mechanisms for support and communication. This meeting represents one example of the kind of gathering for the purposes of sharing and consolidation, a strategy crucial to a critical pedagogy of media praxis. As Trend observes:

> The [political] right's program would disencourage the multiplicity of opinions so necessary to a functioning democracy by asserting an essential stratification of discourses. As a counterargument to such regressive logic, "Teaching TV" emphasized the resistant and antihierarchical aspects of youth culture. Rather than promoting the "functionalist" view of learning (currently favored by conservatives) that obliges students to adapt to existing social mandates, "Teaching TV" presented works that afford students an active role in making and remaking their world.[35]

These experiments also illustrate the progressive potential of the video medium opened up in the spaces created in the dissolution of the dichotomies of reader/writer and source/receiver. Contained within these practices is the possibility of reversing media's current role in contemporary culture and politics: from a source of alienation and silence to a source of collective voice and agency. And these new approaches reveal a strategic point for developing theories of critical pedagogy. It suggests that technology and media are *less determinative of ideology than are the circumstances in which they are applied*.[36]

As theory and practice collapse upon each other into a reformation of a critical media praxis, the transformations of consciousness necessary for a meaningful project of critical media literacy become imaginable. Also imaginable is the growth of media education curricula and the increased role of critical media educators beyond the confines of the classroom and into new interrelations with the various new technologies of LPTV, public access, community radio, and so forth, and with the various community action, environmental, labor, reproductive rights, gay, and lesbian groups who currently use these new media technologies.

As this occurs, notions of media literacy will extend beyond critical viewing and into the creation of new media forms—forms of media practice—that are vital components of the counterhegemony. To further connect this to Freire's ground-breaking *Pedagogy of the Oppressed*, media educators, in their own privileged positions in terms of race, class, and gender, must (as oppressors at least in terms of their untransformed consciousness) undergo their own transformations of consciousness. And their pedagogy must result inevitably in the continued education of the oppressed by the oppressed. Critical media literacy must work to achieve "modes of presentation, imaging, entertainment and argument that are realizations of collective desires, group aspirations, common projects, shared experience, at the same time that they refuse all ideas—all expression—of standing in for and subsuming the heterogeneous individual-sociality/social-individuality of the actual lives of actual men and women."[37]

Conclusion

To call for a new media literacy is to call for new relations to representation and new possibilities for reading and writing. It is to call for a self-constituting practice in which a critical language is used to enable us to "both identify ourselves and recreate ourselves as active subjects in history."[38] It is to call for imagination. This is the possibility to go beyond tomorrow without being naively idealistic. This is utopianism as a dialectical relationship between denouncing the present and announcing the future: it is to anticipate tomorrow by dreaming today.

Notes

1. Williams, R., *The Long Revolution* (New York: Columbia University Press, 1961), p. xxi.

2. A vision of a future "utopia," not in the sense of the imaginary but in Marcuse's sense of a future society of transformed social relations realizable through political action.

3. Kariel, H., *The Disparate Politics of Postmodernism* (Amherst, Mass.: University of Massachusetts Press, 1989), p. xiii.

4. Bogue, R., *Deleuze and Guattari* (New York: Routledge, 1989), p. 102.

5. The right has been particularly successful in achieving a voice of authority by its management of affective commitments through electronic mass media, think tanks, the state educational apparatus, and quasi-public interest groups (Accuracy in Media, etc.) The right's particular "politics of truth" is thus implemented through pedagogical strategies, that is, strategies of maintaining and motivating the appropriation of discourses. This pedagogical dimension is evident in the recent events in the Gulf. The war was horrific enough in itself, but even more horrifying was the 91 percent approval rating of George Bush, itself a reflection of the success of the discursive (pedagogical) campaign of the war in the mobilization of the affective commitment of the populace through the deployment of empty signifiers such as "freedom," "the American way of life," and so on. The greatest loss for the left in this war may be the right's success in cementing its control of the direction of commitment (even though that commitment may be directionless, it is certainly not traveling in the direction of social change).

6. McLaren, P., and Hammer, R., "Critical Pedagogy and the Postmodern Challenge," *Educational Foundations*, 1989, p. 30.

7. As Peter McLaren (1989, p. 161) notes, "In their discussion of "critical thinking" the new conservatives and liberals have neutralized the term *critical* by repeated and imprecise usage, removing its political and cultural dimensions and laundering its analytic potency to mean "thinking skills . . . By defining academic success almost exclusively in terms of creating compliant, productive, and patriotic workers, the new conservative agenda for a 'resurgent America' dodges any concern for nurturing critical and committed citizens."

8. Grossberg, L., "Putting the Pop Back into Postmodernism," in Ross, A. (ed.), *Universal Abandon* (Minneapolis: University of Minnesota Press, 1988), p. 169.

9. See Hebdige, D., *Hiding in the Light* (New York: Routledge, 1988), p. 181.

10. Baudrillard, J., *Selected Writings*, ed. Poster, M. (Stanford: Stanford University Press, 1988).

11. Kroker, A. and Cook, D. *The Postmodern Scene: Excremental Culture and Hyper-Aesthetics* (Montreal: New World Perspectives, 1986).

12. Giroux, H., "Postmodernism and the Discourse of Educational Criticism," *Journal of Education*, 170, 1988a, p. 24.

13. These regressive and nihilistic theorizations of the postmodern condition hold within them the danger of the gradual descent into an intellectual cynicism. Although political apathy in the face of the intricate workings of

the cultural hegemony of late capitalism is one in an array of possible responses, a celebration of difference and a willingness to work for a future you know full well that you will never live to see is another, preferable response. This is a willingness to participate in what Raymond Williams calls the "long revolution."

14. Hebdige, D., "After the Masses," *Marxism Today*, Jan., 1989, p. 51.

15. *Ibid.*, p. 52.

16. Giroux, H., *Schooling and the Struggle for Public Life* (Minneapolis: University of Minnesota Press, 1988b), p. 162.

17. Giroux (1988a), *op. cit.*, pp. 6–7.

18. Not to be confused with the undertheorized notion of "resistance" as in the recent works of Fiske, Jenkins, and others (see Sholle, D., "Resistance: Pinning Down a Wandering Concept in Cultural Studies Discourse," *Journal of Urban and Cultural Studies*, 1, 1990, pp. 87–107).

19. Giroux, H., and Simon, R., *Popular Culture, Schooling and Everyday Life* (Granby, Mass.: Bergin and Garvey, 1989), p. 243. See also Giroux, H., and McLaren, P. (eds.), *Critical Pedagogy, the State, and Cultural Struggle* (Albany: SUNY Press, 1989), p. xxiv.

20. Alvarado, M., "The Place and Purpose of Media Education," Introductory Plenary Presentation, 8 April, 1990, BFI Education Easter School, Liverpool, p. 2.

21. *Ibid.*, p. 3.

22. Wexler, P., "Curriculum in the Closed Society," in Giroux, H., and McLaren, P. (eds.), *Critical Pedagogy, the State, and Cultural Struggle* (Albany: SUNY Press), p. 98.

23. Poster, M., *The Mode of Information* (Chicago: University of Chicago Press, 1990), pp. 14, 46.

24. Shor, I., and Freire, P., *A Pedagogy for Liberation* (Granby, Mass.: Bergin and Garvey, 1987), pp. 10–11.

25. Giroux (1988b), *op. cit.*, p. 175.

26. Heath, S., "Representing Television," in Mellencamp, P. (ed.), *Logics of Television* (Bloomington: University of Indiana Press, 1990), p. 270.

27. *Ibid.*, p. 285.

28. Grossberg, *op. cit.*, p. 285.

29. Jameson, F., "Postmodernism or the Cultural Logic of Late Capitalism," *New Left Review*, 146, 1984, pp. 53–92.

30. Woodward, K., "Introduction," *Discourse*, 13, 1, 1990–91, p. 4.

31. Poster, *op. cit.*, p. 67.

32. Shor and Freire, *op. cit.*, p. 167.

33. Giroux, H., "Liberal Arts Education and the Struggle for Public Life: Dreaming about Democracy," *South Atlantic Quarterly,* 89, 1990, p. 124.

34. Ulmer, G., *Teletheory* (New York: Routledge, 1989).

35. Trend, D., "To Tell the Truth: Strategies for a Critical Media Literacy," *After Image,* March 1991, p. 12.

36. *Ibid.,* p. 14, our underlining.

37. Heath, *op. cit.,* p. 298.

38. McLaren and Hammer, *op. cit.,* p. 49.

11

Feminist literacies: Toward emancipatory possibilities of solidarity

Jeanne Brady and Adriana Hernández

This paper, in its shifting style between the personal and the academic, is the result of our coming together into dialogue. It contains a multiplicity of voices, not only that of a white Anglo woman and that of a Hispanic Argentine one, but also different voices and silences according to the diverse spaces we inhabit—home, the academy—and the varied audiences we engage in this process of coming to voice as subjects engendered in networks of class, gender, race, and ethnicity. Maria C. Lugones and Elizabeth V. Spelman represent a practice of dialogue which situates the forging of differences within unities that characterizes our own work: "We are both the authors of this paper and not just sections of it, but we write together without presupposing unity of expression or experience. So when we speak in unison it means just that—there are two voices and not just one."[1]

Historical experience separates us. It would be unethical to merge our voices in an effort to speak as "women's experience." Rather, ours is an attempt to be partners in a dialogue about issues that affect us as women. We speak from a "representative space"—one grounded in personal experience—within a feminist framework. We do not attempt to examine feminist literacy as a single-issue movement, leading to some form of a totalizing position, but rather we view feminism as occupying multiple spaces, and by recognizing this we also support multiple feminist literacies.

Throughout this paper we engage in a process of reflecting on an already existing body of knowledge on critical literacy. We also theorize our experience and the politics of the different spaces within which we write and speak, struggle with discourses and alien voices, and, in doing so, become subjects naming our own practices. Our paper, then, shifts from the practice of theory to theory as practice, in a diversity of forms and styles, trying to explore a feminist notion of literacy by analyzing central questions about the relationship between voice and public and private space as well as examining a language of multiplicity. For us, these issues represent two aspects of a feminist political project in which a theory of literacy takes up the issue of democratic social change as part of a wider effort to transform the conditions of oppression and discontinuity into emancipatory possibilities.

We begin by recognizing that literacy needs to be defined in political and ethical terms and cannot be disengaged from relations of power. As Henry Giroux points out, "Literacy is a discursive practice in which difference becomes crucial for understanding not simply how to read, write, or develop aural skills, but to also recognize that the identities of "others" matter as part of a progressive set of politics and practices aimed at the reconstruction of democratic public life."[2] Literacy as a form of cultural politics requires us to explore the complexity of power relations that both enable and silence social groups as well as challenge the exclusionary and often colonizing discourse of dominant culture.

Private/public space and the tension around *woman/women*

In seeking to theorize literacy through a feminist approach that addresses issues such as difference and practices of representation, we analyzed critically a diverse range of works on literacy. Thinking within a feminist literacy, it becomes apparent that in the issue of women's voices and discourses there is a tension around *Woman/women* (woman as symbolic category; *women* as social and historical subjects) and the notion of the *private* and the *public*. At present a complex discussion is going on within the academy concerning the discourses that women use and "should" use: a personal one, an academic one (with the risk of being perceived as using the Master's discourse), or a persuasive one? We will address these issues after analyzing the tension between *Woman* and women in relation to private and public spaces.

In the dominant ideology, women are supposed to inhabit or be relegated to private space and men are supposed to inhabit and dominate the public one. How are *public* and *private* being conceptualized within this position? Is it Woman or women who inhabit the private? The politics of the tension between Woman and women is being powerfully recognized in many works, such as those of Gayatri Spivak, Susan Jarratt, and Teresa De Lauretis, and a space is opening where agency and contestation are possible. De Lauretis identifies "the discrepancy, the tension, and the constant slippage between Woman as representation, as the object and the very condition of representation and, on the other hand, women as historical beings, subjects of 'real relations' . . . women are both inside and outside gender, at once within and without representation."[3]

It seems to us that even when feminism, being a plural movement, makes an important turn to recognize differences within women, there is still a strong tendency to fall back into the question of Woman as its main subject. Often this makes it impossible to recognize the multiplicity and flexibility with which women enact roles that have been essentially defined. That is to say, engaging only the paradigm of Woman does not allow one to perceive actual women acting in concrete social, historical, and cultural settings. If we—feminists—persist in concentrating on Woman, just seeing Woman, not *women* in concrete social relations, we lose sight of difference and get caught in the dead end of a binary opposition which does not allow us to articulate "the difference of women from Woman . . . or, perhaps more exactly, the differences within women."[4]

Returning to the public/private dichotomy, it seems to us that the woman that has been relegated to the private—the apolitical—is not women, but rather Woman. We certainly agree with deLauretis that all women go through the process of becoming Woman, but, as she recognizes, we are not just that; we are historical subjects. Furthermore, we/women are constituted through multiple languages and cultural representations; we are subjects "constituted in gender . . . though not by sexual difference alone . . . [subjects] engendered in the experiencing of race and class, as well as sexual relations . . . [subjects] not unified but rather multiple, and not so much divided as contradicted."[5]

Therefore, not only do we need to pay attention to Woman as the one caught in the private, but also to Woman constituted through different representations. Even further, we—feminists—have to see women overflowing those representations as concrete subjects acting within concrete social relations. This certainly problematizes the reductionism of private/female and public/male, offering the possibility of a different and more complex reading of the political, the politics of gender and literacy, and the politics of representation. This is an important step in the process of contesting binary oppositions and flooding the limits of sexual difference.

Within this framework, the private/public tension is constituted as a space of struggle over different meanings and representations, a historical construction that, from a feminist perspective, needs to move toward more egalitarian and fair forms which are certainly multiple and subject to continuous reconstruction. If we deconstruct and contest the specific power relations that work in the Law/Logos male and in Woman as a representation of an essence, then we should also consider that "the historical and social operation of the sexual differential exceed the discursive identification of sexual difference."[6] The public and the private are both part of an ideological process which is enacted in a specific space and time by concrete women and men.

In search of a voice . . . or whose discourse?

> If woman has always functioned "within" the discourse of man, a signifier that has always referred back to the opposite signifier which annihilates its specific energy and diminishes or stifles its very sounds, it is time for her to dislocate this "within," to explode it . . . to make it hers . . . just because there's a risk of identification doesn't mean that we'll succumb. Let's leave it to the worriers, to masculine anxiety and its obsession with how to dominate the way things work.[7]

I became aware of the tyranny of the category *Woman* when writing a paper in which I was confronted with the statement that I was using a male discourse. In a final paper I presented for a feminist course in the spring semester of 1990, I was told that I had used a highly academic discourse—meaning a male discourse—that was totally abstract and, most of all, that I had left my body out. This paper, which I wrote in an inquiring first person, that of a Latin American woman student, analyzed the work of Michelle Le Doeuff on women in philosophy and Margo Culley's and Susan Stanford Friedman's work on women's intellectual authority in the classroom.

I felt silenced, as if being punished for having learned the discourse of the academy (have I?), even when I was aware that my paper did not quite fit within the dominant discourse because I used the radical perspective of critical theory and feminism. When I talked to the professor, she pointed out that I had not referred explicitly to my experience as a teacher in Argentina—recalling concrete events—nor to my life as a graduate student. Therefore, my paper was the copy of a copy, the representation of a representation, a postmodern product where even the women authors I used were accused of being phallocentric. Now, I not only see how I was caught in the binary structures on which the discursive power of patriarchy is built,[8] but I also see how I was positioned as Woman, "the representation of an essence inherent in all women,"[9] and the material conditions of my writing, my own body, were ignored completely.

It seems to me that the questions of voice and discourse are currently being abused in an easy move to delegitimate certain positions, which is very disempowering for women in subject positions such as *Hispanic, lesbian, student,* or *nontenured professor*. At the same time, although the issue of discourse is widely theorized, the issue of voice is still in a stage of under-theorization and, because of this, is essentialized in many ways. Is it always possible or politically powerful to use a personal discourse? How do we call into question different settings and audiences? How do I or you know, when I or you write, that this is my or your voice and not others' voices? Furthermore, is this question of theorizing one of binary opposition—me/you (individualism?)—or rather a collective work? Is an academic discourse a purely male dominion, or rather a site of tension and contradiction that needs to be problematized and historicized?

I understand the importance of reclaiming experiences—feelings in general, and anger in particular—as key elements in women's writing. In addition, the consciousness-raising process as foundational is imperative. I believe this, not because I buy the stereotype of the personal as inherently female, but rather because I consider it as a subversive strategy to contest patriarchal politics of knowledge. This does not mean that I always have to write in a personal discourse. On the other hand, when I use an academic discourse I am not being an accomplice of patriarchy.

When theorizing the concrete problematic around the voice and discourse which confronted me, I found empowering elements in Susan Jarratt's "The First Sophists and Feminism: Discourses of the 'Other'." Here Jarratt considers the Derridean deconstructive analysis of the status of Woman which demystifies the "binary structures on which the discursive power of patriarchy is built."[10] Furthermore, Jarratt recalls Spivak's warning that

> the 'woman' whose displacement is recognized in Derridean deconstructions isn't the real woman whose body is subject to codes of legitimacy and inheritance . . . She uses a dual sense of logos . . . In one sense, the logos to be deconstructed is the founding principle of transcendence, presence, idea, speech. But in another use of the term, logoi are "laws in the normal sense," creating conditions under which humans in social organizations live and write. 'Woman' is oppressed by the former, but women suffer under the latter.[11]

This analysis introduces a necessary tension between a textual exercise and the concrete material conditions of textual production that appears to be absent when a text is taken—my paper, for example—and is automatically portrayed as academic, abstract, male, and just the copy of the Master's discourse. Am I that woman? Through this experience, I understand the possibilities of rhetoric in feminism as opening to consideration the real material situations of discourse performance. I desire to write, I want to theorize, and my writing emerges as a mixture of oral speech—which I learned to repress!—and written text. Cixous tells me that there is no schism between the logic of oral speech and the logic of the text.[12] I have so many questions! My logic and style rise as an ongoing inquiry directed to and from myself and to those who want to listen. If I am silenced, if my voice and

discourse are totally dismissed, I get terrified—I feel ridiculous!—and static, I cannot move, and my body is like a sterile land that cannot even bear a
child. Cixous murmurs: "Decide for yourself on your position in the arena of
contradictions, where pleasure and reality embrace. Bring the other to
life."[13]

I do not believe there is an absolute or unproblematic safe position from
which to speak and always be politically correct. At the same time, this does
not mean we should stop being (methodologically!) self-suspicious and critical among ourselves; rather, we should engage in a collaborative and plural
work for social transformation where diverse voices and discourses can be at
play acknowledging the different rhetorical situations and the different power
relations that place them in dominant or oppressed positions.

A discourse of multiplicity

> In the same way feminists have learned
> to live with multiple meanings so should
> we be initiators of multiple literacies.[14]

In an attempt to explore discourses within feminism that offer alternatives to the language of control, we turn now to the question of difference. By
incorporating difference within the context of literacy, our aim is to provide
an essential component for developing a broader notion of democratic struggle and social justice. Henry Giroux points to the emancipatory implications
of what he calls a "politics of difference."

> If a politics of difference is to be fashioned in emancipatory rather than
> oppressive practices, literacy must be rewritten in terms that articulate
> difference with the principles of equality, justice, and freedom rather than
> with those interests supportive of hierarchies, oppression and exploita-
> tion . . . This is a language in which one speaks WITH rather than FOR
> Others.[15]

Yet if we are to take seriously these emancipatory practices, then we
must think of difference in relation to power. By exploring the complexity of
the relations of power, we are required to understand how relationships are
constructed between ourselves and others and how one's place is historically

and socially constructed. Difference is embedded in cultural spheres that produce knowledge and identities. Central questions underlying difference relating to the notion of power, history, and self-identity must be raised. What knowledge is revered? Whose histories are legitimated? Whose voices are silenced? Mohanty's critique of the language of difference emphasizes how intricately composed and complex this is and is worth quoting at length.

> Difference seen as benign variation (diversity), for instance, rather than as conflict, struggle, or the threat of disruption, bypasses power as well as history to suggest a harmonious, empty pluralism. On the other hand, difference defined as asymmetrical and incommensurate cultural spheres situated within hierarchies of domination and resistance cannot be accommodated within a discourse of "harmony in diversity."[16]

This is complicated because we must consciously acknowledge and understand, not only the barriers that exist between academic and nonacademic women, Third World women, and white women and women of color, but also how positions of center and margin continue to be reproduced. Moreover, power is distributed in ways that divide women from forms of community participation embedded in subordinated and marginalized traditions.

The question of multiplicity is far more complex than a matter of difference. A feminist theory of multiplicity encourages a politics of difference that affirms women's experiences by allowing women to speak as historical subjects from positions within cultural realms. Furthermore, a feminist project of multiplicity attempts to reclaim the alternative histories, identities, and knowledge of marginal people and to view them as authentic and central to emancipatory democracy. In effect, it is an attempt to shift power from the exclusionary and often colonizing discourse of the privileged to those groups in the margins, ultimately, by transforming the margins as multiple sites of power.

Multiple languages and multiple spaces

One occupies many subject positions; each of us is not just "one thing." We speak from multiple places: student, teacher, mother, lover, friend, worker. As feminists we embrace a feminist concern about women, yet as academics we occupy a space of privilege. What role do we play in maintaining and perpetuating these existing social structures? How do we speak in a way that allows people to listen? To dialogue? In an attempt to speak and listen from a position of acceptance, Gayatri Spivak calls for the "unlearning of one's privilege," "so that, not only does one become able to listen to that other constituency, but one learns to speak in such a way that one will be taken seriously by that other constituency."[17]

Engaging in the process of unlearning privilege is a twofold task. First, we must challenge the exclusionary and often colonizing discourse of dominant groups by carefully scrutinizing the legitimation of white, middle-class codes and also by understanding place and identity in relation to issues of power and domination. Our intention is not to reverse the order of things, "but rather to question the formation of the structure."[18] By attempting to shift paradigms rather than appropriate dominant language and space, we can focus on developing strategies of communication and inclusion.

Second, unlearning privilege requires confronting differences constructively and successfully. Western women, of course, are not the only valid subjects in history. The legitimate space that Third World women and women of color occupy marks a further concern. Chandra Mohanty points to the "need for creating an analytical space for understanding Third World women as the subject of our various struggles in history."[19] This requires transforming the ways Third World women and women of color are represented: from fragmented and passive voices to active subjects in the struggles of histories. In establishing this space and celebrating this position, we neither support the homogeneity of cultures nor exoticize or romanticize Third World women or women of color. Rather, we endorse and treat all women as *subjects*. bell hooks advises "Third World women, African American women must work against speaking as 'other', speaking to difference as it is constructed in the white supremist imagination."[20]

Collective work

The political project situated in a feminist theory of literacies attempts to examine and restructure the way we view relations of power so that women are enabled to speak and act as subjects within history. It also seeks to make possible shared literacies and dialogues that allow for multiple solidarities and political vocabularies. For these ends to be realized, however, it is necessary to situate this project in an arena of practice that initiates and encourages collective work. Solidarity and community work constitute the organizing principle for structuring relationships between self and others to analyze the interstructuring of sexism, racism, and economic exploitation. By organizing around a common concern, groups of persons from diverse racial, ethnic, and economic backgrounds can intersect and engage in dialogue that could provide opportunities for community participation, experimentation, and creative cultural production.

Critical feminist literacies

A critical feminist literacy strives for a space that incorporates social practice within a postpatriarchal discourse. It is a radical philosophy that attempts to expose and challenge a hierarchically ordered sexist, classist, and racist worldview by restructuring the relations of power in a way that enables women to speak and act as historical subjects within democratic social relations. Its basic premise is the need to end sexist oppression and sexism while also challenging the politics of domination in areas of not only gender but of race, class, and ethnicity as well. Gender in isolation from these categories of difference gives us an important but disjointed and partial reading of a number of highly complex issues which coexist concurrently within cultural and economic realms. In other words, questions concerning gender foreground forms of oppression and possibility that provide the basis for widening our understanding of how subjectivities, identities, and a sense of worth get constructed within and between various discourses and social relations as they are fought out at the level of everyday life. What this means is that questions of gender and equity provide an essential element in the wider struggle over principles of equity, freedom, and justice. Feminist literacies not only provide new analysis for understanding how subject positions for readers and spectators are constructed, but they also reclaim the importance of linking the personal and the political as a legitimate foundation for how one speaks, what one says, and how one acts.

Any attempt to change the cultural, political, and social aspects of the dominant, patriarchal society will be seen as an attack on democracy. We are willing to risk this, however, because (as this paper suggests) feminist literacies as discourses which initiate multiplicity are fundamental to developing a broader notion of democratic struggle and social justice. Furthermore, without any attempt to change the concept of what constitutes literacy, society will continue to reproduce existing structures of power as well as continue to establish grounds for oppressive relationships. Rather, we want to take responsibility for creating relations between ourselves and others that refuse acts of coercion and transform the conditions of oppression into emancipatory possibilities. For us, these emancipatory possibilities represent freedom, justice, and solidarity.

Notes

1. Lugones, M., and Spelman, E., "Have We Got a Theory for You! Feminist Theory, Cultural Imperialism and the Demand for 'woman's voice,'" *Women's Studies International Forum*, 6,6, 1983, p. 573.

2. Giroux, H., "Literacy, Pedagogy and the Politics of Difference," *College Literature*, 19, 1, 1992, pp. 1–11.

3. deLauretis, T., *Technologies of Gender: Essays on Theory, Film, and Fiction* (Bloomington and Indianapolis: Indiana University Press, 1987), p. 10.

4. *Ibid.*, p. 4.

5. *Ibid.*, p. 2.

6. Jarratt, S., "The First Sophists and Feminism: Discourses of the 'Other,'" *Hypatia*, 5,1, 1990, p. 31.

7. Cixous, H., "The Laugh of the Medusa," in Bizzell, P., and Herzberg, B. (eds.), *The Rhetorical Tradition: Readings from Classical Times to the Present* (Boston: Bedford Books of St. Martin's Press, 1990), pp. 1241–1242.

8. Jarratt, *op. cit.*, p. 30.

9. deLauretis, *op. cit.*, p. 9.

10. Jarratt, *op. cit.*, p. 30.

11. *Ibid.* The reference is to Spivak, G., *The Post-Colonial Critic: Interviews, Strategies, Dialogues*, ed. Harasm, S. (New York: Routledge, 1990).

12. Cixous, *op. cit.*, p. 1236.

13. *Ibid.*, p. 1243.

14. Beckelman, D., "Defining a Feminist Literacy," *Canadian Women's Studies/Les Cahiers de la Femme*, 9, 3/4, p. 133.

15. *Giroux*, op. cit.

16. Mohanty, C., "On Race and Voice: Challenges for Liberal Education in the 1990s," *Cultural Criticism*, Winter 1989–90, p. 181.

17. Spivak, *op. cit.*, p. 42.

18. *Ibid*.

19. Mohanty, *op. cit.*, p. 180.

20. hooks, b., *Talking Back: Thinking Feminist. Thinking Black* (Boston: South End Press, 1989), p. 16.

12

Dis/Connecting Literacy and Sexuality: Speaking the unspeakable in the classroom

Kathleen Rockhill

> I view the telling of our personal stories
> of subordination as an essential political
> act because without our stories recovered
> the past haunts the present and hope-
> lessly claims the future.
>
> (McMahon, 1991, p. 33)

"Dis/connecting literacy and sexuality"—when I write these words, I think of how literacy[1] and sexuality[2] are profoundly connected, especially through their opposition, in women's lives, but, absolutely disconnected in educational discourse and practice. Who speaks of literacy and sexuality in the same space? While this disconnection reflects the erasure of women's experience from the social production of knowledge, it is sedimented by practices of institutionalized heterosexism which regulate sexuality as private, unspeakable, and, for women, in opposition to intellectual performance. It is indicative of these separations that educators who advocate literacy for "empowerment" do not ask, "What does it mean to speak of power for a woman whose subordination is accomplished through sexual objectification?" This question is especially pertinent for critical literacy, for "woman's" sexual subordination hinges upon her not threatening male authority, an authority which is threatened by her attaining higher levels of literacy.

Foucault's (1982) argument that power operates through consensus rather than coercion, in the form of discursive practices that shape the subject's thoughts and regulate conduct, does not appear to have affected the ways in which literacy, even critical literacy, is approached. If power is not "out there" in the form of some external identifiable enemy, but internalized through processes of social inscription that shape the way we think—that is, the landscapes of our subjectivities—then how is it possible to approach the acquisition of literacy as a process of critical learning? Traditional literacy practices have been radically challenged by the work of Paulo Freire and other progressive educators who have recognized that acquisition of "the word" is not a neutral process and that "education for critical consciousness" is important to counter the colonizing effects of literacy acquisition. Still, models of popular education assume that learners are a homogenous group, innocent, free in some way of conflict, and that there is consensus, within and among group participants, who are united in their opposition to "power," which is named as "out there," "external," "coercive" (capitalists, the military, and so on) (Rockhill, 1988). Ironically, in assuming the learner to be a kind of blank slate, traditional conceptions of the learner as lacking in critical knowledge about (his) world and of the teacher as the knower, the one with the unproblematically correct approach to political analysis and action, are reinforced. Although lip service is paid to the subject's ideological inscription, it is assumed that the teacher, somehow, has attained a level of critical consciousness that students have not.

As a feminist concerned about education for radical change, I have been struggling for several years to develop an educational approach that can take up questions of social inscription as integral to processes of critical consciousness through (dis)identifications—experience seen as refracted through prisms of power relations lived as the normalized practices of daily life. How do these processes, relations, and practices differ according to one's social location; that is, how do the class, race, ethnicity, age, physical ability, gender, and sexuality of the learner enter into the challenges posed for literacy work? Although critical approaches to literacy have been important in the development of learner-centered approaches to teaching (Gaber-Katz and Watson, 1991), it is time to recognize that the learner is not a neutral person, but different persons who are gendered, raced, classed, and so on, and located, in all probability, at the margins of mainstream society. Moreover, that person's subjectivity has been formed in such a way that he or she is apt to have "internalized" social prescriptions about what is seen to be desirable behavior; hence racism, sexism, classism, and so on are experienced as inadequacy and self-loathing in relation to white, male-defined standards. Many women, for example, hate themselves for not measuring up to idealized images of feminine beauty at the same time as they desire to be, to match, as closely as possible, those images.

Feminism has scarcely touched the field of adult education; the area of literacy is no exception. This is beginning to shift, but the struggle is a formidable one. In my own faculty the battles have been brutal, fought largely around hirings, with feminist candidates consistently dismissed as "narrow, dogmatic, ideological," their work defined as having nothing to do with adult education, a profound threat to the humanitarian values of "the field." I am struck by the ways in which the current dismissal of feminism strongly replicates the delegitimation of working-class education as a base for practice that took place in the 1930s, when the field of workers' education was captured and defined by professional educators. In a historical study of that era (Rockhill, 1985), I describe how the professional field of adult education was institutionalized through a series of discursive practices that delegitimized class-based education as ideological, separatist, undemocratic, and biased, the very antithesis of liberal egalitarian educational values. Instead of considering a separate, class-based education that might serve to provide a base from which workers collectively could define, study, and critique their class location, educators felt that their responsibility was to provide a place wherein individual adults could be given a second chance to acquire the skills necessary to succeed in the system. These forms continue to define legitimate practice; equality of opportunity through functional literacy is the overarching goal, not literacy for critical consciousness and political action. Separate education for women in which a feminist agenda is the announced goal of the course is virtually unthinkable.

What does all of this have to do with the question of literacy and sexuality? If literacy is about "empowerment" through acquisition and critical awareness of "the word," and if women are subjugated through our sexualization—that is, the manipulation of our desire to be "feminine subjects" who are, by definition, not independent, intelligent, and educated— and if the boundaries of education are set so that literacy and sexuality shall never meet, then what does literacy as empowerment for women mean?

Which women? What does it mean if feminism, the analysis and practice of addressing women's subordination through sexual objectification, is deemed to be "irrelevant" and/or a "threat" to the true values of adult education and literacy?

Literacy, sexuality, and power

> In order to perpetuate itself, every op-
> pression must corrupt or distort those
> various sources of power within the cul-
> ture of the oppressed that can provide
> energy for change. For women this has
> meant a suppression of the erotic as a
> considered source of power and informa-
> tion in our lives.
>
> (Lorde, 1984)

The separation of literacy from sexuality is deeply sedimented in the con-struction of educational work, as well as in the semiotic codes of "woman." To be an educated woman is to be without sex; to be "sexy" is to be desirable, to be vulnerable. To walk into a classroom mandates that we hide our sexual beings (bodies) in the closet. As long as education carries the symbolic meaning of power, it runs against the grain of women's "allowed" (however dangerous and contradictory) domain of "power," her sexual desirability to men.

Catherine MacKinnon (1989) argues that, for women, dominance is eroticized; "woman" does not exist as a "being" independent of the male gaze, which shapes her desire. The meaning of her existence is in her service of and accessibility to men. Sexuality, in this schema, is not limited to narrowly defined sexual acts, but is conceived much more broadly as "a pervasive dimension of social life, one that permeates the whole, a dimen-sion along which gender occurs and through which gender is socially consti-tuted" (p. 130).

> Sexuality . . . is a form of power. Gender, as socially constructed, embod-
> ies it, not the reverse. Women and men are divided by gender, made into
> the sexes as we know them, by the social requirements of its dominant

form, heterosexuality, which institutionalizes male sexual dominance and female sexual submission. If this is true, sexuality is the linchpin of gender inequality . . . sexuality is gendered as gender is sexualized. Male and female are created through the eroticization of dominance and submission." (p. 113)

In their work, F. Haug *et al*. (1987) demonstrate how female socialization is primarily a process of female sexualization. As girls learn how to become women, they learn how to acquire competence as sexualized feminine subjects. Through their collective project in memory work, the authors vividly reveal how "sexuality is represented through a whole set of rules which do not just relate to the genitalia but govern the body as a whole, the way it is treated or clothed, bodily hygiene and so on." They go on to point out that sexuality is regulated through *hetero*sexuality, "which constitutes both the envisaged goal and the framework within which we already move" (p. 212).

To see sexuality broadly, as a full range of beliefs, assumptions, representations, and social practices that regulate women through our (hetero) sexualization, is a controversial move among feminists. In describing the "institution of heterosexuality," Teresa deLauretis (1990) provides a key to understanding why it is everywhere and nowhere at the same time:

> The tenacious mental habit of associating sexuality (as sexual *acts* between people) with the private sphere or individual privacy, even as one is constantly surrounded by representations of sexuality . . . tends to deny the obvious—the very public nature of the discourses on sexuality and what Foucault has called "the technology of sex," the social mechanisms (from the educational system to jurisprudence, from medicine to the media, and so forth) that regulate sexuality and effectively enforce it—*and* that regulate and enforce it as *heterosexuality*. (p. 129)

In education, by and large, sexuality is regulated by its absence, by the severance of the body from the mind, by the relegation of sexuality to the "private" sphere, the sphere of the unspeakable. Even more significantly, I argue that in "our" society women are regulated through the direct opposition of intellectuality to sexuality; to be "woman" is to be sexual, not intellectual. What I am saying is nothing new. Girls learn at a young age not to be too smart if we want to be popular, not to be too sexy if we want to be accepted intellectually. As Michelle Fine (1988) argues, where sexuality does enter educational discourse in high schools, it does so in terms set to regulate girls to be heterosexual, celibate until marriage, and monogamous; sexuality, as a "desire of her own," does not exist in education.[3] For a teenage girl, "achievement" is accomplished through the acquisition of a steady boyfriend of the highest possible status, not school performance. As Angela McRobbie (1991) notes, "One of their [schools'] central functions is to reproduce the sexual division of labour, so that girls come willingly to accept their subordinate status in society" (p. 44). That it is common knowledge that intellectuality and sexuality are opposed for girls and women, and yet never present in discourses about education and literacy, is illustrative of the regulation of sexuality through its absence, and, even further, its unspeakableness, especially if spoken in terms of personal experience in classrooms. This may be especially true of adult education classrooms, which is particularly ironic given that "the field" prides itself on being "experience based" and "learner centered." Whose experience? Which learners?

Intellectuality and sexuality are in opposition for women because education potentially provides an alternative source of power. There is the possibility of independence from men, both materially—in terms of time, space, money, and work—and in thought. That they are opposed partly affirms MacKinnon's argument: what man wants an uppity woman? I think of my own experience, of how men used to phrase my desirability to them in terms of my difference from other academic women, my accessibility, my vulnerability, my tentativeness, my sexiness. In order to counter my intellectuality I learned to deny my mind, to claim "my power" through appearing to be sexually desirable to men. And yet this posed a bind for me in the university, where to appear sexual was to become a target of ridicule, charged with inappropriate behavior and appearance.

To name sex as a power relationship between men and women through which women are subordinated is a threat to deeply sedimented social practices and forms that go far beyond individual male-female relationships, and yet—this is the contradiction—the "power" of this relationship is precisely that it is experienced individually, as one's intimately lived connection to others, to socially sanctioned sources of hope, happiness, and love. Why is there so much resistance to naming heterosexuality as a formative social institution which organizes relations between men and women in "our" society? Does the naming of heterosexism have to mean the erasure of race and class, and/or the invalidation of the possibility of "egalitarian" male-female partnerships? Can the traps of universalism and essentialism be addressed by considering how heterosexism is simultaneously organized according to race and class? How can we shift the ground of the analysis from "innate characteristics" that fix all men as violent and all women as victims to look at the social relations and discursive formations that position men in a dominant relationship to women as mediated by race and class? How is "Woman" framed as "heterosexual" in various societies, and how is that image also codified along the lines of class, race, age, beauty, and so forth?

It is true that theories of women's sexual oppression have not taken into account power differences among women, especially with respect to race and class. This is an important critique. White Western feminist academics—and I am one—cannot claim to speak for all women; we truly do not know, and are not positioned to know, how sexism, racism, and classism work across various social locations. I have no doubt that I am most conscious of my subordination as a woman through my sexual subordination because this is the primary site through which I have lived oppression; the shape of that oppression was influenced by class and to some degree by race.[4] Still, I am uneasy about critiques that would dismiss sexuality as a site of women's oppression because it does not speak to race and class. Instead of throwing out the possibility that women are oppressed through sexuality, I would like to open up the question of *how* the sexual subjugation of women may work, and how it may work very differently according to one's social location. As Mohanty (1988) observes, "Male violence (if indeed that is the appropriate label) must be theorized and interpreted *within* specific societies, both in order to understand it better, as well as in order to effectively organize to change it" (p. 67).

Part of the difficulty with understanding *how*, in Foucault's terms, the "deployment of sexuality" actually works is in its reduction to discourse and, with it, the erasure of the lived bodies of historically located subjects who are lodged in relationships of power (deLauretis, 1987). As MacKinnon (1989) observes, although it has become common to speak of sexuality as socially constructed, "seldom specified is what, socially, it is constructed of, far less who does the constructing or how, when, or where . . . Power is everywhere therefore nowhere, diffuse rather than prevasively hegemonic" (p. 131). And I would add, who receives the constructing, how meaning may be made differently by women in different locations, with different investments in white male-defined mandates of female sexuality. Just as Haug *et al.* begin to open up the "rules" young girls learn to live by, and how they are learned, we need investigations that can begin to explicate how external ordering (social inscription) is lodged in concrete ongoing social relations reproduced differently across social domains over the life span.

Focusing on the social relations that produce women's subordination differently according to race leads Aída Hurtado (1989) to theorize that differences in women's relational position to white male privilege account for differing, contradictory dynamics through which women are subordinated: whereas white women are seduced into "femininity," women of color are rejected.

> White men need white women in a way that they do not need women of color because women of color cannot fulfill white men's need for racially pure offspring. This fact creates differences in the *relational position* of the groups—distance from and access to the source of privilege, white men. Thus, white women, as a group, are subordinated through seduction, women of color, as a group, through rejection. Class position, of course, affects the probability of obtaining the rewards of seduction and the sanctions of rejection. (p. 844)

Although I wonder whether, even for white women, regulation through seduction doesn't depend upon the surety of "rejection" if one cannot live up to or does not follow the norms and rules of white feminine performance, Hurtado makes the crucial point that these dynamics will work very differently depending upon the possibility of access to white male privilege. And, as Mohanty (1988) argues, the category *women of color* has a homogenizing effect that conceals class, cultural, and racial specificities. Cherríe Moraga, writing from within the specificity of Chicano culture, shows how the violation by white males of the Mexicana (Chicana) is taken up among her people in such a way that the Chicana who does not couple with the Chicano male is slandered as a betrayer of her race. Moraga raises the question of the relationship of "women of color" to "men of color," and how that is defined by women's relationship to white male power. As Moraga (1983) argues, the loyalty of the Chicana to her race is defined by her loyalty to the Chicano male, a loyalty that can turn woman against woman:

> What looks like betrayal between women on the basis of race originates, I believe, in sexism/heterosexism. Chicanas begin to turn our backs on each other to gain male approval or to avoid being sexually stigmatized by them under the name of puta, vendita, jota. (p. 98)

> The sexual legacy passed down to the Mexicana/Chicana is the legacy of betrayal, pivoting around the historical/mythical female figure of Malintzin Tenepal. As translator and strategic advisor and mistress to the Spanish conqueror of Mexico, Hernan Cortez, Malintzin is considered the mother of the mestizo people. But unlike La Virgin de Guadalupe, she is not revered as the Virgin Mother, but rather slandered as La Chingada, meaning "fucked one," or La Vendida, sell-out to the white race. (p. 99)

> So little has been documented as to the actual suffering Chicanas have experienced resisting or succumbing to the sexual demands of white men. The ways we have internalized the sexual hatred and exploitation they have displayed against us are probably too numerous and too ingrained to even identify. If the Chicana, like her brother, suspects other women of betrayal, then she must, in the most profound sense, suspect herself. How deep her suspicions run will measure how ardently she defends her commitment, above all, to the Chicano male. As obedient sister/daughter/lover she is the committed heterosexual, the socially acceptable Chicana. Even if she's politically radical, sex remains the bottom line on which she proves her commitment to her race. (p. 105)

Literacy as threat/desire

> In writing close to the other of the other, I can only choose to maintain a self-reflexively critical relationship toward the material, a relationship that defines both the subject written and the writing

> subject, undoing the I while asking
> "what do I want wanting to *know* you or
> me?"
>
> (Minh-ha, 1989)

Some years ago I worked on a research project about the experiences of Spanish-speaking immigrants to West Los Angeles in learning English. Several years later, I published my interpretation of the experiences of the women interviewed, theorizing that the acquisition of English language literacy was highly contradictory for them, a strong desire that also posed a threat to their lives as constructed (Rockhill, 1987b, 1987c). Although my interpretation is necessarily limited by my not being of the same culture and class as the women who told their stories, and I struggle with the racism implicit in that process, still it was in this work that the profound educational bind faced by women came powerfully home to me. Here I first linked what had been separated in my mind—stories of sexual violence—with stories of educational (non)participation. This was ironic in a way, because I knew from my own history the profound threat that the education of women posed to the men with whom they were in relationship; the violence it provoked written in my bones. Still, they remained separated for me. Setting out to study literacy practices, I did not inquire about intimate relationships, but did ask for stories about the experience of immigration, as well as detailed specificities of language situations where English was encountered, which provided concrete settings for understanding the ways in which language learning was interconnected with the structure of daily life.

Because of the gendered structure of the world in which they were lodged, the women interviewed were more dependent than men upon classroom instruction in order to learn English; yet the women were often hampered from participation because of either subtle or overt opposition in the home, their structural location as women. The intricate texture of how heterosexuality is lived as sexual oppression was outlined in bold relief by the extent of the women's isolation and their dependence upon men in the home. The women we interviewed did not drive, did not have access to a car, were not permitted to go out of their homes, and/or were terrified to do so because of crime (woman as target) and not knowing enough English to defend themselves. Unlike men, they could not learn English informally because of the structure of women's work, which is bifurcated between dead-end factory, domestic, and field jobs requiring no talk and highly literacy dependent jobs in clerical, secretarial, and women's caring professions. To advance, literacy in English is crucial, and, since women have less access to learning the language informally, they are extremely dependent upon classes but denied continuing access because of time pressure and/or the threat that their participation can pose to the family; the fear is that the woman will become more educated than her husband, more independent, and be influenced by Western "gringa" feminism. At the same time, the man is more vulnerable than ever, typically with a deplorable short-term heavy manual labor job with a high incidence of disability and unemployment, and at a deficit in not knowing how to work the system. All of these factors are compounded enormously if one's presence in the country is uncertain, either as an illegal immigrant or as a refugee. Literacy is about language and education as well as the specific skills of reading and writing; its meaning is integral to the social relations in which it is embedded. When attending literacy classes represents "becoming educated," for a woman to step out of the house and attend a class can upset the power relations of the traditional family. To "empower" her may be to put her "safety" at risk. In the case of ESL, for the women interviewed, English language literacy was a compelling desire, *and*, as a symbol of educational attainment in a different (dominant) cultural formation, it posed a threat to the stasis of their lives and loves.

In reporting this research, I struggled with my fears that my interpretation was racist and/or would feed into the racist stereotyping of "the other." Although I was absolutely certain that violence is not limited to the population under study, I recognized that it has a particular coloration because of the dynamics of immigration, language, culture, and racism—and that this has to be taken into account in doing educational programming. Since then, other studies have begun to show the dis/connections between education and sexuality for different populations of women. Even today, as I pick up the daily newspaper, there is an account of violence toward Filipino women (Reid, 1991). While pointing out that no community is free of violence against women, one of the workers interviewed for the story goes on to report how, "because of language and cultural barriers, some women remain trapped, not knowing where to turn." Almost as an aside, another of the workers comments, "Being intelligent and vocal is considered masculine in our culture." To be "Woman" is not to be "outspoken." In a study that I am currently engaged in with Patricia Tomic, the community workers interviewed confirm the extreme isolation of Spanish-speaking immigrant and refugee women, the violence some experience in their homes, their terror of going out of the house, calling for help, or participating in educational programs. Often it is not until they separate from their male partners that they act upon their desire to learn English systematically and pursue their educations.

Where not knowing the dominant language is involved, the dis/ connections between education and sexuality can lead to extreme social isolation, even greater dependency upon the male, shame, and self-degradation. What does it mean for a woman suddenly to be rendered "illiterate," to be drastically displaced, without knowledge of "the word" or of the social system to which it refers? And when access to "the word" carries with it access to gringo culture, the image of the educated Western woman with her more "independent" ways, does literacy then pose the possibility of "another way of being woman"?

How do race and class work differently and together in conjunction with sexuality to colonize women? Even where English is the first language, the drama of literacy is about the desire for movement from one class location to another. To what extent are literacy classes, and the life skill training that often accompanies them, really about learning the appearances of white middle-class performance for women (Morton, 1985)? How do these changes, whether real or anticipated, affect the relationships of women to friends, family, and lovers? Is there an underside to the fairytale of Pygmalian, to the romance of literacy as the passport to a life of comfort and success?

It is crucial to emphasize that male violence toward some women who participate in literacy and educational programs is not limited to non-English-speaking families. Presenting initial documentation from a study conducted under the auspices of the Canadian Congress for Learning Opportunities for Women (CCLOW), researcher Betty-Ann Lloyd notes that "many, many women face violence from men if they dare to go back to school." As one participant in the study puts it, "When a woman becomes involved in a literacy program, when she's becoming more independent, the man is losing his grip and he's becoming more violent and more aggressive and attempting more control." Another notes, "Low education does help keep you where you are. That's why men become so threatened when you start to finish your program and you might look at some kind of training. You may not be so dependent" (Lloyd, 1991, p. 33). Significantly, each connects violence to the perceived greater independence of the woman, a "threat" more likely as further educational possibilities develop.

I also wonder at the implication of childhood sexual abuse, as well as of ongoing sexualization/violence in the way many women are treated, for educational performance. "Low self-esteem" has so repeatedly been named as the central problem women must overcome to participate in education that it has the status of commonplace knowledge. What's behind it?

"Stupid! Illiterate! Whore!" How often I heard that refrain in my Los Angeles studies. To be sexualized is to be rendered stupid, the "dumb blonde" in dominant culture, always already accessible: without a thought— or desire—of one's own. Day-in and day-out abuse: what are its effects? As one literacy worker puts it,

> Violence in the home . . . causes a lack of self-worth, a lack of self-esteem, a lack of confidence. If you're being told you're stupid or worthless for so many years you start to believe it . . .. I think every time they're abused it's "How can I go back to school? I'm stupid. How can I make that effort to get out there, that first step to get out there?" (Lloyd, 1991, p. 33)

The privatization of sexuality, its mas(c)ualization as "pleasure," the systemic silencing of women's lived experiences of sex, and the splitting of education from "the personal" keep us from exploring the linkages between sexuality and educational performance. We don't know because we don't ask, don't want to probe, don't want to violate, don't want to know.

Like me, Belenky *et al.* (1986) did not originally think to ask about sexual abuse in their study of "women's ways of knowing." It was midway through their study, after many women had mentioned that sexual trauma had significantly affected their learning, before the researchers began systematically to ask about it. The evidence they have suggests that there may be a strong connection between sexual abuse, lacking a sense of voice, and unquestioned trust in authorities. I know from my own work on incest that it had profound effects upon my sense of self, a deep fear of being seen, of taking up space. This is corroborated by the work of Anne-Louise Brookes (1988). I know only enough to know that the relationship between intellectuality and sexuality must be a complex one for girls who are abused. I "survived" by escaping into my head; I do not know what happens if the head is not experienced as a "safe" place, if one has been controlled by being systematically told that one is stupid, dumb, if one has been asked, "Just who the hell do you think you are to think . . . ?" Consider the erosion of self-esteem, to be told you are a dumb, stupid slut. . .

The argument for culturally specific approaches to literacy is reinforced by Jenny Horsman's sensitive study of literacy in the lives of women in rural Nova Scotia, *Something in My Mind Besides the Everyday* (1990). Detailing a range of violence in women's lives, from sexual abuse to psychological abuse to childhood pregnancy to isolation and poverty, the heartbreaking piece of the story for me is how women take on social judgments and believe that they are to blame for the failures of their lives. Still, Horsman captures the fighting spirit of the women she interviews, their determination to find a place in the world for themselves and their children:

> I think it's probably pretty strange to anyone that doesn't realize the kind of a life that a battered woman lives . . . I made it my little mini war trying to win battle after battle to get my own little place, my own little piece of myself . . . I want to work . . . to work at something that I can enjoy getting up in the morning where I think I'm accomplishing something, where I get paid a reasonable amount to live on . . . I'm asking for the moon and the stars and everything else. (Alice, quoted on back cover)

Horsman observes that the lives of the women she studied are

> organized in relation to the needs of others. This organization is essentially *dis*organization, women living their lives around the demands of their male partners, and children, and sometimes also extended family members . . . Dependence—on men, on inadequately paid work and on social service assistance—is threaded through the lives. (p. 85)

Dependence leads to violence: "The violence of these women's lives is frequently obscured by the illusion that illiteracy creates women's problems—

that it is illiteracy that "disables" women or "chains" them in prison. In that way our attention is focussed not on the disorganizations of women's lives but on women's failure to become literate" (p. 86).

Thus So the "dream" of literacy:—the desire that we as educators, policymakers, and employers co-create that women take on as their own—"become literate, become educated, and your life will change. If you don't, you alone are at fault."

In "Literacy as Threat/Desire" (1987b), I put forth a similar argument. It is not so much a question of whether literacy "in fact" makes any difference in women's (in)dependence as it is the symbolic vision of education as transforming one's life, transporting one into the "safety" of the middle-class home, white picket fence and all. And education may be, "in reality," women's only ticket out of poverty—and it may not make a difference.

Toward a feminist agenda in literacy

> Moving from silence into speech is . . . a gesture of defiance that heals, that makes new life and new growth possible. It is that act of speech, of "talking back," that is no mere gesture of empty words, that is the expression of our movement from object to subject—the liberated voice.
>
> (hooks, 1989, p. 9)

Education is turned to by women in search of a way out of the cycles of dependency in which their lives are enmeshed. This is all we have to offer, really: either that or institutionalization. I recall watching a film by Brenda Longfellow (1981) in which a woman who had been battered finally made her way into a training program. I recall feeling quite sick and angry at the view that this was the "happy ending" of the film, theoretically the romance of the "career" taking the place of romantic love. Although I don't want to deny that education, as a move toward possible economic independence, *is* essential, I also want to ask whether a course or a job is enough to end the cycle of violence in which battered women are caught.

Having spent my life trying to overcome the effects of sexual abuse in my childhood, situations played out over and over as an adult through my (re)positioning as "woman," as sexual object, as one who has and had no worth other than as a body, I want to scream out "No!—Literacy alone is not enough." We need to learn how to resist and refuse our social inscription as "woman," especially since our primary sites of rebellion are also sexually inscribed—as the Whore—the rampantly heterosexual. [5]

So what does "critical literacy" look like for women? If you make it to "our" classes, what do we do? What might explicitly feminist approaches look like? If critical literacy is about "emancipation," "empowerment," how can the various ways in which power works to subordinate women be taken into account? Insofar as power works through our bodies, through our sexual objectification as "feminine," through the formation of our subjectivities, of our consciousnesses, what does this suggest as possibilities for educational approaches to critical consciousness? And what are the implications for women if education is highly charged, posing a threat to our socially designated source of power, "our" (hetero)sexuality?

To address, seriously, the question of women's power, it is essential to open up the ways in which we are implicated in institutionalized heterosexism: the ways in which we live heterosexism, not only in our intimate relationships, but also in public settings, where we are also positioned as the sexualized female, and the ways in which our very identity—our sense of self, our subjectivity—has been shaped by heterosexism, as defined through the prisms of class, race, and culture. Because they are so close to the bone, because they touch our deepest places of emotional investment and wounding, opening up these questions in the classroom can be charged with emotion and conflict, the "danger" of sliding into the slippery domain of therapy ever present. And yet, I know from my teaching that these are critical questions, questions that link what is experienced as personal inadequacy to social positioning and political practices, and that they can be explored in the classroom if personal experiences, disagreements, and confrontations are respected as places from which to begin to talk.

Insofar as we understand power as the ordering of our conduct through the formation of our subjectivities, our identities, as Teresa deLauretis (1990) points out, a key question becomes, how can we *(dis)identify?* If power works through discursive formations of seduction/rejection to manipulate desire, the very construction of "self," of identity, and if the identities formed are in relation to dominant ideologies and deeply sedimented in ongoing social relations, how can we find a standpoint from which to "see through" and resist social inscriptions? And if *"we"* are all so formed, how are we formed differently, according to our social location and positioning relative to white male privilege? I emphasize "we" because teachers do not stand apart from their students, free of social inscription. If anything, teachers may more closely approximate dominant images of power, be more blinded by the possibility of being "seduced," than their students. How do we learn to (dis)identify from hegemonic conceptions of "woman" *as well as* recognize that not all women identify in the same ways? How do we learn to take into account the simultaneity of oppressions through gender, race, class, and sexuality, come to understand and respect their collusion in the constitution of differences through sameness and sameness through difference? Don't differing and complex social locations suggest differing processes of (dis)identifying, as well as multiple and changing (dis)identifications? Doesn't difference in location also suggest differences in the ways and content of knowings, situated knowledges that may differ from dominant conceptions (Luttrell, 1989; Collins, 1989)? Isn't part of the whirl that education poses for those whose experiences have not been fully co-opted by dominant descriptions of their realities immense discomfort, distance, and chaos?[6]

One of the most troubling questions posed by poststructural theory is the question of agency, and the possibility of taking a critical stance, of seeing from a vantage point outside of or alongside our inscription. I want to argue that inscription is totalizing but not total. The "social" is not a monolith, not uniform, often contradictory, and our experience of "it" depends in part upon our locations. This affects both what we know and how we know. As de-Lauretis (1990) argues, there is a place outside of consciousness, perhaps the "unconscious," that resists total inscription. And, as Haug *et al*. point out, discursive formations work through social relations. Using the image of a huge fishing net as what establishes the order of the social whole, the reader is asked to consider *how* the net is woven and *cast*. Herein lies a key for critical approaches to education; social relations are multiple, sometimes contradictory, and, like a net, full of w/holes.

In my work I have used the image of invisible concrete walls that regulate us as in a maze. As I see it, the goal of critical education is to learn how to (re)cognize the walls of the maze and how they are held in place. The bleak vision is seeing that I have been trained like a rat to run through and perform effectively in the maze. As long as I can negotiate the treacherous channels of the maze, I carry in me the illusion of safety, comfort, order, and competence. This is the "negative" theoretical moment, when I must "deconstruct," giving up old safeties. The hopeful vision—the positive moment—is in learning how to see the trap of the maze, to recognize the taken-for-granted rules and assumptions that govern my behavior, to see how they are reproduced and ingrained in everyday practices and relationships, and to see how they are relived in my bodily and emotional responses. The painful reality is that I learn to recognize the boundary of the maze only when I run into its invisible concrete walls head on; as my belief in the course of action prescribed by the walls crumbles, I fall into chaos, disorder, the void of not knowing how to be, how to perform, who I am. In time resistance shifts to more conscious forms of rebellion, of (re)cognition. I know my (re)production when I feel my breath stop, the pressure rise in my head, and the knot form in my gut, when I refuse to be trampled on any longer, saying "NO," finding "support" to resist, to affirm that "I'm not crazy," that what I "know" is valid, . . . and rebuilding . . . rebuilding . . . rebuilding. . . .

Questions about "experience" and the validity of knowledge from experience have plagued me for some time. Although I do not agree with the liberal humanist assumption that experience is in some way "pure," "innocent," or "true," I do recognize a knowing from my experience. I believe that consciousness is ideologically formed, that we have to struggle to understand how our experience is shaped and reproduced through dominant cultural/structural forms. Yet I have worked too long and hard not to recognize that there is a place where I also "know," where my experience has not been totally colonized by ideology, where I have not absolutely "forgotten" in order to survive, to feel "safe," by shaping my experience to fit dominant cultural norms. Perhaps deLauretis is right: it is that part of my "unconscious" that is "eccentric"; it is lodged in my social location as a woman, and it is in that location of difference that the possibility of resistance—of a lesbian stance—rests.

A domain of experience for women that poses an extremely controversial place from which to speak is sexuality, especially if what is spoken challenges dominant constructions that either silence or regulate sexuality as heterosexuality. Although I do not want to argue that "a lesbian stance" is the only place from which inscriptions of heterosexuality can be challenged, I think that the greater a woman's investment in heterosexuality, the more threatening and emotionally laden are its challenges. Still, women who identify as heterosexual can and do challenge their inscription, often from within the frame of heterosexuality, and sometimes in ways that counter it (Williams, 1991).

This brings me back to the question of differences in location and how those differences may speak to less totalizing forms of social inscription, while at the same time the costs of refusing to play according to the rules of the dominant society may be greater. In what kind of a "crazy-making" position would this place one? Is it possible that the processes and possibilities of critical consciousness may play out very differently according to our investment in *not* seeing? Perhaps the greater our privilege is along particular dimensions, the more we have to gain by not seeing, or only seeing so far, or in ways that do not undermine our "loyalties." Yet if sites of rebellion are also socially inscribed (Willis, 1977; McRobbie, 1991), perhaps the picture is more complex. I think that this may be especially true for women where differences in class and race location may pose diametrically opposed possibilities for how one lives the "social outlaw" and/or whether one can choose to trade in sexuality or intellectuality.

Whatever, chances are high that our students know more than their teachers about concrete aspects of their lives that are missing from or (mis)represented in dominant forms of discourse. Unless they can bring their experiences into the classrooms and we can truly learn to listen—to hear their stories—to learn what they know, that they know, and *how* they have come to know what they know, I don't see how we can talk of critical literacy (Razack, 1990). And, through the validation of their experience as knowledge, perhaps they will come to value that they too "know"—and just perhaps "low self-esteem" will be less of a problem. How do we deal with differences in experiential knowings, knowings that are not innocent of ideo-logical inscription, that may be contradictory, that may even violate the knowings of others in the group?

In my work I have found that the implications of truly listening, of encouraging students to speak their exceptionality, to speak their difference, their anger, their pain, has had a revolutionary impact upon my teaching. Like bell hooks (1989) and Audre Lorde (1984), I have come to understand my approach to teaching to be confrontational, and I am learning the impor-tance of listening to the "defiant speech" (hooks, 1989; Ellsworth, 1989) of those who disagree with me, the texts in use, or the generalizing "we" that develops as differences are eclipsed. Painfully, I am coming to know that I do not know. As Ellsworth (1989) learned, all knowledge, even the teacher's, is partial; it is framed through one's social location, one's life experience and history. But this is not easy. To truly allow a space where defiance can be spoken means that classes are conflictual and confrontational. Like most women, I have been sexualized to care for others, not to confront; I am terrified of anger; I struggle to welcome it as a moment of truth.

These moments of speaking exceptionality, of defiant speech, are expe-rienced as emotionally charged interruptions in the classroom. It is not uncommon for a person who has been silent[7] suddenly to erupt, with angry words at last, rupturing silences imposed by seeing one's experience violated or erased by classroom discourse. I recall vividly the moment when I first publicly spoke from my knowledge and location as a sexually abused woman and child, in an emotional torrent unleashing years of tears and rage, and I recall the frenzy that this placed me in because I felt that, as a teacher, I had no right to so ab/use my power, "imposing" my emotions on the women participating in the class. All I had wanted to do was to critique feminist theories of motherhood that explained female socialization in terms of "con-nection" to the mother, while erasing violence, especially the raped violence of the father that I had experienced. I knew painfully of what I spoke and could no longer tolerate the gaping disjuncture between what had been emblazoned in my bones and the abstract theoretical discourse of feminism. As I spoke, years of silenced emotions erupted. In breaking these rules of silence, I've come to see how sexuality, as lived, and emotional outbursts, on the part of the students *and* teacher, are beyond the boundaries of proper classroom conduct. I still struggle with emotional expression and questions of power, and find no easy answer. Although I do not want to impose my emotion, I cannot expect students to enter into the vulnerable place of expressing their feelings if I stay safely masked, hiding behind the role of teacher.

Uma Narayan (1988) argues that the oppressed have "epistemic privilege," "insider knowledge" about the nature of their oppression. She makes a useful distinction between (1) knowledge gained through causal and structural analysis of oppression, and (2) immediate knowledge of everyday life under oppression: "They know first-hand the detailed and concrete ways in which oppression defines the spaces in which they live and how it affects their lives" (p. 36). Moreover, the insider (the oppressed) knows these in an emotionally embodied way, as a "truth" which the outsider may seek to understand but can never fully know in the same way. Although Narayan's description does not take into account differences in consciousness of the oppressed, or multiple social locations among the oppressed that mean that knowledge is always partial, shifting, and changing, her distinction is still useful in thinking about education for critical consciousness. I don't want to risk separating theory from experience, but it seems to me that education for critical consciousness is about the integration of both kinds of knowledge identified by Narayan. It means that experiences as emotionally embodied must be linked to poststructural analyses of one's experience as socially mediated and constructed. The poststructural turn, which argues that subjectivities are ideologically formed, means that we must hold in question even what we think we know through experience. So to Narayan's two distinctions I would add critical self-reflexivity, or developing the capacity to see *how* one's subjectivity, one's interpretation of experience, one's knowledge, is lodged in social relations and shaped by discursive formations.

That the emotions are central to critical consciousness I've come to understand in two ways: one is the emotional tenacity of our attachment to how we have learned to become. As Haug *et al*. point out, in the process of learning *how* to become a sexualized female, one acquires a competence, a sense of safety and pleasure in that competence; to let go is to feel incompetent, to lose one's sense of self, to fall into an abyss. And our emotions are deeply etched in our bodies; to "understand" what is happening does not mean we can change it. We are deeply invested in the "safety" of the ways we have learned to be, the "safety" of the known, the familiar of the (hetero)sexualized feminine. It is quite terrifying to upset this, especially since those ways of being are not individual to us, but socially prescribed, mandated. Our fear of change, our sense of impending threat, is justified. Minnie Bruce Pratt (1984) writes of the exclusions, the denials, that this sense of safety, of home, depends upon, a safety that does not get called into question until old ways of being become untenable. Pratt describes how, when she became a lesbian, she stepped "outside the circle of protection" she had taken for granted. She writes that "we experience change as loss" "because it is: the old lies and ways of living, habitual, familiar, comfortable, fitting us like our skin, were *ours*. Our fear of losses can keep us from changing. What is it, exactly, that we are afraid to lose?" (p. 39). Fears of loss are not limited to our psychic lives. Every time we interrupt, speak defiantly, and/or name our differences, we risk the loss of our community, home, and friends. So too in the classroom, difference is spoken at great risk—but what is this "safety" which depends upon silence, politeness, and "comfortable" speech?

Berenice Fisher (1987) notes that emotions are integral to the process of consciousness raising and of feminist pedagogy, but we know very little about how to work with them; we assume that in some way, once we understand the social roots of our emotions, our "true" emotions will emerge. Fisher draws upon the work of Audre Lorde, on the power of the erotic and of anger as liberatory, to ask how we can learn to use the emotions in approaches to feminist teaching, and describes her use of theatrical forms to encourage classroom participants to "embody" the standpoints of others and to talk about their feelings about doing so.

I have also struggled for many years now to bring a full range of emotions into the classroom. I have wanted to provide a space where participants can embody our learning, speak from and challenge our experiences as women, find the courage to name our exceptionality from the normalizing "we" of the classroom even with respect to feminism. I know of no model for this kind of education. I refuse to run from pain, conflict, and anger in the classroom; I refuse to set up safeties that are predicated upon false assumptions of trust, of an inclusive "we." I want us to bring our bodies, our sexualities, the full "strength of the erotic" (Lorde, 1984), into our classroom. The more I push, the more I've come to see the deep chasm that's developed between the mind and the body, education and therapy. The extent to which the sexual, the body, and the emotional are seen as the domain of therapy and not of education becomes clearer as these boundaries are pushed.

These divisions are reflected in some of the reactions I've had to my written work. When I read the "Chaos" (1987a) piece, in which I write emotionally about my experience and the erasure of incest and sexual abuse from educational and scholarly work, I am urged to go into therapy, to work through my pain and anger. When I speak about literacy as threat/desire, I am told, "But we cannot possibly take up that kind of work in the classroom." To address that doubleness of threat and desire, to take seriously the possibility that educational participation can be a site of violence for women, cannot be done within the framework of education; that is the domain of therapy.

Consciousness raising is a painful process. It upsets our world as we know it. If literacy poses a threat to women, how much greater will that threat be if it is also tied to a critical analysis of our situations? The power we confront is not some alien enemy but ourselves, the ways we have learned to be as feminized objects, our life as we have understood it, including the hope for safety and salvation through romance, the home, and the family.

These longings for safety are reproduced in the classroom. As educators, we do all we can to stave off conflict, to avoid unpleasant emotional experiences, to make everyone feel comfortable, liked. We shun disruption—and yet, it is only through disruption, I believe, that critical learning can take place. As Magda Lewis (1990) observes,

> We cannot expect that students will readily appropriate a political stance that is truly counter-hegemonic, unless we also acknowledge the ways in which our feminist practice/politics *creates*, rather than ameliorates, feelings of threat: the threat of abandonment, the threat of having to struggle with unequal power relations, the threat of psychological/social/sexual, as well as economic and political marginality; the threat of retributive violence—threats lived in concrete embodied ways. (p. 485)

Does this feel too hot to touch? Perhaps. Over the years I have found researchers and educators arguing that questions of violence toward women cannot be taken up, for we are unprepared to deal with the consequences of what might be opened. Although I see this as a legitimate concern, I am also appalled by the arrogance of the assumption that silence is safer for the woman who is being abused. Although I don't want to deny the need for more resources, more training, who exactly are we protecting when we ignore the bruises on the woman before us? Imagine what it is like to live in the isolation of violence sealed tightly behind the "safety" of four walls—to have absolutely no corner in which to hide.

Women's stories are coming into literacy classrooms (Doiron, 1987; Gaber-Katz and Horsman, 1988; Green, 1990). Whether this is due to "learner-centered" curricular approaches that encourage students to write their stories, to increasing numbers of feminist teachers who create safer spaces for these stories to be told, and/or to the sharp rise in public discourse about sexual abuse, the boundaries of the speakable have been shifting in education. When women do speak out, especially when they talk together in women's groups, issues of violence are frequently raised; but, as Garber, Horsman, and Westall (1991) point out, generally teachers feel ill-equipped to deal with these situations, want to be able to rescue the women and/or are fearful of the pain that talking may evoke. As literacy workers, they stress the necessity of finding ways to collaborate with those who work in the area of violence against women, and of paying more attention to teachers' stories, for they too are often in struggle. I think that this is a crucial point, not only to see the teacher's standpoint and to provide bases for support, but also to undo the idea of the "illiterate other," as though in some way the teacher—bound to be a woman—is exempt from, above, or beyond the violence of her own social inscriptions.

This raises the question posed by Uma Narayan of power and the epistemic privilege of the oppressed. The reality is that the classroom is not the same as a CR group. Participants do not freely choose each other, safety and trust cannot be assumed, and there are power differences—between teacher and student, but also among students. Especially troublesome in my teaching has been learning how to allow for power differences in knowledge, whether due to the "epistemic privilege" of social location, to assumptions of the greater "political correctness" of one position over another, or to differences in access to the privileged discourse operating in any particular classroom. To disagree, or to speak with authority, is difficult for women and can be very painful. In her thesis, Marian McMahon (1987) vividly describes the conflict she has experienced between caring for others and speaking with authority. I see this as another way in which the opposition between sexuality and intellectuality is played out: a key aspect of our sexual inscription as women is caring for others, including taking responsibility for the nurturing, flattering, and nonthreatening support of their egos, whereas intellectuality implies authority, the possibility of disagreeing, seeing things differently. This can be quite terrifying for women, since to disagree, to challenge, runs counter to our desire to be nice, to take care of others, to make things run smoothly, to feel comfortable for all.

In order to form an identity in opposition, or as deLauretis puts it, to (dis)identify, I believe it is necessary to have separate spaces in which to work collectively to see how what is taken for granted as natural and normal, as the way one must be, is socially inscribed and can be resisted—and, most important, is not a function of individual disorder, but of social ordering. Although not "safe," separate spaces are at least "safer," and it is in these spaces that women begin to talk without feeling they must take care of men and/or be silenced by male prescriptions of the talkable. Although classrooms are deeply inscribed by patriarchal relations whether or not men are present, at least the nonphysical presence of males makes it possible to take up female sexualization in a way that their presence hinders. Significantly "women-only" programs are typically viewed as an "impossibility," for "what about the men?" (Lloyd, 1991). Still, some question how the work of literacy can be done successfully unless the emotional and situational issues and violences faced by women are addressed (Garber, Horsman, and Westall, 1991). In the research it has supported, CCLOW recommends "woman-positive" programming in literacy, with local programs deciding on the approach. Clearly "woman positive" is an important beginning, but we need also to learn how to maintain vigilance in asking "which women?"

How do we approach this work in ways that do not repeat the mistake of assuming universal woman—that all women are the same? How do we teach in ways that encourage rather than conceal differences, and how do we relate these to differences in power among women? What is the relevance of more work that takes on feminist analyses of privilege with respect to race and class for women whose lives are lived as anything but privilege? Are there other approaches that can open up questions of difference and show how these are lodged in relations of power? Ellsworth (1989) suggests the formation of affinity groups to address dynamics of oppression as they are reenacted in the classroom. Also stressing the necessity of using classroom dynamics as a place from which to work, Lewis (1990) articulates the irony that the "feminist critique of social relations reproduces exactly the practices we are critiquing" (p. 486). I agree with Ellsworth and Lewis, and would add that I have found it crucial that I become sensitive to my power as a teacher; my words take on the power of teacher, no matter how hard I work to divest myself of that power.

I have found memory work or storytelling to be the process that works best for me. In this work, I also participate in the writings, revealing my inner struggles with inscription. I use the term *memory work* rather than *autobiography* because I want to stress the possibility of this work as having a social and political dimension. Garber, Horsman, and Westall (1991) question endless autobiography and storytelling, asking where it gets us. In a disturbing but important review of the stories of incest survivors, Louise Armstrong (1990) goes so far as to argue that "the personal is apolitical." I rebel against this, especially coming at a time when women are just beginning to speak our stories. When our stories are left to the domain of therapy, they are depoliticized. As educators, I think the crucial question is, how can we politicize the personal? Collective memory work may hold a key.

In this, I've found the work of Haug *et al.* (1987) to be especially suggestive. In their approach, participants write individual and then collective stories based upon childhood experiences of various parts of the body—for example, legs, hair, "the body." In my teaching, I've found that photographs are especially evocative as we study each other's progressive accomplishment in acquiring "the look"—how it is that we learn how we must be, what photographs we have, why they were taken and chosen, and what lies outside the frame, the story behind the pictures chosen.

In talking about our memories, I work with participants to situate stories in time and place, to recall specific details, physical appearances, people present or absent, their probable stories, the beliefs and activities that frame the remembered event, its perceived significance, and so on. In this way, we work at historically and socially locating our stories, uncovering commonalities and differences, looking for the ways in which processes of regulation work through "taken-for-granted-as-normal" beliefs and practices that continue to shape our lives.

I've also used "memory work" to push through impasses and conflicts in the classroom. Here I ask whether participants would like to write something brief to express what the situation evokes for them; then, the next time we meet, we read our words one after another, without interruption or discussion, until all voices have filled the room like a cacophony of sound. First we hear, really try to hear, from where each person speaks, and then we talk, searching for dis/connections between our experience of the current situation and past events, and among our collective experiences. These moments are powerful ones emotionally as well as intellectually, as we begin to see beyond the personal of our private stories to trace the ways in which we have been socially and politically shaped. So memory serves as a lever to see how our subjectivities have been and continue to be constructed, even in classroom practices, how we struggle with resistance, and the risks of refusal.

Endings

I don't know what relevance my experience of teaching at the graduate level has for literacy teaching. In this writing I feel frustrated by my lack of experience in teaching literacy, and yet I cannot separate my research and thinking on the topic from my teaching. Perhaps the final challenge of the postmodern critique is to the ways in which expertise and knowledge get constructed. How is it that I am the one invited to write on critical literacy, and why do I agree? The latter question is especially troubling to me. I feel passionately about the contradictions of which I write, about the challenge that sexuality as power poses for literacy and the education of women, about the importance of emotional embodiment, of the erotic, to learning. I refuse to let go of the violence that women face, and I want to learn how to see locational differences in how that violence is lived, but whether I am an "authority" on literacy is another question.

I end because I cannot go on any longer; I have no conclusion. To tie all of the foregoing together would be to bring closure where there can be none. To quote Nancy Simms (1991), "I see literacy as political. An advocacy role is very much a part of it. The issues aren't coming together. We have to talk about how literacy connects with racism, homophobia, classism, sexism" (p. 28).

In my work, I continue to use autobiography and memory work. To some extent, this paper is one form of that approach. As Arlene Schenke (1991) contends, "A genealogy of memory-work should offer strategies of commitment that are relational, provisional, deliberately ambivalent and continuously in process" (p. 13). It should be an opening, ideally, to continuing reflection and critique, a story that "never stops beginning or ending. It appears headless and bottomless for it is built on differences. Its (in)finitude subverts every notion of completeness and its frame remains a non-totalizable one" (Minh-ha, 1989, p. 2).

Notes

* So many conversations and confrontations have shaped my thinking over the years. My deepest debt is to the Latina and Chicana women who participated in the Los Angeles research. Since then, students in my classes, members of CCLOW's Literacy Advisory Board, participants in my "memory work" groups, friends within and without these groups, have been crucial to my work. A special thanks to Becky, who labored through several drafts of this paper with me.

1. I use the term *literacy* broadly, to mean discrete sets of reading and writing practices, as well as symbolically, as in "to be literate," "to be educated." Hence, *literacy* and *education* are sometimes used interchangeably when the reference is to the symbolic, that is, the intellectual- and/or class-associated dimensions of literacy. Furthermore, I think of literacy as a "process of acquiring more education" for women which signals a change in a woman's relationship to education in her life.

2. I also use the term *sexuality* broadly as the full range of institutionalized social practices, beliefs, and assumptions that define woman as woman—as the object of desire and/or caretaker of men. This is developed more fully in the text. Although I do not want to argue that all men are violators and all women are victims, I do see, in the social construction of "woman," that she has been "essentialized" as an object of male desire. In

this paper, I speak of sexuality primarily in terms of violence because, as constructed in opposition to education and women's increased independence from men, that is how it is lived. This does not mean that sexuality cannot also be experienced as pleasure, even in forms that some consider to be violent. What would "a desire of her own" look like for women?

3. Fine's work raises the question of the relationship of desire to violence in the representation of sexuality in schooling. She argues that girls are presented with an image of heterosexual relations in which men are depicted as violent and women as victims. In contrast to Fine's research, the life skills curricula with which I am familiar do not take up the question of sexuality as violence at all; the underlying framework appears to be lodged in libertarian approaches to sexuality as pleasure. Hence, even when sexual learnings from parents are presented, they are given in terms of parental openness about bodies, touch, and so on; the possibility of violence, or of sex as a power relation, is not suggested. See, for example, Zaph et al. (1983). My appreciation to Becky Anweiler for bringing this work to my attention.

4. How do we bring race, class, and sexuality together in our analysis? In my work, I have found that the closer I am to dominant standards, or "privilege," the harder it is to see how the "isms" work. I see class as deeply tied to the sexual drama I lived as a child: my parents' determination to move into the middle class, the importance of my mother's education as the daughter of working-class Italian immigrants to that movement, and the very conflictual position in which this placed my father, who was from a dirt-poor farming background and who worked as a laborer, taking out his sense of male inadequacy, his rage, through violence against his children. Threatened by the developing class difference between him and my mother, her intellectual development, did he turn to me?

5. My thesis is that, in Western societies, the dominant way available to girls and women to live out their "rebellion" against straight middle-class norms is through being "wild," a wildness defined through sexual power— the sexier, the more available, the greater a woman's sense of power. How this varies according to social location, especially with respect to class and race, is an important question. The work of Angela McRobbie on working-class girls in England suggests the relevance of looking at girls' sexual desires in terms of perceived possibilities for educational pursuit.

6. I think of my own experiences of sexual abuse, the educational mandate that I leave my body, sexuality, and experience out of the classroom, and the deep pain and chaos that I felt in having systematically to separate what I knew in my history from what I was allowed to present and produce in the classroom. Finally, one day I was able to find the clarity to name, to stand by the "integrity" of, my experience, to take exception without turning the

blame inward as my shame and inadequacy, and to at last find the courage to speak my difference publicly.

7. In emphasizing the importance of defiant speech, I do not want to lose sight of the communicative presence and power of silence. See Arlene Schenke's work for a critique of "voice" in critical pedagogy. Also highly suggestive is her use of Foucault's genealogy as a method from which to approach critical teaching through memory work in ESL classes.

References

Armstrong, L. (1990). "The personal is apolitical." *Women's Review of Books*, March 1991, 7(6), 1–4.

Belenky, M.F., *et al*. (1986). *Women's Ways of Knowing: The Development of Self, Voice and Mind*. New York: Basic Books.

Brookes, A.-L. (1988). *Feminist Pedagogy: A Subject In/formation*. Unpublished doctoral dissertation, University of Toronto.

Collins, P.H. (1989). "The Social Construction of Black Feminist Thought." *Signs*, 14(4), 745–773.

deLauretis, T. (1987). *Technologies of Gender: Essays in Theory, Film and Fiction*. Bloomington: Indiana University Press.

———. (1990). "Eccentric Subjects: Feminist Theory and Historical Consciousness." *Feminist Studies*, 16(1), 115–150.

Doiron, R. (1987). *My Name is Rose*. Toronto: East End Literacy.

Ellsworth, E. (1989). "Why Doesn't This Feel Empowering? Working Through the Repressive Myths of Critical Pedagogy." *Harvard Educational Review*, 59(3), 297–324.

Fine, M. (1988). "Sexuality, Schooling and Adolescent Females: The Missing Discourse of Desire." *Harvard Educational Review*, 58(1), 29–53.

Fisher, B. (1987). "The Heart Has Its Reasons: Feelings, Thinking and Community-Building in Feminist Education." *Women's Studies Quarterly*, 15(3–4), Fall/Winter, 47–58.

Foucault, M. (1982). "The Subject and Power." In H.L. Dreyfus and Paul Rabinow (eds.), *Beyond Structuralism and Hermeneutics*. Chicago: University of Chicago Press, pp. 208–226.

Gaber-Katz, E., and Horsman, J. (1988). "Is It Her Voice If She Speaks Their Words?" *Canadian Woman Studies: Woman and Literacy*, 9(3–4), 117–120.

Gaber-Katz, E., and Watson, G.M. (1991). *The Land That We Dream* of . . . *A Participatory Study of Community-Based Literacy*. Toronto: OISE Press.

Garber, N., Horsman, J., and Westall, T. (1991). "Feminism and Literacy." In N. Breen (ed.), *Women, Literacy and Action: A Handbook*. Toronto: Ontario Literacy Coalition, pp. 6–21.

Green, A.R. (1990). *Coming Out of My Shell*. St. John's Newfoundland: Rabittown Literacy Program.

Haug, F., *et al*. (1987). *Female Sexualization: A Collective Work of Memory*. London: Verso.

hooks, b. (1989). *Talking Back: Thinking Feminist. Thinking Black*. Boston: South End Press.

Horsman, J. (1990). *Something in My Mind besides the Everyday: Women and Literacy*. Toronto: Women's Press.

Hurtado, A. (1989). "Relating to Privilege: Seduction and Rejection in the Subordination of White Women and Women of Color." *Signs*, 14(4), 833–855.

Lewis, M. (1990). "Interrupting Patriarchy: Politics Resistance and Transformation in the Feminist Classroom." *Harvard Educational Review*, 60(4), 467–488.

Lloyd, B.-A. (1991). *Discovering the Strength of Our Voices: Women and Literacy Programs*. Toronto: Canadian Congress for Learning Opportunities for Women.

Longfellow, B. (1981). *Breaking Out*. 27 min./16 mm. Toronto: Development Education Center.

Lorde, A. (1984). *Sister/Outsider*. New York: The Crossing Press.

Luttrell, W. (1989). "Working-Class Women's Ways of Knowing: Effects of Gender, Race and Class." *Sociology of Education*, 62 (Jan.), 33–46.

MacKinnon, C.A. (1989). *Towards a Feminist Theory of the State*. Cambridge: Harvard University Press.

McMahon, M. (1987). *Telling Tales out of School: The ABC's of Repression in Education*. Unpublished master's thesis, University of Toronto.

———. (1991). "Nursing Histories: Reviving Life in Abandoned Selves." *Feminist Review*, 35, 23–37.

McRobbie, A. (1991). *Feminism and Youth Culture: From 'Jackie' to 'Just Seventeen.'* Boston: Unwin Hyman.

Minh-ha, T. (1989). *Woman, Native, Other*. Bloomington: Indiana University Press.

Mohanty, C. (1988). "Under Western Eyes: Feminist Scholarship and Colonial Discourses." *Feminist Review*, 30, 62–88.

Moraga, C. (1983). *Loving in the War Years*. Boston: South End Press.

Morton, J. (1985). *Assessing Vocational Readiness in Low Income Women: An Exploration into the Construction and Use of Ideology*. Published master's thesis, University of Toronto.

Narayan, U. (1988). "Working Together Across Difference: Some Considerations on Emotions and Political Practice." *Hypatia*. 3(2), 31–47.

Pratt, M.B. (1984). "Identity: Skin Blood Heart." In E. Bulkin, M.B. Pratt, B. Smith, *Yours in struggle*. New York: Long Haul Press, pp. 9–63.

Razack, S. (1990). Storytelling for social change. Unpublished draft manuscript.

Reid, S. (1991). "Filipino Women Battle Abuse: Victims Urged to End Silence Imposed by Cultural and Language Barriers." *Toronto Star*. (March 14, 1991) p. A23.

Rockhill, K. (1985). "Ideological Solidification and Liberalism in University Adult Education: Confrontation Over Workers' Education in the USA." In R. Taylor, K. Rockhill and R. Fieldhouse *University Adult Education in England and the USA*. London: Croom Helm, pp. 175–220.

———. (1987a). "The Chaos of Subjectivity in the Ordered Halls of Academe." *Canadian Woman Studies*. 8(4), 12–17.

———. (1987b). "Literacy as Threat/Desire: Longing to be SOMEBODY." In J. Gaskell and A. McLaren (eds.), *Women and Education: A Canadian Perspective*. Calgary: Detselig Enterprises, pp. 315–331.

———. (1987c). "Gender, Language and the Politics of Literacy." *British Journal of Sociology of Education* 8(2), 153–167.

———. (1988). "e-MAN-ci-patory Literacy." *Canadian Woman Studies*, 9(3–4), 113–115.

Schenke, A. (1991). *Speaking the Autobiographical "I" in Poststructuralist Practice: A Pedagogy of Voice and Memory-Work*. Unpublished master's thesis, University of Toronto.

Simms, N. (1991). "Looking at 'Ism's': Visible Minority Women and Literacy." Interview by M. Breen (ed.), *Women Literacy and Action: A Handbook*. Toronto: Ontario Literacy Coalition, pp. 22–30.

Williams, B.J. (1991). *Notes Passed between Hostages: Feminist Writing and the Politics of Self-Representation*. Unpublished doctoral thesis, University of Toronto.

Willis, P. (1977). *Learning to Labor: How Working Class Kids Get Working Class Jobs*. New York: Columbia University Press.

Zaph, M.B., *et al*. (1983). *Discovering Life Skills*. Vol. 3. Toronto: YWCA.

13

Literacy and the politics of difference

Henry Giroux

In this essay I want to analyze some central questions relevant to the debate that is increasingly being waged around the relationship between literacy, culture, and difference, particularly in terms of what it means for restructuring school curricula in order to address the needs of those groups who traditionally have been excluded within the dominant discourse of schooling. In what follows I want to explore a number of issues about the importance of redefining literacy as a form of cultural citizenship and politics that provides the conditions for subordinate groups to learn the knowledge and skills necessary for self and social empowerment, that is, to live in a society in which they have the opportunity to govern and shape history rather than be consigned to its margins. Literacy in this sense is not just a skill or knowledge, but an emerging act of consciousness and resistance.[1]

Literacy in its varied versions is about the practice of representation as a means of organizing, inscribing, and containing meaning. It is also about practices of representation that disrupt or rupture existing textual, epistemological, and ideological systems. Hence, literacy becomes critical to the degree that it makes problematic the very structure and practice of representation; that is, it focuses attention on the importance of acknowledging that meaning is not fixed and that to be literate is to undertake a dialogue with others who speak from different histories, locations, and experiences. Literacy is a discursive practice in which difference becomes crucial for understanding not simply how to read, write, or develop aural skills, but also how to recognize that the identities of "others" matter as part of a progressive set of politics and practices aimed at the reconstruction of democratic public life. Literacy as part of a broader politics of difference and democracy points, at the very least, to two important considerations. First, it makes visible the historically and socially constructed strengths and limitations of those places and borders we inherit and which frame our discourses and social relations. Second, literacy is a form of ethical address that structures how we construct relationships between ourselves and others. It marks out the boundaries of difference and inscribes them in borders that "define the places that are safe and unsafe, [that] distinguish *us* from *them*."[2] Borders signal in the metaphorical and literal sense how power is inscribed differently on the body, culture, history, space, land, and psyche. When literacy is defined in monolithic terms, from the center, within a linear logic that erases uncertainty, it only recognizes the borders of privilege and domination. What is crucial here is that the discourse of literacy cannot be abstracted from the language of difference and power. Literacy cannot be viewed as merely an epistemological or procedural issue but must be defined primarily in political and ethical terms. It is political in that how we "read" the world is always implicated in relations of power. Literacy is ethical in that people "read" the world differently depending, for instance, on circumstances of class, gender, race, and politics. They also read the world in spaces and social relationships constructed between themselves and others which demand actions based on judgments and choices about how one is to act in the face of ideologies, values, and experiences that constitute "otherness." It is these shifting relations of knowing and identity which frame our "different modes of response to the other (e.g., between those that transfigure and those that disfigure, those that care for the other in his/her otherness and those that do not)."[3]

If a politics of difference is to be fashioned in emancipatory rather than oppressive practices, literacy must be rewritten in terms that articulate difference with the principles of equality, justice, and freedom rather than with those interests supportive of hierarchies, oppression, and exploitation. In this case, literacy as an emancipatory practice requires people to read, speak, and listen in the language of difference, a language in which meaning becomes multiaccentual and dispersed, and resists permanent closure. This is a language in which one speaks *with* rather than *for* Others, and has serious implications not only for students but also for teachers, particularly around the issue of authority, pedagogy, and politics.

In this case, knowledge and power come together not to merely reaffirm experience and difference but to also interrogate it, to open up broader theoretical considerations, to tease out its limitations, and to engage a vision of community in which student voices define themselves in terms of their distinct historical and social formations and their broader collective hopes. For critical educators, this entails speaking *to* important social, political, and cultural issues from a deep sense of the politics of their own location and the necessity to engage and often unlearn the habits of institutional (as well as forms of racial-, gender-, and class-specific) privilege that buttress their own power while sometimes preventing others from becoming questioning subjects.[4] This does not suggest that as educators we should abandon our authority as much as we should transform it into an emancipatory practice that provides the conditions for us to speak and be taken seriously. Of course, as teachers we can never speak inclusively *as* the Other, though we may be the Other with respect to issues of race, class, or gender; but we can certainly work *with* diverse Others to deepen both our own and their understanding of the complexity of the traditions, histories, knowledges, and politics that they bring to the schools. More specifically, although teachers may not speak as others whose experiences they do not share, they certainly can speak about and to the experiences of racism, sexism, class discrimination, and other concerns as historical and contingent issues that affect public life. In other words, as a heterosexual, white, middle-, and working-class educator, I cannot, for example, speak for African Americans or women. But I can speak self-reflectively from the politics of my own location about the issues of racism and sexism as ethical, political, and public issues which implicate in their web of social relations all those who inhabit public life, though from different spheres of privilege and subordination. Such a position reconstructs teachers as intellectuals whose own narratives must be situated and examined as discourses that are open, partial, and subject to ongoing debate and revision.

Put differently, the discourse of critical literacy is one that signals the need to challenge and redefine the substance and effects of cultural borders, the need to create opportunities for students to be border crossers in order to understand otherness on its own terms, and the need to create borderlands in which diverse cultural resources allow for the fashioning of new identities within existing configurations of power. [5]

In what follows, I want to highlight briefly what I call a postmodern discourse of literacy and difference. The emphasis here will be on the importance of the relationship between literacy and difference rather than on the specific substance and effects of the various approaches that characterize the burgeoning field of literacy. But before I develop these issues, I think it is important to address briefly the broader political context in which the debates over cultural difference and literacy have been framed during the last decade. It is to this consideration that I now turn.

Cultural literacy as eurocentrism

The ideological parameters of the current debate over culture and difference took shape during the Reagan era. During the last decade, the terms of this debate have been principally set by conservatives such as Allan Bloom, Diane Ravitch, and E.D. Hirsch, Jr.[6] All of these critics have presented in different ways an agenda and purpose for shaping public schooling and higher education under the terms of a cultural discourse in which the concept of difference is seen as a threat to what is labeled as Western culture. Within this discourse, the issue of culture and schooling is taken up primarily in terms aimed at overpowering or erasing difference rather than incorporating it as part of an ongoing democratic and pedagogical project. The conservative position has arisen from the recognition by some of its followers that the United States is in the midst of a cultural crisis which can be traced to the broader ideological tenets of the radical social movements that emerged during the 1960s along with the more recent emergence and influence of diverse forms of postmodern, feminist, and poststructuralist theory. The villains include, among others, those who hold that intellectuals should engage public life in oppositional terms, those who reject universal reason as a foundation for human affairs, those who oppose totalizing narratives, those who refuse to accept Eurocentric notions of Western culture as being synonymous with the very notion of civilization, those who argue that student experience should qualify as a legitimate form of knowledge, and those who claim that racial, class, gender, and ethnic differences extend, rather than threaten, the most basic principles of a democratic society.

In response to these developments, neoconservatives have attempted to reduce the politics of difference and schooling to forms of character education in which the call to pluralism becomes a euphemism for educating students to learn how to follow the rules and to adapt rather than to critically engage the values that reproduce existing structures of power. In this view, the concept of cultural difference, especially racial difference, is seen as threatening to the integrative character of the American polity, a threat to the merits of individualism, and disrespectful of the "high culture" of the West.

Removed from the language of social justice, difference is associated with a notion of literacy in which a critique of Eurocentrism, racism, or cultural domination is dismissed as merely an instance of a vile form of particularism that threatens to undermine the basis of what is unproblematically labeled as Western Civilization. Related to this perspective, there is a general tendency to view "otherness" as threatening to the notion of equality and tolerance central to the neoconservative view of national unity and security. The call to literacy has become a powerful weapon used by neoconservatives in their fight against the diverse groups attempting to rewrite the cultural, political, and social codes of the dominant society. Fearful of the threat to its physical (immigration), linguistic (bilingualism), academic (curriculum and canon), and racial (segregation) borders, neoconservatives have constructed a notion of cultural literacy that abstracts equity from difference while framing educational policies in a language that represents a new form of nativism. Consequently, literacy is often defined by the pedagogical imperative to learn knowledge, skills, and values that transcend the difficulties of race, color, ethnicity, language, and religion. Within this view, Diane Ravitch, for example, attacks those who analyze how cultural differences have been structured in forms of dominance and subordination as particularists and separatists who have not learned how to treat her notion of literacy and the "common culture" with reverence and respect.[7]

In my mind, this approach to difference, literacy, and schooling raises a fundamental challenge to how educators and others might view the role of educating students for critical citizenship in a democratic society. At risk in this debate is neither the "tradition" of Western culture as it is represented in school curricula nor the issue of whether subordinate students will be given the appropriate skills to function adequately in the labor market. Of course, these are important issues, but they should not be the concerns that define the purpose and meaning of literacy and schooling in this country. That is, the purpose and meaning of schooling extend beyond the function of a museum safeguarding the treasures of cultural tradition or the needs of the corporate state for more literate workers.

What is at stake in this debate is the status of literacy defined in relation to the radical responsibility of ethics, a responsibility that takes seriously educating students with the knowledge, skills, and values necessary for establishing relations between the self and others that refuse acts of violence, aggression, and subjugation. In question are those democratic values which provide the possibility for drawing attention to the languages, histories, and voices of those groups who have traditionally been excluded or marginalized from the discourse and citadels of power. More specifically, the importance of the debate on literacy, difference, and schooling raises important questions about the fragile nature of democracy itself. This suggests that any debate about schooling and difference is inseparable from a wider concern with the reconstruction of democratic public life.

Rewriting the discourse of literacy and difference

In opposition to the emerging neoconservative view, which defines democracy against cultural difference and literacy as a politics of equality, justice, and representation, I want to develop a rationale, along with some pedagogical principles, for developing a politics of difference responsive to the imperatives of a critical democracy. In doing so, I want to emphasize that public schools and institutions of higher learning cannot be viewed simply as instructional sites; they must be more broadly defined as contradictory agencies engaged in specific forms of moral and political regulation. That is, they produce knowledge and they provide students with a sense of place, worth, and identity. In doing so, they offer students selected representations, skills, social relations, and values that presuppose particular histories and ways of being in the world. The moral and political dimension at work here is revealed in the question: Whose history, story, and experience prevails in the school setting? In other words, who speaks for whom, under what conditions, and for what purpose? Educational institutions and the processes in which they engage are not innocent. Simply stated, schools are not neutral institutions designed for providing students with work skills or with the privileged tools of culture. Instead, they are deeply implicated in forms of inclusion and exclusion that produce particular moral truths and values. In effect, they both produce and legitimate cultural differences as part of their broader project of constructing particular knowledge/power relations and producing specific notions of citizenship. To some, this may sound commonsensical and a bit tiresome. But I think it is imperative to locate all levels of education within a moral and social context in order to assess how a politics and pedagogy of difference might be engaged as part of a discourse fundamental to the reconstruction of a critical democracy.

The problems facing education around the issue of difference in the United States need to be reformulated as a crisis in citizenship and ethics. This suggests that the solution to these problems lies ultimately in the realms of values and politics, not in simplistic calls for the creation of a common culture, a monolithic notion of cultural literacy, or a pluralism divorced from the issues of power and struggle. What is at stake is not the semantic difference between pluralism and particularism, but the creation of a democratic society in which differences are affirmed and interrogated rather than dismissed as essentialist or disruptive. It is no small irony that many conservatives who oppose a politics of difference to the discourse of pluralism are also arguing for measuring citizenship competencies through standardized cultural literacy tests and dismissing the voices of those who have been left out of dominant versions of academic discourse by suggesting that they are incapable of being more than self-referential and doctrinaire. Within this formulation, justice is subordinated to a plea for academic balance while at

the same time the school curriculum (canon) is defended as being representative of a version of Western history that is self-righteously equated with the
meaning of civilization itself. There is something ironic in the charge by
those in power (white academic males), especially in higher education, that
they have been pushed to the margins as a result of their defense of a
Eurocentric-based curriculum. In the face of an upsurge of racism across the
country, this type of logic translates into the self-indulging act of mistaking
the call to defend one's views as a form of aggression. So much for the spirit
of critical inquiry. The sentiment echoes what the dominant curriculum
suggests and what blacks, women, and other subordinate groups generally
accept as a given: it is only the voices of white males that count.

At the risk of overstating this issue, the crisis of literacy in this country
must be framed as part of a politics of difference that provides students with
the opportunity to engage in a deeper understanding of the importance of
democratic culture while developing classroom relations that prioritize the
importance of diversity, equality, and social justice. The ethical imperative
that links difference, schooling, and democracy in institutions of public and
higher education should educate students primarily for the responsibilities of
learning how to govern. This means organizing curricula in ways that enable
students to make judgments about how society is historically and socially
constructed, how existing social practices are implicated in relations of
equality and justice as well as how they structure inequalities around racism,
sexism, and other forms of oppression. It also means offering students the
possibilities for being able to make judgments about what society might be,
what is possible or desirable outside existing configurations of power.

Students need more than information about what it means to get a job or
pass standardized tests that purport to measure cultural literacy. They need
to be able to critically assess dominant and subordinate traditions so as to
engage their strengths and weaknesses. What they don't need is to treat
history as a closed, singular narrative that simply has to be revered and
memorized. Educating for difference, democracy, and ethical responsibility
is not about creating passive citizens. It is about providing students with the
knowledge, capacities, and opportunities to be noisy, irreverent, and vibrant.
Central to this concern is the need for students to understand how cultural,
ethnic, racial, and ideological differences enhance the possibility for dia-

logue, trust, and solidarity. Within this perspective, difference can be analyzed and constructed within pedagogical contexts that promote compassion and tolerance rather than envy, hatred, and bigotry. The pedagogical and ethical practice which I am emphasizing is one that offers opportunities for students to be border crossers; as border crossers, students not only refigure the boundaries of academic subjects in order to engage in new forms of critical inquiry, but they are also offered the opportunities to engage the multiple references that construct different cultural codes, experiences, and histories. In this context, a pedagogy of difference provides the basis for students to cross over into diverse cultural zones that offer a critical resource for rethinking how the relations between dominant and subordinate groups are organized, how they are implicated and often structured in dominance, and how such relations might be transformed in order to promote a democratic and just society. Difference in this case does not become a marker for deficit, inferiority, chauvinism, or inequality; on the contrary, it opens the possibilities for constructing pedagogical practices that deepen forms of cultural democracy that serve to enlarge our moral vision.

It is crucial for educators to link a politics of literacy and difference to a theory of social welfare and cultural democracy. At the very least, this means that educators can work to insert the idea of difference into the curriculum as part of an attempt to rearticulate the ideas of justice and equality. A politics of literacy and difference not only offers students the opportunity for raising questions about how the categories of race, class, and gender are shaped within the margins and center of power; it also provides a new way of reading history as a way of reclaiming power and identity. This is no small matter for those students who have generally been either marginalized or silenced by the dominant ideologies and practices of public schooling. Educators need to acknowledge that the radical responsibility of a politics of literacy and difference necessitates an ongoing analysis by students of the contradictions in American society between the meaning of freedom, the demands of social justice, and the obligations of citizenship on the one hand, and the accumulated suffering, domination, force, and violence that permeates all aspects of everyday life on the other. Such an analysis necessitates forms of literacy grounded in the ethical imperative to challenge the prevailing social order while simultaneously providing the basis for students to deepen the intellectual, civic, and moral understanding of their role as agents of public formation.

This means that the debate over the politics of literacy, difference, and culture might be reconstructed to engage the broader issue of how learning that goes on in American education is truly attentive to the problems and histories that construct the actual experiences students face in their everyday lives. A pedagogy of literacy and difference is not based merely on providing students with conflicting paradigms or the dispassionate skills of rhetorical persuasion; on the contrary, it points to pedagogical practices which offer students the knowledge, skills, and values they will need to critically negotiate and transform the world in which they find themselves. The politics of critical literacy and cultural difference engages rather than retreats from those problems that make democracy messy, vibrant, and noisy. Of course, literacy and difference when defined in these terms appear dangerous to neoconservatives and others who believe that social criticism and social justice is inimical to both the meaning of American education and the lived experience of democratic public life. This is precisely why educators cannot let the politics of literacy and difference be subordinated to cleansing and comforting self-righteous appeals made in the name of a common culture or the false equality of a pluralism devoid of the trappings of struggle, empowerment, and possibility. Our students do not deserve an education constrained by the smothering dictates of monolithic and totalizing views of culture, literacy, and citizenship; they deserve an education that acknowledges its role in the preparation of critical political subjects, that prepares them to be agents capable of locating themselves in history while simultaneously being able to shape it.

A postmodern discourse of literacy and difference provides readers with diverse elements of a critical approach to literacy that ruptures universal versions of reason and linear notions of history; it points to decentering margins as spaces that offer the opportunity for other voices to be spoken and heard. Within this perspective, literacy is not engulfed in a stifling regime of knowledge that refuses to recognize its own partiality, but in a view of uncertainty that makes dialogue and debate possible. At the same time, the call for literacies rather than literacy does more than displace regimes of certainty; it also, as Iain Chambers points out in a different context, "suggests an ecological frame in which the Other continues to simultaneously exist apart from us and yet be part of us in a shared responsibility for living in difference, for being responsible, just as we are for ourselves and the ethics that sustain such a relationship."[8] This points to a view of literacy that extends rather than cuts off the possibilities of acknowledging a world forged in differences that matter, that addresses the memories, traces, and voices of those who think and act in the struggle for an extension of human dignity. This is a pedagogy of literacy in which "differences are recognized, exchanged and mixed in identities that break down but are not lost, that connect but remain diverse."[9] It is a literacy that both affirms and disrupts in the name of hope, committed to the radical possibility of politics and ethics that inform the struggle for a better future.

Notes

1. Clarke, S., "Discipline and Resistance: The Subject of Writing and the Discourse of Instruction," *College Literature*, 18, 2, 1991, p. 123.

2. Anzaldüa, G., *Borderlands/La Frontera: The New Mestiza* (San Francisco: Spinsters/Aunt Lute, 1987), p. 3.

3. Kearney, R., *The Wake of Imagination* (Minneapolis: University of Minnesota Press, 1988), p. 369.

4. Spivak, G., "The Making of Americans, the Teaching of English, and the Future of Culture Studies," *The New Literary History*, 21, 4, 1990, pp. 781–798.

5. These themes are developed extensively in Aronowitz, S., and Giroux, H., *Postmodern Education: Politics, Culture and Social Criticism* (Minneapolis: University of Minnesota Press, 1991). See also Henry A. Giroux, *Border Crossings: Cultural Workers and the Politics of Education* (New York: Routledge, 1992).

6. Bloom, A., *The Closing of the American Mind* (New York: Simon and Schuster, 1987); Hirsch, E.D., Jr., *Cultural Literacy: What Every American Needs to Know* (Boston: Houghton Mifflin, 1987); Ravitch, D., "Multiculturalism: E Pluribus Plures," *The American Scholar*, Summer 1990, pp. 337–354.

7. Ravitch, D., "What's at Stake with Multicultural Education?" *Clipboard*, no. 4, February 1990, pp. 1–2. See also Ravitch, *ibid.*

8. Chambers, I., *Border Dialogues: Journeys in Postmodernity* (New York: Routledge, 1990), p. 115.

9. *Ibid.*, p. 114.

14

Critical literacy and
the postmodern turn*

Peter L. McLaren and
Colin Lankshear

Educators have become increasingly aware that, far from being a sure means to attaining an accurate and "deep" understanding of the world and one's place within it, the ability to read and write may expose individuals and entire social groups to forms of domination and control by which their interests are subverted. During the past two decades important advances have been made in understanding the ideological role of literacy within the production and "allocation" of economic, political, and cultural power. The "two-sided" character of literacy has been revealed. Developments in the "new" sociology of knowledge and the wider application of Marxist theory to education during the 1970s and 80s greatly enhanced our knowledge of how literacy in particular, and education in general, can serve to domesticate populations and reproduce hierarchies of inequality and injustice. At much the same time, such educational events as the dramatically successful Cuban and Nicaraguan literacy campaigns, and other initiatives throughout the world inspired by Paulo Freire's approach to literacy, showed what can be contributed to social transformation when educators revise their conceptions and practices of literacy and consciously turn reading and writing toward expansive and emancipatory ends.

Critical literacy is grounded in these insights as well as in the ethical and political commitment to democratic and emancipatory forms of education. As evident from earlier chapters, two main perspectives can be identified within the critical literacy project at present. One is a radical tradition, influenced particularly by Freirean and neo-Marxist currents, with strong links to modernist social theory. The other is an emerging Anglo-American theory development drawing on a variety of contributions from continental philosophy, poststructuralist currents, social semiotics, reception theory, neopragmatism, deconstruction, critical hermeneutics, and other post-modern positions.

This chapter deals with recent theoretical advances and research approaches from this latter perspective, especially developments in poststructuralist theory, and asks how they might contribute to the ongoing theory and practice of critical literacy. Our discussion ranges over several questions: What *is* the postmodern turn in social theory? What are the points of strength and disputation in postmodern theoretical developments as viewed from a *critical* perspective? What can postmodern insights contribute to emancipatory projects, specifically critical literacy? In what ways does postmodern social theory enhance our *conception* of critical literacy and point to important elements of a critical literacy *research* agenda?

To stake out more firmly the theoretical position of research practices which lead to a poststructuralist view of critical literacy, let us describe briefly some of the most basic theoretical conceptions of critical research in its various manifestations (participatory research, critical ethnography, action research, and so on). Operating within a theoretical subterrain outside of the policing structure of sovereign research discourses, the tradition of critical research continues to make unconventional alliances between descriptions and meanings.

From a critical standpoint, knowledge is never self-authenticating, self-legitimating, or self-ratifying. Critical research is not a process which can determine its own effects or speak its own truth in a manner which transcends its relations to the sociopolitical context in which learning takes place. It is always a creature of cultural limits and theoretical borders, and as such is necessarily implicated in particular economies of truth, value, and power. Consequently, critical researchers need to remind themselves of the following: Whose interests are being served in social acts of doing research? Where is this process situated ethically and politically in matters of social justice? What principles should we choose in structuring our pedagogical efforts?

To not ask these questions is to risk being reduced to custodians of sameness and system-stabilizing functions which serve the collective interests and regimes of truth of the prevailing power elite(s). Similarly, to seek a neutral balance of perspectives by refusing to capitulate to the discourses of either left or right is to support those whose interests prevail within the status quo.

Critical research works from a view of culture that focuses on *disjuncture, rupture, and contradiction*. Culture is best understood as a *terrain of contestation* that serves as a locus of multivalent practical and discursive structures and powers. Knowledge is construed as *a form of discursive production*. As understood here, discourses are modalities which to a significant extent govern what can be said, by what kinds of speakers, and for what types of imagined audiences.[1] The rules of discourse are normative and derive their meaning from the power relations in which they are embedded. Discourses organize a way of thinking into a way of doing. Unlike language, they have both a subject and an object, and actively shape the social practices of which they are mutually constitutive.

At the level of research, discourses are always indexical to the context of researchers and their interpretations. All research discourses are conflictual and competitive. As such they embody particular interests, "establish paradigms, set limits, and construct human subjects."[2] Discourse "constitutes the guarantee and limit of our understanding of *otherness*."[3] Moreover, *discourse* refers to the conditions of any social practice.[4] The process of constructing knowledge takes place within an unevenly occupied terrain of struggle in which the dominative discourses of mainstream research approaches frequently parallel the discursive economies of the larger society, and are reinforced by the asymmetrical relations of power and privilege which accompany them.

A critical approach to analysis and research makes it clear that all knowledge consists of rhetorical tropes. These both reflect and shape the way that we engage and are transformed by the manner in which we consciously and unconsciously identify ourselves with our roles as researchers, and with the subjects we study. This process has been detailed in the work of Paulo

Freire, Henry Giroux, Linda Brodkey, Patricia Bizzell, Donaldo Macedo, Jim Berlin, Jim Gee, and others. They have advanced the notion that reality does not possess a presignifying nature but is an interactive, cultural, social, and historical process. They have also described the relationship between discourses of literacy, research practices, and the workings of power, and revealed the various ways in which power operates as a regulating force which conforms to its dominant ideologies and their institutionalized supports as well as centralizes and unifies often conflicting and competing discourses in the interests of capitalist social relations.

The idea here is that discourses are not single-minded positivities but are invariably mutable, contingent, and partial. Their authority is always provisional as distinct from transcendental. The real is not transparent to the world; the real and the concept are insurmountably asymmetrical.[5] Truth has no real name other than the meanings rhetorically or discursively assigned to it. Discourses may in fact *possess* the power of truth, but in reality they are historically contingent rather than inscribed by natural law; they emerge out of social conventions. In this view, any discourse of conducting is bounded by historical, cultural, and political conditions and the epistemological resources available to articulate its meaning. Educators involved in critical research remind us that people do not possess power but produce it and are produced by it in their relational constitution through discourse.

Critical research is not limited to any one methodology and can incorporate both qualitative and quantitative approaches. What characterizes research as "critical" is an attempt to recognize its own status as discourse and to understand its role as a servant of power. Critical researchers try to understand how the research design and process are themselves implicated in social and institutional structures of domination. They must also recognize what conflicts might exist within their subjective formation without sacrificing or hiding the political or ethical center of gravity that guides the overall research project. Research undertaken in a critical mode requires recognizing the complexity of social relations and the researcher's own socially determined position within the reality he or she is attempting to describe. Critical research must be undertaken in such a way as to narrate its own contingency, its own situatedness in power/knowledge relations. Critical researchers attempt to become aware of the controlling cultural mode of their research and the ways, often varied and unwitting, in which their research subjects and their relationship to them become artifacts of the *epistemes* that shape the direction of their research by fixing the conceptual world in a particular way and by selecting particular discourses from a range of possibilities.

Postmodernism and postmodern social theory

The term *postmodernism* straddles several definitional boundaries. It refers at once to a sensibility, a political perspective, a state of mind, and a mode of social analysis. Taking these as an amalgam, we may speak of the postmodern *age:* an era wherein democratic imperatives have become subverted, originary values simulated, and emancipatory symbols and their affective power commodified. It is an age in which the modernist quest for certainty and meaning and the liberal humanist notion of the individual as a unified and coherent essence and agency are being forcefully challenged.

Much of the discourse of postmodernism has been criticized for betraying a dry cynicism in which irony and pastiche become politics' last recourse at social change. It often reveals an uncompromising distaste for the masses, adopts a form of high-brow, antibourgeois posing, and occasionally assumes the role of a self-congratulatory vanguardism which resonates dutifully with the "high seriousness" of the academy, at times appearing as dressed-up restatements of Nietzsche and Heidegger.

In the postmodern age, breaks and disjunctures in contemporary social reality have led to the retreat of democratic forms of social life. MacCannell speaks of the "implosive reduction of all previously generative oppositions: male/female, rich/poor, black/white . . . into a single master pattern of dominance and submission . . . with . . . no semiotic or institutional way of breaking the patterns of advantaging one class, ethnic group or gender over another." The result is a proliferation of gender and racial inequality, all within the framework of apparently progressive legislation and administration which, in reality, seems to be doing the opposite.[6]

The turmoil of late capitalism is perhaps best displayed by the surging impulses of media images—from which the postmodern subject can hardly escape the cruel insistence of their ever-presentness—and the tragic liaison between the media industry and the viewing public, the former arrogating the right to legislate, produce, and serve up the latter's daily reality. Increasing youth alienation is evident, brought about by what Voss and Schutze refer to as "a world blanketed with signs and texts, image and media of all kinds . . . which has brought forth a culture . . . based on an overproduction of sensations that dulls our sensory faculties."[7]

Attendant characteristics of the postmodern condition also include the rejection of truth claims that have a grounding in a transcendent reality independent of collective human struggle, an abandonment of the teleology of science, the construction of lifestyles out of consumer products and cultural bricolage, and cultural forms of communication and social relations that have evolved from the disorganization of capitalism.[8] The postmodern condition signals the undecidability, plurality, or "thrownness" of culture rather than its homogeneity or consensual nature. Indeed, some characteristics of postmodernity seem to affirm Benjamin's equation of fascism and the aestheticization of politics, which includes the demise of a public democratic sphere of rational debate "replaced by a consumerist culture of manipulation and acclamatory politics."[9] From this standpoint, postmodernism represents a "'cultural' logic that correlates political-economic and social-psychological changes in late capitalism."[10]

As social theory, postmodernist perspectives attempt to advance an oppositional stance against the policing structures of modernist discourse. Of particular importance here are appropriations by postmodernist social theory of various currents of poststructuralist social theory. From these emerge numerous issues that have an important bearing on critical literacy and the development of critical research on literacy. Two central issues are especially noteworthy: the new social theories have radicalized the conception of the subject as social agent by relativizing the authority of the text-in-itself; and they have deterritorialized and deauthorized the task of conducting research as it is generally understood. We will try to draw out some implications of these shifts in terms of how they affect our theoretical approaches to the study of critical literacy.

Poststructuralism can be distinguished from its structuralist predecessor as follows. Structuralists typically conceive of language as an arbitrary system of differences in which meaning is *guaranteed* by the linguistic system itself and the values given to signifying practices within particular linguistic communities. In other words, given the signs and linguistic practices, meanings follow. For structuralists, meaning is *uncovered* by "cracking" the code that explains how elements of a social text function together. Often, these codes are granted a transcendental status, serving as privileged referents around which other meanings are positioned.

Poststructuralism is less deterministic. Much more emphasis is placed on meaning as *a contested event*, a terrain of struggle in which individuals take up often conflicting subject positions in relation to signifying practices. Poststructuralists acknowledge explicitly that meaning consists of more than signs operating and being operated in a context. Rather, there is struggle over signifying practices. This struggle is eminently *political* and must include the relationship among discourse, power, and difference. Poststructuralists put much more emphasis on discourse and the contradictions involved in subjective formation. They regard transcendental signifieds as discursive fictions.

In addition, poststructuralism draws attention to the significant danger of assuming that concepts can exist independently of signifying systems or language itself, or that meaning can exist as a pure idea, independently of its contextual embeddedness in the materiality of speech, gesture, writing, and so on. Poststructuralism does not locate the human subject within the structure of language, that is, within the rules of signification. Rather, the subject is an effect of the structure of language and the signifying system. Just as there exists no unified, monolithic, and homogeneous sign community which produces and interprets signs, so too there exists no self that precedes its social construction through the agency of representation. As Judith Butler explains,

> The subject is a consequence of certain rule-governed discourses that govern the intelligible invocation of identity. The subject is not *determined* by the rules through which it is generated because signification is *not a founding act, but rather a regulated process of repetition* that both conceals itself and enforces its rules precisely through the production of substantializing effects . . . There is no self that is prior to the convergence or who maintains "integrity" prior to its entrance into this conflicted cultural field.

There is only a taking up of the tools where they lie, where the very "taking up" is enabled by the tool lying there.[11]

According to poststructuralists, we construct our future selves, our identities, through the availability and character of signs of possible futures. The parameters of the human subject vary according to the discursive practices, economies of signs, and subjectivities (experiences) engaged by individuals and groups at any historical moment. We must abandon the outmoded and dangerous idea that we possess as social agents a timeless essence or a consciousness that places us beyond historical and political practices. Rather, we should understand our "working identities" as an effect of such practices. Our identities as subjects are not tied to or dependent upon some transcendental regime of truth beyond the territory of the profane and the mundane. Rather, they are constitutive of the literacies we have at our disposal through which we make sense of our day-to-day politics of living.

From the postmodernist position, discourses are always saturated in power. Jane Flax says, "Postmodern discourses are all 'deconstructive' in that they seek to distance us from and make us sceptical about beliefs concerning truth, knowledge, power, the self, and language that are often taken for granted within and serve as legitimation for contemporary Western culture."[12] Postmodern thinking takes as its object of investigation issues such as "how to understand and (re)constitute the self, gender, knowledge, social relations, and culture without resorting to linear, teleological, hierarchical, holistic, or binary ways of thinking and being."[13]

A key feature of postmodern discourse has been its ability to effect a decentering of the authority of the text, and also a decentering of the reader. Readers are revealed to be restricted by the tropes and conventions of their reading practices just like, for instance, historians are constrained by the discourses available in the act of writing history.

Postmodernist social theory has much to offer the critique of colonial discourses within literacy research because it assumes the position that the age of modernism was characterized by the geopolitical construction of the center and the margins within the expansive hegemony of the conqueror. It was, in other words, marked by the construction through European conquest of the foundational "I."[14] Postmodern criticism has significantly revealed how even the language of critical theory, which has its roots in European history and philosophy, carries with it a debilitating Eurocentric bias that continues to privilege the discourse of the white male colonizer. All discourses, even those of freedom and liberation, carry with them ideological traces and selective interests which must be understood and transformed in the interests of greater justice and equality.

Moreover, from a postmodernist perspective, knowledge does not constitute decoded transcriptions of "reality" separable into the grand postulates of Western thought and what is left over: the lesser, vulgar, popular, and massified knowledges of the "barbarians." Rather, all knowledge is considered to be framed by interpretation and controlled by rhetorical devices and discursive apparatuses. It is an approach to knowledge that is perturbing and unsettling, especially to those who hold "objectivist" perspectives on reality. Derrida, for example, reveals the metaphorical character of knowledge and attacks the objectivism in our understanding of social relations inherited from the tradition of sociology: the notion that society can be reduced to a "metaphysics of presence," or an objective and coherent ensemble of conceptually formulated laws. He has uncovered the discrepancy between meaning and the author's assertion by rupturing the "logocentric" logic of identity,[15] and has highlighted the status of philosophy as writing which, following Nietzsche, entails a deconstruction of the history of metaphysics.

The postmodern turn in the study of English has moved beyond late modernist attempts to rupture realist narrative conventions. It now faces the chalenge of historiographic metafiction and interactive fiction. Mainstream literary theorists and English educators are witnessing serious attacks on dominant forms of literary discourse such as modernist notions of the original and originating author. They are further facing postmodernist critical practices which consist of a dethroning of totalized thought; the problemization of forms of autorepresentation; the transparency of historical referentiality; and an emphasis on the enunciative situation—text, producer, receiver, historical, and social context—and double-voicing or implied readers.[16] The ideological situatedness of all literary practices is now being highlighted, with a recognition of the impossibility of the disinterestedness of any discursive claim or cultural practice.

Postmodern social theory: Obstacles from within

Although our aim in this chapter is to seek the contribution of postmodern social theory for the ongoing development and practice of critical literacy, it must be conceded that poststructuralism has met with trenchant criticism on several grounds and from several directions. To appreciate the potential inherent in the postmodern turn for further progress toward developing critical literacy as a mainstream rather than a marginalized educational engagement, it is necessary to rehearse some of these criticisms, most of which have an overtly *political* emphasis. These critiques identify limitations within postmodern theory which need to be overcome and, at the same time, help us clarify further the criteria and requirements of critical literacy in theory and practice.

Several of the criticisms which follow pertain to two of the central advances made by postmodern theory: the decentering of the subject and the decentering of the text. These ideas will be elaborated in our account of those objections which seem to us most important.

Of course, the criticisms of poststructuralism which follow do *not* preclude the development of a critical project in educational research and practice that can accommodate poststructuralism. Indeed, the contemporary world is largely *unintelligible* without a poststructuralist perspective. Here we share Jameson's view that although poststructuralism represents "the ideology of a new multinational stage of capitalism" and therefore shares certain counterrevolutionary tendencies, it nevertheless "contains some of the elements for the beginning of a critical analysis of the present."[17] Poststructuralism does, however, pose some difficult challenges for those committed to a critical emancipatory project: How can we construct narratives of cultural difference that affirm and empower and that do not undercut the efforts of other social groups to win self-definition? In what way are our own discourses as literacy researchers disguised by self-interest and defined by the exclusion of the voices of others? In what ways must we rewrite the stories which guide our research and our interpretations of these stories in relation to shifting cultural boundaries and new political configurations? How can we redefine research practices so that they no longer describe the discourses and practices of white, Western males who are charged to speak on behalf of everyone else? How do we position the "other" in the semantic field of our research so that he or she does not become a "silent predicate" that gives birth to Western patriarchal asumptions of what constitutes truth and justice?

Decentering the subject

Poststructuralist theorists, among others (notably, feminists), have criticized educators for working within a discourse of critical rationalism which reifies the humanist subject—the rational, self-motivating, autonomous agent—as a subject of history, change, and resistance. They maintain that what separates being an individual from being a subject is a linguistic membrane known as discourse. Discourses provide individuals with identifications which convert them into subjects. By contrast, the rationalist position associated with the modern Enlightenment rests on a "metaphysics of presence" which constitutes the individual as a noncontradictory, rational, self-fashioning, autonomous being: Descartes' fully conscious "I" immediately transparent to itself. There is a logic of identity here in which the self defines itself in opposition to the "other." The forced unity of this position and the unilinearity of its progressive rationality work to deny the specificity of difference and heterogeneity. The subject is projected as a unity, but this disguises and falsifies the complex disunity of experience.[18]

The debate over postmodernity is largely related to the advent of multinational or late capitalism, which has formed, from its "centerless ubiquity,"[19] a new postmodern subject out of the pathological jumble of consumer myths and images fed by the global dispersal of capital and its constant promises of fulfillment through an ever-expanding market economy which structures the shape and direction of our desire. The debate, moreover, is about the construction of our identities as raced, classed, and gendered beings which have been decentered irrevocably, thereby giving ominous weight to Brenkman's observation that "the obligation to criticize and transform outer reality wanes as authentic meanings and values are granted a purely inner reality."[20]

Postmodernist efforts to decenter the subject have met with criticisms and cautions. Hartsock sounds a note of deep suspicion that just at a time when many groups are engaged in "nationalisms" which involve redefining them as marginalized Others, the academy begins to legitimize a critical theory of the "subject" which holds its agency in doubt and which casts a general scepticism on the possibilities of a general theory which can describe the world and institute a quest for historical progress.[21] Henry Louis Gates, Jr., echoes a similar concern. He argues that in rejecting the existence of a subject, poststructuralist theorists are denying those who have been subjugated and made voiceless and invisible by the high canon of Western literature the chance to reclaim their subjectivity before they critique it.

> To deny us the process of exploring and reclaiming our subjectivity before we critique it is the critical version of the grandfather clause, the double privileging of categories that happen to be *preconstituted*. Such a position leaves us nowhere, invisible and voiceless in the republic of Western letters. Consider the irony: precisely when we (and other third world peoples) obtain the complex wherewithal to define our black subjectivity in the republic of Western letters, our theoretical colleagues declare that there ain't no such thing as a subject, so why should we be bothered with that? In this way, those of us in feminist criticism or African-American criticism who are engaged in the necessary work of canon deformation and reformation, confront the skepticism even of those who are allies on other fronts, over the matter of the death of the subject and our own discursive subjectivity.[22]

Elsewhere, postmodernist discourse has met the charge that its over-determination of the subject through discourse renders the social agent as politically innocuous as the liberal humanist. The obsession of both post-structuralists and the new historicists to formulate the self as an effect of discourse rather than as its origin necessarily submits human subjects to determinations over which they have little control. Frank Lentricchia targets "a literary politics of freedom whose echoes of Nietzsche and his joyful deconstructionist progeny do not disguise its affiliation with the mainline tradition of aesthetic humanism, a politics much favored by many of our colleagues in literary study, who take not a little pleasure from describing themselves as powerless. This is a literary politics that does not . . . [answer] . . . the question: So what?"[23]

Decentering the text

Another major contribution of poststructuralist theory has been its revelation that texts need to be understood in their historical, political, and cultural specificity. There are no texts which are meant in the same way by readers because readers occupy different subjective positions of articulation. The rhetorical claims of the text are integrated or transformed through the parallel rhetorics of common sense and the everyday against which they are read.

Poststructuralism has provided a necessary shift from a critical focus on text alone to the dynamics of culture and consumption reflected in the reader. Bennett[24] cuts across the notion of the unitary experience of reading in suggesting how subjects approach a text with already coded perceptions of "reading formations." These consist of a set of discursive and textual determinations which organize and animate the practice of reading. Reading formations, says Bennett, may be shaped by social positionality (such as the role of class and gender relations in organizing reading practices), intertextual determinations (readers' experience of other texts), and culturally determined genre expectations (the dominant codes that govern the popular text, or subcultural codes such as feminism, trade unionism, Marxism, moral majority thinking, and so forth). Readers are thus placed in a position in which they can potentially refuse the subject position which the text "coaxes" them to adopt. In this theoretical move, which sees the determinant text supplanted by the recipient of the text, no text can be so penetrative and pervasive in its authority as to eliminate all grounds for contestation or resistance.

Eagleton, however, urges moderation here, rejecting a swing from the all-powerful authority of the text to a total decentering of text. He satirizes the Readers' Liberation Movement and its fetishistic concern with consumer rights in reading, and describes the dominant strategy of this movement as an "all-out *putsch* to topple the text altogether and install the victorious reading class in its place." He argues that reader power cannot answer the question of what one has power over. For this reason he ridicules the ascendancy of reader reception theory, which transforms the act of reading into "creative enclaves, equivalent in some sense to workers' cooperatives within capitalism [in which] readers may hallucinate that they are actually writers, reshaping government handouts on the legitimacy of nuclear war into symbolist poems."[25]

There is much to commend this bold move to decenter the authorial discretion of the writer and the projection of the reader as a passive, acted-upon object. Yet the very act of desituating and dehistoricizing the reader actually brings it into line with the humanist position. As Scully puts it, in each position "the work's specious authority will derive from the illusion that it is not value-bound, not historically conditioned, not responsible . . . its authoritativeness will depend not on the making of its particular human source but on the implicit denial that it comes from anywhere at all, or that it is class couched."[26]

What gets lost unavoidably in preoccupation with the construction of meaning at the point of reception is sufficient acknowledgment of the ways in which privileged forms of representing experience come to serve as regimes of truth. Reception theory permits us to disattend the various forms of competing interpellations which are at play simultaneously within a given text or social formation.

Collins reveals the self-legitimating aspects of interpellations which compete for our identification and involvement within any text or cultural form. He argues that within the fragmentary cultures of the postmodern condition, "competing discourses must differentiate themselves according to style and function."[27] He points out how, for instance, literary style may serve as an aesthetic ideology which valorizes certain ideologies competing in a cultural text as a means of converting individuals into subjects. Even though we are not free to choose as independent autonomous readers which discourses we wish to identify with, we still participate in a process of *selection*. This is an important truth. Because of the vast array of competing discourses which offer themselves as a means of completing the subject, by giving it a temporarily fixed identity, it is necessary for the subject to hierarchize and arrange them.

The process of selecting the most politically transformative discourses in endless competition for "completing" the subject has never been more urgent, since we are presently in times when culture's unifying characteristics seem irrevocably decentered. Disparate discourses may be managed through multiple aesthetics and multiple styles: by a means of *bricolage* by which ideologies and representations may be selected and combined in new, transformative ways.[28] This has an important implication for developing a critical literacy, since it raises the following questions: *To what extent do conventional literacy practices duplicate the ideologies embedded in literary texts and the already constructed reading formations of teachers and students?* If reading formations are not always already fixed, *how can educators help their students develop reading formations which will enable them to resist the authority of the dominative ideologies produced within required texts?*

To reduce reading to the subjective act of the reader has dangerous consequences. It can blind us to the means by which power works on and through subjects and ignores the way in which textual authority is constructed as a form of production linked to larger economies of power and privilege in the wider social order. If the meaning of a text is reduced to individual interpretation, then the act of reading itself can be reduced to a textual palliative in which the material conditions of existence, the suffering of certain select groups in our society, can be turned into a fantasy of personal resolution. Furthermore, it enables us to engage in self-recuperation in a move that smoothly sidesteps collective participation in social transformation. It produces a mode of subjectivity that can participate gleefully in troubling the hegemony of social silence while avoiding the task of reconstructing the social practices which produce such silence. It can create an optimism that is strictly personal, removed from historical context. In this way the dominant culture can achieve both the individualism and poverty of theory necessary for it to escape the threat of resistance.

Left social and political theorists within the academy vary greatly in their opinion and appropriation of postmodern strategies of critique. Jameson warns against a simplistic, reductionistic view of the political,[29] and Merod regrets that much academic work falling into the category of "postmodernism" decidedly fails to move the reader "from the academic world of texts and interpretations to the vaster world of surveillance, technology, and material forces."[30] Harsher antagonists claim that the deconstructive enterprise often operates as a kind of left mandarin terrorism, displacing "political activism into a textual world where anarchy can *become* the establishment without threatening the actual seats of political and economic power," and sublimating political radicalism "into a textual radicalism that can happily theorize its own disconnection from unpleasant realities."[31]

Feminist theorists have identified a range of concerns associated with extreme versions of decentering text and/or subject. Mascia-Lees, Sharpe, and Cohen, for example, pose a crucial issue for social theory:

> Once one articulates an epistemology of free play in which there is no inevitable relationship between signifier and signified, how is it possible to write an ethnography that has descriptive force? . . . Once one has no metanarratives into which the experience of difference can be translated, how is it possible to write any ethnography?[32]

Feminists, among others, have also noted how in its assault on the classic figure of Western humanism—the rational, unified, noncontradictory, and self-determining individual—poststructuralist discourse has erased the suffering, bleeding, breathing subject of history. Poststructuralism's infatuation with the dancing signifier whose meaning is always ephemeral, elusive, disperse, and mutable, and the emphasis which it places on textualizing the reader as an intricate composition of an infinite number of codes or texts,[33] can be subversive of its potentially empowering and transformative agenda. Knowledge can be depotentiated and stripped of its emancipatory possibilities if it is acknowledged only as a form of textualization. Moreover, such a facile treatment of discourse can lead to the subject's encapsulation in the membranes of his or her rationalizations, leading to a soporific escape from the pain and sensations of living, breathing, human subjects. As Alan Megill warns:

> All too easy is the neglect or even the dismissal of a natural and historical reality that ought not to be neglected or dismissed . . . For if one adopts, in a cavalier and single-minded fashion, the view that everything is discourse or text or fiction, the realia are trivialized. Real people who really died in the gas chambers at Auschwitz or Treblinka become so much discourse.[34]

Clearly there is danger in assuming a literal interpretation of Derrida's "there is nothing outside of the text." We are faced with the postmodern "loss of affect" which occurs when language attempts to "capture the 'ineffable' experience of the Other."[35] We risk textualizing gender, denying sexual specificity, or treating difference as merely a formal category with no empirical and historical existence.[36]

Further criticisms

Various other obstacles to a political agenda of justice and emancipation have been discerned within postmodern social theory. Barbara Christian's critique of postmodern discourse takes aim at the *language* of literary critical theory. She condemns this language on the grounds that it "mystifies rather than clarifies our condition, making it possible for a few people who know that particular language to control the critical scene—that language surfaced, interestingly enough, just when the literatures of peoples of color, of black women, of Latin Americans, of Africans, began to move to 'the center.'"[37]

Still further problems are seen to arise from postmodern attacks on the unified, transcendental ego and the rejection of theoretical procedures for arriving at ontologically and metaphysically secure truth claims. In particular, postmodern theorists are seen as at risk of lapsing into an ethical relativism and a burgeoning nihilism. French versions of postmodernism have been seen as reflecting "a disturbing kinship with facism," and Jürgen Habermas has actually accused Bataille, Foucault, and Derrida of being "young conservatives."[38]

Peter Dews has taken up this latter line, revealing its ethical and political implications. He targets poststructuralism, with its "Nietzsche-inspired assault on any putatively universal truth" and its tendency to implicitly equate the rational principle of modernity with cognitive instrumental thought. Poststructuralist invocations of the radical other of Enlightenment reason and social modernization produce a radical other which takes the form of an expressive subjectivity—"the untamed energies of mind and body—of madness, intensity, desire." This is a subjectivity freed from the demands of utility and morality and economic and administrative rationality. In this way, says Dews, poststructuralism "curiously coincides with neo-conservatism, although the polarity of values is reversed from one position to another."[39] He rejects the one-sidedness of poststructuralism's "cult of immediacy, the deflation of noble forms, anarchism of the soul," in favor of a stress on human and civil rights.

A way ahead: Beyond the obstacles of postmodern theory

Feminist contributions

If feminists have advanced some of the more strident critiques of postmodern social theory on behalf of a politics of material engagement in the cause of freedom and justice, they have also given clear pointers to a way ahead. In resisting "the dangers inherent in a complete decentering of the historical and material" and in their task of "changing the power relationships that underlie women's oppression," feminists offer postmodernist discourse a way of dealing with contradictions which do not decenter their own categories of analysis in such a way that political reform is immobilized. Feminist discourse can move analysis away from the word and toward the world, since, according to Mary Hawkesworth, "feminist accounts derive their justificationary force from their capacity to illuminate existing social relations, to demonstrate the deficiencies of alternative interpretations, to debunk opposing views." It is "precisely because feminists move beyond texts to confront the world" that they are able to give "concrete reasons in specific contexts for the superiority of their accounts." From the perspective of feminist theory, postmodern anthropology may actually "erase difference, implying that all stories are really about one experience: the decentering and fragmentation that is the current experience of Western white males."[40] The dangers are obvious:

> If the postmodernist emphasis on multivocality leads to denial of the continued existence of a hierarchy of discourse, the material and historical links between cultures can be ignored, with all voices becoming equal, each telling only an individualized story. The history of the colonial, for example, can be read as independent of that of the colonizer. Such readings ignore or obscure exploitation and power differentials and therefore offer no ground to fight oppression and effect change.[41]

By revealing how women are constituted as voiceless and powerless through dominant conceptions of the subject, feminist theorists challenge us to recuperate a non-Western, nonmale subject-agent likewise removed from modernist philosophy's essentializing search for origins and a universal sovereign consciousness. In heeding this challenge, Giroux argues that modernism, postmodernism, and feminism can be articulated in terms of the interconnections between their differences and the common ground they share for being mutually corrective. All three discourses can and should be used to mutually inform ways of advancing a new politics of literacy research.[42]

Subjectivity and subjects/agency and agenthood: Problems with identity politics in emancipatory research

Recent work by Larry Grossberg on the relationship between structure and agency offers valuable insights for further developing a critical poststructuralist agenda in literacy research and practice. The structure-agency debate has haunted critical social theory for decades: initially in its modernist "moment," but later within poststructuralist theorizing as well.

Grossberg detects the carryover of an Althusserian view of subject formation into dominant strands of poststructuralism, resulting in an unwanted determinism. The subject becomes essentially a passive occupant of a particular discursive construction, although individuals are not all constructed equally. Social groups are positioned differentially within domains of subjectivity—that is, places from which one experiences the world—and according to discursively constituted systems of social differences (black/white, gay/hetero, poor/rich, female/male, and so on). Different discourses (economic, educational, legal, medical) enable or constrain the power that allows subjects to give voice to their experiences within specific systems of language and knowledge. The process of ideology constructs sets of "cultural identities" which determine the meaning and experience of social relations within fields of difference such as race, gender, class, and sexual preference.

Grossberg is critical of the determinism in such poststructuralist conceptions of the formation of the historical subject. Within them

> the individual appears to be weightless, thrown about by the weighty fullness of cultural texts. In the end, history is guaranteed in advance. Ideology (and history) seem to hold the winning hand, determining as it were, in

its own spaces and structures, the subject-ion of the individual, hailing them into places it has already identified for them within its maps of meaning. It appears to guarantee that history will constantly reproduce the same experiences over and over, constantly replaying the same psychic or social history that is always already in place.[43]

Such a view denies the possibility of resistance to ideological hegemony, since agency is structured into the very reproduction of history. Finding little solace in the concept of the fractured or decentered subject, Grossberg sees no solution to the paradox of subjectivity because it derives from a conceptual model that identifies individuals with both the subjects and agents of history. He attempts to escape the paradox by distinguishing subjectivity, agency, and agenthood.

By *subjectivity* Grossberg means "the site of experience and of the attribution of responsibility." *Agency* refers to "the active forces struggling within and over history." *Agenthood* signifies "actors operating, whether knowingly or unknowingly, on behalf of particular agencies."[44] Grossberg's account of agency is large. It refers to *historical* agency as well as to the location of individuals in systems of discourse and difference. Historical agency has less to do with social identity than with historical effectivity, or what Gramsci called "tendential forces"—such as capitalism, industrialism, technology, democracy, nationalism, and religion. Tendential forces "map out the long-term directions and investments which have already been so deeply inscribed upon the shape of history that they seem to play themselves out in a constantly indeterminate future."[45]

Agency, however, calls for historical and cultural agents to accomplish specific activities. In other words, it presupposes *agenthood*. Agents may be individuals or nominal groups such as organizations and political parties. Although these may have their own political agendas, such agendas depend ultimately on the apparatuses of agency.

For Grossberg, the important question concerns the link connecting ideological subjects to agents. What kinds of investments of subjectivity occur in the formation of nominal groups and social organizations? Grossberg speaks here of "the domain of affective individuality." This is the individual of "affective states" rather than the individual of "identities."

The affective individual exists within its nomadic wandering through the ever-changing places and spaces, vectors and apparatuses of daily life. Its shape and force are never guaranteed; its empowerment (i.e., its possibilities for action—in this case, for investment) depends in part on where it is located, how it occupies its places within specific apparatuses, and how it moves within and between them. The affective individual always moves along different vectors, always changing its shape. But it always has an affective shape as a result of its struggles to win a temporary space for itself within the places that have been prepared for it. Such nomadic travels are not random or subjective; the nomad often carries not only its maps but its places with it, through a course determined by social, cultural and historical knowledges. The affective individual is both an articulated site and a site of ongoing articulation within its own history . . . The nomadic individual is the subject and the agent of daily life, existing within an affective economy of investment which makes daily life the link between private experiences and public struggles.[46]

This account of the affective or nomadic subject has important implications for political struggle. In particular, it suggests the limitation of identity politics based on gender, race, class, religion, or nationality for large-scale social transformation. Identity politics are grounded in the direct experience of particular groups. Strategies of alliance within identity politics face serious problems. Specifically, Grossberg argues that

the various strategies of alliance are all attempts to construct a "We" which can represent and speak for different individuals and groups, a collective identity which transcends differences and speaks for them as well. "We" speaks as a unity from the position which the other has already constructed for it (i.e., the essentialist view). "We" speaks from an imaginary place (the site of alliance) located in the midst of the differences (i.e., the postmodern view). The discourse of representation involves the circulation of a sign which articulates specific effects (e.g., it often activates a discourse of guilt or authenticity) in specific contexts (e.g., anti-abortion ads).[47]

Grossberg suggests that in creating a politics of transformation it is more important to mobilize affective subjects than to create a politics of identity or discourse of representation. Grossberg calls for the strategic and provisional deployment of a "We" that does not purport to represent anyone but rather is used as a "floating sign," not of unity or identity, "but of common authority and commitment to speak and act." This involves the ability to "structure the commitments which fashion everyday life and its relations to the social formation." A transformative politics needs to mobilize individuals through their affective investments in certain issues rather than through essentialist claims around the authenticity of identity through direct experience. This is not to claim that identity struggles are not important, since people invest in what they identify with, be it race, creed, or political party. The problem is that the building of coalitions based on multiple sites of identity collapses under the weight of calls for authenticity and "linguistic self-righteousness" and "political purity."

Grossberg's concern is distinctively postmodern. Fred Pfeil gets to the heart of it in recognizing that "the problem to be worked through and, ultimately, strategized" is that of "the *dis*unified and *de*-centered subject": "a vast array of ideological apparatuses, from advertizing to education, politics to MTV . . . work as much to *dis*-articulate the subject as to interpellate it, [offering] not the old pleasures of 'self-understanding,' of knowing and accepting our place, but the new delights of ever-shifting bricolage and blur."[48]

Ernesto Laclau speaks to a position that affirms Grossberg's unease with the Althusserian residue in poststructuralism and the importance of subjectivity as a hegemonic-articulatory process. Laclau writes that

> the Althusserian theory of interpellation . . . leaves out the fact that interpellation is the terrain for the production of discourse, and that in order to "produce" subjects successfully, the latter must identify with it. The Althusserian emphasis on interpellation as a functional mechanism in social reproduction does not leave enough space to study the construction of subjects from the point of view of the individuals receiving those interpellations.[49]

Laclau, like Grossberg, attempts to eliminate the dualism between agent and structure by noting that social agents are always partially internal to institutions. However, since institutions never constitute closed systems but are always riven with antagonisms, social agents are always constituted within the gaps of institutional structures. The institutionalization of the social is always partial and contingent, and only to a relative degree does this constitute the subjectivity of the agents themselves.

The perspective advanced by Grossberg has much to offer transformative research agendas, especially as it concerns the role of the literacy teacher as an agent of transformative social change. Clearly, the perspective itself requires considerable further refinement and critical appraisal. Enough has been said, however, to demonstrate the fruitfulness of further research in this area on the part of those concerned with the theory and practice of critical literacy in the postmodern age.

Pedagogy in the postmodern age

The United States as global educator; constructing the "other". The United States is fast becoming the global educator par excellence. This is of growing concern for those interested in developing critical research practices for the study of literacy. Through its ideologies of individualism and free enterprise, it is fostering tutelary democracies among the "barbaric" and "uncivilized." This raises the following questions: How can we avoid reconstituting the "Other" in the language of a universal, global discourse (in this case an uncritical acceptance of liberal humanism)? How can we refrain from keeping the "Other" mute before the ideals of our own discourse? What research practices must exist in order to restore the marginalized and disenfranchized to history?

Inden argues that U.S. pedagogy is underpinned by a commonsense theory of the mind which assumes that most students are converted to the American way of life before entering school. Except in the most stubborn cases, the teacher need merely convey to the students' reasoning faculties through books (which mirror the world rather than deal with physical objects situated in the world) information needed to live in a natural, rational universe of commonsense enlightenment whose social analogue is U.S. civic culture.[50] Here educators confront the legacy left by the colonizer, especially in relation to minority populations in U.S. schools, where there are concealed attempts to integrate the oppressed into the moral imperatives of the ruling elite.[51]

We have inherited a legacy in which blacks, Latinos, and other groups are essentialized as either biologically or culturally deficient and treated as a species of outsiders. Yet the postmodernist perspective, while addressing the contingent, contradictory, and conflictual characteristics of subject formations, sometimes itself falls prey to a neocolonizing logic by dictating the terms by which we are to speak of the marginal and subaltern.

Although modernity has been haunted by the bourgeois historical subject which remains oblivious to its roots in oppression, the solution should not simply be to embrace the demise of the contemporary subject, reduced to "a dispersed, decentered network of libidinal attachments, emptied of ethical substance and psychical interiority, the ephemeral function of this and that act of consumption, media experience, sexual relationship, trend or fashion."[52] This strips the subject of authorship of its own will, yet leaves nothing in its place but a passive subject *always already determined* by discourse. Here again we must acknowledge the feminist critique, which raises the issue of whether or not women "can afford a sense of decentered self and a humbleness regarding the coherence and truth of their claims."[53] As Di Stefano points out, postmodernism depends on a notion of a decentered subjectivity, whereas feminism depends on a relatively unified notion of the social subject as "woman."[54] We should follow Eagleton and agree that "the subject of late capitalism . . . is neither simply the self-regulating synthetic agent posited by classical humanist ideology, nor merely a decentered network of desire, but a contradictory amalgam of the two."[55] This points once more to the importance of critical poststructuralist, neo-Marxist, and postmodern feminist discourses working together as self-correcting theoretical enterprises.[56]

Poststructuralist pedagogy versus political pedagogy

Eagleton argues that the discourse of modernism in the teaching of English constitutes both a moral technology and a particular mode of subjectivity. Dominant forms of teaching English serve to create a bourgeois body/subject that values subjectivity *in itself*. This occurs through "particular set[s] of techniques and practices for the instilling of specific kinds of value, discipline, behaviour and response in human subjects."[57] Within liberal capitalist society the lived experience of "grasping literature" occurs within a particular form of subjectivity which values freedom and creativity as ends in themselves, whereas the more important issue should be: freedom and creativity *for what?* It would seem that one alternative to the modernist pedagogy decried by Eagleton would be a poststructuralist approach to teaching. But poststructuralist pedagogy, although an improvement on modernist approaches, can *appear* politically progressive while still serving the interests of the dominant culture.

Mas'ud Zavarzadeh[58] has recently attacked poststructuralist theory and pedagogy, arguing that the dominant humanist and poststructuralist pedagogies used in the academy are similar in that both reflect *a resistance to theory.* Whereas humanist pedagogy constructs a subject that is capable of creating meaning, poststructuralist pedagogy offers textuality as a panhistorical truth that exists beyond ideology. According to Zavarzadeh, humanist and poststructuralist pedagogies are both united against what he calls "political pedagogy," which is based on theory as the critique of intelligibility.

The effect of humanist and poststructuralist pedagogy is to recover and protect the subject of patriarchal capitalism. This is achieved by privileging individual experience over theory through a "pedagogy of pleasure." Pleasure becomes an experience for containing and subverting the political, yielding a politics of liberation underwritten by "playfulness" and "fancy" which is at odds with bourgeois norms and social practices, but without really *challenging* the social logic of those norms. Liberation becomes a "relief" from the fixity of the social rather than a form of emancipation that comes with seriously challenging existing social relations. The dominant logic is temporarily displaced in an *illusion of freedom*.

According to Zavarzadeh, poststructuralist pedagogy concerns itself with the "how" or "manner" of knowing, whereas humanist pedagogy generally concerns itself with the "what" of knowing (such as the canon, great books). Neither approach deals with the "why" or the "politics" of representation. At their best, poststructuralist and humanist pedagogies address how a given discourse is *legitimated* but avoid asking about its *legitimacy* and how this is embedded in the prevailing economies of power. The pedagogy of poststructuralism is about using "laughter," "parody," "pastiche," and "play" as strategies of subversion which, although they decenter bourgeois relations, do not fundamentally transform them. Such strategies serve merely as a fanciful way of recruiting students into subject positions which maintain existing social relations.

By contrast, radical pedagogy does not simply bracket reality, but radically restructures it, dismantling secured beliefs and interrogating social practices and the constituents of experience while foregrounding and rendering visible the power/knowledge relation between the teacher and the student. In the radical classroom, students are "made aware of how they are the sites through which structures of social conflict produce meanings."[59] Theory becomes posited as a form of resistance, a means of understanding how cultural practices transform the actual into the real. Theory is used as a means to situate tropes socially and historically according to specific practices of intelligibility through which they can be read. The subject of knowledge in this case is always theoretically positioned in the context of class, race, and gender relations.

Zavarzadeh uncovers various ways in which the discourses of poststructuralism and humanism actually work to *enforce* the larger economies of power, even though they profess to assisting social emancipation. His critique of poststructuralist pedagogy shows why we seek a "*critical* postmodernism" or "*critical* poststructuralism" which appropriates the socially emancipatory potential of postmodern social theory but refuses its tendency to reproduce forms of liberal humanism.

Critical literacy in the age of postmodernism

In this section we outline some of the theoretical advantages of the critical postmodernist position.[60] Developing a critical literacy which can appropriate important insights from critical postmodernism means recognizing the limitations of this perspective while building on its strengths. We try to bring together here some summary positions on critical literacy research, while considering some of the advances that postmodern social theory might bring to this research.

(1) Research on critical literacy carries with it an important historical function: namely, to discover the various complex ways in which ideological production occurs, especially the way in which subjective formations are produced on a level which is often referred to as "common sense." Common sense, or "practical consciousness," is most commonly manufactured at the level of language production and language use, and a critical literacy must be

able to account for the "mutual intelligibility of acts and of discourse, achieved in and through language."[61] Furthermore, critical literacy research needs to be able to identify the characteristics of an individual's "ethno-methods"—the routine actions, unconsciousness knowledge, and cultural memory from which community members draw in order to engage in a politics of daily living. This means developing participatory field approaches that can engage, interpret, and appropriate such knowledge.

(2) Critical literacy research needs to approach the process of becoming literate as something more than simply becoming rational. It must understand literacy as the means by which reality is constructed as being morality, truth, beauty, justice, and virtue, given the *social habitus* of society and the means by which society is able to reproduce and manage its symbolic and emotional economies. In this way, the literacy researcher needs to disrupt unconscious routines rather than simply report them, and bring into relief the politics which inhere in the dialectics of daily life and struggle.

(3) Literacy researchers must take an oppositional stance toward privileged groups within the dominant culture who have attained a disproportionately large share of resources, who are ceaselessly driven by self-perpetuatng ideologies, and who are able to incapacitate opposition by marginalizing and defaming counterdiscourses while legitimating their own. To accomplish this means understanding the production of subjectivity as something more than simply an ensemble of sliding, shifting signifiers constructed against a hyperrealistic backdrop of simulated meanings devoid of origins. Rather, it means grappling with the complex relationship between power and knowledge and how this works to affirm the interests of certain privileged groups against others.

(4) Critical literacy researchers need to seek means toward the political empowerment of oppressed groups, while at the same time avoiding discursive practices that are compatible with dominant social, economic, and political formations or congenial to the market order. They must assist groups and individuals seeking empowerment in clarifying their historical experience of oppression and subjugation and connect individual narratives of specific instances of oppression to an ever larger historical framework in order to recover social memory and an awareness of the struggle of other

groups. Histories of survival and resistance must be recalled and efforts made to clarify "how the structural interaction among dynamics of oppression have differently affected the lives and perceptions of our own group and others."[62] A liberation ethics must be developed which includes solidarity with the marginal and oppressed and, in some instances, our co-suffering with them.[63]

In establishing the groundwork for a critical literacy, however, the tendency within poststructuralism to privilege the experience of the particular over the theoretical should be avoided. It must be remembered that experience is not something that speaks for itself, but is an understanding which is constructed as a particular interpretation over time of a specific concrete engagement with the world of symbols, social practices, and cultural forms. How we think and talk about our world through the particular language of theory largely shapes our understanding of experience. All our experiences are held accountable within a particular system of interpretation; they are not free of political, economic, social, and linguistic constraints.[64] Individual and group experiences should be taken seriously because these constitute the voices students bring with them into the classroom. They should not, however, be celebrated unqualifiedly. Rather, it is important to understand how the voices (experiences) of both the students and the teacher have been subject to historical and cultural constraints which help to shape their identities.

We believe the primary referent for the empowerment of dispossessed groups should not be their moral, ethnic, gender, or political strangeness or displacement outside the boundaries of the dominant and familiar, but rather the location of criteria which can distinguish claims of moral, ethnic, gender, or political superiority which we exercise as outsiders. 'Others' have a hermeneutical privilege in naming the issues before them and in developing an analysis of their situation appropriate to their context. How our research subjects name experience and place labels on their sense of reality should be the primary elements which inform our research. The marginalized have the first right to name reality, to articulate how social reality functions, and to decide how the issues are to be organized and defined.[65] Welch claims that "it is oppressive to free people if their own history and culture do not serve as the primary sources of the definition of their freedom." She warns that "the temptation to define others' hopes for liberation must be avoided." Furthermore, "a concept of freedom is most effective as it is rooted in the imagination of the people to be freed, if it does indeed speak to something in their experience and their history."[66]

Since the experiences of those with whom we study can never be regarded as self-evident—experience always being the seat of ideology and never a state of unmediated innocence—researchers need to help students understand the literalness of their reality, the context in which such a reality is articulated, and how their experiences are imbricated in contradictory, complex, and changing vectors of power.

(5) Literacy researchers need to explore seriously the idea that there is not just one way to become literate, but that there are multiple literacies. This idea comes from poststructuralism and feminist theory, as well as from certain modernist studies.[67] It suggests that literacy can be articulated in more than one form, depending on the cultural, historical, and ideological ways in which it unfolds within particular social formations and settings. To be a literate Latino living in a community in eastern Los Angeles may reflect qualitatively different interactions and skills than to be a Chicano living in upscale Manhattan. In a related sense, to be a minority woman in a minority culture or a woman in the dominant culture also carries profound implications for what counts as literacy.

The notion of being literate must also take into account the poststructuralist insight that every individual consists of an ensemble of multiple, shifting positions within discourses and social practices. This means that individuals can acquire knowledge from a variety of subject positions *and* a number of theoretical perspectives. Many of these positions, of course, can be articulated as positions of resistance to the dominant discourse on literacy, which labels them as illiterate or semiliterate.[68]

All this has implications for our understanding of critical literacy. Within critical literacy the personal is always understood as social, and the social is always historicized to reveal how the subject has been produced in particular. Subjectivity is understood, therefore, as a field of relations forged within a grid of power and ethics, knowledge and power. Literacy research provides a context for research subjects to analyze their identity as a product of larger social and historical struggles.

(6) Critical literacy research must counter the essentialization of difference reflected in the liberal humanist (and some postmodernist) positions, which consist of little more than a facile celebration or tolerance of the multiplicity of voices of the marginalized. It is worth emphasizing that celebrating difference without investigating the ways in which difference becomes constituted in oppressive asymmetrical relations of power often betrays a simpleminded romanticism and "exoticization" of the Other.[69]

The serious issue ahead for literacy researchers struggling to work through the pluralistic implications of postmodernist social theory is to elaborate a position for the human subject which acknowledges its embeddedness and contingency in the present political and historical juncture without, however, relinquishing the struggle against domination and oppression and the fight for social justice and emancipation. In the context of postmodernism, literacy researchers must ask "how . . . the discourse of theory [may] intervene in practice without bolstering domination."[70]

To further avoid falling into a laissez-faire pluralism, literacy researchers must develop a more detailed account of what Fraser calls "interpretive justification" of people's needs.[71] This means examining the inclusivity and exclusivity of rival interpretations and analyzing the hierarchy and egalitarianism of the relations among the rivals who are engaged in debating such needs. Fraser maintains that consequences should also be taken into consideration by comparing alternative distributive outcomes of rival interpretations. This should take the form of procedural considerations concerning the social processes by which various competing interpretations are generated. Fraser asks:

> Would widespread acceptance of some given interpretation of a social need disadvantage some groups of people vis-a-vis others? Does the interpretation conform to, rather than challenge, societal patterns of dominance and subordination? Are rival chains of in-order-to relations to which competing need interpretations belong more or less respectful, as opposed to trans-

gressive, of ideological boundaries that delimit "separate spheres" and thereby rationalize inequality?[72]

Two autobiographical sources help enhance our theoretical understanding of subjectivity while helping us avoid the trap of a poststructuralist or liberal relativism: the idea of expansive otherness developed by Rigoberta Menchú, and Gloria Anzaldúa's concept of borderlands.[73]

Menchú's struggle as a Guatemalan Indian sees her participating in the regeneration of her culture by learning Spanish, but also by identifying with poor *ladinos*, incorporating two ethnicities in her struggle against oppression and exploitation. This resonates with perspectives contained in Anzaldúa's work, *Borderlands/La Frontera*, written from a Chicana lesbian stance. Anzaldua rejects the classic "authenticity" of cultural purity in favor of the "many-stranded possibilities of the borderlands."[74] She is able to transform herself into a complex persona which "incorporates Mexican, Indian, and Anglo elements at the same time that she discards the homophobia and patriarchy of Chicano culture." Anzaldúa writes that the new *mestiza* (person of mixed ancestry) "copes by developing a tolerance for ambiguity. She learns to be Indian in Mexican culture, to be Mexican from an Anglo point of view. She learns to juggle cultures. She has a plural personality, she operates in a pluralistic mode—nothing is thrust out, the good the bad and the ugly, nothing rejected, nothing abandoned. Not only does she sustain contradictions, she turns the ambivalence into something else."[75]

Undertaking critical research on literacy means being able to rupture effectively the charmed circle of exchange among cultural forms, historical consciousness, and the construction of subjectivity which coincide in the authorized version of the humanistic subject. It must, moreover, be an approach to critical literacy which does more than simply celebrate the infinite play of textual inscription or discover "double readings" in literary texts.

Toward critical poststructuralist literacy research

To address the antecedents and implications of new social theory in connection with formulating new advances in critical literacy research will mean a searching reevaluation of the Western metaphysical tradition, not a spurious rejection of it. The truths which modernity struggled so hard to justify, either with an objectivist world or upon transcendental grounds, should certainly be granted a provisional status, but it is incautious and politically imprudent to abandon them outright. The development of critical analyses of literacy will mean a continuing interchange with a wide variety of contemporary currents in social theory. Theorists will have to become discursive cross-dressers, always probing their own "secret heart" that undercuts the politics they are attempting to construct.

We are arguing, then, for the development of a *critical* poststructuralist research. This recognizes that the space between the actual and the real, between consciousness and identity, between the word and the world, is the space of experience: the space of giving voice to one's world. It is a space for restaging the ordinary and the mundane by giving it a name. A critical literacy must recognize that this space is always already occupied: a space in which the colonizer always owns a share. This colonizer, of course, is often the conquering white male of Western history.

In its critique of mainstream research, critical poststructuralist research does not argue that empirical verifiability or evidential supports are unimportant. Rather, it stresses the contingency of the social rather than "higher" forms of objectivity, the primacy of the discursive rather than the search for epistemological foundations, the transgression of the social as distinct from its positivity, and the splintering of the self-mirroring aspects of the social mundane rather than the scrutinizing of the adequacy of evidential claims.

Literacy researchers need to rethink and extend the notion of literacy to include "forms of linguistic experience that are peculiar to the twentieth century, and in particular the structures of domination they contain."[76] This means greater awareness of the development of new modes of information which "designates the way symbols are used to communicate meanings and to constitute subjects."[77] Literacy educators must address the following questions raised recently by Poster:

> What happens in society when the boundaries of linguistic experience are drastically transformed? How are social relations altered when language is

no longer limited to face to face speech or to writing? What assumptions about the nature of society need to be revised when the already complex and ambiguous aspects of language are supplemented by electronic mediation?[78]

In our pursuit of a literacy that is truly critical, we need to understand that we are living in an epochal transition to an era of multiple feminisms, liberalisms, and Marxisms. These, on the one hand, hold the enabling promise of liberation from sexist subjugation and a loosening of the bonds of cultural and sociopolitical white supremacy, misogyny, and class privilege. On the other hand, they threaten to splinter the left irrevocably in a maze of often mutually antagonistic micropolitics.

This risk of splintering calls for some kind of totalizing vision—what McLaren has referred to as "an arch of social dreaming"—that spans the current divisiveness we are witnessing within the field.[79] An arch of social dreaming gives shape, coherence, and protection to the unity of our collective struggles. It means attaining a vision of what the total transformation of society might mean. When we refer to a totalizing vision, however, it must be clear that we intend what Laclau[80] calls "the search for the universal in the contingent" as well as the "contingency of all universality." The arch of social dreaming attempts to make "ambiguous connections" rather than foster "underlying systematicities." As Jameson remarks, "Without some notion of a *total* transformation of society and without the sense that the immediate project is a figure for that total transformation, so that everybody has a stake in a particular struggle, the success of any local struggle is doomed, limited to reform."[81] Jameson makes clear that in our research efforts *we cannot dismiss the search for totality.*

We must continue to seek multiple discourses (African-American pedagogy, Marxist pedagogy, feminist pedagogy) which mutually enhance the political project of each. But such nontotalizing alternatives to liberal humanist discourse must not reject the dream of totality outright. Although there may be a number of public spheres from which to wage an oppositional politics, and although the micropolitical interests of groups that fleck the horizon of the postmodern scene may have overwhelmingly separate and distinct agendas, we should—*all of us*—work together toward a provisional, perhaps evanescent or even *ephemeral, totality* to which we can all aspire, as paradoxical as this may seem.

The real challenge of postmodernity is to steer an ethical and political course in times of shifting theoretical borders and unstable systems of meaning and representation. We must heed Hartsock's challenge to build "an account of the world as seen from the margins, an account which can expose the falseness of the view from the top and can transform the margins as well as the center." This is not a theory of power in which one can afford to retreat from all that is oppressive and inhuman. It is "an engaged vision . . . a call for change and participation in alterning power relations."[82]

The proper response to the challenge of postmodernism is not to wish ourselves back to the halcyon days of the male subject's quest for total control of his subjectivity, but rather to return to a renewed sense of our own obligation to the other. Before we raise the epistemological question "Who are you?" we must first raise the ethical question "Where are you?" We cannot forget our commitment to the other. For, as Kearney notes, "When a naked face cries 'Where are you?,' we do not ask for identity papers. We reply, first and foremost, 'Here I am.'"[83]

It is important to remember that literacies are always brittle and that through the cracks seeps the stuff of possibility. Confronting the wall of subjective determination is Derrida's "gap"—*dehiscence*—the gap that allows and necessitates the further construction of subjectivity through language, even in the face of an always and already disappearing present.

It is in this sense that a poststructuralist approach to literacy can help students develop narratives of identity that do not abandon the reality of human suffering and struggle in a world rife with pain and suffering. It is a process that can help them develop *phronesis*—the competence to choose among seemingly incompatible values in situations where no a priori standard can be invoked.[84] A poststructuralist approach to literacy can assist us in answering the question: How do essentially arbitrarily organized codes, products of historical struggle among not only regimes of signs but regimes of material production, come to represent the "real" and the "natural" and the "necessary"? Part of the answer is that our "practical consciousness" masks the materiality of socially contested social relations by presenting norms to explain reality that purport to be self-referential, that appear to refer to immanent laws of signification, that are reflected away from being considered as the effects of social struggle. A critical poststructuralism recognizes that signs do not correspond to an already determined metaphysical reality, nor are they transhistorically indeterminable or undecidable. Rather, their meaning-making possibilities and their meaningfulness are legitimized through the specificity of discursive and material struggles, and the political linkages between them.

A poststructuralist perspective on literacy can help us understand the danger that arises when literacy is seen as a private or individual competency or set of competencies rather than a complex circulation of economic, political, and ideological practices that inform daily life—competencies that invite or solicit students to acquiesce in their social and gendered positions within a highly stratified society and accept the agenthood assigned to them along the axes of race, class, and gender.

Critical literacy, as we are using the term, becomes the interpretation of the social present for the purpose of transforming the cultural life of certain groups, for questioning tacit assumptions and unarticulated presuppositions of current cultural and social formations and the subjectivities and capacities for agenthood that they foster. It aims at understanding the ongoing social struggles over the signs of culture and over the definition of social reality—over what is considered legitimate and preferred meaning at any given historical moment. Of course, aesthetic concerns mediate such struggles, but their outcomes are largely ideological and economic. Through such struggles historically and ideologically contested class and social relations are naturalized. In this way, critical literacy can be described as investigating those communicational devices that reinscribe the human subject into prevailing social relations so that these relations are seen as conventional and uncontested. That is, critical literacy asks: How is cultural reality encoded within familiar grids or frames of intelligibility so that literacy practices that unwittingly affirm racism, sexism, and heterosexism, for example, are rendered natural and commonsensical?

Teachers and students engaged in the process of critical literacy recognize that dominant social arrangements are dominant not because they are the only possible arrangements but because those arrangements exist for the advantage of certain privileged groups. Critical literacy is not satisfied that students should know the 4,700 items that all Americans need to know according to E.D. Hirsch, Jr., or that they can reflect the cultural capital of an Allan Bloom or Roger Kimball. Critical literacy doesn't lament the dearth of bourgeois salons for cultivating allegiances to Western culture but rather asks: Creativity, culture, and literacy for what?

Critical literacy as a pedagogy of empowerment does not seek a universal truth, or a truth whose ideological effects permit some groups to survive at the expense of others. Critical literacy rather seeks to produce partial, contingent, but necessary historical truths that will enable the many public spheres that make up our social and institutional life to be emancipated— truths which are acknowledged for their social constructedness and historicity and the institutional and social arrangements and practices they legitimate.

For educators, this means constructing a place of hybrid pedagogical space where students do not feel that they need any longer the colonizer's permission or approval to narrate their own identities, a space where individual identities are not essentialized on the basis of race, gender, or nationality, but where these expressions of identity can find meaning in collective engagement with conditions which threaten to undermine the authority and power of individuals to speak and to live with dignity and under conditions of equality and social justice.[85]

Critical literacy enables us to rearticulate the role of the social agent so that he or she is able to make affective alliances with forms of agency that will provide new grounds of popular authority from which to speak the neverending narratives of human freedom. Poststructuralist educators must not abandon their rootedness in the struggles of the popular classes in favor of joining a patrician priesthood of left mandarin metropolitan intellectuals. They must never abandon Volosinov's recognition of the materiality of the sign as a product of social forces and relations of power, as a lived embodiment of both oppression and possibility, subordination and emancipation.

In the final analysis, we must reject any notion of the human subject which seals itself off from its own history, its own link to the community of multiple selves which surrounds it, its narratives of freedom. To construct a truly critical literacy, we need to make despair less salutary and economic, social, racial, and gender equality politically conceivable and pedagogically possible.

Notes

*This is a reworked and greatly expanded version of Peter McLaren, "Literacy Research and the Postmodern Turn: Cautions from the Margins," In Richard Beach *et al.* (eds.) *Multidisciplinary Perspectives on Literacy Research*, Urbana, Illinois: National Conference on Research in English and the National Council of Teachers of English, 1992, pp. 319–339.

1. Weedon, C., *Feminist Practice and Poststructuralist Theory* (Oxford and New York: Basil Blackwell, 1987).

2. Collins, J., *Uncommon Cultures* (London: Routledge, 1990).

3. Frow, J. *Marxism and Literary History* (Cambridge, Mass: Harvard University Press, 1986).

4. Laclau, E., and Mouffe, C., *Hegemony and Socialist Strategy* (London: Verso, 1985).

5. Laclau, E., "Building a New Left: Interview with Ernesto Laclau," *Strategies*, 1, pp. 10–28.

6. MacCannell, D., "Baltimore in the Morning . . . After: On the Forms of Post-Nuclear Leadership," *Diacritics*, 1984, pp. 33–46.

7. Voss, D., and Schutze, J., "Postmodernism in Context: Perspectives of a Structural Change in Society, Literature and Literacy Criticism," *New German Critique*, 47, 1989, pp. 119–142.

8. Lash, S., and Urry, J., *The End of Organized Capitalism* (Madison: University of Wisconsin Press, 1987); McLaren, P., "Postmodernity and the Death of Politics: A Brazilian Reprieve," *Educational Theory*, 36, 4, 1986, pp. 389–401, and "Schooling the Postmodern Body: Critical Literacy and the Politics of Enfleshment," *Journal of Education*, 170, 3, 1988, pp. 53–83; McLaren, P., and Hammer, R., "Critical Pedagogy and the Postmodern Challenge: Towards a Critical Postmodernist Pedagogy of Liberation," *Educational Foundations*, 3, 3, 1989, pp. 29–62; Giroux, H., "Postmodernism and the Discourse of Educational Criticism," and "Border Pedagogy in the Age of Postmodernism," *Journal of Education*, 170, 3, 1988, pp. 5–30 and 162–181.

9. Berman, R., *Modern Culture and Critical Theory* (Madison: University of Wisconsin Press, 1989), p. 41.

10. Voss and Schutze, *op. cit.*, p. 120.

11. Butler, J., *Gender Trouble* (London and New York: Routledge, 1987), p. 145.

12. Flax, J., "Postmodernism and Gender Relations in Feminist Theory," *Signs*, 12, 4, 1987, p. 624.

13. Flax, J., "Postmodernism and Gender Relations in Feminist Theory," in Nicholson, L.J. (ed), *Feminism/Postmodernism* (New York and London: Routledge, 1990), p. 39.

14. Cf. Dussel, E., *Philosophy of Liberation* (Maryknoll, N.Y.: Orbis Books, 1980).

15. Cf. Sarup, M., *Poststructuralism and Postmodernism* (Athens, Ga.: University of Georgia Press, 1989), p. 57.

16. Cf. Hutcheon, L., *A Poetics of Postmodernism* (London and New York: Routledge, 1988).

17. See Poster, M., *Critical Theory and Poststructuralism* (Ithaca, N.Y.: Cornell University Press, 1989), pp. 28–29.

18. Cf. Butler, J., *Subjects of Desire: Hegelian Reflections in Twentieth Century France* (New York: Columbia University Press, 1987).

19. Connor, S., *Postmodernist Culture* (Oxford and New York: Basil Blackwell, 1989), p. 48.

20. Brenkman, J., "Theses on Cultural Marxism," *Social Text*, 7, 1983, p. 27.

21. Hartsock, N., "Rethinking Modernism: Minority vs. Majority Theories." *Cultural Critique* 7: p. 106.

22. Gates, H. L., Jr., "The Master's Pieces: On Canon Formation and the African-American Tradition," *The South Atlantic Quarterly*, 89, 1, 1990, pp. 89–111.

23. Lentricchia, F., *Ariel and the Police* (Madison: University of Wisconsin Press, 1988), p. 100.

24. Bennett, T., "Texts in History: The Determinations of Readings and Their Texts," in Attridge, D., and Bennington, G. (eds.), *Post-structuralism and the Question of History* (Cambridge: Cambridge University Press, 1986).

25. Eagleton, T., *Against the Grain* (London: Verso, 1989), p. 184.

26. Scully, J., *Line Break* (Seattle: Bay Press, 1988), p. 66.

27. Collins, *op. cit.*, p. 89.

28. *Ibid*.

29. Jameson, F., "Interview," *Diacritics*, 12, 3, 1982, p. 75.

30. Merod, J., *The Political Responsibility of the Critic* (Ithaca and London: Cornell University Press, 1987), p. 284.

31. Scholes, R., "Deconstruction and Communication," *Critical Inquiry*, 14, Winter 1988, p. 284. Compare also Cornell West's position: Stephanson, A., "Interview with Cornell West" in Ross, A. (ed.), *Universal Abandon?* (Minneapolis: University of Minnesota Press, 1989), p. 274.

32. Mascia-Lees, F., Sharpe, P., and Cohen, C.B., "The Postmodern Turn in Anthropology: Cautions from a Feminist Perspective," *Signs*, 15, 1, 1989, p. 27.

33. Barthes, R., *S/Z* (London: Cape, 1975).

34. Megill, A., *Prophets of Extremity* (Berkeley: University of California Press, 1985), p. 345.

35. Yudice, G., "Marginality and the Ethics of Survival," in Ross, A. (ed.), *Universal Abandon?* (Minneapolis: University of Minnesota Press, 1989), p. 225.

36. deLauretis, T., *Technologies of Gender* (Bloomington: Indiana University Press, 1987), p. 25.

37. Christian, B., "The Race for Theory," *Cultural Critique*, 6, 1987, p. 55.

38. Kellner, D., "Postmodernism as Social Theory: Some Challenges and Problems," *Theory, Culture and Society*, 5, 2–3, 1988, p. 263.

39. Dews, P., "From Post-Structuralism to Postmodernity: Habermas' Counter-Perspective," *ICA Documents*, 4, published by Institute for Contemporary Arts, London, 1986, p. 15.

40. Hawkesworth, M., "Knowers, Knowing, Known: Feminist Theory and Claims of Truth," *Signs*, 14, 3, 1989.

41. Mascia-Lees et al., *op. cit.*, p. 29.

42. Giroux, H., "Modernism, Postmodernism and Feminism: Rethinking the Boundaries of Educational Discourse," in his (ed.), *Postmodernism, Feminism, and Cultural Politics* (Albany: SUNY Press, 1991), pp. 1–59.

43. Grossberg, L., *We Gotta Get Out of This Place*, working manuscript, forthcoming.

44. *Ibid.*

45. *Ibid.*

46. *Ibid.*

47. *Ibid.* The quotations in the following paragraph are from the same source.

48. Pfeil, F., *Another Tale to Tell* (London and New York: Verso, 1990), p. 256.

49. Laclau, E., *New Reflections on the Revolution of Our Time* (London and New York: Verso, 1990), p. 210.

50. Inden, R., "America Teaches the World Order," paper delivered at the seminar "Intellectuals and Social Action," University of North Carolina, 1989.

51. McLaren, P., *Life in Schools* (New York: Longman, 1989); Giroux, H., and McLaren, P., "Schooling, Cultural Politics, and the Struggle for Democracy: Introduction,: in Giroux, H., and McLaren, P. (eds.), *Critical Pedagogy, the State, and Cultural Struggle* (Albany: SUNY Press, 1989).

52. Eagleton, T., *Against the Grain* (London: Verso, 1986), p. 145.
53. Nicholson, L., "Introduction," in her (ed.), *Feminism/Postmodernism* (London and New York: Routledge, 1990), p. 6.
54. Di Stephano, C., "Dilemmas of Difference: Feminism, Modernity, and Postmodernism," in Nicholson, L. (ed.), *ibid.*, pp. 63–82.
55. Eagleton (1986), *op. cit.*, p. 145.
56. Giroux (1991), *op. cit.*
57. Eagleton (1986), *op. cit.*, pp. 96–97.
58. Zavarzadeh, M., "Theory as Resistance," *Rethinking Marxism*, 2, 1, 1989.
59. *Ibid.*, p. 66.
60. McLaren (1987) and McLaren and Hammer (1989), both *op. cit.*
61. Thompson, K., *Beliefs and Ideology* (New York and London: Tavistock and Ellis Horwood, 1986), p. 116.
62. See Harrison, B. W., *Making the Connections*, ed. Carol S. Robb) (Boston: Beacon Press, 1985).
63. Giroux (1988), *op. cit.*
64. Morton, D., and Zavarzadeh, M., "The Cultural Politics of the Fiction Workshop," *Cultural Critique*, 11, 1988, pp. 155–173.
65. Milhevc, J., "Interpreting the Debt Crisis," *The Economist*, 28, 1, 1989, pp. 5–10.
66. Welch, S., *Communities of Resistance and Solidarity* Maryknoll, N.Y.: Orbis Books, 1985), p. 83.
67. See, for example, Graff, H., *The Literacy Myth* (New York: Academic Press, 1979); Street, B., *Literacy in Theory and Practice* (Cambridge: Cambridge University Press, 1984); Lankshear, C., with Lawler, M., *Literacy, Schooling and Revolution* (London and New York: Falmer Press, 1987).
68. Cf. Giroux (1988), both *op. cit.* (see note 8).
69. *Ibid.*
70. Poster, *op. cit.*, p. 27.
71. Fraser, *op. cit.*, p. 182.
72. *Ibid.*
73. Menchú, R. *I, Rigoberta Menchú: An Indian Woman in Guatemala*, ed. and Introduction by Burgos-Debray, trans. Ann Wright (London: Verso, 1984); Anzaldúa, G., *Borderlands/La Frontera: The New Mestiza* (San Francisco: Spinsters/Aunt Lute, 1987).
74. Rosaldo, R., *Culture and Truth: The Remaking of Social Analysis* (Boston: Beacon Press, 1989), p. 216.
75. Anzaldúa, cited in *ibid.*, p. 216.
76. Poster, *op. cit.*, p. 132.
77. *Ibid.*, p. 131.

78. *Ibid.*, p. 129.

79. McLaren (1988), *op. cit.*

80. Laclau (1988), *op. cit.*, p. 23.

81. Jameson, F., "Cognitive Mapping," in Nelson, C., and Grossberg, L. (eds.), *Marxism and the Interpretation of Culture* (Urbana: University of Illinois Press, 1988), p. 360.

82. Hartsock, *op. cit.*, p. 172.

83. Kearney, R., *The Wake of Imagination* (Minneapolis: University of Minnesota Press, 1988), p. 362.

84. Fererra, A., "On Phronesis," *Praxis International*, 7, 3–4, 1987, pp. 246–267.

85. One of the difficulties that radical educators who work from a postmodern perspective have to face is a specious attack on their work as mere "textualism" or "aestheticism." Many of these attacks are launched by Marxist educators who seek the moral high ground by claiming that only they are really interested in the suffering and emancipation of oppressed groups. Many of these attacks are inadequately theorized and researched and carefully select out those works that specifically run counter to their claims. For a prime example, see Landon E. Beyer and Daniel P. Liston, "Discourse or Moral Action? A critique of Postmodernism." *Educational Theory*, Vol. 42, No. 4, pp. 371–393. Criticism such as this, which fails to adequately distinguish between ludie and resistance strands of postmodernism, cannot hope to appreciate the emancipatory possibilities of postmodern discourse. For works that not only address similar criticisms of postmodernism, but seek to establish a postmodernism of resistance—especially with respect to the development of a moral imagination—see Peter McLaren, "Multiculturalism and the Postmodern Critique: Towards a Pedagogy of Resistance and Trans-formation," *Cultural Studies*, in press; Peter McLaren and Rhonda Hammer, "Critical Pedagogy and the Postmodern Challenge: Towards a Critical Post-modernist Pedagogy of Liberation," *Educational Foundations*, Vol 3, No. 3 (1989), pp. 29–62; Peter McLaren, "Postmodernity, Postcolonialism and Pedagogy," *Education and Society*, Vol.9, No. 2 (1991), pp. 136–158; and Henry Giroux, *Border Crossings*, (London and New York: Routledge, 1992). To acknowledge pedagogies informed by resistance or critical postmodernism would undercut Beyer and Liston's arguments so this strand of postmoder-nism remains absent in their critique.

Postscript to "critical literacy and the postmodern turn"

Peter L. McLaren and Colin Lankshear

In his recent book, *Common Culture*,[1] Paul Willis argues that we live in an era in which high culture or official culture has lost its dominance. Official culture—the best efforts of Allan Bloom and E.D. Hirsch, Jr., notwithstanding—cannot hope to colonize, dominate, or contain the everyday and the mundane aspects of life. Formal aesthetics have been replaced by a grounded aesthetics. The main seeds of cultural development are to be found in the commercial provision of cultural commodities.

Indeed, as Scott Lash points out,[2] postmodern culture permits us to see the economy itself as a kind of culture, a regime of signification. On the "demand side" of a post-Fordist economy we have specialist consumption and "sign value" rather than "use value"—and there are, seemingly, virtually no limits to sign value. We have an era of mass advertising with an oversupply of cultural significations in what is basically a self-service economy. The shift from producer capitalism to consumer capitalism, and the privileging of distribution over production, has created new restrictions and possibilities alike for identity formation and social change. Willis says,

> We must start from unpalatable truths or no truths at all. The time for lies is gone. We need worse truths, not better lies. The "arts" are a dead letter for the majority of young people. Politics bore them. Institutions are too often associated with coercion or exclusion and seem, by and large, irrelevant to

what really energizes them. "Official culture" has hardly recognized informal everyday culture, still less has it provided usable materials for its dialectical development. Worse, the "holiness" of "art" has made the rest of life profane.[3]

According to Willis, one way to work for the "best side" of this trend is to give everyday culture "back to its owners" and letting them develop it. "Let them control the conditions, production, and consumption of their own symbolic resources."[4] This, however, is no easy task, and there are no guarantees, especially since symbolic resources "are lodged in their own historical patterns of power and logics of production." But if the grounded aesthetics of everyday cultural life for youth are concretely embedded in the sensuous human activities of meaning making, there are implications for a critical approach to literacy. Literacy must help students "to increase the range, complexity, elegance, self-consciousness and purposefulness of this involvement" in symbolic work.[5] It must provide them with the symbolic resources for creative self and social formation so that they can more critically reenter the broader plains of common culture.

Symbolic work within informal culture is unlike the symbolic work of school in fundamental ways.

> Where everyday symbolic work differs from what is normally thought of as "education" is that it "culturally produces" from its own chosen cultural resources. Psychologically, at least, the informal symbolic workers of common cultures feel they really "own" and can therefore manipulate their resources as materials and tools—unlike the books at school which are "owned" by the teachers.[6]

For these reasons, creative symbolic work within informal culture offers important possibilities for "oppositional, independent or alternative symbolizations of the self." Moreover, human beings must not be regarded merely as human capital or labor power, but as "creative *citizens*, full of their own sensuous symbolic capacities and activities and taking a hand in the construction of their own identities." The pursuit of emancipation and equality, therefore, requires more than being made equal as workers. It calls for all to be fully developed as *cultural producers*.[7]

Critical literacy is essential to this struggle in several ways. We need to be literate enough to deny the injunctions by which identities are constructed through official culture, in whatever form it appears. This presupposes that we create what Judith Butler calls "alternative domains of cultural intelligibility . . . new possibilities . . . that contest the rigid codes of hierarchical binarisms."[8] Within such hybrid pedagogical spaces educators can give greater attention to the everyday artifacts of popular culture and forms of knowledge that avoid the elitist tyranny of the center. Critical literacy enables us to rearticulate the role of the social agent so that she or he can make affective alliances with forms of agency that provide new grounds of popular authority, ground to stand on from which to give voice to narratives of human freedom.

What educators like Hirsch and Bloom seemingly fail to understand is that schools are failing large numbers of minority and otherwise marginalized students precisely because too much emphasis is already placed on trading in the status of one's cultural capital. Ironically, students who populate urban settings in places like New York's Howard Beach, Ozone Park, and El Barrio are likely to learn more about the culture of Eastern Europe in settings designed by metropolitan intellectuals than they are about the Harlem Renaissance, Mexico, Africa, the Caribbean, or Aztec or Zulu culture. The sad irony is that test scores based on information decanted from the vessel of Western values and bourgeois cultural capital are used to justify school district and state funding initiatives.

Critical literacy helps us identify and answer the question: How do essentially arbitrarily organized cultural codes, products of historical struggle among not only regimes of signs but regimes of material production, also come to represent the "real," the "natural," and the "necessary"? A critical literacy reveals that signs do not correspond to an already determined metaphysical reality, nor are they transhistorically indeterminable or undecidable. Rather, their meaning-making possibilities and their meaningfulness are legitimized through the specificity of discursive and material struggles, and the political linkages between them. A critical perspective on reading and writing also enables teachers and students to understand the dangers in considering literacy to be a private or individual competency—or set of competencies—rather than a complex circulation of economic, political, and ideological practices that inform daily life, that invite or solicit students to acquiesce in their social and gendered positions within a highly stratified society and accept the agenthood assigned to them along the axes of race, class, and gender.

To this extent critical literacy becomes the interpretation of the social present for the purpose of transforming the cultural life of particular groups, for questioning the tacit assumptions and unarticulated presuppositions of our current cultural and social formations and the subjectivities and capacities for agenthood that they foster. Critical literacy is directed at understanding the ongoing social struggles over the signs of culture and over the definition of social reality, over what is considered legitimate and preferred meaning at any given historical moment.

The critical literacy we envisage does not suggest that diversity in and of itself is necessarily progressive; but it does suggest that curricula should be organized in ways that encourage and enable students to make judgments about how society is historically and socially constructed, both within and outside of a politics of diversity, how existing social practices are implicated in relations of equality and justice as well as how they structure inequalities around racism, sexism, economic exploitation, and other forms of oppression.

Students need to be able to cross over into different zones of cultural diversity for rethinking the relationship of self and society, self and other, and for deepening the moral vision of society. Moreover, the question arises: How are the categories of race, class, and gender shaped within the margins and center of society, and how can students engage history as a way of reclaiming power and identity?

Trinh T. Min-ha talks about constructing hybrid and hyphen-ated identities, identities which simultaneously affirm difference and unsettle every definition of otherness.

> The moment the insider steps out from the inside she's no longer a mere insider. She necessarily looks in from the outside while she's looking out from the inside. Not quite the same, not quite the other, she stands in that undermined threshold place where she constantly drifts in and out. Undercutting the inside/outside opposition, her intervention is necessarily that of

both not-quite an insider and not-quite an outsider. She is, in other words, this inappropriate other or same who moves about with always at least two gestures: that of affirming "I am like you" while persisting in her difference and that of reminding "I am different" while unsettling every definition of otherness arrived at.[9]

Critical literacy is built on the notion of border identities and a politics of location as border crossers[10]. It is also grounded in the ethical imperative of examining the contradictions in society between the meaning of freedom, the demands of social justice, and the obligations of citizenship, on the one hand, and the structured silence that permeates incidences of suffering in everyday life. The politics of difference that undergirds critical literacy is one in which differences rearticulate and reshape identity so that identities are transformed and in some instances broken down, but never lost. That is, they are identities immersed not in the effete objections of a centrist politics which leaves individuals to function as obeisant servants of the power brokers, but identities which affirm them as reshapers of their own histories.

Notes

1. Willis, P., *Common Culture* (Boulder, Colo.: Westview Press, 1990).
2. Lash, S. *Sociology of Postmodernism* (London and New York: Routledge, 1990).
3. Willis, *op. cit.*, p. 129.
4. *Ibid*.
5. *Ibid*., pp. 130–131.
6. *Ibid*., p. 136.
7. *Ibid*., p. 150.
8. Butler, J. *Gender Trouble* (New York and London: Routledge, 1990), p. 145.
9. Min-ha, Trinh T., "Not You/Like You: Post-Colonial Women and the Interlocking Questions of Identity and Difference," *Inscriptions*, 3–4, 1988, p. 76.
10. Giroux, H. *Border Crossings*. (New York and London, 1992).

Contributors

Gary L. Anderson is Assistant Professor in the Department of Educational Administration in the College of Education at the University of New Mexico. His research interests include critical ethnography, Latin American education, and cultural and institutional analysis of schooling. Recent articles include 'Critical Ethnography in Education: Origins, Current Status, New Directions' (*Review of Educational Research*) and 'Towards a Critical Constructivist Approach to School Administration' (*Educational Administration Quarterly*).

Michael W. Apple is the John Bascom Professor of Curriculum and Instruction and Educational Policy Studies at the University of Wisconsin, Madison. A former elementary and secondary school teacher and past president of a teachers union, he has worked with dissident groups, unions, and progressive governments to democratize educational research and practice. Among his many books are *Ideology and Curriculum*, *Education and Power*, *Teachers and Texts*, and *The Politics of the Textbook*. He is also editor of Critical Social Thought.

Barbara Bee has extensive teaching experience in primary and tortiary education systems in Australia, and has for many years been closely and actively involved in the areas of women's and immigrant women's literacy, education and employment. She has designed curriculum theories based on Freirean concepts and is currently developing an international literacy kit for women with limited reading skills.

James Berlin taught elementary school in Detroit and Flint, Michigan for six years before receiving his doctorate in Victorian literature from the University of Michigan. He has taught at Wichita State University, the University of Cincinnati, the University of Texas at Austin, Pennsylvania State University, and, since 1987, at Purdue. He has published two histories of writing instruction in American colleges and is coeditor with Michael Vivion of *Cultural Studies in the English Class*.

Jeanne F. Brady teaches at the Pennsylvania State University. She is a former elementary school teacher, having taught in Roxbury, Boston and in Ohio schools. She is the author of a number of articles on feminist literacies and is working on a book-length manuscript. She received her Ph.D. at Miami University of Ohio.

Dennis Carlson is Assistant Professor in the Department of Educational Leadership and the Center for Education and Cultural Studies at Miami University, Ohio. He is author of *Teachers and Crisis: Urban School Reform and Teachers' Work Culture,* and has published articles on curriculum and culture in a number of journals including *Curriculum Inquiry, Harvard Educational Review,* and *Journal of Education*.

Stan Denski is Assistant Professor of Communication and Theatre at Indiana University, Indianapolis, where he teaches in media theory and video production. His writing appears in *The Journal of Film and Video, Popular Music and Society,* and *Tracking: Popular Music Studies,* as well as in edited anthologies. He is currently completing work on two books: *Media Education and the (Re)Production of Culture,* and *Authenticity in Cultural Studies*.

James Paul Gee received his Ph.D. in linguistics from Stanford University in 1975 and subsequently taught in the School of Language and Communication at Hampshire College and the School of Education at Boston University. He is currently Professor of linguistics at the University of Southern California and a member of the executive board of the Literacies Institute in Newton, Massachusetts. Professor Gee has worked in a variety of areas in linguistics, most recently including discourse theory, sociologuistics, sociocultural theories of multiple literacies, and educational linguistics. Recent books include *Social Linguistics: Ideology in Discourses* (Falmer, 1990) and *The Social Mind* (Bergin and Garvey, 1992).

Henry Giroux holds the Waterbury Chair in Secondary Education at the Pennsylvania State University. He is a former high school teacher from Rhode Island and his work on critical pedagogy is internationally renowned. He is the winner of numerous awards for his writings on liberatory education and is an active international speaker. His most recent book is *Border Crossings*.

Kevin Harris is Professor of Education at Macquarie University in Sydney, Australia. He has previously taught in schools and in teacher education. One of the co-founders of *Radical Education Dossier* (now *Education Links*), Kevin Harris has been active in educational politics throughout his career and played a key role in developing the 'Sydney Marxist' school within educational philosophy from the mid 1970s. He has published extensively in a wide range of education journals, and his books include *Education and Knowledge, Teachers and Classes*, and *Sex, Ideology and Religion*.

Adriana Hernandez is a doctoral Fulbright-LASPAU student from Argentina (University of Comahue) at Miami University, Ohio. She has recently completed her dissertation on the issue of public and private spheres from a feminist perspective. Her interest include cultural studies, education, and feminism.

Patricia Irvine is interested in the social context of literacy and has coauthored articles on that topic which were published in *Harvard Educational Review* and several anthologies (*The Social Construction of Written Communication*, B. Rafoth and D. Rubin, eds.; *Freire in the Classroom*, I. Shor, ed.;

and *Bilingualism and Language Contact*, E. Brandt and F. Barkin, eds.). She has taught critical literacy projects in New Mexico, on the Navajo reservation, and in the West Indies.

Didacus Jules was former Head of the National Commission of the Center for Popular Education and later served as Chief Education Office and the Permanent Secretary for Education in the Grenada Revolution. Expelled from Grenada after the U.S. invasion, he was actively involved in promoting literacy in the Caribbean, representing that region on the International Task Force on Literacy in preparation for the International Year of Literacy. He is currently a doctoral student at the University of Wisconsin-Madison.

Colin Lankshear has recently been appointed to the School of Language and Literacy Education at the Queensland University of Technology, Australia. He is the author of several books and numerous articles, mainly on the politics of education and literacy. He has been involved over several years with development and education projects in Nicaragua, including an investigation of the links between women's literacy and children's health.

Peter McLaren is Associate Professor and Renowned Scholar in Residence in the School of Education and Allied Professions at Miami University, Ohio, and Director of the Center for Education and Cultural Studies. He is a former teacher and union activist and has served on task forces to improve conditions in urban schools. He is the author of numerous books on education including *Life in Schools* and *Schooling as a Ritual Performance*. He is co-editor of *Paulo Freire: A Critical Encounter*, Routledge, 1993. Several of his books have been translated into Spanish and Portuguese and he is a regular speaker in Mexico, Brazil, and other Latin American countries. He has also made speaking trips to Eastern Europe where his work is becoming increasingly popular. His classroom diary, *CRIES from the Corridor*, was a Canadian best seller and *Life in Schools* was winner of the Critics Choice award by the American Educational Studies Association.

Kathleen Rockhill has been teaching at the Ontario Institute for Studies in Education since 1983, in the Department of Adult Education where she specializes in Feminist Studies. She first began to conduct research in the area of literacy in 1972 in the U.S.A. Her current research focuses on the political possibilities of autobiographical research.

Chris Searle is a teacher and writer, at present a Headteacher of a comprehensive school in Sheffield, England. He has also taught in Hast London, Mozambique, Canada and the Caribbean. His books include *The Forsaken Lover: White Words and Black People* (Winner of the Martin Luther King Award 1972), *Classrooms of Resistance, The World in a Classroom, We're Building a New School* (on education in post-independence Mozambique), *Words Unchained: Language and Revolution in Grenada, Grenada Morning,* and *A Blindfold Removed: Ethiopia's Struggle for Literacy*. He is a member of the Editorial Advisory Committee, and a frequent contributor to the international journal, *Race and Class*.

David Sholle is Assistant Professor in the Department of Communication at Miami University, Ohio. His articles on cultural studies, the media critical pedagogy and popular culture have appeared in the *Journal of Urban and Cultural Studies, Journal of Education, Cultural Studies, Wide Angle,* and other places. He is currently working on two books: *Critical Pedagogy and Media Education,* and *The Question of Authenticity in Cultural Studies*.

Author Index

Subject Index